T0178579

Lecture Notes of the Institute for Computer Sciences, Social Informatics and Telecommunications Engineering 559

The LNICST series publishes ICST's conferences, symposia and workshops.

LNICST reports state-of-the-art results in areas related to the scope of the Institute. The type of material published includes

- Proceedings (published in time for the respective event)
- Other edited monographs (such as project reports or invited volumes)

LNICST topics span the following areas:

- General Computer Science
- E-Economy
- E-Medicine
- Knowledge Management
- Multimedia
- Operations, Management and Policy
- Social Informatics
- Systems

Celimuge Wu · Xianfu Chen · Jie Feng · Zhen Wu
Editors

Mobile Networks and Management

13th EAI International Conference, MONAMI 2023
Yingtan, China, October 27–29, 2023
Proceedings

Springer

Editors
Celimuge Wu
The University of Electro-Communications
Tokyo, Japan

Xianfu Chen
VTT Technical Research Centre
Helsinki, Finland

Jie Feng
Xidian University
Xi'an, China

Zhen Wu
Jiangxi University of Technology
Nanchang, China

ISSN 1867-8211   ISSN 1867-822X (electronic)
Lecture Notes of the Institute for Computer Sciences, Social Informatics
and Telecommunications Engineering
ISBN 978-3-031-55470-4   ISBN 978-3-031-55471-1 (eBook)
https://doi.org/10.1007/978-3-031-55471-1

This Springer imprint is published by the registered company Springer Nature Switzerland AG
The registered company address is: Gewerbestrasse 11, 6330 Cham, Switzerland

Paper in this product is recyclable.

Preface

We are delighted to present EAI MONAMI 2023, the 13th EAI International Conference on Mobile Networks and Management. This conference served as a significant gathering for researchers, developers, and practitioners hailing from all corners of the globe. They converged here to harness the diverse facets of mobile networks and management technologies and apply them to their respective domains, all with the overarching objective of enriching the quality of end-user experiences.

The technical program of EAI MONAMI 2023 comprised 24 comprehensive papers, inclusive of 3 invited papers, thoughtfully organized into three thematic keynote sessions. These papers traverse a multitude of domains, encompassing Wireless Communication and Networks, Image Processing and Computer Vision, Network Security, and various other fields. In addition to the high-caliber technical paper presentations, the technical program was enriched by the inclusion of three distinguished keynote addresses. The three keynote speeches were delivered by Celimuge Wu from The University of Electro-Communications, Siyang Lu from Beijing Jiaotong University, and Xun Shao from Osaka University. We take immense pleasure in introducing EAI MONAMI 2023. This conference was truly a remarkable achievement, and we wholeheartedly acknowledge the support and guidance provided by our committee members, as well as the unwavering dedication of our organizing committee team.

We extend our profound gratitude to the Technical Program Committee (TPC), who meticulously oversaw the peer review process of the technical papers and curated a program of exceptional quality. Additionally, we express our sincere appreciation to all the authors who contributed their research to EAI MONAMI 2023.

We hold firm in our belief that EAI MONAMI 2023 not only provided a remarkable platform for researchers, developers, and practitioners to learn and engage in discussions spanning various facets of science and technology, but it also set the stage for future conferences to be equally successful and inspiring, as evidenced by the outstanding contributions within this volume.

A.P. Jie Feng
Celimuge Wu
Xianfu Chen
Zhen Wu

Organization

Steering Committee

Organizing Committee

General Chair

Celimuge Wu   University of Electro-Communications, Japan

General Co-chairs

Liefa Liao   Jiangxi University of Science and Technology,
                               China
Ning Zhang   University of Windsor, Canada
Yuanlong Cao   Jiangxi Normal University, China
Baixiong Liu   Jiangxi University of Science and Technology,
                               China

TPC Chairs and Co-chairs

Li Yu   Huazhong University of Science and Technology,
                               China
Peng Yang   Huazhong University of Science and Technology,
                               China
Zhaoyang Du   University of Electro-Communications, Japan
Yong Luo   Jiangxi Normal University, China
Yang Zhou   Information and Communication Branch of State
                               Grid Jiangxi Electric Power Co, Ltd, China
Qiuming Liu   Jiangxi University of Science and Technology,
                               China
He Xiao   Jiangxi University of Science and Technology,
                               China
Xiaohong Qiu   Jiangxi University of Science and Technology,
                               China
Chen Guo   Jinggangshan University, China
Yuanlong Cao   Jiangxi Normal University, China

Yangfei Lin	University of Electro-Communications, Japan
Heli Zhang	Beijing University of Posts and Telecommunications, China
Celimuge Wu	University of Electro-Communications, Japan
Peng Li	University of Aizu, Japan
Junbo Wang	Sun Yat-sen University, China
Bo Gu	Sun Yat-sen University, China
Wei Zhao	Anhui University of Technology, China
Yu Gu	Hefei University of Technology, China
Lu Chen	Kyoto Institute of Technology, Japan
Ryohei Banno	Tokyo Institute of Technology, Japan
Lei Zhong	Toyota R&D, Japan
He Li	Muroran Institute of Technology, Japan
Ziji Ma	Hunan University, China
Rui Yin	Zhejiang University City College, China
Huiming Chen	Jiangxi University of Science and Technology, China
Liefa Liao	Jiangxi University of Science and Technology, China
Zhen Wu	Jiangxi University of Science and Technology, China

Sponsorship and Exhibit Chair

Xiangpeng Xiao	Jiangxi University of Science and Technology, China

Local Chairs

Huiming Chen	Jiangxi University of Science and Technology, China
Guhui Wan	Yingtan Science and Technology Bureau, China

Workshops Chair

Yang Zhou	Information and Communication Branch of State Grid Jiangxi Electric Power Co, Ltd, China

Publicity and Social Media Chairs

Musheng Chen	Jiangxi University of Science and Technology, China
Daopei Zhu	Jiangxi University of Science and Technology, China
Xiaoshun Wu	Jiangxi University of Science and Technology, China

Publications Chair

Zhen Wu	Jiangxi University of Science and Technology, China

Web Chair

He Xiao	Jiangxi University of Science and Technology, China

Posters and PhD Track Chair

Zhen Wu	Jiangxi University of Science and Technology, China

Panels Chair

Xiaohong Qiu	Jiangxi University of Science and Technology, China

Demos Chair

Yong Luo	Jiangxi Normal University, China

Tutorials Chairs

Lei Wang	Jiangxi University of Science and Technology, China

Technical Program Committee

Chen Guo   Jinggangshan University, China
Shumin Liu   Jiangxi University of Science and Technology,
                            China

Contents

Emerging Applications

Wireless Communication and Networks

An Occlusion Signal-Processing Framework Based on UAV Sampling for Improving Rendering Quality of Views

Qiuming Liu[1,2(✉)] [ID], Ke Yan[1] [ID], Yichen Wang[1] [ID], RuiQin Li[1] [ID], and Yong Luo[3]

[1] School of Software Engineering, Jiangxi University of Science and Technology, Nanchang 330013, China
liugiuming@jxust.edu.cn, 6720210691@mail.jxust.edu.cn
[2] Nanchang Key laboratory of Virtual Digital Factory and Cultural Communications, Nanchang 330013, China
[3] School of Software, Jiangxi Normal University, Nanchang 330022, China

Abstract. Using unmanned aerial vehicles (UAV) for large-scale scene sampling is a prevalent application in UAV vision. However, there are certain factors that can influence the quality of UAV sampling, such as the lack of texture details and drastic changes in scene geometry. One common factor is occlusion, which is a surface feature in 3D scenes that results in significant discontinuity on the scene surface, leading to transient noise and loss of local information. This can cause degradation in the performance of computer vision algorithms. To address these challenges, this paper proposes a UAV sampling method that takes into account occlusion. The method is based on the principle of quantizing occlusion information and improves the aerial light field (ALF) technology. It establishes a UAV ALF sampling model that considers scene occlusion information and calculates the minimum sampling rate of UAV sampling by deriving the exact expression of the spectrum. The proposed model is used to sample and reconstruct large-scale scenes in different occlusion environments. Experimental results demonstrate that the model effectively improves the reconstruction quality of large-scale scenes in occluded environments.

Keywords: Unmanned aerial vehicle · Occlusion scene · Aerial light field · Spectrum analysis

1 Introduction

Using Unmanned Aerial Vehicles (UAV) for image sampling and scene reconstruction is a prevalent application in computer vision [1–5]. UAV sampling offers greater flexibility and a wider sampling range compared to traditional camera sampling in large-scale scenes. However, it also faces some challenges,

C. Wu et al. (Eds.): MONAMI 2023, LNICST 559, pp. 3–15, 2024.
https://doi.org/10.1007/978-3-031-55471-1_1

such as a lack of texture detail, drastic surface changes in the scene, and so on. One particular issue is occlusion - a feature in 3D scenes that causes significant discontinuities on object surfaces, resulting in transient noise and loss of local information. The absence of these crucial details can lead to a degradation in the performance of computer vision algorithms.

To address these challenges and enhance the quality of novel view reconstruction in large-scale scenes, we propose a method based on the quantification of occlusion information. Meanwhile, our proposed method improves the aerial light field (ALF) technique and obtains an ALF sampling model for UAV. This model can reduce the impact of occlusion on large-scale scene reconstruction. The procedures are as follows: First, we conduct an in-depth analysis of the UAV sampling characteristics, based on which we establish the occlusion signal model of the ALF. According to the model, the occlusion degree in the scene is quantified. Then we derive the precise expression of the ALF based on the established sampling model, enabling us to obtain the necessary spectral support for ALF. Additionally, we analyze the signal bandwidth according to spectral support to determine the minimum sampling rate for UAV sampling. Finally, we solve the sampling problem of the real obscured scenes to prove the practicality of the model.

2   Related Work

2.1   UAV Sampling and Rendering

In recent years, there has been a great deal of research about techniques for sampling and reconstructing large-scale scenes from UAV, and these techniques are also widely used in a variety of fields. Schedl et al. [6] utilized airborne optical sectioning (AOS) image integration technology to locate missing or injured individuals within dense forests, thereby paving the way for future advancements in search and rescue techniques. Khaloo et al. [7] employed UAV-captured images along with SFM algorithms to create three-dimensional (3D) models of bridges for unmanned aerial vehicle inspections. This approach facilitates the evaluation of bridge structural integrity and ensures the safety of transportation infrastructure. Liu et al. [8] proposed an image-based crack assessment method for bridge piers using unmanned aerial vehicles and 3D scene reconstruction algorithms. Through this approach, UAV technology is utilized to evaluate and maintain the safety of bridge piers by detecting and analyzing cracks. Prosekov et al. [9]developed techniques and software for 3D thermal imaging and mapping of coal warehouses and coal mining facilities. This advancement aims to swiftly identify potential fire ignition points, thus enabling prompt fire prevention measures and minimizing extinguishing time. Fernando et al. [10] implemented a UAV photogrammetry scheme based on Structure from Motion (SfM) and Multiple View Stereo (MVS) algorithms. By utilizing this method, they successfully modeled the topography of surfaces, established structural foundations, and connecting channels. The resulting data aided in reconstructing and understanding intricate archaeological sites, ultimately contributing to their restoration and preservation.

To improve the quality of UAV image reconstruction, various methods have been proposed to make an improvement, especially for the prevalent occlusion problem in large-scale scenes, Guan *et al.* [11] introduced a UAV-YOLO vehicle detector that utilizes depth-separable convolution and resolution adjustment techniques. They also proposed a multi-view occlusion optimization algorithm to enhance the quality and speed of reconstruction by determining the optimal spatial distribution of image sequences. Schneider *et al.* [12] developed a TLS-based 3D structure measurement method specifically designed for dense tropical and temperate forests. This approach effectively quantifies the 3D structure and occlusion within the forests, resulting in improved quality for 3D measurement and reconstruction of forest environments. Zhao *et al.* [13] put forth an improved YOLOV5 method for accurate detection of wheat spikes in UAV images. This method addresses the issue of occlusion-induced spike detection errors and missed detections, leading to more reliable and precise results.

These works have made significant contributions to the research on sampling and reconstruction of UAVs for large scenes. However, it is worth noting that there has been limited focus on specific factors that are prevalent in large-scale scenes, such as occlusion and shadows. These factors play a crucial role in the overall quality of sampling and reconstruction in large-scale scenes. Furthermore, some reconstruction methods that overlook the sampling rate while prioritizing the enhancement of reconstruction quality. This oversight often results in data redundancy and consumes excessive memory during the reconstruction process.

2.2 Light Field Sampling and Reconstruction

With the increasing application of 3D reconstruction and other technologies, many related methods have been proposed to reduce the sampling rate of light field and improve the rendering quality of view. To reduce the redundancy of light field sampling and improve the reconstruction efficiency, Qi *et al.* [14] proposed the feature ray under-sampling (FRUS) method, and studied the influence of the under-sampling methods, flame dividing voxels, noise levels and light field camera parameters. Gilliam *et al.* [15] employed a set of inclined planes to approximate the scene's geometry and derived a precise closed expression for the complete optical spectrum of a finite width inclined plane. Additionally, they developed a novel reconstruction filter to enhance the reconstruction process. Wu *et al.* [16] conducted a study and discovered that the fundamental issue behind the challenges of large disparities and non-Lambertian surfaces is the problem of aliasing. They introduced an alternative framework for performing anti-aliasing reconstruction in the image domain, which demonstrated excellent results.

Although there have been many researches related to light field sampling and reconstruction, the techniques related to light field reconstruction are still limited to small scenes.

3 A Framework for Occlusion Signal Based on UAV Sampling

3.1 Aerial Light Field Parameterization

For light rays, a 7-dimensional function(POF) $\Phi\left(x,y,z,\theta,\phi,\lambda,\tau\right)$ [17] is usually used to parameterize it (Fig. 1), where(x,y,z) is the position of the UAV, (θ,ϕ) is the direction of light transmission, λ is the wavelength of the rays and τ is the time.

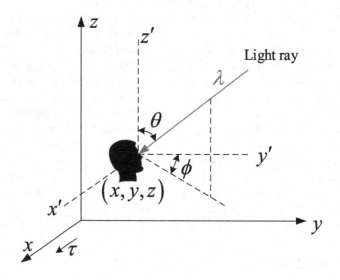

Fig. 1. 7-dimensional plenoptic function. A light in space is described with seven parameters centered on the human eye.

The 7D functions are complex when it comes to mathematical calculations and Fourier transforms. Therefore, it can be simplified to 5D in the process of describing the actual 3D scene, as $F\left(x,y,z,\theta,\phi\right)$.

3.2 Aerial Light Field Occlusion Signal Model

In this paper, we analyse the scene information captured by the UAV to quantify the degree of occlusion in the scene. The field of view (FOV) of the UAV camera represents the range of scene information that can be captured, as shown in Fig. 2. The FOV can be represented by cone $U-ABCD$, $U\left(x,y,z,\theta,\phi\right)$represents the information captured by the camera, and the occlusion field is represented by cone $U-A'B'C'D'$. Obviously the occlusion field is also a part of the FOV.

Zhu *et al.* in the literature [18], define a novel view of the rendering of the captured scene information based on the camera to improve the rendering quality

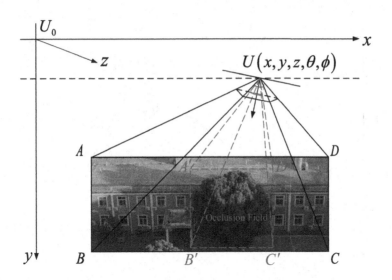

Fig. 2. 3D Aerial light field occlusion signal model. The red box area indicates the occlusion coverage range in the scene. (Color figure online)

by compensating for the OCD function [19]. The expressions are as follows,

$$P(x, y, z, \theta, \phi) = \int \Phi(C(x, y, z, \theta, \phi), O(x, y, z, \theta, \phi)) \cdot B(x, y, z, \theta, \phi) \, dx dy dz d\theta d\phi \tag{1}$$

where $P(x, y, z, \theta, \phi)$ represents the new view after rendering, $C(x, y, z, \theta, \phi)$ is the scene information captured by the UAV, $\Phi(\cdot)$ is a compensation function implemented in a certain relationship, and $B(\cdot)$ is the rendering kernel function. The function $O(x, y, z, \theta, \phi)$ represents the degree of occlusion in the scene captured by the UAV. The expression for $O(x, y, z, \theta, \phi)$ is as follows,

$$O(x, y, z, \theta, \phi) = \beta \frac{V_O(x, y, z, \theta, \phi)}{V_F(x, y, z, \theta, \phi)} \tag{2}$$

where β is determined by the FOV $V_F(x, y, z, \theta, \phi)$ of the UAV. $V_F(x, y, z, \theta, \phi)$ and $V_O(x, y, z, \theta, \phi)$ are the volumes of cone $U - ABCD$ and cone $U - A'B'C'D'$. Based on this theory, we develop an ALF occlusion signal model. In order to improve the computational efficiency and reduce the complexity of the quantitative expression of occlusion, we further simplify the 5D light field according to the principle of unstructured light fields [20]. By choosing a position parameter (x, z) and a direction parameter θ, the 5D function is then reduced to a 3D function. The expression (1) is simplified as follows,

$$P(x, z, \theta) = \int \Phi(C(x, z, \theta), O(x, z, \theta)) \cdot B(x, z, \theta) \, dx dz d\theta \tag{3}$$

Thus, the model in Fig. 2 can be simplified to Fig. 3, where the degree of occlusion can be expressed as the ratio of the area of the occlusion field to the area of the FOV, and their area can be quantified in terms of the number of rays.

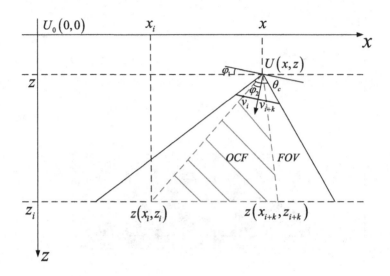

Fig. 3. 2D Aerial light field occlusion signal model. The red box region represents the set of rays of the occluded range. (Color figure online)

The light rays can be defined by their intersection with the camera plane at position x and imaging planes corresponding to pixel position v [15]. Thus there is,

$$\tan \varphi_2 = \tan \left(90° - (\varphi_1 + \theta_1)\right) = \frac{\cos \varphi_1 (x_0 - x_1) - \sin \varphi_1 (z_1 - z_0)}{\sin \varphi_1 (x_0 - x_1) + \cos \varphi_1 (z_1 - z_0)} \quad (4)$$

$$v = f \tan \varphi_2 = f \left(\frac{\cos \varphi_1 (x_0 - x_1) - \sin \varphi_1 (z_1 - z_0)}{\sin \varphi_1 (x_0 - x_1) + \cos \varphi_1 (z_1 - z_0)} \right) \quad (5)$$

From this we get an exact expression for the pixel position, which we can then substitute into a simplified expression for the degree of occlusion. Finally, we get the expression of scene occlusion degree expressed by UAV position and pitch angle.

$$O(x, z, v) = \beta \frac{K(x, z, v)}{N(x, z, v)} \approx \beta \frac{|v_{i+k} - v_i|}{2 v_m}$$

$$= \frac{\beta}{2 f \tan \frac{\theta_c}{2}} \left| \frac{f \cos \varphi_1 (x - x_i) + f \sin \varphi_1 (z - z_i)}{\sin \varphi_1 (x - x_i) + \cos \varphi_1 (z_i - z)} - \frac{f \cos \varphi_1 (x - x_{i+k}) + f \sin \varphi_1 (z - z_{i+k})}{\sin \varphi_1 (x - x_{i+k}) + \cos \varphi_1 (z_{i+k} - z)} \right| \quad (6)$$

where f is the distance between the camera plane and the image plane, as the focal length. φ_2 is the pitch angle of the unmanned aerial vehicles. v_m is the maximum pixels in the image plane.

3.3 Fourier Transform of the ALF Occlusion Signal Model

A spectral transformation of the sampling model of the occlusion signal allows the effect of occlusion on the signal to be analyzed, and a Fourier transform of the occlusion function gives as follows,

$$
O\left(\omega_x,\omega_z,\omega_v\right) = \int_{-\infty}^{\infty}\int_{-\infty}^{\infty}\int_{-\infty}^{\infty} O\left(x,z,v\right) \times \exp\left(-j\left(\omega_x x + \omega_z z + \omega_v v\right)\right) dx dz dv
$$
(7)

where the $E = \exp\left(-j\left(\omega_x x + \omega_z z + \omega_v v\right)\right)$, and in the following we will abbreviate $O\left(\omega_x,\omega_z,\omega_v\right)$ to $O(\cdot)$. Substituting (6) into (7) and we get,

$$
O(\cdot) = \iiint \frac{\beta E}{2f \tan\frac{\theta_c}{2}} \left[\begin{array}{c} \dfrac{f\cos\varphi_1\left(x-x_i\right)+f\sin\varphi_1\left(z-z_i\right)}{\sin\varphi_1\left(x-x_i\right)+\cos\varphi_1\left(z_i-z\right)} - \\[2ex] \dfrac{f\cos\varphi_1\left(x-x_{i+k}\right)+f\sin\varphi_1\left(z-z_{i+k}\right)}{\sin\varphi_1\left(x-x_{i+k}\right)+\cos\varphi_1\left(z_{i+k}-z\right)} \end{array} \right] dx dz dv
$$

$$
= \frac{\beta}{2f\tan\frac{\theta_c}{2}} \left[\begin{array}{c} \iiint \dfrac{f\cos\varphi_1\left(x-x_i\right)+f\sin\varphi_1\left(z-z_i\right)}{\sin\varphi_1\left(x-x_i\right)+\cos\varphi_1\left(z_i-z\right)} E dx dz dv \\[2ex] -\iiint \dfrac{f\cos\varphi_1\left(x-x_{i+k}\right)+f\sin\varphi_1\left(z-z_{i+k}\right)}{\sin\varphi_1\left(x-x_{i+k}\right)+\cos\varphi_1\left(z_{i+k}-z\right)} E dx dz dv \end{array} \right]
$$
(8)

By analyzing (8) and applying properties of calculus, we decompose it into two triple integrals. We further proceed to decompose and simplify each triple integral, taking into account the symmetry of the Fourier transform. Ultimately, we obtain formula (9), which represents the spectral expression of the occlusion function.

$$
\begin{aligned}
O(\cdot) = {}& \frac{j\beta\pi^2 \operatorname{sgn}\left(\omega_x\right)}{f\cdot\tan\theta_c/2} \left(\begin{array}{l} \exp\left(j\omega_x\left(\dfrac{\omega_v-\omega_x d_{i+K}-\omega_z t_{i+K}}{\omega_z}\right)\right)\left(x_{i+K}+d_{i+K}\right) \\[2ex] -\exp\left(j\omega_x\left(\dfrac{\omega_v-\omega_x d_i-\omega_z x_i}{\omega_z}\right)\right)\left(x_i+d_i\right) \end{array} \right) \\[3ex]
&+\pi^2 f \left(\begin{array}{l} 1+\pi\delta\left(\omega_v-2\right) \\ +\pi\delta\left(\omega_v+2\right) \end{array} \right) \left(\begin{array}{l} \left(\dfrac{d_i\delta\left(\omega_z\right)\operatorname{sgn}\left(\omega_x\right)-j\delta'\left(\omega_z\right)\operatorname{sgn}\left(\omega_x\right)}{\omega_x}+ \right. \\[2ex] \left. \dfrac{d_i\delta\left(\omega_x\right)\operatorname{sgn}\left(\omega_z\right)-j\delta'\left(\omega_x\right)\operatorname{sgn}\left(\omega_z\right)}{\omega_z} \right) \\[2ex] -\left(\dfrac{d_{i+K}\delta\left(\omega_z\right)\operatorname{sgn}\left(\omega_x\right)-j\delta'\left(\omega_z\right)\operatorname{sgn}\left(\omega_t\right)}{\omega_x}+ \right. \\[2ex] \left. \dfrac{d_{i+K}\delta\left(\omega_x\right)\operatorname{sgn}\left(\omega_z\right)-j\delta'\left(\omega_x\right)\operatorname{sgn}\left(\omega_z\right)}{\omega_z} \right) \end{array} \right) \\[3ex]
&+j\pi^2\left(\delta\left(\omega_v+2\right)-\delta\left(\omega_v-2\right)\right) \left(\begin{array}{l} \left(\begin{array}{l} \delta\left(\omega_z\right)\left(t_i\operatorname{sgn}\left(\omega_x\right)-2\pi\delta\left(\omega_x\right)\right) \\ +\left(t_i\operatorname{sgn}\left(\omega_z\right)-2\pi\delta\left(\omega_z\right)\right) \end{array} \right) \\[2ex] -\left(\begin{array}{l} \delta\left(\omega_z\right)\left(t_{i+K}\operatorname{sgn}\left(\omega_x\right)-2\pi\delta\left(\omega_x\right)\right) \\ +\left(t_{i+K}\operatorname{sgn}\left(\omega_z\right)-2\pi\delta\left(\omega_z\right)\right) \end{array} \right) \end{array} \right)
\end{aligned}
$$
(9)

3.4   ALF Occlusion Signal Sampling and Reconstruction

The spectrum of the occlusion function from (9) contains ω_x, ω_z and ω_v. Where ω_z depends on the depth between the UAV and the subject. We only analyze the occlusion function through ω_x and ω_v. Applying the concept of fundamental bandwidth, the bandwidths along the ω_x-axis and the ω_v-axis of the occlusion function are derived as follows,

$$B_x = \left\{ \omega_x : |\omega_x| \leq \frac{1}{2\pi |x_i - x_{i+k}| \cdot |d_i - d_{i+k}| + \text{sgn}(\theta)} \right\} \tag{10}$$

$$B_v = \left\{ \omega_v \in \left[\frac{\Omega_x |x_i - x_{i+k}| z_{\max}}{f}, \frac{\Omega_x |x_i - x_{i+k}| z_{\min}}{f} \right] \right\} \tag{11}$$

where Ω_x denotes the maximum value of B_x along the ω_x-axis, as

$$\Omega_x = \frac{1}{2\pi |x_i - x_{i+k}| \cdot |d_i - d_{i+k}| + \text{sgn}(\theta)} \tag{12}$$

Depending on the bandwidth, an adaptive filter is designed to eliminate the interference caused by the occlusion signal. Tilting filter is still used in the reconstruction, with two filter expressions are as follows,

$$H_{opt}(\omega_x, \omega_v) = \frac{F^*((\omega_x + \omega_v))}{B_x + B_v} e^{-j(\omega_x T_x + \omega_v T_v)} \tag{13}$$

$$F_R = \frac{|x_i - x_{i+k}| \cdot |z_{\max} + z_{\min}|}{2\pi f} \tag{14}$$

Referring to the occlusion scoring method proposed by Zhu *et al.* in the literature [18], the case where occlusion has the least impact on the quality of the scene reconstruction can be deduced. The expression for the occlusion scoring is as follows,

$$S_R = \min_{(x,z,v)} \left(\hat{O}(x,z,v) \right) = \min_{(x,z,v)} \left(\frac{|v_{i+k} - v_i|}{2f \cdot \tan \theta_c / 2} \right) = \min_{x = x_0, \theta = \theta_0} \left(\frac{|v_{i+k} - v_i|}{2f \cdot \tan \theta_c / 2} \right) \tag{15}$$

4   Experiment

4.1   Experimental Sampling Methods

The experiment of large-scale aerial shooting scene conducted in this paper is based on the mathematical theory derivation above. By determining the spectral bandwidth of ALF, the maximum sampling spacing of UAV sampling can be deduced, that is, the minimum sampling rate can be obtained, and the reconstruction filter can be obtained at the same time. According to the minimum sampling rate, the sampling interval can be determined. The inter-frame estimation method in [21] takes frames from the UAV sampling video to obtain the images required for the experiment, and then renders new views according to the sampled images.

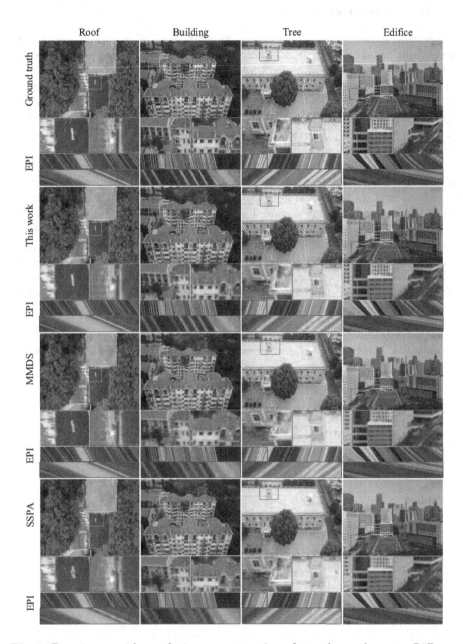

Fig. 4. Experiment with novel view reconstruction of complex real scenes. Different sampling methods have different quality results for four different experimental scenarios. Changes in EPI can reflect the quality of the reconstructed view by the corresponding method. Some Magnified details help us to clearly compare the rendering quality of different methods.

4.2   Real Scene Experiment

In this experiment, we selected several different types of occlusion scenes and successfully reconstructed them. These scenes involved various scenarios, such as trees obstructing buildings, multiple buildings obstructing each other, and unique vertical views in aerial scenes. To ensure the credibility of our findings, we conducted comparative experiments with other relevant methods, including Maximum and Minimum Depth of the Scene (MMDS) [22] and Single Slanted Plane Analysis (SSPA) [15]. Additionally, we employed the EPI (Epipolar Plane Image) [23] to verify the view reconstruction quality of different methods.

As depicted in Fig. 4, we present the reconstructed views and corresponding EPIs of four scenes for comparison. Notably, these scenes featured large-scale dimensions and intricate surface textures, representing a key characteristic of complex aerial photography scenes. The results demonstrate that the proposed sampling method in this study significantly enhances the quality of reconstructed views, particularly when considering the occlusion present in real-world scenes. This indicates the effectiveness of our proposed sampling method for large-scale complex aerial photography scenes. Moreover, when zooming in on specific scene details, it becomes evident that our proposed method also outperforms other approaches in terms of reconstruction accuracy.

Table 1. PSNRs for rendering of four real scenes using three different methods.

Method	Scene			
	Roof	Building	Tree	Edifice
This work	30.413	27.696	28.306	27.083
MMDS	29.564	26.735	27.415	26.374
SSPA	29.222	26.466	27.105	26.095

Table 2. SSIMs for rendering of four real scenes using three different methods.

Method	Scene			
	Roof	Building	Tree	Edifice
This work	0.889	0.914	0.890	0.897
MMDS	0.861	0.890	0.858	0.872
SSPA	0.850	0.883	0.847	0.867

To intuitively compare the rendering quality of different methods, we compared the Peak Signal-to-Noise Ratio (PSNR) and Structural Similarity Index (SSIM) of four sets of experiments, and the average values of the PSNR and SSIM are shown in Table 1 and Table 2. By comparing the Peak Signal-to-Noise Ratio (PSNR) and Structural Similarity Index (SSIM) obtained from our real scene experiments, we observe that the UAV sampling method proposed in this paper consistently produces superior rendering effects for generating novel viewpoints. This result further proves the superiority of our sampling method. Overall, the experimental results affirm the reconstruction capabilities of the UAV sampling method across a wide range of scene types.

5   Conclusion

Based on the principle of quantizing occlusion information, this paper presents a novel UAV sampling method that considers occlusion to improve the technology of ALF. We establish a UAV ALF sampling model that takes into account scene occlusion information, enabling us to calculate the minimum sampling rate required for UAV sampling by deriving the exact expression of the spectrum. Additionally, we determine the reconstruction filter suitable for large-scale aerial photography. The experimental results demonstrate the model's effectiveness in mitigating the impact of occlusion on large-scale scene reconstruction, and shows the superiority of this model in reconstructing large-scale scenes in occluded environment.

However, it is important to note that our discussion solely focuses on the UAV sampling method considering occlusion. During the ALF sampling process, the presence of sunlight can create shadow areas within the scene, while light reflections may occur on the external walls of certain buildings. These factors can potentially impact the overall quality of scene reconstruction for large-scale scenes. In our future research, we will focus on exploring various improvement methods to further enhance the quality of occlusion scene novel view reconstruction.

Acknowledgment. This work was supported in part by National Natural Science Foundation of China (No. 62067003), in part by Culture and Art Science Planning Project of Jiangxi Province (No. YG2018042), in part by Humanities and Social Science Project of Jiangxi Province (No. JC18224).

References

1. Yan, F., Xia, E., Li, Z., Zhou, Z.: Sampling-based path planning for high-quality aerial 3D reconstruction of urban scenes. Remote Sens. **13**(5) (2021). https://doi.org/10.3390/rs13050989. https://www.mdpi.com/2072-4292/13/5/989
2. He, Y., Liang, Q., Lu, H., Chai, C.: Based on unmanned aerial vehicle real-scene 3D design and implementation of virtual simulation experiment system for mine smart supervision in large-scale applications. In: 2021 2nd International Conference on Information Science and Education (ICISE-IE), pp. 1406–1413. IEEE (2021)
3. Hermawan, S., Purnomo, J., Tjandra, D., Purnomo, Y.C.: The use of unmanned aerial vehicles (UAV) for reconstruction of topography and bathymetry maps: consideration for civil construction against coastal adaptation due to climate changing. In: MISEIC 2018 (2018)

4. Mancini, F., Dubbini, M., Gattelli, M., Stecchi, F., Fabbri, S., Gabbianelli, G.: Using unmanned aerial vehicles (UAV) for high-resolution reconstruction of topography: the structure from motion approach on coastal environments. Remote Sens. **5**(12), 6880–6898 (2013)

5. Qiao, G., Yuan, X., Florinsky, I., Popov, S., He, Y., Li, H.: Topography reconstruction and evolution analysis of outlet glacier using data from unmanned aerial vehicles in Antarctica. Int. J. Appl. Earth Obs. Geoinf. **117**, 103186 (2023)

6. Schedl, D.C., Kurmi, I., Bimber, O.: Search and rescue with airborne optical sectioning. Nat. Mach. Intell. **2**(12), 783–790 (2020)

7. Khaloo, A., Lattanzi, D., Cunningham, K., Dell'Andrea, R., Riley, M.: Unmanned aerial vehicle inspection of the placer river trail bridge through image-based 3D modelling. Struct. Infrastruct. Eng. 1–13 (2018)

8. Liu, Y.F., Nie, X., Fan, J.S., Liu, X.G.: Image-based crack assessment of bridge piers using unmanned aerial vehicles and three-dimensional scene reconstruction. Comput.-Aided Civ. Infrastruct. Eng. **35**(5), 511–529 (2020)

9. Prosekov, A.Y., Rada, A., Kuznetsov, A., Timofeev, A., Osintseva, M.: Environmental monitoring of endogenous fires based on thermal imaging and 3D mapping from an unmanned aerial vehicle. In: IOP Conference Series: Earth and Environmental Science, vol. 981, p. 042016. IOP Publishing (2022)

10. Carvajal-Ramírez, F., Navarro-Ortega, A.D., Agüera-Vega, F., Martínez-Carricondo, P., Mancini, F.: Virtual reconstruction of damaged archaeological sites based on unmanned aerial vehicle photogrammetry and 3D modelling. Study case of a Southeastern Iberia production area in the bronze age. Measurement **136**, 225–236 (2019)

11. Guan, J., et al.: Full field-of-view pavement stereo reconstruction under dynamic traffic conditions: incorporating height-adaptive vehicle detection and multi-view occlusion optimization. Autom. Constr. **144**, 104615 (2022)

12. Schneider, F.D., Kükenbrink, D., Schaepman, M.E., Schimel, D.S., Morsdorf, F.: Quantifying 3D structure and occlusion in dense tropical and temperate forests using close-range lidar. Agric. Forest Meteorol. **268**, 249–257 (2019). https://doi.org/10.1016/j.agrformet.2019.01.033. https://www.sciencedirect.com/science/article/pii/S0168192319300267

13. Zhao, J., et al.: A wheat spike detection method in UAV images based on improved YOLOv5. Remote Sens. **13**(16) (2021). https://doi.org/10.3390/rs13163095. https://www.mdpi.com/2072-4292/13/16/3095

14. Qi, Q., Hossain, M.M., Li, J.J., Zhang, B., Li, J., Xu, C.L.: Approach to reduce light field sampling redundancy for flame temperature reconstruction. Opt. Express **29**(9), 13094–13114 (2021)

15. Gilliam, C., Dragotti, P.L., Brookes, M.: On the spectrum of the plenoptic function. IEEE Trans. Image Process. **23**(2), 502–516 (2013)

16. Wu, G., Liu, Y., Fang, L., Chai, T.: Revisiting light field rendering with deep anti-aliasing neural network. IEEE Trans. Pattern Anal. Mach. Intell. **44**(9), 5430–5444 (2021)

17. Adelson, E.H., Bergen, J.R., et al.: The plenoptic function and the elements of early vision. Comput. Models Vis. Process. **1**(2), 3–20 (1991)

18. Zhu, C., Zhang, H., Liu, Q., Zhuang, Z., Yu, L.: A signal-processing framework for occlusion of 3D scene to improve the rendering quality of views. IEEE Trans. Image Process. **29**, 8944–8959 (2020)

19. Durand, F., Holzschuch, N., Soler, C., Chan, E., Sillion, F.X.: A frequency analysis of light transport. ACM Trans. Graph. (TOG) **24**(3), 1115–1126 (2005)

20. Buehler, C., Bosse, M., McMillan, L., Gortler, S., Cohen, M.: Unstructured Lumigraph rendering. In: Proceedings of the 28th Annual Conference on Computer Graphics and Interactive Techniques, pp. 425–432 (2001)
21. Liu, Q., Wang, Y., Wei, Y., Xie, L., Zhu, C., Zhou, R.: Spectral analysis of aerial light field for optimization sampling and rendering of unmanned aerial vehicle. In: 2022 IEEE International Conference on Visual Communications and Image Processing (VCIP), pp. 1–5. IEEE (2022)
22. Chai, J.X., Tong, X., Chan, S.C., Shum, H.Y.: Plenoptic sampling. In: Proceedings of the 27th Annual Conference on Computer Graphics and Interactive Techniques, SIGGRAPH 2000, pp. 307–318. ACM Press/Addison-Wesley Publishing Co., USA (2000). https://doi.org/10.1145/344779.344932
23. Bolles, R.C., Baker, H.H., Marimont, D.H.: Epipolarplane image analysis: an approach to determining structure from motion. Int. J. Comput. Vis. 1(1), 7–55 (1987)

YOLOv5-LW: Lightweight UAV Object Detection Algorithm Based on YOLOv5

He Xiao[1,2(✉)], Kai Zhao[1], Xiaomei Xie[1], Peilong Song[1], Siwen Dong[1], and Jiahui Yang[1]

[1] School of Software Engineering, Jiangxi University of Science and Technology, Nanchang 330013, Jiangxi, People's Republic of China
xiaohe804@gmail.com, {kewitt,mavia}@jxust.edu.cn, adsw@mail.jxust.edu.cn
[2] Nanchang Key Laboratory of Virtual Digital Factory and Cultural Communications, Nanchang 330013, People's Republic of China

Abstract. UAV object detection task is a highly popular computer vision task, where algorithms can be deployed on unmanned aerial vehicles (UAVs) for real-time object detection. However, YOLOv5's performance for UAV object detection is not entirely satisfactory due to the small size of the detected objects and the problem of occlusion. To address these two issues in the YOLOv5 algorithm, we propose the YOLOv5-LW algorithm model. Building upon YOLOv5, we replace the FPN-PAN network structure with the FPN-PANS structure. This modification helps mitigate the issue of feature disappearance for small objects during the training process while reducing the model parameters and computational complexity. Additionally, within the FPN-PANS structure, we employ a multistage feature fusion approach instead of the original feature fusion module. This approach effectively corrects the erroneous information generated during the upsampling stage for certain objects. Finally, we replace the SPPF module with the SPPF-W module to further increase the receptive field while maintaining almost unchanged parameters. We conducted multiple experiments and demonstrate that YOLOv5-LW performs exceptionally well in lightweight small object detection tasks using the VisDrone dataset. Compared to YOLOv5, YOLOv5-LW achieves a 4.7% improvement in mean average precision (mAP), reduces the model size by 40%, and decreases the parameters by 40%.

Keywords: Object detection · UAV object detection · Lightweight model · Small object detection

---

This work was supported by Jiangxi Province Office of Education.

C. Wu et al. (Eds.): MONAMI 2023, LNICST 559, pp. 16–26, 2024.
https://doi.org/10.1007/978-3-031-55471-1_2

1   Introduction

UAV object detection tasks have been widely applied in various scenarios, such as plant protection [1,2], wildlife conservation [3,4], and EU regulation monitoring [5,6]. However, our focus lies more on the development of lightweight real-time object detection.

In recent years, significant progress has been made in object detection tasks using deep convolutional neural networks [7–10]. Benchmark datasets like MS COCO [11] and PASCAL VOC [12] have played a crucial role in promoting the advancement of object detection applications. However, most previous deep convolutional neural network works were designed for natural scene images, and directly applying these models to handle object detection tasks in UAV-captured scenes presents challenges. Some examples in Fig. 1 illustrate this point. Firstly, the scale of objects varies significantly due to different flight altitudes, causing drastic changes in object sizes. Secondly, images captured by UAVs contain dense objects, leading to object occlusion. Lastly, UAV-captured images often contain a large amount of confusing background due to coverage. These three issues make object detection in UAV-captured images highly challenging.

The YOLO [13–17] series of one-stage detectors plays a crucial role in object detection. In this paper, we propose a new lightweight detection model called YOLOv5-LW based on YOLOv5. The proposed model addresses the problem of feature loss for small objects during feature fusion and the generation of erroneous information due to the disappearance of certain object features during the upsampling process. Additionally, we increase the receptive field of the network and reduce the algorithm parameters and model size. Compared to YOLOv5, our algorithm achieves higher accuracy with fewer parameters and model size (as shown in Fig. 1).

Our contributions are as follows:

- We propose the FPN-PANS network structure, which not only reduces the model parameters but also enhances detection accuracy with multiple detection heads.
- We introduce a multistage feature fusion module that effectively reduces information loss during convolution and upsampling processes.
- We propose the SPPF-W module, which increases the field of view compared to the original SPPF module while keeping the parameters unchanged.
- We conduct extensive and effective experiments to demonstrate the superiority of our algorithm compared to related algorithms.

2   Related Work

2.1   Object Detection Algorithm

Object detection algorithm is an important research direction in the field of computer vision. With the development of deep learning technology, object detection

Fig. 1. As shown in the figure, due to the far-distance top-down shooting under different lighting conditions in the VisDrone [5] dataset, it differs from other datasets in terms of shooting angles. Moreover, the objects are small and densely packed, significantly increasing the difficulty of detection.

algorithms have also made significant progress. This article will introduce the development of object detection algorithms and the classification of object detection algorithms.

The development of object detection algorithms can be divided into two stages. The first stage is traditional object detection algorithms, which mainly include template matching, edge detection, color features, and other methods. These methods have limitations in terms of accuracy and robustness. The second stage is the application of deep learning technology, mainly including object detection algorithms based on convolutional neural networks, such as RCNN [18], Fast RCNN [19], Faster RCNN [20], YOLO, etc. These algorithms have greatly improved in terms of accuracy and speed.

The classification of object detection algorithms can be divided into two categories: region-based object detection algorithms and one-stage object detection algorithms. Region-based object detection algorithms mainly generate a series of candidate regions in the image and then classify and regress each candidate region. One-stage object detection algorithms directly classify and regress the entire image. Among them, region-based object detection algorithms include RCNN, Fast RCNN, Faster RCNN, etc.; one-stage object detection algorithms include YOLO, SSD [21], etc.

2.2   Neck

In object detection, the role of the Neck layer is to fuse features from different layers to improve the model's performance. As the field of object detection continues to evolve, there are now various types of Neck layers commonly used. Here are a few examples:

1. Feature Pyramid Network (FPN) [22]: FPN is a widely-used feature pyramid structure that aims to simultaneously capture features at different scales by utilizing both top-down and bottom-up pathways for feature fusion, thereby improving detection accuracy.

2. Path Aggregation Network (PAN) [23]: PAN is another feature pyramid-based Neck structure that focuses on information aggregation and expansion between different feature pyramids, enabling better feature fusion and improving detection accuracy.
3. Neural Architecture Search FPN (NAS-FPN) [24]: NAS-FPN is a feature pyramid structure automatically designed using neural architecture search algorithms, which outperforms traditional FPN structures in terms of performance.
4. Bi-Directional Feature Pyramid Network (BiFPN) [25]: BiFPN is a bi-directional feature pyramid structure that enables feature communication and propagation in both top-down and bottom-up directions, facilitating better information exchange and feature fusion.

In conclusion, with the advancement of deep learning techniques, object detection algorithms have made significant progress. Object detection algorithms can be categorized into region-based and one-stage approaches. These algorithms have wide-ranging applicability in various domains.

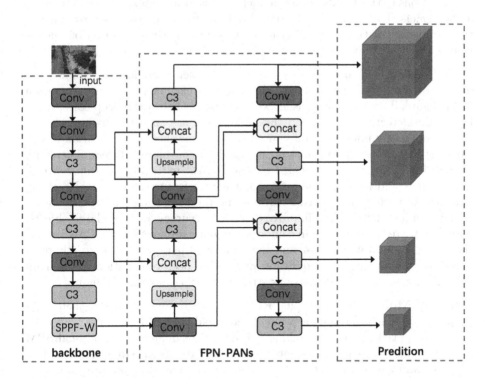

Fig. 2. The network structure of our algorithm consists of three parts: the main network structure, FPN-PANs, and the Head, as shown in the figure above.

3 YOLOv5-LW

3.1 Overview of YOLOv5

For YOLOv5, it includes multiple models such as YOLOv5s, YOLOv5m, YOLOv5l, YOLOv5n, and YOLOv5x. These models only differ in terms of their width and depth, while the overall model structure remains the same. Generally, YOLOv5 uses the architecture of CSPDarknet53 with an SPPF layer as the backbone, PANet as the Neck, and YOLO detection head. In our experiments, we conducted comparisons using models of different sizes, and the results showed significant improvements in our algorithm across multiple models. Please note that the translation might not capture the complete technical details accurately, as it is a complex domain-specific topic.

3.2 YOLOv5-LW

The network architecture of YOLOv5-LW is shown in Fig. 2. We have made some modifications to the YOLOv5 base model to make it more suitable for unmanned aerial vehicle (UAV) object detection. We have also made some adjustments to the parameters of the network structure to prioritize the extraction of shallow features.

FPN-PANS Structure. For the VisDrone dataset, there are only a few large objects present. We have visualized the output of each layer's features as shown in the figure. Through comparison, we have found that in the deep convolution layers, the detection targets and the background are almost indistinguishable, while more useful information is concentrated in the shallow convolution layers. There is limited useful information in the deep convolution layers. Therefore, in the FPN stage, we have decided to abandon the extraction of deep convolution features and focus on the fusion of shallower features. In the PANS stage, however, we perform deeper convolutions and retain the original detection head for large object detection to improve detection accuracy for those large objects. Although there is an increase in computation and parameters in the PANS stage, the overall computational cost and the number of parameters are greatly optimized as we eliminate the significant overhead of deep convolution in the main network stage. The specific network structure is illustrated in the figure.

SPPF-W Module. For SPP [26], RFB [27], SPPF, and SimSPPF, their main purpose is to enhance the perception of the visual field. SPP modules have their origins in spatial pyramid matching (SPM) [28] techniques. The original SPM method divides the feature map into equally sized blocks with dimensions of d*d, where d can take values such as 1, 2, 3, and so on. This division forms a spatial pyramid, and then the bag-of-words features are extracted. In the YOLO series, SPP (implemented in YOLOv3) consists of three parallel max-pooling outputs with sizes of $k \times k$, where $k = 5$, 9, and 13, respectively. SPPF (employed in YOLOv4) consists of three max-pooling outputs with a fixed size of $k \times k$, where $k = 5$. SPPF provides the same field enhancement as SPP but with fewer structural parameters and faster computation. In YOLOv6, the SimSPPF module

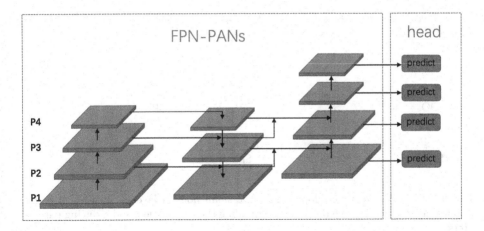

Fig. 3. In the FPN-PANs structure, we primarily focus on integrating shallow-level information and adding a small object detection head. This design enables better performance in unmanned object detection tasks.

simply replaces the SiLU activation function used in SPPF with the ReLU activation function. To further enhance the field of view, we modified the SPPF module in YOLOv6 by setting k to 7 and observed significant improvements in training performance. However, this modification also increased the model's parameter count (Fig. 3).

In this paper, a novel pooling module called SPPF-W is proposed (see Fig. 4). The SPPF-W module is composed of three SPOOL modules, with each SPOOL module consisting of three SP modules. Each SP module comprises a k × k max-pooling operation and a SiLU activation function. For instance, if we assume the input image size is 28 × 28 and apply a 5 × 5 pooling layer with a step size of 1, the resulting feature map size would be $(28 - 5)/1 + 1 = 24$. Similarly, using a 77 pooling layer with a step size of 1, we would obtain a feature map size of $(28 - 7)/1 + 1 = 22$. Finally, when three successive 3 × 3 pooling layers are applied, the feature map sizes would be as follows: $(28 - 3)/1 + 1 = 26$ for the first layer, $(26 - 3)/1 + 1 = 24$ for the second layer, and $(24 - 3)/1 + 1 = 22$ for the third layer. It is noteworthy that the 7 × 7 pooling layer provides a similar field of view as the combination of three 3 × 3 pooling layers. In terms of parameter count, the three 3 × 3 pooling layers have a total of 3 × (3 × 3) channels, the 5 × 5 pooling layer has 5 × 5 channels, and the 7 × 7 pooling layer has 7 × 7 channels. Therefore, the SPPF-W module achieves a larger perceptual field of view with minimal parameter growth. Specifically, it has approximately 45% fewer parameters compared to using a 7 × 7 pooling layer.

Multi Level Feature Fusion Module (MLF). In the original PAN network architecture, only the relevant features in FPN are fused. However, we found that for small object detection, a significant amount of valuable information is lost during the convolution and upsampling processes. Even with fusion,

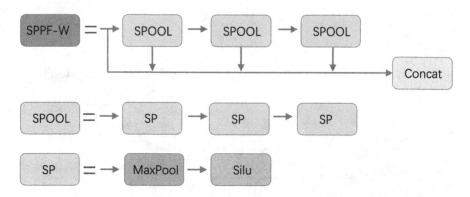

Fig. 4. SPPF-W: We have adopted multiple small pooling layers instead of a larger pooling layer to achieve the purpose of expanding the field of view and reducing parameters.

the fused features are often contaminated with a considerable amount of noise. This is mainly because in deeper convolutions, the detection of the target and background becomes indistinguishable, and upsampling alone is not effective in restoring the features. To mitigate the impact of this noise on the model's accuracy, we propose the PANS network architecture, as shown in Fig. 1. In the convolution process, we incorporate fusion with the features from the main network, allowing a larger amount of valuable information to correct erroneous information and improve the accuracy of the algorithm. Please refer to Fig. 1 for the model structure

4 Experiments

4.1 Experimental Environment

Implementation Details In aerial object detection experiments, we used the pytorch framework and the Ubuntu 22.04 operating system. The model parameters are set as follows: lr = 0.01, epoch = 1000, batch size = 28. All experiments were trained on the GTX3070 GPU.

4.2 Experimental Data

We evaluated our model using the testing challenge and testing development subsets of the Vis-Drone2021 dataset. We reported the mean Average Precision (mAP) across all 10 IoU thresholds ranging from 0.5 to 0.95, as well as the mAP at IoU threshold 0.5 (mAP50). In this chapter, we conducted control experiments, including different model sizes of the same algorithm, and ablation experiments to validate the superiority of our algorithm.

4.3   Comparisons with the State-of-the-Art

In this section, we trained and tested multiple YOLOv series models along with our algorithm model on the VisDrone dataset (with images uniformly resized to 512×512). The final results are shown in Table 1, which demonstrates the superiority of our algorithm. From the data in the table, it can be observed that our model outperforms most algorithm models in terms of accuracy and has fewer parameters and a smaller model size. Although the YOLOv7 series algorithm models achieve higher accuracy than our model, with a 0.3% higher mAP0.5:0.95 and a 2.2% higher mAP0.5 for the S-sized model, our model only has around 27% of the parameters and approximately 29% of the model size compared to YOLOv7. In terms of model size, our model is slightly less accurate than YOLOv7, with a 2.7% lower mAP0.5 and a 0.8% lower mAP0.5:0.95. However, our model's parameters are only around 27% of YOLOv7, and the model size is about 36% of YOLOv7. Compared with other algorithms, our algorithm is not only more lightweight but also achieves higher accuracy. In conclusion, our model demonstrates better advancement.

Table 1. During the training process, we use 512×512 images for training. The bold font represents the best metrics.

VisDrone				
Methods	mAP0.5	mAP0.5:0.95	parameters	model size
Yolov5s	0.286	0.152	7037095	14.4 MB
Yolov6s	0.327	0.191	–	38.0 MB
Yolov7s	**0.398**	**0.214**	9344734	19.0 MB
Yolov8s	0.354	0.208	11129454	22.5 MB
YOLO-LWs	0.376	0.211	**2499348**	**5.5 MB**
Yolov5n	0.242	0.119	1772695	3.8 MB
Yolov6n	0.275	0.156	–	6.2 MB
Yolov7n	**0.33**	0.165	2353014	5.0 MB
Yolov8n	0.301	**0.172**	3007598	6.2 MB
YOLO-LWn	0.303	0.157	**634340**	**1.8 MB**

4.4   Ablation Studies

In this section, we conducted ablation experiments on the VisDrone test dataset to validate the effectiveness of each proposed module. We used the Yolov5 S model for all experiments. The valuable data obtained from these experiments are presented in Table 2.

Effect of SPPF-W: After improving the FPN to FPNS in the model (using Yolov5 S model as an example), there were no significant changes in computational complexity, parameters, or model size. However, the detection performance of the model improved. The mAP at a IoU threshold of 0.5 increased by 0.8%, and the mAP at a IoU threshold of 0.5:0.95 increased by 0.3%. Overall, compared to SPPF, SPPF-W is a superior choice.

Effect of FPN: After modifying the FPN module, the model parameters decreased from over 7 million to just over 2 million. The number of model layers decreased from 214 to 201, and the model size reduced from 14.4 MB to 5.3 MB. However, there was a significant improvement in mAP at a IoU threshold of 0.5 and mAP at a IoU threshold of 0.5:0.95. The mAP at a IoU threshold of 0.5 increased by 7.4%, and the mAP at a IoU threshold of 0.5:0.95 increased by 5.1%. These results indicate that our FPN+ module is more efficient for UAV object detection.

Effect of Multi-Level Fusion: After adding the multi-level fusion module to our algorithm, there was only a slight increase in model parameters and computational complexity, while the model size remained the same. However, there was a significant improvement in the detection results. The mAP at a IoU threshold of 0.5 increased by 0.8%, and the mAP at a IoU threshold of 0.5:0.95 increased by 0.5%.

Table 2. In the ablation experiments, we validate our proposed modules using the S-sized model, and the results demonstrate the advanced performance of each module.

VisDrone				
Methods	mAP0.5	mAP0.5:0.95	parameters	model size
Yolov5s	0.286	0.152	7037095	14.4 MB
Yolov5s+FPN-PANs	0.363	0.204	2401044	5.3 MB
Yolov5s+FPN-PANs+SPPF-W	0.368	0.206	2401044	5.3 MB
YOLO-LWs	**0.376**	**0.211**	2499348	5.5 MB

From the table, it can be observed that compared to Yolov5, our model is more lightweight, and when applied to UAV detection tasks, it achieves higher accuracy and has greater potential for industrial applications.

References

1. Hird, J.N., et al.: Use of unmanned aerial vehicles for monitoring recovery of forest vegetation on petroleum well sites. Remote Sens. **9**(5), 413 (2017)
2. Shao, Z., Li, C., Li, D., Altan, O., Zhang, L., Ding, L.: An accurate matching method for projecting vector data into surveillance video to monitor and protect cultivated land. ISPRS Int. J. Geo Inf. **9**(7), 448 (2020)

3. Kellenberger, B., Volpi, M., Tuia, D.: Fast animal detection in UAV images using convolutional neural networks. In: 2017 IEEE International Geoscience and Remote Sensing Symposium, IGARSS 2017, Fort Worth, TX, USA, 23–28 July 2017, pp. 866–869. IEEE (2017)
4. Kellenberger, B., Marcos, D., Tuia, D.: Detecting mammals in UAV images: best practices to address a substantially imbalanced dataset with deep learning. Remote Sens. Environ. **216**, 139–153 (2018)
5. Audebert, N., Le Saux, B., Lefèvre, S.: Beyond RGB: very high resolution urban remote sensing with multimodal deep networks. ISPRS J. Photogrammetry Remote Sens. **140**, 20–32 (2018)
6. Gu, J., Su, T., Wang, Q., Du, X., Guizani, M.: Multiple moving targets surveillance based on a cooperative network for multi-UAV. IEEE Commun. Mag. **56**(4), 82–89 (2018)
7. Ren, S., He, K., Girshick, R., Sun, J.: Faster R-CNN: towards real-time object detection with region proposal networks. In: Advances in Neural Information Processing Systems, vol. 28, pp. 91–99 (2015)
8. Redmon, J., Divvala, S., Girshick, R., Farhadi, A.: You only look once: unified, real-time object detection. In: Proceedings of the IEEE Conference on Computer Vision and Pattern Recognition, pp. 779–788 (2016)
9. Lin, T.-Y., Goyal, P., Girshick, R.B., He, K., Dollar, P.: Focal loss for dense object detection. In: IEEE International Conference on Computer Vision, ICCV 2017, Venice, Italy, 22–29 October 2017, pp. 2999–3007. IEEE Computer Society (2017)
10. Zhang, H., Wang, Y., Dayoub, F., Sunderhauf, N.: VarifocalNet: an IoU-aware dense object detector. In: Proceedings of the IEEE/CVF Conference on Computer Vision and Pattern Recognition, pp. 8514–8523 (2021)
11. Lin, T.Y., et al.: Microsoft COCO: common objects in context. In: Fleet, D., Pajdla, T., Schiele, B., Tuytelaars, T. (eds.) ECCV 2014. LNCS, vol. 8693, pp. 740–755. Springer, Cham (2014). https://doi.org/10.1007/978-3-319-10602-1_48
12. Everingham, M., Van Gool, L., Williams, C.K.I., Winn, J.M., Zisserman, A.: The pascal visual object classes (VOC) challenge. Int. J. Comput. Vis. **88**(2), 303–338 (2010)
13. Redmon, J., Farhadi, A.: YOLO9000: better, faster, stronger. In: Proceedings of the IEEE Conference on Computer Vision and Pattern Recognition (CVPR), pp. 7263–7271 (2017)
14. Redmon, J., Farhadi, A.: YOLOv3: an incremental improvement. arXiv preprint arXiv:1804.02767 (2018)
15. Alexey, B., Chien-Yao, W., Mark, L.H.-Y.: YOLOv4: optimal speed and accuracy of object detection, arXiv preprint arXiv:2004.10934 (2020)
16. Wang, C.-Y., Bochkovskiy, A., Liao, H.-Y.M.: Scaled-YOLOv4: scaling cross stage partial network. In: Computer Vision and Pattern Recognition, pp. 13029–13038 (2021)
17. Junyang, C., et al.: A multiscale lightweight and efficient model based on YOLOv7: applied to citrus orchard. Plants-Basel **11**(23) (2022)
18. Pang, J., Chen, K., Shi, J., Feng, H., Ouyang, W., Lin, D.: Libra R-CNN: towards balanced learning for object detection. In: Proceedings of the IEEE Conference on Computer Vision and Pattern Recognition (CVPR), pp. 821–830 (2019)
19. Girshick, R.: Fast R-CNN. In: Proceedings of the IEEE International Conference on Computer Vision (ICCV), pp. 1440–1448 (2015)
20. Ren, S., He, K., Girshick, R., Sun, J.: Faster R-CNN: towards real-time object detection with region proposal networks. In: Advances in Neural Information Processing Systems (NIPS), pp. 91–99 (2015)

21. Liu, W., et al.: SSD: single shot multibox detector. In: Leibe, B., Matas, J., Sebe, N., Welling, M. (eds.) LNCS. ECCV 2016, vol. 9905, pp. 21–37. Springer, Cham (2016). https://doi.org/10.1007/978-3-319-46448-0_2

22. Lin, T.-Y., Dollar, P., Girshick, R., He, K., Hariharan, B., Belongie, S.: Feature pyramid networks for object detection. In: Proceedings of the IEEE Conference on Computer Vision and Pattern Recognition (CVPR), pp. 2117–2125 (2017)

23. Liu, S., Qi, L., Qin, H., Shi, J., Jia, J.: Path aggregation network for instance segmentation. In: Proceedings of the IEEE Conference on Computer Vision and Pattern Recognition (CVPR), pp. 8759–8768 (2018)

24. Ghiasi, G., Lin, T.-Y., Le, Q.V.: NAS-FPN: learning scalable feature pyramid architecture for object detection. In: Proceedings of the IEEE Conference on Computer Vision and Pattern Recognition (CVPR), pp. 7036–7045 (2019)

25. Tan, M., Pang, R., Le, Q.V.: EfficientDet: scalable and efficient object detection. In: Proceedings of the IEEE Conference on Computer Vision and Pattern Recognition (CVPR) (2020)

26. He, K., Zhang, X., Ren, S., Sun, J.: Spatial pyramid pooling in deep convolutional networks for visual recognition. IEEE Trans. Pattern Anal. Mach. Intell. (TPAMI) **37**(9), 1904–1916 (2015)

27. Liu, S., Huang, D., et al.: Receptive field block net for accurate and fast object detection. In: Proceedings of the European Conference on Computer Vision (ECCV), pp. 385–400 (2018)

28. Lazebnik, S., Schmid, C., Ponce, J.: Beyond bags of features: spatial pyramid matching for recognizing natural scene categories. In: Proceedings of the IEEE Conference on Computer Vision and Pattern Recognition (CVPR), vol. 2, pp. 2169–2178. IEEE (2006)

29. Visdrone Team. Visdrone 2020 leaderboard (2020). http://aiskyeye.com/visdrone-2020-leaderboard/

Client Selection Method for Federated Learning in Multi-robot Collaborative Systems

Nian Ding[1,3]([⊠]), Chunrong Peng[2], Min Lin[3], Yangfei Lin[1], Zhaoyang Du[1], and Celimuge Wu[1]

[1] Graduate School of Informatics and Engineering, The University of Electro-Communications, 1-5-1 Chofugaoka, Chofu, Tokyo 182-8585, Japan
3192720267@qq.com, celimuge@uec.ac.jp
[2] Library, Inner Mongolia University of Finance and Economics, Xincheng District, Hohhot, Inner Mongolia Autonomous Region, People's Republic of China
[3] College of Computer Science and Technology, Inner Mongolia Normal University, Saihan District, Hohhot, Inner Mongolia Autonomous Region, People's Republic of China

Abstract. Federated Learning (FL) has recently attracted considerable attention in multi-robot collaborative systems, owning to its capability of enabling mobile clients to collaboratively learn a global prediction model without sharing their privacy-sensitive data to the server. In a multi-robot collaboration system, an approach that ensures privacy-preserving knowledge sharing among multiple robots becomes imperative. However, the application of FL in such systems encounters two major challenges. Firstly, it is inefficient to use all the network nodes as federated learning clients (which conduct training of machine learning model based on own data) due to the limited wireless bandwidth and energy of robots. Secondly, the selection of an appropriate number of clients must be carefully considered, considering the constraints imposed by limited communication resources. Selecting an excessive number of clients may result in a failure in uploading important models. To overcome these challenges, this paper proposes a client selection approach that considers multiple metrics including the data volume, computational capability, and network environment by integrating fuzzy logic and Q-learning. The experimental results validate the theoretical feasibility of the proposed approach. Further empirical data can be derived from training experiments on public datasets, enhancing the practical applicability of the proposed method.

Keywords: Federated Learning · Fuzzy Logic · Q-learning Algorithm · Multi-robots Collaboration

1 Introduction

Artificial intelligence (AI) has become an indispensable element of modern society, owing to the recent advancements in machine learning (ML) technology that have enabled successful implementations in various domains, such as image recognition and natural language processing [1]. ML models require a large amount of data to update the

C. Wu et al. (Eds.): MONAMI 2023, LNICST 559, pp. 27–41, 2024.
https://doi.org/10.1007/978-3-031-55471-1_3

model to achieve the desirable accuracy [2]. In traditional ML model training, a cloud centric approach is adopted to gather data collected by mobile devices and train the ML model on a powerful cloud server or data center [3]. However, the data transmission process raises security concerns, as it increases the risk of data breaches and compromises user privacy when data is aggregated in the cloud. The current trend in machine learning is shifting towards decentralized edge clouds, leading to the emergence of FL. FL allows the efficient training and utilization of ML models while ensuring user data localization [4, 5].

In order to protect the security of local data for each robot, prevent the leakage of important or sensitive data, and achieve information sharing between robots, FL has been applied in the field of multi-robot collaboration. Unlike the independent and identically distributed (IID) data environment of traditional machine learning, FL operates in a complex and heterogeneous environment, with significant differences in sample size and data distribution among different clients. This indicates that there is a Non-Independent and Identical Distribution (Non-IID) feature between the local data of the client in FL [6]. There are two key challenges in the application of FL in multi-robots collaborative systems. Firstly, the local data of each robot (client) is inconsistent in practical applications, and some robots may not be helpful or even ineffective for collaborative systems. Hence, it is crucial to select clients based on their performance to optimize information exchange. Selecting robots with better performance for information sharing is currently a challenging and active research area. Secondly, in multi-robots collaborative systems, communication between the clients (robots) and the central server occurs via network connections, which may be unstable and prone to temporary disconnections. Due to the limitations of network resources, the selection of an appropriate number of clients for information exchange becomes critical. Choosing an optimal client count depends on factors such as network status, computational resource capabilities, and FL model accuracy. Consequently, determining the appropriate number of clients for information exchange represents another research challenge and focal point. To address the above two challenges, this paper proposes a client selection method based on fuzzy logic and Q-learning for FL in multi-robot collaborative systems. The purpose of the paper is to select high-performance clients based on the local data volume and computing resource capabilities and to select an appropriate number of clients based on network status, computing resource capabilities and model accuracy of FL. The main contributions of the paper are listed below:

- The paper proposes a client evaluation approach based on fuzzy logic to tackle the challenge of selecting clients with better performance. This approach considers the data volume and computational capability of each client. By setting the corresponding fuzzy combination based on local data size and model training time, the approach obtains fuzzy results through fuzzification and fuzzy reasoning. These fuzzy results are then converted into numerical values, enabling the evaluation of all candidate clients. By utilizing a fuzzy logic algorithm, the proposed approach effectively selects clients with superior performance.
- The paper addresses the problem of determining the appropriate number of clients for FL by proposing an approach based on the Q-learning algorithm. The Q-table and R matrix are initialized, and the initial action is chosen based on the R matrix

and initial state. Subsequently, the Q-table is iteratively updated using feedback from the environment until the appropriate number of clients is determined. This approach contributes to client selection by finding the optimal number of clients, taking into account factors such as network status, computational resource capabilities, and FL model accuracy.

• To verify the effectiveness of the proposed scheme, this paper conducts empirical training experiments on GTSRB (The German Traffic Sign Benchmark). The simulation results show that the proposed scheme outperforms other baseline methods.

The remainder of the paper is organized as follows. Related works are listed in Sect. 2. The overview of the system model is introduced in Sect. 3. A method for selecting federated learning clients based on fuzzy logic is described in Sect. 4. A method for selecting federated learning clients based on Q-learning is described in Sect. 5. Following, we present the performance of the proposed scheme using a simulator in Sect. 6. Finally, we conclude our work in Sect. 7.

2 Related Work

FL has gained significant attention and widespread application in multi-robot collaborative systems, as it enables collaborative machine learning without the need for centralized data storage [7]. FL can use data collected by a set of robots distributed in different locations to train ML models. Reference [8] studies a new federated deep reinforcement learning method called F-DRL. This method addresses issues such as signal strength attenuation caused by obstacles and the dynamic environment caused by robot movement. By utilizing a dynamic long-term goal, each robot autonomously plans its own path and downlink power, reducing training dimensions and saving computational costs [8]. Reference [9] proposes a distributed federated learning method for networked multi-robots called dFRL. This method solves the inherent problems of centralized federated learning methods such as central node failures and channel bandwidth bottlenecks. Unlike traditional centralized methods that rely on a limited number of cloud servers to aggregate models, dFRL performs model aggregation through parameter transfer among robots, providing a decentralized and scalable approach [9].

Another key issue is that a group of robots typically collect data at different rates, which affects the frequency of robot participation in shared model updates. Reference [10] proposes a data-driven approach where robots update their local model only when sufficient data has been collected. However, an important challenge in FL for multi-robots systems lies in selecting the most suitable client to participate in the training process [10]. Because each client may have different data distribution and computational capability, this may affect the overall performance of the model. McMahan et al. reveal that the convergence performance of FL depends on the importance of client updates [11]. In the context of client selection, reference [12] investigates the problem from the perspective of minimizing average model exchange time. Meanwhile, reference [13] points out that selecting clients with higher local loss can achieve faster convergence in the learning process. They propose an efficient client selection method that considers factors such as convergence speed, result bias and communication/computation cost [13]. Furthermore,

FL is applied to multi-robots reinforcement learning in reference [14]. They focus on establishing a collaborative model in the context of 5G HetNet, which can quickly and stably complete tasks while ensuring security performance [14].

Although these studies have contributed to addressing various challenges in FL for multi-robot systems, there are still opportunities for improvement in terms of efficiency, scalability, and robustness. This paper focuses on investigating client selection methods for federated learning in multi-robots collaborative systems, aiming to enhance the quality of trained models and reduce communication overhead.

3 System Overview

3.1 Task Scenario

As shown in Fig. 1, multiple robots collaborate to move goods in a multi-robots collaborative system. Robots collaborate through navigation technology to transport goods from point A to point B. To enhance their navigation capabilities, traffic signs are placed on both sides of the road.

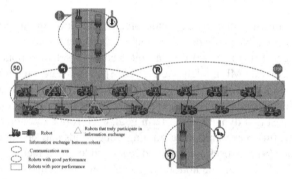

Fig. 1. Application scenario of FL client selection method for multi-robots collaborative systems.

In order to preserve the security of local data, FL is used for information exchange in a multi-robots collaborative system. Choosing some useless or weakly correlated robots as clients for FL may waste communication resources and lead to a decrease in the performance of the global model. It is necessary to select clients with better performance to participate in FL, which can help improve performance of FL. Due to network resource constraints, different clients' numbers are selected based on the requirements of different scenarios, such as selecting 20, 40, 60 or 80 clients for information exchange. It is necessary to select high-performance robots for information exchange while also choosing an appropriate robots' numbers according to different scenarios requirements.

3.2 The Workflow of Fuzzy Logic

We have designed a FL client method based on fuzzy logic. As shown in Fig. 2, it mainly consists of the following two modules:

- Clients' local training. Each client trains a local model using its local dataset. The client's local data volume (LDV) and resource computation time (local model training time, RCT) serve as two factors that are considered together to assess the client's performance.
- Fuzzy logic model. The client's LDV and RCT are used as inputs. Then, fuzzy results are obtained through fuzzy inference. The final client selection result is obtained through defuzzification.

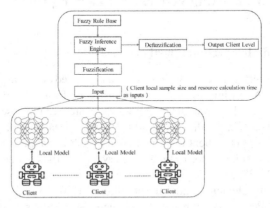

Fig. 2. Workflow of fuzzy logic.

3.3 The Workflow of Q-Learning

The proposed FL client selection method incorporates the utilization of Q-learning.

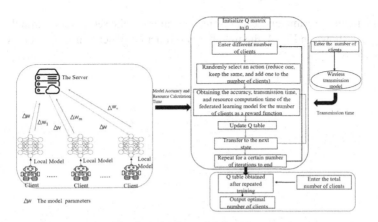

Fig. 3. Workflow of Q-learning.

As shown in Fig. 3, it consists of the following three key modules:

- FL model. FL accuracy (ACC) and clients' RCT are obtained through FL are used as inputs for the Q-learning algorithm.
- Wireless transmission model (WT). In FL, model parameters are transmitted between the client and server through WT. The obtained transmission time through WT is used as an input for the Q-learning algorithm.
- Q-learning algorithm. Obtain the final Q-table. Enter a total clients' numbers. Output an optimal clients' numbers.

4   A Method for Selecting Federated Learning Clients Based on Fuzzy Logic

4.1   Fuzzy Set and Membership Functions

The comprehensive performance of a client is evaluated based on two aspects: the client's LDV and its RCT. According to the comprehensive performance of the client, it is divided into three levels: high, middle, and low. There are two fuzzy sets, namely LDV set 'Num' and RCT set 'Time'. The set 'Num' is {many, middle, few}, and the set 'Time' is {high, middle, low}. The client data is Non-IID, with a maximum of 1200 images and a minimum of 100 images for LDV. The interval [0, 500] is defined as the element "few" in set 'Num'. [300, 900] is defined as the element 'middle' in set 'Num'. [700, 1200] is defined as the element 'many' in set 'Num'. [64, 68] is defined as the element 'low' in set 'Time'. [66, 62] is defined as the element 'middle' in set 'Time'. [70, 74] is defined as the element 'high' in set 'Time'.

When the value of LDV belongs to the set 'Num', the membership function is defined as follows:

$$F_{Num}(X) \begin{cases} 1/(1 + e^{-a(x-c)}) & x \in [0, 500] \\ 1/(1 + e^{-a((x-300)-c)}) & x \in [300, 900] \\ 1/(1 + e^{-a((x-700)-c)}) & x \in [700, 1200] \end{cases} \tag{1}$$

a and c are feature parameters. x represents the values of the set 'Num' within the range [0, 1200]. As shown in Fig. 4, the membership function of set 'Num' for values within the range [0, 1200].

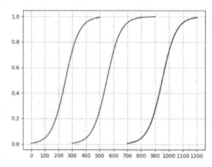

Fig. 4. The membership function of the set 'Num' for values within the range [0, 1200].

When the value of the element 'low' in the set 'Time' is [64, 68], the membership function is defined as follows:

$$F_{Time}(X) = (\frac{x-s}{b-s})^4 \tag{2}$$

s and b are feature parameters. x represents the values of the set 'Time' within the range [64, 68].

When the value of the element 'middle' belongs to the set 'Time', the membership function is defined as follows:

$$F_{Time}(X)\begin{cases}(\frac{x-c}{d-c})^4 & x \in [66, 68]\\ \frac{x}{x} & x \in [68, 70]\\ (\frac{t-x}{t-u})^4 & x \in [70, 72]\end{cases} \tag{3}$$

d, c, t, and u are feature parameters. x represents the values of the set 'Time' within the range [66, 72].

When the value of the element 'high' belongs to the set 'Time', the membership function is defined as follows:

$$F_{Time}(X)\begin{cases}\frac{x}{x} & x \in [70, 72]\\ (\frac{p-x}{p-k})^4 & x \in [72, 74]\end{cases} \tag{4}$$

p and k are feature parameters. x represents the values of the set 'Time' within the range [70, 74].

As shown in Fig. 5, the membership function of the set 'Time' for values within the range [64, 74].

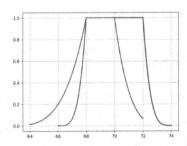

Fig. 5. The membership function of the set 'Time' for values within the range [64, 74].

4.2 Fuzzification and Defuzzification

For the set 'Num' {few, middle, many}, each element in 'Num' corresponds to a membership degree. Define them as N_0, N_1 and N_2 in sequence. For the set 'Time' {low, middle, high}, each element in 'Time' corresponds to a membership degree. Define them as T_0, T_1 and T_2 in sequence. The combination of the value from 'Num' and the value

Table 1. Fuzzy reasoning.

Serial Number	Num	Time	Rule Results	Membership degree
1	few(N_0)	low(T_0)	low	Min(N_0, T_0)
2	few (N_0)	middle(T_1)	middle	Min(N_0, T_1)
3	few (N_0)	high (T_2)	middle	Min(N_0, T_2)
4	middle(N_1)	low (T_0)	low	Min(N_1, T_0)
5	middle(N_1)	middle (T_1)	middle	Min(N_1, T_1)
6	middle(N_1)	high (T_2)	high	Min(N_1, T_2)
7	many(N_2)	low (T_0)	low	Min(N_2, T_0)
8	many(N_2)	middle (T_1)	high	Min(N_2, T_1)
9	many(N_2)	high (T_2)	high	Min(N_2, T_2)

from 'Time' can trigger the relevant rules. For example, if the client' LDV is 'few' and RCT is 'high', the performance of the client is low. Fuzzy rule base is shown in Table 1.

The relationship between LDV and RCT is 'and', so the minimum value method is used to determine the strength of the rule. It can be observed that there are identical rule results, such as the first rule and the fourth rule. If several rules have the same result, the maximum membership degree of these rules is obtained using the maximum value method. The maximum value among the membership degrees of different rules is taken as the final determined output result, which is used to determine the level of the client.

5   A Method for Selecting Federated Learning Clients Based on Q-Learning

5.1   Design of Q-Table

We build a Q-matrix in the research, which is used to store all the learning performed by the clients through a series of actions and state transitions. The initial state of the Q-matrix represents a situation where it has no knowledge about the external environment, so all the values in the Q-matrix are set to 0. The rows represent states, which represent the current number of clients, ranging from 1 to 100. The columns represent actions, ranging from 1 to 100. However, only three actions are valid: increasing the number of clients by 1, decreasing the number of clients by 1, and keeping the number of clients unchanged. Other actions are considered invalid. For example, if the current state respectively is 10 clients, the corresponding valid actions are 9, 10 and 11.

5.2   Design of Reward Function

A simple WT is designed. The bandwidth is defined as 10 Mbps and converting it to bytes is 1310720 Bps. This means that 1310720 bytes can be transmitted in one second. A client network model size is calculated as model_ size $= 2495610$ bytes. As the number of clients increases, the utilization of bandwidth also changes accordingly. When clients' numbers are less than or equal to 10, the transmission time is defined as follows:

$$y = model\_size / (bandwidth * a) \tag{5}$$

The constant a represents the proportion of space in the bandwidth allocated for data transmission.

When clients' numbers are greater than 10, the transmission time y is defined as follows:

$$y = model\_size / (bandwidth * (a - (n/10) * rate) \tag{6}$$

n represents the number of clients and $rate$ represents a decrease rate for data transmission space.

The transmission time is defined as y. The accuracy of FL is acc. RCT is c. The reward function r is defined as follows:

$$r = 0.5 * (\frac{1}{100} * acc) + 0.2 * (\frac{1}{3.02} * y) + 0.3 * (\frac{1}{7360} * c) \tag{7}$$

5.3 An Iterative Process of Q-Learning

The iterative process of Q-learning begins by entering a different number of clients for each iteration. The FL model is then employed to obtain the corresponding FL accuracy, Round Completion Time (RCT), and transmission time for the given number of clients. These values are subsequently used as inputs to the reward function. Equation (8) represents the update rule for the Q-table in each iteration:

$$Q(s, a) = Q(s, a) + \alpha[r(s, a) + \gamma \max_A Q(s', a) - Q(s, a)] \tag{8}$$

α is the learning rate. $Q(s, a)$ represents the estimated value of the current state-action pair. $Q(s', a)$ represents the estimated value of the next state-action pair. $\max_A Q(s', a)$ selecting an action in action set A that maximizes $Q(s', a)$. γ represents the discount factor for the reward value. $r(s, a)$ represents the reward value immediately given by the environment when an action is executed in the current state.

6 Experimental Result

6.1 Experimental Dataset and Preprocessing

The dataset is the German Traffic Sign Recognition Benchmark. As shown in Fig. 6, the first row from left to right is speed limits of 20, 50, 60, 70 and 80. The second row from left to right is left turn, right turn, warning, no entry and STOP.

The client IDs for 1–100 are set to 0–99. If ID is 1, 31 or 61, the assigned LDV is greater than or equal to 600. If ID is divisible by both 3 and 5, the assigned LDV is greater than or equal to 200. If ID is divisible by 7, the assigned LDV is greater than or equal to 300. If ID is divisible by 8, the assigned LDV is greater than or equal to 400. As shown in Table 2, the assigned LDV is greater than or equal to 50 for IDs that do not meet the above conditions.

Fig. 6. Partial presentation of the GTSRB dataset.

Table 2. Client local data volume allocation results.

Local data volume	Clients' numbers
100	46
200	3
400	31
600	10
800	5
1000	4
1200	1

6.2 Metrics

We introduce a metric called the average resource computation time (ARCT) to assess the performance of the FL model. To define the $ARCT$, we first consider the total training completion time of the FL model, denoted as T_{FL}, and the number of clients participating in the training, represented by N. The ARCT is defined as follows:

$$ARCT = \frac{T_{FL}}{N} \tag{9}$$

6.3 A Method for Selecting Federated Learning Clients Based on Fuzzy Logic

The experimental results of the proposed scheme about selecting high-performance clients based on fuzzy logic are shown in Table 3.

To verify the effectiveness of the proposed scheme, we chose three baselines for comparison, namely, client selection method based on local data volume, client selection method based on resource computation time, and client selection method based on random sampling. The details are as follows.

If only considering clients' LDV, the clients with LDV in the range of 800 to 1200 are classified as high performance, and the clients with LDV in the range of 400 to 600 are classified as middle performance, and the clients with LDV in the range of 100 to 200 are classified as low performance. The results are shown in Table 4.

If only considering clients' RCT, the clients with RCT in the range of 64 to 67 are classified as high performance, the clients with RCT in the range of 67 to 71 are classified

Table 3. Client level classification (Client selection method based on fuzzy logic).

Client classification	Client ID
High	0, 1, 33, 65
Middle	4, 6, 8, 10, 12, 13, 14, 18, 25, 26, 29, 31, 36, 40,49, 50, 52, 54, 57, 60, 61, 63, 68, 69, 71, 78, 79, 82, 89
Low	2, 3, 5, 7, 9, 11, 15, 16, 17, 19, 20, 21, 22, 23, 24, 27, 28, 30, 32, 34, 35, 37, 38, 39, 41, 42, 43, 44, 45, 46, 47, 48, 51, 53, 55, 56, 58, 59, 62, 64, 66, 67, 70, 72, 73, 74, 75, 76, 77, 80, 81, 83, 84, 85, 86, 87, 88, 90, 91, 92, 93, 94, 95, 96, 97, 98, 99

Table 4. Client level classification (Client selection method based on local data volume).

Client classification	Client ID
High	0, 1, 8, 16, 32, 33, 40, 65, 80, 88
Middle	3, 6, 7, 9, 12, 14, 15, 18, 21, 24, 28, 30, 35, 36, 39, 42, 45, 48, 49, 51, 54, 56, 57, 60, 63, 66, 69, 70, 72, 75, 77, 78, 81, 84, 87, 90, 91, 93, 98, 99
Low	2, 5, 10, 11, 13, 17, 19, 20, 22, 23, 25, 26, 29, 31, 34, 37, 41, 43, 44, 46, 47, 50, 52, 53, 55, 58, 59, 61, 62, 64, 67, 68, 71, 73, 74, 76, 79, 82, 83, 85, 86, 89, 92, 94, 95, 96, 97

as middle performance, and the clients with RCT in the range of 71 to 74 are classified as low performance. The results are shown in Table 5.

Table 5. Client level classification (Client selection method based on RCT).

Client classification	Client ID
High	1, 2, 5, 6, 10, 11, 13, 15, 16, 20, 22, 23, 24, 32, 33, 34, 38, 39, 41, 43, 44, 46, 47, 50, 51, 53, 54, 56, 57, 58, 59, 62, 63, 66, 68, 71, 74, 75, 76, 77, 78, 79, 80, 84, 85, 88, 90, 91, 92, 93, 96, 98, 99
Middle	0, 4, 7, 8, 9, 12, 14, 17, 18, 19, 21, 25, 26, 27, 28, 29, 30, 31, 35, 36, 40, 45, 48, 49, 52, 55, 60, 61, 64, 65, 67, 69, 72, 73, 81, 82, 83, 86, 87, 89, 94, 95, 97
Low	3, 37, 42, 70

The results of selecting clients using random sampling are shown in Table 6.

The evaluation metrics for this experiment are ARCT and the training data volume of the global model. The shorter ARCT of the selected clients in this group, the stronger the computational capability. The larger the training data volume of the global model of selected clients, the better the training performance of FL. The comprehensive analysis results of the experiments are shown in Fig. 7 and Fig. 8.

Table 6. Client level classification (Client selection method based on random sampling).

Client classification	Client ID
High	88, 19, 24, 34, 15, 74, 3, 22, 86, 60
Middle	45, 44, 53, 14, 52, 31, 61, 8, 46, 73, 30, 54, 32, 20, 21, 12, 40, 39, 27, 16, 18, 78, 26, 94, 17, 42, 89, 36, 99, 2, 85, 67, 84, 83, 1, 79, 82, 87, 49, 98, 23, 11, 77, 4, 7
Low	0, 5, 6, 9, 10, 13, 25, 28, 29, 33, 35, 37, 38, 41, 43, 47, 48, 50, 51, 55, 56, 57, 58, 59, 62, 63, 64, 65, 66, 68, 69, 70, 71, 72, 75, 76, 80, 81, 90, 91, 92, 93, 95, 96, 97

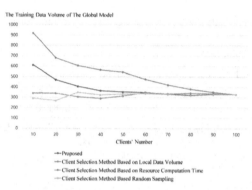

Fig. 7. Performance comparison of client level classification in global model training data volume for different methods.

There are a total of 100 clients, with 10, 20, 30 and up to 100 selected in sequence. Therefore, when all 100 clients are selected, the results of all methods are the same.

As shown in Fig. 7, client selection method based on LDV has a higher global model training data volume compared to the proposed method. However, as the number of clients increases, the difference between the two methods gradually diminishes until they become the same. The global model training data volume of client selection method based on RCT and client selection method based on random sampling is generally lower than that of the proposed method.

As shown in Fig. 8, the evaluation results indicate that the client selection method based on RCT has a higher ARCT compared to the proposed method. However, it is worth noting that as the number of clients increases, the difference between the two methods gradually diminishes, eventually converging to the same results. The abscissa of point A is x and the ordinate is y in Fig. 8. Specifically, when the number of clients is less than x, ARCT of client selection method based on LDV is lower than the proposed method. When the range of clients' number is x ~ 50, ARCT of client selection method based on LDV is higher than the proposed method. When the clients' number is greater than 50, both methods become similar and eventually converge to the same results. When clients' number is less than 40, ARCT of client selection method based on random sampling is lower than the proposed method. When the clients' number is greater than 40, both methods become similar and eventually converge to the same results. These findings highlight the capability of the proposed method to effectively optimize client selection in the context of federated learning in multi-robot collaborative systems.

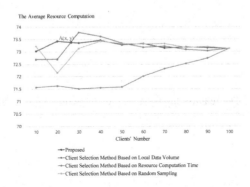

Fig. 8. Performance comparison of client level classification in ARCT for different methods.

6.4 A Method for Selecting Federated Learning Clients Based on Q-Learning

In a collaborative system of multiple mobile robots (clients), there are several robots collaborating to transport goods. Each robot has varying volumes of local data consisting of traffic sign images. The communication bandwidth between the robots is 10 Mbps. However, when the robots' numbers are greater than 10, the data transmission portion of the bandwidth decreases at a rate of 0.02. Due to limited network resources, it is not necessary to select all mobile robots for communication. In the first scenario, there are a total of 30 robots working Collaboratively, the optimal number of robots determined is 15 according to the proposed method. In the second scenario, there are a total of 50 robots working Collaboratively, the optimal number of robots determined is 40 according to the proposed method.

The evaluation metrics for this experiment are ACC and ARCT. As the number of clients increases, the changes in model accuracy and ARCT are respectively shown in Fig. 9 and Fig. 10.

The experimental results obtained by the proposed method are 15 robots in the first scenario. From ACC perspective, the result is a local optimal solution in between 5 and 30. From ARCT perspective, the result is a local optimal solution between 16 and 30.

The experimental results obtained by the proposed method are 40 robots in the second scenario. From ACC perspective, the ACC of the result is low. From ARCT perspective, the result is a local optimal solution between 41 and 50.

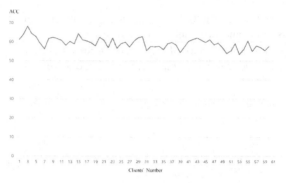

Fig. 9. The relationship between clients' numbers and ACC.

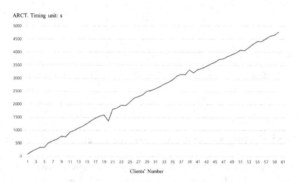

Fig. 10. The relationship between clients' numbers and ARCT.

7 Conclusion

In this paper, we propose a client selection method for federated learning in multi-robots collaborative systems. The proposed method combines fuzzy logic and Q-learning to address the challenges of selecting high-performance clients and determining the appropriate number of clients for FL. By employing fuzzy logic, the method effectively identifies and selects high-performance clients based on their data volume and computational capabilities. This selection process improves communication efficiency and overall work performance within the collaborative system. Moreover, the integration of Q-learning enables the determination of the optimal number of clients for FL. By considering factors such as network constraints, computational resource capabilities, and FL model accuracy, the method achieves a balance between the number of clients and their performance. This approach ensures efficient resource utilization and enhances the overall effectiveness of FL. The effectiveness of the proposed method is verified through experimental results and comparative analysis. In this research, the number of robots selected based on different scenarios is considered to be a local optimal solution. Consequently, our subsequent efforts will be focused on further optimizing it towards a global optimum solution.

Acknowledgments. This research was supported in part by the Inner Mongolia Science and Technology Key Project No. 2021GG0218, ROIS NII Open Collaborative Research 23S0601, and in part by JSPS KAKENHI Grant No. 21H03424.

References

1. Krizhevsky, A., Sutskever, I., Hinton, G.E.: ImageNet classification with deep convolutional neural networks. In: Proceedings of the Annual Conference on Neural Information Processing Systems, pp. 1097–1105 (2012)
2. Sun, C., Shrivastava, A., Singh, S., Gupta, A.: Revisiting unreasonable effectiveness of data in deep learning era. In: Proceedings of the IEEE International Conference on Computer Vision (ICCV), pp. 843–852 (2017)
3. Yadav, R., Zhang, W., Kaiwartya, O., Song, H., Yu, S.: Energy-latency tradeoff for dynamic computation offloading in vehicular fog computing. IEEE Trans. Veh. Technol. **69**(12), 14198–14211 (2020)
4. McMahan, H.B., Ramage, D., Talwar, K., et al.: Learning differentially private recurrent language models. arXiv preprint arXiv:1710.06963 (2017)
5. Apple Differential Privacy Team. Learning with privacy at scale. In Apple Machine Learning Journal (2017)
6. Hartmann, F., Suh, S., Komarzewski, A., et al.: Federated learning for ranking browser history suggestions. arXiv preprint arXiv:1911.11807 (2019)
7. Zhu, H., Xu, J., Liu, S., et al.: Federated learning on non-IID data: a survey. Neurocomputing **465**, 371–390 (2021)
8. Zhao, Y., Li, M., Lai, L., et al.: Federated learning with non-IID data. arXiv preprint arXiv: 1806.00582 (2018)
9. IEEE J. Sel. Areas Commun. **41**(4), 915–928 (2023). https://doi.org/10.1109/JSAC.2023.324 2720
10. Zhang, W., Wang, X., Zhou, P., Wu, W., Zhang, X.: Client selection for federated learning with non-IID data in mobile edge computing. IEEE Access **9**, 24462–24474 (2021)
11. Qu, Z., Duan, R., Chen, L., Xu, J., Lu, Z., Liu, Y.: Context-Aware online client selection for hierarchical federated learning. IEEE Trans. Parallel Distrib. Syst. **33**(12), 4353–4367 (2022)
12. Huang, T., Lin, W., Shen, L., Li, K., Zomaya, A.Y.: Stochastic client selection for federated learning with volatile clients. IEEE Internet Things J. **9**(20), 20055–20070 (2022)
13. Asad, M., Moustafa, A., Rabhi, F.A., Aslam, M.: THF: 3-way hierarchical framework for efficient client selection and resource management in federated learning. IEEE Internet Things J. **9**(13), 11085–11097 (2022)
14. Shi, F., Hu, C., Lin, W., Fan, L., Huang, T., Wu, W.: VFedCS: optimizing client selection for volatile federated learning. IEEE Internet Things J. **9**(24), 24995–25010 (2022)

Network Security and Blockchain

Cross-Chain Model of Notary Group Based on Verifiable Random Functions

Can OuYang[1]([✉]) and Xiaohong Qiu[2]

[1] Jiangxi University of Science and Technology, Nangchang 330013, China
ouyangcan0127@163.com
[2] Nanchang Key Laboratory of Virtual Digital Factory and Cultural Communications,
Nanchang 330013, People's Republic of China

Abstract. In response to the issues of high centralization, slow transaction rates, and high security risks in the cross-chain mechanism of notary groups, this paper proposes an identity-based, non-interactive cross-chain model for notary groups. The model introduces notary groups to reduce centralization and divides the nodes within the notary group into transaction nodes, validation nodes, and supervisory nodes using verifiable random functions, significantly improving the fault tolerance of the optimized model. Additionally, the model introduces Merkle tree structures to locally store transaction information, enabling the processing of multiple cross-chain transactions at once and reducing transaction latency caused by multiple verifications, thereby improving transaction rates. Experimental results demonstrate that compared to traditional models, the optimized model significantly reduces transaction security risks and increases transaction rates by 55.8%.

Keywords: blockchain · blockchain · verifiable random function · notary mechanism

1 Introduction

With Bitcoin becoming a hot topic of discussion, Blockchain 1.0 quietly arrived, and society entered the era of blockchain. The emergence of open-source platforms like Ethereum [1] enabled various industries to combine the characteristics of blockchain technology, such as decentralization, high security, and immutability, with their specific industry requirements. The continuous implementation of various DApps also heralded the arrival of the blockchain 2.0 era. As blockchain 3.0, represented by EOS, became the core of value interconnection, every piece of information and byte representing value in the Internet can undergo ownership confirmation, measurement, and storage, enabling assets to be tracked, controlled, and traded on the blockchain. However, in different application scenarios, issues such as information circulation and large-scale blockchain data storage have emerged, often requiring costly third-party fees to address. With the advent of cross-chain technology, the consumption of financial and material resources has been reduced, facilitating asset interaction and information circulation.

© ICST Institute for Computer Sciences, Social Informatics and Telecommunications Engineering 2024
Published by Springer Nature Switzerland AG 2024. All Rights Reserved
C. Wu et al. (Eds.): MONAMI 2023, LNICST 559, pp. 45–54, 2024.
https://doi.org/10.1007/978-3-031-55471-1_4

Currently, numerous implementation solutions have been proposed for cross-chain technology. The founder of Ethereum has put forward three different implementation methods for cross-chain technology [2]: the notary mechanism, sidechain/relay chain technology, and hash locking technology. Additionally, as the number of blockchain applications increases, a new cross-chain technology called distributed private key control has emerged. The notary mechanism is relatively simple to implement but overly relies on the trust of notaries, leading to low security and high centralization. Sidechain/relay chain technology primarily extends the main chain and its security depends on the main chain, but it imposes certain requirements on the structures of the cross-chain parties, making it challenging to implement. Hash locking technology is widely used and achieves cross-chain asset exchange through smart contracts, but it is limited in its ability to transfer assets. Distributed private key control technology separates asset ownership and usage rights to facilitate asset circulation and value transfer between heterogeneous chains, offering high security but posing challenges for implementation and wider adoption.

Compared to the other three cross-chain technologies, the notary mechanism has lower costs, is easy to implement, and is suitable for large-scale application in various scenarios. Therefore, this paper proposes an improved cross-chain model using a notary group to address the issues of high centralization, slow transaction rates, and high security risks in traditional notary cross-chain mechanisms.

2   Blockchain Cross-Chain Technology

In blockchain, each node typically joins an independent blockchain network, and different blockchain networks, in their initial design and development, do not support interconnectivity and lack the characteristic of the Internet of Everything. To promote interconnection in blockchain and prevent different blockchain networks from being value silos, cross-chain technology has gained increasing attention. The following will introduce four common types of cross-chain technology.

2.1   Notary Scheme

The Notary Mechanism refers to the introduction of a trusted third-party notary node between mutually untrusted blockchains. This notary node is responsible for verifying the consistency and legality of the transaction information exchanged between the parties.

The specific process is as follows: Firstly, a user, Alice, on Chain A transfers the assets to the notary node. The notary node verifies and locks Alice's assets. Finally, the transaction information is confirmed by Bob on Chain B to complete the transfer of the previously confirmed and locked assets. The Notary Mechanism operates on a simple principle without the need for complex Proof-of-Work (PoW). However, the simplicity of the Notary Mechanism's structure and its high reliance on notary nodes result in a higher degree of centralization. Many scholars also question its compatibility with the decentralized nature of blockchain. Currently, the representative projects of mature Notary Mechanisms include Interledger [3, 4].

2.2 Sidechain/Relay Chain Technology

Currently, there are mature cross-chain projects implemented using Sidechain/Relay Chain Technology. These include Rootstock and BTC-Relay [5], both of which are considered sidechain solutions that enhance the performance of the Bitcoin network. In this approach, the existing running blockchain network serves as the main chain, while the sidechain is constructed on top of it by anchoring to the main chain. The main chain offloads its pressure to the sidechain, thereby improving its own performance and scalability. To alleviate the pressure on the Bitcoin mainnet and increase virtual currency payment channels, the BTC-Relay project was proposed as a solution using Sidechain/Relay Chain Technology. It enables one-way cross-chain payments using Bitcoin on the Ethereum network, reducing the limitations of transactions and effectively addressing issues such as low throughput and long transaction confirmation times in the Bitcoin network.

In the Relay Chain cross-chain model, the relay chain acts as a forwarding hub that simply relays transactions without the need to maintain data. It can be regarded as a network hub. Moreover, in the forwarding of inter-chain transaction information, the receiving party verifies the messages without the need to download block header data, which improves the transmission speed. The flexibility and scalability of the relay mode are unique compared to other cross-chain solutions. One of the currently mature relay cross-chain solutions is Cosmos [6].

2.3 Hash Locking Technology

Time locks and hash locks are the core components of Hash Locking Technology [7]. When using hash locks to lock user assets on the corresponding chain, a time lock is also set to restrict the transaction within a specified time period. The time lock ensures that only if both parties provide the correct hash value within the designated transaction time, the assets can be unlocked and the transfer can be completed. The Lightning Network [8] utilizes hash locking technology to address issues such as low transaction throughput and long confirmation times in the Bitcoin network, optimizing Bitcoin transactions through off-chain channels.

While Hash Locking Technology achieves asset exchange between heterogeneous chains by reducing the amount of information disclosed between transaction parties and minimizing their knowledge of each other, there are still challenges that need to be addressed, including low transaction efficiency, high payment costs, and limited scalability.

2.4 Distributed Private Key Control Technology

The core idea of Distributed Private Key Control Technology is to map the assets of different nodes onto an intermediate chain and achieve interoperability between various blockchain networks through the distributed control of private keys by multiple nodes. This technology enables the seamless exchange of assets between different blockchains by allowing distributed nodes to control the private keys associated with each node.

Distributed Private Key Control Technology shares many similarities with the notary mechanism in terms of the overall process. However, in the context of distributed private key cross-chain solutions, users retain control over their own assets. Similar to the notary mechanism, this technology offers broad applicability and ease of implementation.

Representative projects implementing this technology include Wanchain and Fusion [9].

2.5   The Current State of Improvements in the Notary Mechanism

Currently, scholars such as Xue [10] have proposed improvements to the traditional notary model to address issues such as high centralization, slow transaction speed, and high security risks. They have introduced a cross-chain interaction model based on a notary group. Compared to the traditional notary cross-chain model, the complexity of the transaction result's signature count has been reduced from O(n) to O(1), thus lowering the degree of centralization in the notary mechanism. Additionally, this model does not require the verification of every transaction, leading to improved transaction speed.

Scholars like Dai [11] have collected relevant information about multiple notary nodes and utilized an improved PageRank algorithm to rank the credibility of these nodes. By prioritizing highly credible notary nodes for transactions, the security of the model is enhanced.

Cao [12] proposed a cross-chain data traceability mechanism for addressing the issue of data flow across different trust domains. The mechanism establishes a cross-domain access and traceability mechanism by constructing a global authorization chain and access chains within each trust domain. By integrating cross-chain technology based on notary groups, the mechanism enables global authorization and transactions of data assets, as well as cross-domain data access and traceability.

3   VRF-Based Notary Group Cross-Chain Model

In response to the high degree of centralization, slow transaction speeds, and high security risks in the public notary group cross-chain mechanism, this paper proposes an improved model of the public notary group cross-chain mechanism based on Verifiable Random Function (VRF). The model consists of four parts: the public notary group, VRF-based random selection, public notary incentive mechanism, and Merkle tree verification.

Unlike the traditional public notary group model where all notary nodes have the same functions, the optimized model divides the notary group nodes into three categories: validation nodes, transaction nodes, and supervisory nodes. In the mechanism for extracting node identities, the current interactive validation scheme for node identity disclosure is vulnerable to attacks and lacks security. The optimized model introduces VRF-based random selection function to locally extract node identities. Transaction nodes only need to provide a proof pi, generated from the private key SK and a random number alpha, to all supervisory nodes for identity verification. This prevents precise attacks on nodes and improves security. Unlike traditional public notary cross-chain interaction models, the optimized model proposed in this paper ensures that even if a single node is attacked or goes offline, as long as the number of malicious nodes does not exceed half of the transaction nodes, it does not impact the transaction results. It possesses a Byzantine fault tolerance of $f = 2n + 1$.

3.1 Cross-Chain Model of the Public Notary Group

For the issues encountered in the traditional notary model, we have implemented the following optimizations:

1) Introducing a public notary group and dividing the notary nodes' roles to reduce the centralization and single point of failure issues in the traditional notary model.
2) Utilizing the VRF algorithm to partition the nodes' identities, with the remaining nodes acting as verification nodes and supervision nodes for validating the legitimacy of transactions and the identities of transaction nodes. This prevents identity spoofing attacks and enhances the security of the model.
3) Instead of querying the blockchain for each transaction during information verification, we construct a Merkle tree locally to enable fast verification of block data. This reduces communication and computational overhead, thereby improving transaction speed.

The specific cross-chain process is illustrated in Fig. 1.

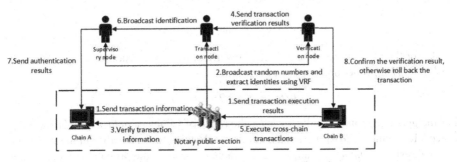

Fig. 1. Cross-chain Transaction Process Flowchart

In Fig. 1, the traditional model is described in detail using dashed boxes, while the optimized model makes certain improvements in certain steps compared to the traditional model. The specific descriptions are as follows:

1) When the cross-chain group receives the transaction information, it proceeds to Step 2. All nodes in the group perform a hash operation on the random number alpha broadcasted by the system and extract their node identities using the VRF algorithm. Unlike the traditional model where node identities are publicly known, in each cross-chain operation, no one can determine the exact identity of the transaction node. Each node only knows its own identity and verifies the broadcasted identity proof pi. This effectively solves the problem of malicious attacks resulting from the public disclosure of node identities in the traditional model.

2) After the completion of Step 2, the verification nodes perform a breadth-first search on the local Merkle tree structure to quickly verify the legality of the transaction. After each merge of the local Merkle tree to obtain the Merkle tree root node, it is compared with the Hash value and PreHash value in the block header of Chain A. Compared to the traditional model that directly compares and searches for the Hash value in the block header of Chain A, the optimized model reduces a significant amount of ineffective searches and reduces system redundancy.

3) Regarding transaction confirmation, the optimized model adopts a dual verification mechanism. In addition to verifying the legality of the transaction information in the traditional model, the optimized model includes the verification of the transaction node identity, as shown in Steps 7 and 9 in Fig. 1. A cross-chain request can only succeed if both types of verification yield positive results. Otherwise, the transaction will be rolled back through the execution of smart contracts using the SDK provided by both transaction chains, thereby enhancing system stability.

3.2   Verifiable Random Functions

The verifiable random function (VRF), proposed by Silvio et al. [20], is an encryption scheme that maps inputs to verifiably pseudo-random outputs. For a given input random value *alpha*, different nodes output a corresponding random value *beta* and a random proof *pi* based on their own private key *SK*, the specific functions are as follows:

$$beta = VRF\_Hash(SK, alpha) \tag{1}$$

$$pi = VRF\_Prove(SK, alpha) \tag{2}$$

As for the random value *beta*, it can be verified using the proof *pi* as input through the *Proof2Hash* function.

$$beta = Proof2Hash(pi) \tag{3}$$

For the generated random value of *beta*, the range of values is: $beta \in [0, 2bits(beta)]$, Since VRF cannot accomplish a fixed number of drawing tasks, the algorithm introduces a new threshold *gamma*. By adjusting the value of *gamma*, the probability of selecting transaction nodes can be modified. When the *beta* is divided by $2^{bits(beta)}$ is less than *gamma*, the node is selected as a transaction node. VRF requires different private keys from different transaction nodes, which ensures that each node generates unique *beta* and *pi* values. This prevents the design of a unified standard that would make a random result uniquely meet a certain condition. It also enhances resilience against external attacks on transaction nodes.

$$result = VRF\_Verify(alpha, beta, pi, PK) \tag{4}$$

The validation result of the transaction node's identity is obtained through *VRF_Verify*, and *pi* provides a zero-knowledge proof for the validation of the random value, which includes the private key signature of the generator. The verifier calculates the hash by using the globally broadcasted random number alpha and the public key *PK* of the transaction node, then compares the result with the output random number to obtain a Boolean value, *result*, for the validation of the transaction node's identity.

4 Analysis of Experimental Results

4.1 Software and Hardware Test Environment

The software and hardware environment for the testing in this paper is shown in Table 1.

Table 1. The software and hardware testing environment.

Name	Version/Model
OS	macOS Monterey (12.3)
CPU	2 GHz 4 Core Inter Core i5
RAM	16 GB 3733 MHz LPDDR4X
Programming language	Golang 1.17.8
Blockchain framework	Fabric 2.4.3, FISCO BCOS 2.7.1

4.2 Experiment and Result Analysis

Identity Extraction Experiment

After a detailed analysis of VRF in Sect. 3.2, it is not difficult to determine that the selection of transaction nodes is completely random. There is also a certain probability of having zero transaction nodes, which is calculated as $p = (1 - gamma)^n$. The model can adjust the probability of notary nodes being selected as transaction nodes by setting an appropriate threshold value, $gamma$. Due to hardware limitations in the experimental environment, the maximum number of deployable notary nodes in the current setup is 13, with a CPU usage rate reaching 95.6%. Under the condition of ensuring the normal completion of the experiment without any crashes, the impact of different numbers of notary nodes and the values of $gamma$ on the absence of transaction nodes was analyzed. The analysis results are shown in Fig. 2.

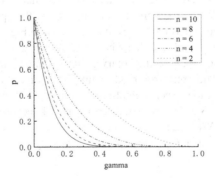

Fig. 2. No transaction node probability graph is generated

The analysis of Fig. 2 reveals that when *gamma* is fixed, the probability of no transaction nodes decreases as the value of n increases. When the value of n is fixed, the probability of no transaction nodes decreases as the value of *gamma* increases. Under the condition of fully utilizing resources, this paper sets the number of notary nodes to n = 10. Analyzing the curve for n = 10 in Fig. 2, it is observed that as *gamma* increases, the downward trend of *p* becomes stable when *gamma* reaches around 0.4. Therefore, in the subsequent experiments, *gamma* = 0.4 is set as a constant, under which the theoretical probability of not generating transaction nodes is 0.0001. To address the situation of no transaction nodes being generated, the optimized model sets up a transaction timer within the notary node group. When a transaction request is received, the timer starts counting, and if no transaction nodes are generated within the set time, a new round of identity extraction is initiated. In this case, the probability of no transaction nodes occurring is given by $p = (1 - gamma)^{2n}$. The specific test results are presented in Table 2.

Table 2. No transaction node statistics table

Number Of Transaction	Set Transaction Timer(Y/N)	Transaction Node Not Specified
1000	N	1
10000	N	8
1000	Y	0
10000	Y	0

Based on the experimental data statistics, it is observed that when the transaction timer is not set within the notary group, the probability of having no transaction node is 0.08%. However, after implementing the transaction timer within the notary group, the occurrence of no transaction node is eliminated.

Defense Against Malicious Attack Experiment

To test the system's ability to resist malicious node improvements, we set the number of nodes in the notary group as n = 10, with half of the nodes being malicious and the other half being normal. We conducted separate tests to evaluate the transaction security of both the traditional notary group cross-chain model and the optimized model under malicious conditions. The experimental results are shown in Fig. 3.

The experimental results indicate that when the number of malicious nodes reaches 50% of the total number of nodes in the notary group, all initiated transactions fail with a probability of 100%. The optimized model outperforms the traditional model when facing attacks. Analyzing the experimental results reveals that the average number of transaction failures in the VRF-based notary group model decreases by 94% compared to the traditional model. With an increase in the number of transactions, the failure rate slightly increases, averaging at 6%. This demonstrates a significant improvement in the ability to resist malicious attacks.

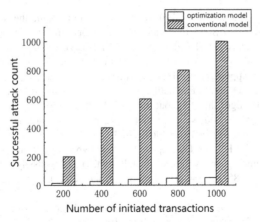

Fig. 3. Number of successful attacks by malicious nodes

5 Conclusion

This paper proposes a notary group cross-chain transaction model based on a random verifiable function to address the issues of low transaction efficiency, poor resistance to malicious attacks, and long verification time in traditional notary cross-chain mechanisms. The model is tested for the possibility of not generating transaction nodes and proposes the addition of a transaction timer to solve the problem of zero transaction nodes. Subsequently, the security and transaction processing time of the traditional model and the optimized model are tested, and the experimental results are analyzed and explained. The experimental results demonstrate that the improved notary mechanism, under the same hardware conditions, exhibits better security performance and faster transaction processing speed compared to the traditional notary mechanism.

References

1. Butterin, V.: Ethereum: A Next-Generation Smart Contract and Decentralized Application Platform 2014 (2022)
2. Buterin, V.: Chain interoperability. R3 Research Paper, 9 (2016)
3. Schwartz, E.: A payment protocol of the web, for the web: or, finally enabling web micro-payments with the interledger protocol. In: Proceedings of the 25th International Conference Companion on World Wide Web, pp. 279–280 (2016)
4. Hope-Bailie, A., Thomas, S.: Interledger: creating a standard for payments. In: Proceedings of the 25th International Conference Companion on World Wide Web, pp. 281–282 (2016)
5. Qun, W.A.N.G., Fujuan, L.I., Xueli, N.I., Lingling, X.I.A., Guangjun, L.I.A.N.G., Zhuo, M.A.: Research on blockchain interoperability and cross-chain technology. J. Front. Comput. Sci. Technol. **1**
6. Kwon, J., Buchman, E.: Cosmos: a network of distributed ledgers (2016). https://cosmos.net work/whitepaper
7. Zhang, S.T., Qin, B., Zheng, H.B.: Research on multi-party cross chain protocol based on hash locking. Cyberspace Secur. **9**(11), 57–62
8. Poon, J., Dryja, T.: The bitcoin lightning network: scalable off-chain instant payments (2016)

9. Fujimoto, S., Higashikado, Y., Takeuchi, T.: ConnectionChain: the secure interworking of blockchains. In: 2019 Sixth International Conference on Internet of Things: Systems, Management and Security (IOTSMS), pp. 514–518. IEEE (2019)

10. Jiang, C., Fang, L., Zhang, N., Zhu, J.: Cross-chain interaction safety model based on notary groups. J. Comput. Appl. **42**(11), 3438–3443 (2022)

11. Dai, B., Jiang, S., Li, D., et al.: Evaluation model of cross-chain notary mechanism based on improved PageRank algorithm. Comput. Eng. **47**(2), 26–31 (2021)

12. Cao, L., Zhao, S., Gao, Z., Du, X.: Cross-chain data traceability mechanism for cross-domain access. J. Supercomput. **79**(5), 4944–4961 (2023)

13. Esgin, M.F., Steinfeld, R., Liu, D., Ruj, S.: Efficient hybrid exact/relaxed lattice proofs and applications to rounding and VRFs. In: Handschuh, H., Lysyanskaya, A. (eds.) CRYPTO 2023. LNCS, vol. 14085, pp. 484–517. Springer, Cham (2023). https://doi.org/10.1007/978-3-031-38554-4_16

14. Xiong, A., Liu, G., Zhu, Q., Jing, A., Loke, S.W.: A notary group-based cross-chain mechanism. Digit. Commun. Netw. **8**(6), 1059–1067 (2022)

15. Sun, Y., Yi, L., Duan, L., Wang, W.: A decentralized cross-chain service protocol based on notary schemes and hash-locking. In: 2022 IEEE International Conference on Services Computing (SCC), pp. 152–157. IEEE (2022)

16. Wang, Z., Li, J., Chen, X.B., Li, C.: A secure cross-chain transaction model based on quantum multi-signature. Quantum Inf. Process. **21**(8), 279 (2022)

17. Chen, L., Fu, Q., Mu, Y., Zeng, L., Rezaeibagha, F., Hwang, M.S.: Blockchain-based random auditor committee for integrity verification. Futur. Gener. Comput. Syst. **131**, 183–193 (2022)

Enhancing Cloud Data Integrity Verification Scheme with User Legitimacy Check

Dong Wu[1]($\boxtimes$), Chao Peng[1], Meilan Zheng[1], Chen Fu[1], Hua Wang[1], Hua Zhong[1], Qiuming Liu[2,3], He Xiao[2,3], and Siwen Dong[3]

[1] Information and Communication Branch of Jiangxi Electric Power Co., Ltd., Nanchang, China
972452554@qq.com
[2] Nanchang Key Laboratory of Virtual Digital Factory and Cultural Communications, Nanchang 330013, People's Republic of China
[3] School of Software Engineering, Jiangxi University of Science and Technology, Ganzhou, China
liuqiuming@jxust.edu.cn

Abstract. Users employ cloud servers to store data and depend on third-party audits to guarantee data integrity. However, this auditing system poses certain risks, as it may have vulnerabilities that attackers can exploit for intrusion. To address these concerns and achieve decentralization, a cloud data integrity verification scheme is proposed. This scheme is based on a verifiable random function and aims to eliminate the need for third-party auditing. Before performing data integrity verification, a blockchain smart contract is employed to calculate bilinear pairs, serving the purpose of verifying the user's legitimacy. If the user successfully completes this verification, the integrity of the cloud data is then verified using the verifiable random function. The simulation results demonstrate that this scheme is effective in detecting the legitimacy of users and significantly reduces the computational and communication overhead associated with verifying data integrity.

Keywords: User verification · Data integrity · Smart contract · Verifiable random functions

1 Introduction

With the rapid advancement of information technology and manufacturing industry, various high-performance storage and computing devices have been developed. Additionally, computer networks have made significant progress [1]. Service providers have started merging the benefits of large storage and computing devices with high-speed networks to offer cloud computing services to users, such As AliCloud (Alibaba Cloud) and Amazon AWS. These cloud computing services have gained popularity due to their on-demand service delivery, easy network access, extensive storage resources, and high flexibility. As a result, more and more organizations and individual users are drawn to these services, considering them as one of the most influential innovations [2].

C. Wu et al. (Eds.): MONAMI 2023, LNICST 559, pp. 55–69, 2024.
https://doi.org/10.1007/978-3-031-55471-1_5

Cloud computing allows users to save a substantial amount of storage and computing resources by migrating data storage to cloud servers or delegating computing tasks to cloud service providers. Moreover, cloud computing has found widespread applications in various fields, including e-commerce, automotive networking, and medical care, where large volumes of data and demanding computational tasks are involved [3]. Hence, it is crucial to ensure the completeness and reliability of cloud data, as well as to verify the legitimacy of users, ensuring that only authorized individuals with no malicious intent can access the data [4].

The traditional method involves the utilization of a trusted Third Party Audit (TPA) to serve as an intermediary that verifies the legitimacy of accessing users and the integrity of the data [5]. However, relying on TPAs comes with its own set of drawbacks. There are inherent risks associated with TPAs. Firstly, the TPA's system might have undiscovered vulnerabilities or weaknesses that can be exploited by attackers to gain unauthorized access. This can arise from faulty software, misconfiguration, or a failure to timely update the system. Secondly, attackers may employ social engineering techniques to manipulate employees of the audit organization into revealing sensitive information or exploiting their privileges. Additionally, Distributed Denial of Service (DDoS) attacks can target the network infrastructure of TPAs, resulting in the unavailability of their systems. An attacker executes a DDoS attack by overwhelming the target system with a flood of requests, surpassing its processing capacity. Blockchain, being a decentralized ledger, offers the capability to store, compute, verify, and share data through consensus mechanisms and other technologies [6]. By leveraging the strengths of blockchain technology, it is possible to achieve greater efficiency and security compared to other data integrity verification methods. Previous studies [5, 13, 14] have explored the use of blockchain to protect data integrity, addressing the issue of single points of failure in TPAs and implementing Measurement Hash Trees (MHT) to ensure data completeness. However, none of these studies have considered the verification of unauthorized and malicious users.

We propose a new approach to improve upon the traditional method by utilizing zero-knowledge proofs. Zero-knowledge proofs allow for the verification of a claim without revealing any additional information to the verifier. In this approach, the data owner (DO) stores their data in a cloud storage server (CSP) to save local storage space. When the DO needs to retrieve the data from the CSP, it is verified using a Verifiable Random Function (VRF). If the verification is successful, the data is downloaded from the CSP. Essentially, this method allows users to encrypt their data and store it in the cloud, while also providing a verification mechanism to ensure data integrity. This scheme combines the functions of encryption and integrity verification. Users can encrypt their data using an encryption key and generate authentication tags. When data integrity needs to be verified, the user can provide the key and data, and the cloud performs decryption and verification label calculations to confirm the data integrity.

2 Prerequisite

2.1 Bilinear Pair

A bilinear pair is defined as follows: $e : G \times G \to G_T$ where G, G_T are multiplicative cyclic groups, and the bilinear map should have the following properties:

(1) Bilinear $\forall x, y \in G \Rightarrow e(x^a, y^b) = e(x, y)^{ab}$
(2) Non-degeneracy: $\forall x \in G, x \neq 0 \Rightarrow e(x, x) \neq 1$.
(3) Computability: e exists and is efficiently computable.

2.2 Elliptic Curve Encryption Algorithm

Elliptic Curve Cryptography (ECC) is based on the concept of utilizing operations between points on an elliptic curve to create a secure public key cryptosystem. ECC involves a finite field and an elliptic curve defined over it, where the set of points on the curve serves as the key space. The operations performed on these points on the elliptic curve adhere to properties such as the law of exchange, the law of union, and the law of distribution. These properties are utilized to carry out encryption and decryption operations.

The main steps of ECC include:

1. Parameter selection: Selection of appropriate elliptic curves and related parameters, which include the equations defining the curves, the size of the finite domain, the base point (generating element), etc.
2. Key generation: Generate public and private key pairs. The private key is a randomly chosen value and the public key is another point on the curve obtained by multiplying the base point by the private key.
3. Encryption: the plaintext message is converted into points on the curve and combined with the other party's public key to perform point operations to generate the ciphertext.
4. Decryption: Use your own private key to perform point operations with the ciphertext sent by the other party to restore the points on the curve and convert it to a plaintext message.

2.3 Homomorphic Hash Algorithm

For a given base g, exponent r, modulo N, the corresponding modulo power is g^rmod N. This is shown below:

$$H(m) = g^m \bmod N \tag{1}$$

The function hash satisfies the following laws, as follows:

$$H(m_i + m_j) = g^{m_i + m_j} \bmod N$$
$$= (g^{m_i} \bmod N) \times (g^{m_j} \bmod N)$$
$$= H(m_i) \times H(m_j) \tag{2}$$

H Similarly, it can be obtained:

$$H(a_i m_i + a_j m_j) = g^{a_i m_i + a_j m_j} \bmod N$$
$$= H(m_i)^{a_i} \times H(m_j)^{a_j} \tag{3}$$

2.4 Verifiable Random Functions

A Verifiable Random Function (VRF) is a cryptographic construction that combines a random function with verifiability properties. It allows a generator to produce a pseudo-random function that can be verified by a verifier without disclosing the generator's internal secrets.

The VRF is composed of three algorithms: generation, proof, and verification.

1. Generation Algorithm: This algorithm takes a key pair (public and private keys) as input and generates a pseudo-random function output based on random numbers and messages. Only the generator with the private key can compute the function, ensuring its pseudo-random nature.
2. Proof Algorithm: Given the output produced by the generation algorithm, along with the related input message and private key, the proof algorithm generates an additional proof value. This proof value can be used by the verifier to check the correctness and unpredictability of the output.
3. Verification Algorithm: The verification algorithm takes the public key, the message, the output generated by the generation algorithm, and the proof value generated by the proof algorithm. It verifies the correctness of the proof and determines whether the generated output was indeed produced by the generating algorithm.

3 System Modeling

The system model in the paper comprises three entities: data holder (DO), blockchain platform (BC), and cloud storage server (CSP). Before conducting data integrity verification, the user stores the data in the cloud server, while the blockchain stores homomorphic digital tags containing user information and data digest information.

To verify the data integrity of the cloud server, DO must first undergo identity legitimacy testing and send the identity verification information to BC. Once the verification is passed, BC sends a data integrity query to the cloud server. The cloud server returns the data integrity proof to BC, which then checks it and sends the verification result to DO. This process is made more reliable and trustworthy than TSP due to the use of a reliable blockchain platform and smart contracts, which document every verification. As a result, DO and CSP can trust each other completely, unlike the unreliable and untrustworthy TPA (Fig. 1).

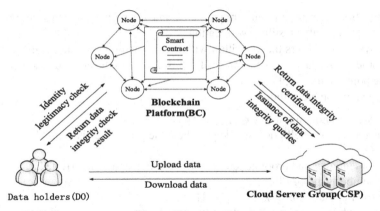

Fig. 1. System model

3.1 Data Integrity Threat Model

(1) Intentional data tampering by unauthorized users is a potential risk. Malicious individuals may manipulate validation results to gain false claims during the data integrity verification process.

(2) Cloud server failure can stem from different factors like hardware issues, software glitches, and network attacks. Such failures can lead to data corruption on the cloud server. Notably, corruption of validation information can impact both data validation and recovery.

(3) To mitigate replay attacks and minimize storage requirements, cloud servers may opt to store only data tags for integrity verification purposes.

4 Data Integrity Protection Program

Scheme overview: firstly, we design elliptic curve cryptographic verifiable random function, and then combine it with smart contract for data integrity verification, which mainly includes (1) data uploading; (2) user legitimacy checking; (3) data integrity verification; and (4) data recovery.

4.1 Elliptic Curve Verifiable Random Function Design

The verifiable random function algorithm based on elliptic curves consists of four main algorithms:

System initialization algorithm: given the system security parameter π, the algorithm produces the public parameters.

Key generation algorithm: The input includes the public parameter params, and the output comprises the public key pk and private key sk.

Random Number and Proof Generation Algorithm:The input consists of the public parameter params, message m, and private key sk. The output includes a random number value and its corresponding proof.

Verification algorithm: inputs are public parameters params, message m, proof and public key pk, output is result of verification.

The system initializes the algorithm with the following parameters: GF(q): a finite field of order q. q: a large prime number of π bits. E: an elliptic curve defined on GF(q). g: a base point on the elliptic curve.

Key generation algorithm:

A1: Choose a random number $x \in [1, q - 1]$.

A2: Generate a pair of elliptic curve keys, where the private key is x and the public key is $Y = xG$.

Random number and proof generation algorithm: message m, private key x. Output: random number v, proof PROOF.

B1: Choose random number $k \in [1, q - 1]$.

B2: Compute h = H1(m) using the hash function H1 to map message m to a point H on the elliptic curve;

B3: compute kH, kG;

B4: encode the input into an integer $c = H3((kH, kG)$; using function H3.

B5: Calculate $s = (k - c * x) mod n$;;

B6: Compute$\Gamma = xH$;

B7: Use the function H2 to encode the points on the elliptic curve as an integer to obtain the random number $\Gamma = xH$, proving that proof is (Γ, c, s).

Verification algorithm: input: message m', proof proof'. Output: legitimacy (*valid or invalid*).

C1: Map the message m' to a point H' on the elliptic curve using the hash function H1;

C2: Compute $U = c'Y + s'G; V = c'\Gamma + s'H'$;

C3: Calculate $c' = H3(U, V)$;

C4: If $c = c'$, then it indicates that the random number is valid and the verification passes, and outputs *valid*; otherwise it indicates that the random number is invalid and the verification fails, and outputs *in valid*.

4.2 Data Upload

The user-side operation:In the user operation, the user initially applies the ECDSA algorithm to obtain the private key (sk) and public key (pk). Following this, the data is segmented into chunks for integrity verification purposes, allowing each block to be verified individually. Each data block generates a corresponding value.

Concurrently, corrective code encoding is executed to produce a recovery block. This recovered block is then combined with the original data block and uploaded to the cloud server. The set of data blocks is denoted as $D = \{d_i\}(i \in (1, n))$.

Each data block d_i is processed using the homomorphic hash algorithm and public key pk, as outlined in the preparatory knowledge, to create the label$T_i = (H(d_i))^e$. A hash operation is then performed on d_i to generate the data summary informationH_i, $H_i = H_1(d_i)$, The label T_i, H_i, and index i are uploaded to the blockchain.

Each data block also has a corresponding VALUE. The data owner uses the private key SK to calculate this VALUE of the data and stores it in the cloud along with the data.

Subsequently, the user carries out integrity verification. If the result is inconsistent, it indicates improper data storage, and distinct server is selected. If the results are consistent, both parties are in agreement.

As the data tags are stored on the blockchain, any node can access and notarize this data. This process ensures that data deletion is agreed upon and does not result in data loss.

4.3 User Legitimacy Check

Users who want to operate on the data should first verify the legitimacy of the user, and prohibit subsequent operations if they are unauthorized users, and similarly prohibit further operations if they are malicious users. An unauthorized user is a user who has not been given a sk and a malicious user is a user who intentionally denies data integrity and uses a g_s that does not match x, resulting in an error in the server-side data integrity check, and thus begging for compensation from the data repository.

The user first sends x and g_s to the blockchain legitimacy checking smart contract (SC_L).

$$x = d \times s \tag{4}$$

$$g_s = g^s \tag{5}$$

d comes from the user's private key $sk = (d, N)$, $s \in Z_p^*$, g is the generator of G_1.x is used to hide the private key sk, and g_s is used to check the user's legitimacy and data integrity.

When (SC_L) receives x and g_s from the user, it can determine whether the user is legitimate or not by verifying whether the following equation holds:

$$e\left(H^e, g^x\right) mod N = e(H, g_s) \tag{6}$$

according to the curve $h : \{0, 1\}* \rightarrow G_1$ where $H = h(v), \forall v \in R$.

If the condition stated above is satisfied, it proves that the user is authorized and is a normal user. A set of random coefficients $A = \{a_i\}, i \in [1, n]$ is generated using (SC_L) for data integrity verification.

4.4 Data Integrity Validation

The user verifies the VRF value of the downloaded data block using the public key pk and a verifiable random function. The public key is used to verify the correctness of the VRF value and ensure that the data has not been tampered with. During the verification process, the generated proof value is compared with the downloaded VRF value Based on the result of verification of VRF value, the integrity of the data block is determined.

A successful match indicates that the data block remains intact and unaltered. If the VRF values do not match, it indicates that the data block may have been tampered with or corrupted.

4.5 Data Recovery

$$D = \begin{bmatrix} d_1 \\ d_2 \\ d_3 \\ d_4 \\ d_5 \end{bmatrix} = \begin{bmatrix} 0 & 1 & 0 & 0 & 0 \\ 0 & 0 & 1 & 0 & 0 \\ 0 & 0 & 0 & 0 & 1 \\ B_{11} & B_{12} & B_{13} & B_{14} & B_{15} \\ B_{31} & B_{32} & B_{33} & B_{34} & B_{35} \end{bmatrix}^{-1} \times \begin{bmatrix} d_2 \\ d_3 \\ d_5 \\ c_1 \\ c_3 \end{bmatrix} \quad (7)$$

B is the invertible Cauchy matrix, and C is the array of recovered blocks. The above method reveals that only the correct block can restore the original data. Initially, the server identifies and excludes the incorrect block by locating the index of the erroneous block in the scattered data storage. By comparing the summary information of the blockchain storage, which consists of non-modifiable data uploaded in the blockchain H_i the server can determine the serial number index of the data block where the error occurred. This summary information serves as a reliable reference for data recovery.

To begin the recovery process, the server performs a Hash operation on the original data it stores:$H_i^* = H_1(d_i)$. The server then transmits the index, user public key, and hash value of the stored data to the data recovery smart contract (SC_D). SC_D utilizes the index and public key to locate the summary information H_i of the data block stored on the blockchain. It compares this information with the received H_i^* and returns the index of the incorrect block to the server.

In the event that $H_i^* = H_i$, it indicates that the i-th block of the original data remains intact. Conversely, if they do not match, the i-th block of data is identified as the incorrect block.

5 Security Analysis

5.1 User Legitimacy

According to the proposed scheme, smart contracts with verifiable random functions are unforgeable and unpredictable, and only authorized and non-malicious users satisfy Eq:

$$e\left(H^e, g^x\right) modN = e(H, g_s) \quad (8)$$

Proof:
$e(H^e, g^x) modN = e(H, g)^{ex} modN = e(H, g)^{eds} modN = \left(e(H, g)^s\right)^{ed} modN$ By Euler's theorem:

$$m^{\varphi(n)} \equiv 1(modn) \quad (9)$$

$$m^{k\varphi(n)+1} \equiv m(modn) \quad (10)$$

$$ed \equiv 1(mod(\varphi(n))) \quad (11)$$

$ed = k\varphi(n) + 1$, with k an arbitrary constant.

$$(e(H, g)^s)^{ed} modN$$
$$= (e(H, g)^s)^{k\varphi(N)+1} modN \quad (12)$$
$$= e(H, g)^s$$

By the bilinear pair mapping property, it follows that:

$$e(H, g_s) = e(H, g)^s \tag{13}$$

so that the equation holds for

$$e\left(H^e, g^x\right) mod N = e(H, g_s) \tag{14}$$

If a non-authorized user is agnostic, Euler's theorem will not be satisfied and the above equation will not hold.

If the user has malicious intent, the following equation will not be satisfied:

$$g_s \neq g^{\frac{x}{d}} \tag{15}$$

Ultimately, only authorized and legitimate users with no malicious intent can be satisfied; In all other cases, the condition does not apply.

5.2 Data Integrity

Users in the data download stage, due to hardware and software failure or network delay and other factors, the downloaded data may be lost or damaged during transmission, or the server may be subjected to hacking attacks, etc., resulting in some data being tampered with, and all of these factors make the data less than complete.

According to the integrity of verifiable random function: if the inputs to the generation algorithm and the proof algorithm are legitimate, The verification algorithm will consistently accept and validate the accuracy of the proof. In the original scheme, the client will cross-verify all received data results, and only when they are all identical, the verification process will succeed Therefore, even if the attacker successfully attacks only one data node, the client will fail to validate the proof because of the inconsistency of the received data results. Even if the determination strategy is changed to more than half of the data results are consistent, the endorsement result is valid, in this case, when the number of malicious nodes in the data nodes is more than half of the number of malicious nodes, the attacker can completely control the result of the inconsistency of the data. In the optimization scheme, the client no longer needs to get all the results of the data nodes, so that the attacker affects the probability of the transaction is reduced. The same is the success of the attack on a candidate data node, if the adversary tries to influence the data, It is essential to endorse only one node from the candidate set of nodes, specifically the node that was successfully targeted by the adversary, to achieve a probability of success.

$$Pr = \frac{1}{n}C(1 - \gamma)\gamma^{(n-1)} = (1 - \gamma)\gamma^{(n-1)} \tag{16}$$

Prevent the attack from succeeding with a very low probability.

5.3 Preventing Replay Attacks

Once the cloud server has computed the data labels, it deletes the stored raw data and stores only the data labels g^{m_i}. The case is also not likely to pass validation because the g_s sent to the cloud server is randomized each time. There is no way for the cloud server to $g_s \rightarrow s$, which at this point converts to a discrete logarithm problem.

Discrete Logarithm (DL) problem: Let G_1 be a cyclic multiplicative group of order q on an elliptic curve with large prime q, g is a generator of G_1, $s \in Z_q$, and it is known that $g, g, g^s \in G_1$ and computing s is difficult. Namely

$$Pr\left(A_{dl}(g, g_s) \rightarrow a \in Z_q, s.t.g_s = g^s\right) \leq \varepsilon \qquad (17)$$

Therefore, it is impossible for the server to give a correct verification proof with only the data labels saved.

If $P = STmodN$, it means that the cloud server saves the complete data.

Proof.

$$P = g_s^{a_1m_1+a_2m_2+.....+a_nm_n}$$

$$= g_s^{a_1m_1} \times g_s^{a_1m_1} \cdots \times g_s^{a_nm_n}$$

$$= \prod_{i=1}^{n} g^{a_im_is} \qquad (18)$$

$$ST = T_1^{a_1x} \times T_2^{a_2x} \times .... \times T_n^{a_nx}$$

$$= \prod_{i=1}^{n} T_i^{a_ix} = \prod_{i=1}^{n} g^{m_iea_ids} \qquad (19)$$

According to Eqs. (13) and (14), it can be obtained:

$$STmod \ N = \prod_{i=1}^{n} g^{m_iea_ids} mod \ N$$

$$= \prod_{i=1}^{n} g^{m_ia_is}$$

$$= p \qquad (20)$$

Therefore, $P = STmodN$ holds in the case where the cloud server stores complete data.

It is also impossible for the cloud server to compute the labels on the blockchain ahead of time because s is already hidden by $x = d \times s$.

6 Performance Analysis and Experimental Evaluation

The cloud data integrity verification scheme proposed in this experiment becomes VRF-Y. The comparative literature for this experiment [5] is based on MHT to verify the integrity and is called MHT-V; and literature [13] is based on a variant of MHT and BLS and is called MB. The experiment uses elliptic curve verifiable random function and bilinear pair nature for data block signing and verification, and the hash function is SHA-256, and the hash function is SHA-256, and the hash function is SHA-256, on a A PC configured with Intel Core Duo, i7-7200U CPU with 2.50 GHz and 8 GB of RAM, calling CryptGenRandom library and OpenSSL library for key generation.

6.1 Fuel Consumption of Smart Contracts

We will assess the fuel consumption (gas) of the smart contract SC_L in the integrity verification protocol, where the test platform of the smart contract is Remix, and its programming language is Solidity of version 0.4.19. In this scheme, the inputs of the smart contract SC_L are mainly in the form of the seed value Q, the current timestamp QN, and the identity Bid of the current database. In particular, the integer type of the seed value Q selected in the experiment is int64 data type, which varies from 10 to 10^15 (Fig. 2).

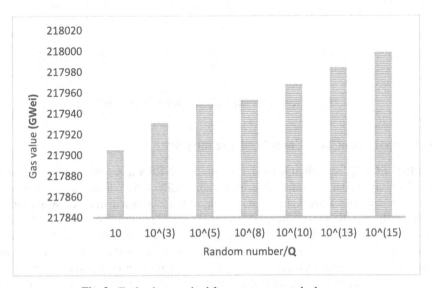

Fig. 2. Fuel value required for smart contract deployment

6.2 Comparison of Time Required to Generate Labels

MHT-V, on the other hand, does not employ labels, and thus, there is no comparison of its label generation time. The experimental results are shown in Fig. 4, which shows that VRF-Y is significantly faster than MB generation. While both utilize the modulo power operation, MB's label generation includes additional curve hash operation and MHT tree root generation, whereas VRF-Y only involves extra hash operations. As a result, VRF-Y is more efficient (Fig. 3).

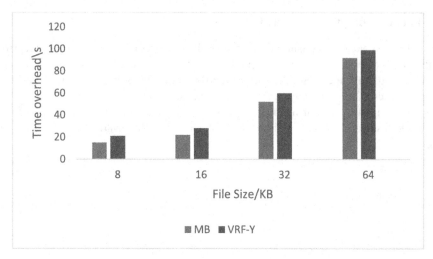

Fig. 3. Time overhead of label generation for different file sizes

6.3 Comparison of Time Spent Verifying Integrity

In VRF-Y, ECDSA algorithm is used, compared with RSA algorithm used in MB and VRF-Y Firstly, under the same security length, ECDSA has shorter key length and signature length than RSA digital signature algorithm, and in a distributed system such as blockchain, the shorter signature length can effectively reduce the content of the data transmission and lower the cost of system communication. Secondly, ECDSA is also better than RSA in terms of signature generation speed. Key nodes, as the generators of proofs and random numbers, need to perform a large number of signature operations, using ECDSA can reduce the algorithm running time and lower the impact of VRF algorithm on system throughput. Among the three methods, MHT-V demonstrates the fastest processing speed but incurs the highest communication overhead, whereas MB is the slowest with comparatively lower communication overhead, and VRF-T is in between with the lowest communication overhead. MHT-V is the fastest because it mainly performs hash operation, but it has to send the raw data to the blockchain every time, but the storage of the blockchain is limited after all. MB not only involves the modulo-power operation but also requires hash and MHT generation operations, making the entire process the most time-consuming. On the other hand, VRF-T only performs the modulo-power and hash operations, resulting in shorter processing time. Since it only needs to transmit the modulo-power calculation result to the blockchain, VRF-T incurs the least communication overhead. As shown in Fig. 5:

6.4 Error Finding

The experimental results illustrating the time overhead of error block identification under various file sizes are presented in Fig. 6. MHT-V is an error block identification method based on the MHT tree, which requires passing auxiliary information and a data block each time. It continually hashes upwards until obtaining a new root, which

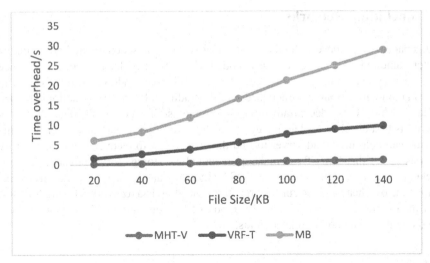

Fig. 4. Time overhead of verifying integrity with different file sizes

is then compared with the old root on the blockchain to determine block correctness. In contrast, VRF-T directly hashes the data block and compares it with the corresponding block label on the blockchain, making it a simple and efficient approach.

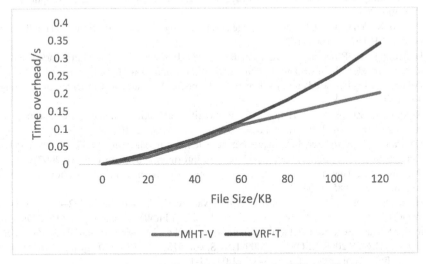

Fig. 5. Time overhead of error block lookup for different file sizes

7 Concluding Remarks

In this paper, we propose a cloud data integrity verification scheme based on verifiable random functions. The stored data is encoded with corrective deletion code to enhance data recovery capability. At the same time, the verifiable random function is used in combination with a smart contract instead of the traditional third-party auditor to realize the idea of blockchain decentralization. Before the user's access to the data, the user's identity is first checked for legitimacy. After the integrity of cloud data is verified, this scheme can help the cloud server to find the error block to recover the data. Security analysis shows that VRF-T can make users and cloud storage servers trust each other. Replacing the RSA algorithm with ECDSA algorithm also reduces the integrity verification time overhead and the computational overhead of data recovery. Moving forward, we will continue to pay attention to the trend of edge computing and continue to study cloud computing and other related fields.

References

1. Liang, H., Li, M., Chen, Y., et al.: Architectural protection of trusted system services for SGX enclaves in cloud computing. IEEE Trans. Cloud Comput. **9**(3), 910–922 (2019)
2. Zhang Guipeng. Research on cloud data security storage technology based on blockchain [D]. Guangdong:Guangdong University of Technology (2022(
3. Xu, Y., Ren, J., Zhang, Y., Zhang, C., Shen, B., Zhang, Y.: Blockchain empowered arbitrable data auditing scheme for network storage as a service. IEEE Trans. Serv. Comput. **13**(2), 289–300 (2020)
4. Yinhao, X., Yizhen, J., Chunchi, L.: Edge computing security: state of the art and challenges. Proc. IEEE **107**(8), 1608–1631 (2019)
5. Dongdong, Y., Ruixuan, L., Yan, Z.: Blockchain-based verification framework for data integrity in edge-cloud storage. J. Parallel Distrib. Comput. **146**, 1–14 (2020)
6. Zhang, Y.: Identity-based integrity detection scheme for cloud storage. Computer Engineering. **44**(3) (2018)
7. Xiuqing, L., Zhenkuan, P., Hequn, X.: An integrity verification scheme of cloud storage for internet-of-things mobile terminal devices. Comput. Secur. **92**, 101686 (2020)
8. Deswarte, Y., Quisquater, J., Saidane, A.: Remote integrity checking. In: The Sixth Working Conference on Integrity and Internal Control in Information Systems (IICIS) (2007)
9. Wutong, M., Zhang, D.: Hyperledger Fabric consensus mechanism optimization scheme. J. Autom. **47**(8), 1885–1898 (2007)
10. Hovav, S., Brent, W.: Compact proofs of retrievability. J. Cryptol. **26**(3), 442–483 (2013)
11. Wang, Q., Wang, C., Li, J., Ren, K., Lou, W.: Enabling Public Verifiability and Data Dynamics for Storage Security in Cloud Computing. In: Backes, M., Ning, P. (eds) Computer Security – ESORICS 2009. ESORICS 2009. LNCS, vol. 5789, pp. 355–370. Springer, Heidelberg (2009).https://doi.org/10.1007/978-3-642-04444-1_22
12. Zheng, Z., Xie, S., Dai, H.: An overview of blockchain technology: architecture, consensus, and future Trends, pp. 557–564 (2017)
13. Li, J., Wu, J., Jiang, G.: Blockchain-based public auditing for big data in cloud storage. Inf. Process. Manage. **57**(6), 102382 (2020)
14. Wang, Y.: Research on data integrity auditing in cloud storage[D]. Chongqing University (2021)

15. Vujičić, D,, Jagodić, D., Ranđić, S.: Blockchain technology,bitcoin,and ethereum:a brief overview. In: Proceedings of the 2018 17th International Symposium on Infoteh-Jahorina, pp. 1–6 (2018).https://doi.org/10.1109/INFOTEH.2018.8345547

16. Xiao, Y., Zhang, N., Lou, W.J., et al.: A survey of distributed consensus protocols for blockchain networks. IEEE Commun. Surv. Tutorials **22**(2), 1432–1465 (2020)

17. Zheng, M., Wang, H., Liu, H., et al.: Survey on consensus algorithms of blockchain. Netinfo Secur. **7**, 8–24 (2019)

18. Hai-yang, D., Zi-chen, L., Wei, B.: (k, n)halftone visual cryptography based on Shamir's secret sharing. J. China Univ. Posts Telecommun. **25**(2), 60–76 (2018)

19. Qi-feng, S., Zhao, Z., Yan-chao, Z., et al.: Survery of enterprise blockchains. J. Softw. **30**(9), 2571–2592 (2019(

20. Yong, Y., Xiao-chun, N., Shuai, Z., et al.: Block consensus algorithms: the state of the art and future trends. Acta Automatica Sinica, **44**(11), 2011–2022 (2018)

21. Shao, Q.F., Jin, C.Q., Zhang, Z., et al.: Blockchain: architecture and research progress Chinese. J. Comput. **41**(5), 969–988 (2018)

22. Bo, Y.: A chameleon hash authentication tree optimisation audit for data storage security in cloud calculation. Int. J. Innovative Comput. Appl. **11**(2–3), 141–146 (2020)

23. Mehibel, N., Hamadouche, M.H.: Authenticated secret session key using elliptic curve digital signature algorithm. Secur. Priv. 4(2), e148 (2021)

24. Khalili, M., Dakhilalian, M., Susilo, W.: Efficient chameleon hash functions in the enhanced collision resistant model. Inf. Sci. **510**, 155–164 (2020)

25. Wang, Q., Wang, C., Li, J., Ren, K., Lou, W.: Enabling public verifiability and data dynamics for storage security in cloud computing. In: Backes, M., Ning, P. (eds.) Computer Security – ESORICS 2009. ESORICS 2009. Lecture Notes in Computer Science, vol. 5789, pp. 355–370. Springer, Heidelberg (2009).https://doi.org/10.1007/978-3-642-04444-1_22

26. Zhang, Y., Xu, C.X., Yu, S., et al.: SCLPV: secure certificateless public verification for cloud-based cyber-physical-social systems against malicious auditors. IEEE Trans. Comput. Soc. Syst. 2(4), 159–170 (2015)

Decoupled 2S-AGCN Human Behavior Recognition Based on New Partition Strategy

Liu Qiuming[1,2], Chen Longping[1(✉)], Wang Da[1], Xiao He[1,2], Zhou Yang[3], and Wu Dong[3]

[1] School of Software Engineering, Jiangxi University of Science and Technology, Nanchang 330013, China
liuqiuming@jxust.edu.cn, {6720220666, 6720220658}@mail.jxust.edu.cn
[2] Nanchang Key Laboratory of Virtual Digital Factory and Cultural Communications, Nanchang 330013, China
[3] Information and Communication Branch of Jiangxi Electric Power Co., Ltd., Nanchang 330095, China

Abstract. Human skeleton point data has better environmental adaptability and motion expression ability than RGB video data. Therefore, the action recognition algorithm based on skeletal point data has received more and more attention and research. In recent years, skeletal point action recognition models based on graph convolutional networks (GCN) have demonstrated outstanding performance. However, most GCN-based skeletal action recognition models use three stable spatial configuration partitions, and manually set the connection relationship between each skeletal joint point. Resulting in an inability to better adapt to varying characteristics of different actions. And all channels of the input X features use the same graph convolution kernel, resulting in coupling aggregation. Contrary to the above problems, this paper proposes a new division strategy, which can better extract the feature information of neighbor nodes of nodes in the skeleton graph and adaptively obtain the connection relationship of joint nodes. And introduce Decoupled Graph Convolution (DC-GCN) to each partition to solve the coupled aggregation problem. Experiments on the NTU-RGB+D dataset show that the proposed method can achieve higher action recognition accuracy than most current methods.

Keywords: 2S-AGCN · New partition strategy · DC-GCN · Action recognition · NTU RGB+D

1 Introduction

As a research hotspot in the field of computer vision, human action recognition has a wide range of applications in many fields such as video surveillance, human-computer interaction, and social security. Therefore, people are more and more interested in research in this field. According to the form of input data, action recognition methods can be

C. Wu et al. (Eds.): MONAMI 2023, LNICST 559, pp. 70–82, 2024.
https://doi.org/10.1007/978-3-031-55471-1_6

roughly divided into two categories: one is image-based, and the other is skeleton-based. In image-based recognition methods, RGB data is usually used as input to realize action recognition by extracting image features. In the recognition method based on human skeleton data, the skeleton data composed of two-dimensional or three-dimensional coordinates of joint points of the human body is extracted, and the action is recognized by feature extraction technology [1].

Human action recognition is a complex task because it requires a deep understanding of image content. Due to the diversity and complexity of human behavior and postures, as well as possible occlusions and other problems. Human action recognition is more challenging and complex than merely recognizing or detecting objects in images. The study of image information works well under simple background conditions. However, in reality, it may be affected by noise such as illumination. The action recognition method based on human skeleton information uses posture information to represent human characteristics, which can effectively reduce the impact of illumination [2]. With the rise and wide application of depth cameras, it becomes easier to obtain precise coordinates of joint points of the human skeleton. The action recognition method based on skeleton data has the characteristics of robustness and insensitivity to changes in lighting conditions, and can show better and excellent performance when given accurate joint point coordinates.

Researchers mainly use three deep techniques to learn actions in skeleton sequences, namely traditional convolutional neural network (CNN), recurrent neural network (RNN), and graph convolutional network (GCN). CNN has a strong ability to extract spatio-temporal features, while RNN is suitable for modeling temporal information [3]. Both approaches, RNN and CNN, have been widely used in skeleton-based action recognition and achieved impressive results. However, these two types of methods always represent bones in a grid-like manner, which cannot fully express the spatial structure information between human joints. Recently, graph convolutional networks (GCNs) have gradually received more attention, which are very suitable for processing non-Euclidean data. Skeletons can be naturally represented as graphs in non-Euclidean spaces. GCN-based methods have made substantial improvements in skeleton-based action recognition tasks. Therefore, Yan et al. first introduced the graph convolutional network into skeletal action recognition, and proposed the spatio-temporal graph convolutional network (ST-GCN) [4], which uses the natural connection relationship between human joints for action modeling, which does not require Manually design and divide skeleton parts or make human skeleton joint point traversal rules, so this method achieves better performance than previous methods.

In recent years, GCN has been rapidly developed and applied to process graph data. It usually has two kinds of construction ideas, which follow different principles. One is the spectral domain idea, whose principle is to perform graph convolution similarly in the frequency domain with the help of Fourier transform; the other is the spatial domain idea, whose principle is to use convolution directly on the nodes and their neighborhoods of the topological graph filter to extract features [5]. The graph convolutional network (GCN) that has emerged in recent years can make full use of the connection relationship between nodes to model data, which is very suitable for action recognition applications based on skeleton point data. Shi et al. [6] proposed the 2S-AGCN network, which adds an adaptive topological graph to each graph convolutional layer to enhance the long-range spatial modeling capability of the graph convolutional layer. Zhang et al. [7] proposed the SGN network, which uses the semantic information of human body joints and frames to enrich the expressive ability of skeleton features, thereby improving the recognition accuracy of the model. In any case, neither RNN network nor CNN network can fully characterize the spatial structure of skeleton data, because skeleton data is not a sequence of vectors or a two-dimensional grid, which has the structure of a graph of natural connections of human body structure. Compared with the former two methods, the GCN-based method does not need to manually divide the skeleton into multiple parts and design joint traversal rules, and can preserve the skeleton topology in the process of modeling skeleton space and time dependencies. Therefore, the GCN-based action recognition method has more advantages in modeling the spatiotemporal characteristics of the skeleton and has gradually become the preferred framework in this field.

However, most GCN-based methods still have some shortcomings, which have not been considered by current research. The above GCN for skeleton-based action recognition models all use stable three spatial configuration partitions and manually set the connection relationship between each skeletal joint point, which cannot better adapt to the changing characteristics of different actions. To solve this problem, in order to better extract the feature information of neighbor nodes of the nodes in the skeleton graph and adaptively obtain the connection relationship of joint nodes, this paper proposes a new partition strategy based on the original 2S-AGCN space-time model. In addition, for the coupling aggregation phenomenon caused by the feature channels of the input X sharing the same adjacency matrix, by introducing decoupling graph convolution to each partition, the feature channel information is fully utilized to improve the network's ability to model human bone information.

2 Related Work

2.1 ST-GCN Model

The input of the spatiotemporal graph convolutional network can be expressed as a spatiotemporal graph $G = (V, E)$, as shown on the left side of Fig. 1. $V = \{V_{ti} \mid t = 1, \cdots, T; i = 1, \cdots, v\}$, T represents the sequence frame, v represents the joint position, and V_{ti} represents the 2D or 3D coordinate data of the i-th joint in the t-th frame [8]. E includes E_S and E_F, $E_S = \{V_{ti}V_{tj} \mid (i, j) \in H\}$ represents the connection between human joints in a skeleton data frame, H is the joint natural connection set, $E_F = \{V_{ti}V_{(t+1)i}\}$ means that the same joints are interconnected in the time latitude. After ST-GCN obtains the skeleton sequence data composed of coordinates, it models the structured information between these joints along the space and time dimensions. The space dimension refers to the dimension where the joints in the same frame are located, and the time dimension refers to a certain One row is the dimension in which the same joint is located for all frames.The spatiotemporal graph convolutional neural network is composed of 9 ST-GCN units, each ST-GCN unit is composed of GCN and temporal convolutional network (temporal convolutional network, TCN), and a residual mechanism is added between ST-GCN units (residual).The main process is: given a skeleton sequence of an action video, first construct the graph structure data expressing the sequence, and use it as the input of ST-GCN; then extract high-level spatiotemporal features through a series of spatiotemporal graph convolution operations; Finally use the Softmax classifier gets the classification result.The core idea of ST-GCN is to combine the graph convolutional network (Graph Convolutional Network, GCN) with the temporal convolutional network (Temporal Convolutional Network, TCN), among them, GCN convolution space dimension data, TCN convolution time dimension The data.The skeleton spatiotemporal graph is shown in Fig. 1.

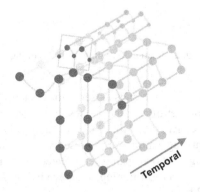

Fig. 1. Skeleton spatiotemporal diagram

The convolution of the single-frame skeleton graph above is represented by the following for Eq. (1):

$$f_{out} = \sum_{k}^{K_v} W_k \left(f_{in} A_k \right) \odot M_k \tag{1}$$

Among them, f_{in} is used as the input of the network, and the input is the skeleton sequence V in the space-time graph, and f_{out} is the output of the ST-GCN network, which is the behavior category output by the fully connected layer. K_v is the number of subsets divided by neighbor nodes, that is, the number of partitions. The partition strategy used by ST-GCN is space configuration partition, and the size of K_v is set to 3. The three configuration partitions are respectively represented by the adjacency matrix A_k, where $k \in \{1, 2, 3\}$, and the size of A_k is N × N. W_k is the weight function of graph convolution, which is a two-dimensional convolution with a convolution kernel size of 1 × 1. M_k is an N × N attention matrix used to learn the importance weights of node connections in the adjacency matrix, and $\odot$ represents the dot product.

ST-GCN proposes three partition strategies, namely Uni-labelling, Distance partitioning, and Spatial configuration partitioning. Uni-labelling is the simplest strategy, where each node has the same label (0) and K = 1; Distance partitioning is also simple, it divides the adjacent nodes according to their distance from the root node, if D = 1, then this means that the root node is always 0 and all other nodes are 1. This enables the algorithm to simulate local differential behavior. K = 2 and lti(vti) = d(vti, vti); Spatial configuration partitioning division is a little more complicated, and the 1 neighborhood of node i is divided into three subsets. The first subset is the node i itself, the second

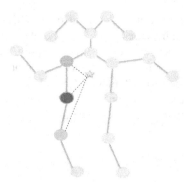

Fig. 2. Spatial configuration partitioning

subset is a set of neighbor nodes, which is closer to the center of the skeleton than node i, and the third subset is the set of neighbor nodes farther away from the center of the skeleton than node i, respectively denoting Motion characteristics such as static state, centripetal motion and centrifugal motion. K represents the number of partitions, and the space-time graph node neighborhood span is represented by D. The strategy adopted by ST-GCN is Spatial configuration partitioning, as shown in Fig. 2. This partition strategy can be expressed by Eq. 2 below.

$$l_{ti}(v_{ti}) = \{ \begin{array}{l} 0 \ if \ r_j = r_i \\ 1 \ if \ r_j < r_i \\ 2 \ if \ r_j > r_i \end{array} \tag{2}$$

where r_j is the distance from adjacent node j to the root node, and r_i is the distance from root node i to the center of gravity.

2.2 2S-AGCN Model

Since the adjacency matrix A_k in ST-GCN is shared in each spatiotemporal graph convolutional network layer, and only the natural connection relationship of the human body can be used, non-existent connections cannot be established. However, many bone nodes that are not directly connected in the process of action will also have actions related to each other. For example, clapping and other actions, the bone joint points between the two hands will have a relationship, that is, there will be a connection relationship other than the natural structure joint points of the human body. At this time, the predefined adjacency matrix that only includes the natural connection relationship of human bone points will not guarantee learning. The obtained bone point connection relationship is optimal. In order to solve the problem that ST-GCN only contains first-order information of bones, lacks second-order information and uses a stable graph structure, Shi et al. [14] proposed an adaptive graph volume called 2S-AGCN Productive dual-stream network structure. 2S-AGCN still follows the method of constructing spatio-temporal graph in ST-GCN, which is used to extract the features of joints in spatial and temporal dimensions. However, different from ST-GCN, Adaptive Spatio-Temporal Graph

Convolutional Network (2S-AGCN) tries to adaptively learn non-existing connection relations while trying to learn data correlation between samples.The form of Eq. (1) is changed so that the structure of the graph can be adjusted adaptively.

$$f_{out} = \sum_k^{Kv} W_k f_{in}(A_k + B_k + C_k) \tag{3}$$

In Eq. (3), A_k, which is the same as in Eq. (1), represents the normalized adjacency matrix of the physical structure of the human body. During training, elements of B_k and other parameters are parameterized and optimized together. It does not have any effect on the value of B_k, which indicates that the graph is learned entirely from the training data. With this data-driven approach, the model can fully learn the graph to complete the recognition task and be more personalized to the different information contained in different layers. It can be noted that the elements in the matrix can have arbitrary values. It not only indicates whether two joints are connected, but also how strong the connection is. C_k is the attention map between sample data, which can be obtained by Eq. (4), making the model fully data-driven, where $W\theta$ and $W\varphi$ are the weights of the Gaussian embedding function. The output of the two Gaussian embedding functions is multiplied to obtain a joint similarity weight matrix with a size of $N \times N$. The similarity matrix is passed through the softmax activation function [9] to obtain the similarity score between any two joints in the sample. Different samples will have considerable differences even with the same motion characteristics under the influence of subjects and cameras.

$$C_k = \tanh(f_{in}^T W_{\theta k}^T W_{\varphi k} f_{in}) \tag{4}$$

3 Decoupled 2S-AGCN Based on New Partition Strategy

3.1 2S-AGCN with New Partition Strategy

Most of the current GCN-based models often use a stable space configuration partition strategy and manually set the connection relationship between each bone joint point, which cannot better adapt to the changing characteristics of different actions. The 2S-AGCN also uses the same spatial configuration partitioning as the above-mentioned ST-GCN. To solve this problem, under the condition that the time domain is consistent with the traditional strategy, the new partition strategy proposed in this paper expands the node neighborhood span D in the space domain to 2, and changes the partition from the original three partitions to four partitions. Different partition strategies are equivalent to changing the size of the convolution kernel. At the same time, the proposed segmentation strategy can cover most of the motion joint points in the human skeleton, such as arms, thighs, etc., so it is no longer limited to adjacent joint points, but can be effectively extended to other joints [10]. The original partition strategy and the new partition strategy are shown in Fig. 3:

The division strategy of the original space configuration is shown in Fig. 3(a). Under the original partition strategy, the space-time graph is divided into three parts according to the distance from each node to the center of gravity of the skeleton: root node, centripetal

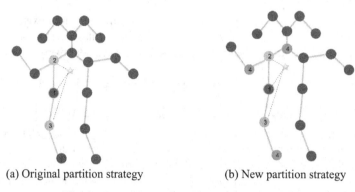

(a) Original partition strategy   (b) New partition strategy

Fig. 3. Comparison of partition strategies

node, and centrifugal node [11]. 1 is the root node, 2 is the centripetal node, and 3 is the centrifugal node. The center of gravity of the skeleton is represented by a star in the figure, which is the average coordinate of all joints in the coordinate system. The new partitioning strategy proposed in this paper is shown in Fig. 3(b). Expressed as follows:

1: Root node.
2: Centripetal node, closer to the center of gravity of the skeleton than the root node.
3: Centrifugal node, which is further away from the center of gravity of the skeleton than the root node.
4: A node whose root node neighborhood span D is 2.

The implementation process of the adaptive graph convolution layer in 2S-AGCN is shown in Fig. 4 where each layer has three graph subsets A_k, B_k, and C_k. The orange box indicates that the parameters can be learned, and k_v indicates the number of partitions. In 2S-AGCN, k_v is 3. After using the new partition strategy, the k_v of the adaptive graph convolution layer changes from 3 to 4.

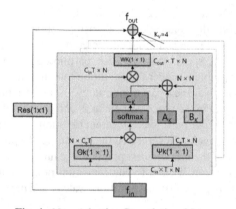

Fig. 4. New Adaptive Convolutional Layers

3.2 Decoupling GCN

Graph convolution consists of two matrix multiplication processes: AX and XW. AX calculates aggregated information between different skeletons, so we call it spatial aggregation. XW calculates the correlation information between different channels, so we call it channel correlation.

As the picture shows. In Fig. 5, the spatial aggregation (AX) can be decomposed to compute the aggregation on each channel separately. Note that all channels of feature X share an adjacency matrix A (drawn in the same color), which means that all channels share the same convolution kernel. We call this coupled aggregation. Since the human body has multiple degrees of freedom, the correlation between joints is very complex, and the correlation between different actions is also different, which limits the expressive ability of graph convolution spatial aggregation. While most of the existing GCN-based skeletal action recognition methods use coupling aggregation, such as ST-GCN [4], non-local adaptive GCN, AS-GCN [12], Directed-GNN [13], 2S-AGCN [6]. We collectively refer to them as coupled graph convolutions.

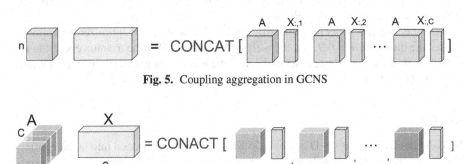

Fig. 5. Coupling aggregation in GCNS

Fig. 6. Decoupling aggregation in GCNS

In this paper, we adopt Decoupled Graph Convolution (DC-GCN) for skeletal action recognition, where different channels have independent trainable adjacency matrices, as shown in Fig. 6. Decoupled graph convolutions greatly increase the diversity of adjacency matrices. Similar to the redundancy of CNN kernels [14], decoupled graph convolutions may introduce redundant adjacent matrices. Therefore, we divide the channels into g groups. Channels in a group share a trainable adjacency matrix. When g = C, each channel has its own spatial aggregation kernel, which leads to a large number of redundant parameters; when g = 1, the decoupled graph convolution degenerates into a coupled graph convolution [15]. So we can temporarily set g to 8. The equation for decoupling graph convolution is as follows:

$$\mathbf{X}' = \widetilde{\mathbf{A}}^d{}_{:,:,1}\mathbf{X}^{\mathbf{w}}{}_{:,:,\lfloor\frac{C}{g}\rfloor}\|\widetilde{\mathbf{A}}^d{}_{:,:,2}\mathbf{X}^{\mathbf{w}}{}_{:,\lfloor\frac{C}{g}\rfloor:\lfloor\frac{2C}{g}\rfloor}\|\cdots\|\widetilde{\mathbf{A}}^d{}_{:,:,9}\mathbf{X}^{\mathbf{w}}{}_{:,\lfloor\frac{(g-1)C}{g}\rfloor:} \tag{5}$$

where $\mathbf{X}^{\mathbf{w}} = \mathbf{XW}$, $\mathbf{A}^d \in \mathbb{R}^{n \times n \times g}$ is the decoupled adjacency matrix. The indices of $\mathbf{A}^d$ and $\mathbf{X}^{\mathbf{w}}$ are in Python notation, representing channel-level connections.

DC-GCN can be naturally extended to the case of multiple partitions by introducing a decoupled graph convolution to each partition. Note that our DC-GCN differs from the multi-partition strategy, which integrates multiple graph convolutions with different adjacency matrices. Combining DC-GCN with the new partitioning strategy proposed above for experiments shows the complementarity between multi-partitioning strategies and DC-GCN.

4 Experiment and Analysis

This paper uses the large-scale public behavior dataset NTU-RGB+D [16] to conduct ablation experiments to verify the effectiveness of the model components; compare the method with some current mainstream and advanced methods to verify the performance level of the method proposed in this paper. Experiments show that the model has achieved high recognition accuracy on the NTU-RGB+D dataset, which verifies the effectiveness of the method proposed in this paper. The experimental platform used is: Window10 system, the CPU is i5-12500H, the graphics card is RTX3090, the memory is 8 GB, and the deep learning framework is Pytorch.

All models in this paper use stochastic gradient descent (SGD) optimizer for training, and set the momentum is 0.9, and the weight decay is 0.0001. The training epochs is set to 50. The initial learning rate is set to 0.1, and the learning rate decays with a coefficient of 0.1 at the 20th epoch and 40th epoch, and the batch size is set to 32.

4.1 Datasets

NTU-RGB+D. NTU RGB+D contains 56,880 motion clips grouped into 60 categories. They invited 40 different volunteers to perform the moves. Use three cameras simultaneously to capture three different horizontal views of the same action. These actions were recorded by 40 volunteers in a laboratory environment using three cameras simultaneously. Detect and provide annotations through Kinect depth sensors, and provide 3D joint positions (X, Y, Z) in the camera coordinate system, mainly including 25 joint points of the human body.The 3D coordinates of 25 body joints are captured to form a skeleton sequence. The structure diagram of NTU human body is shown in Fig. 7.The authors of this dataset used two evaluation schemes:

(1) cross-subject (CS): The training set contains 40,320 samples from 20 subjects, and the test set has 16,560 samples from other subjects.
(2) cross-view (CV): The training set contains 37,920 samples from two camera views, while the test set from another camera view contains 18,960 samples.

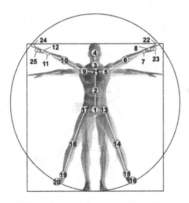

Fig. 7. NTU Dataset Anatomy of the Human Body

4.2 Ablation Experiment

In order to verify the improvement effect of the different improvements proposed in this paper on the original 2S-AGCN model, comparative experiments were carried out on the NTU-RGB + D dataset using new partition strategies and using decoupled graph convolution. The specific experimental results are shown in Table 1, where X-Sub and X-View represent the results obtained from different targets or different camera angles for the test samples, respectively. In order to verify whether the new partition strategy can improve the performance of the model, in the original 2S-AGCN model, the original partition strategy is replaced with the new partition strategy, namely 2S-AGCN + NPS in the table. At the same time, in order to test the performance of decoupled graph convolution (DC-GCN), DC-GCN is added to the original 2S-AGCN, that is, 2S-AGCN + DC in the table. Our proposed model is represented by 2S-AGCN + NPS + DC.

Table 1. Accuracy comparison experiment results of different model structures

Backbone	+ NPS	+ DC	X-Sub (%)	X-View (%)
2S-AGCN			88.5%	95.1%
2S-AGCN	✔		88.7%	95.2%
2S-AGCN		✔	88.8%	95.3%
2S-AGCN	✔	✔	**90.1%**	**95.8%**

It can be clearly seen from Table 1 that the accuracy rate on the NTU-RGB + D data set has been improved after using the new division strategy, which has increased by 0.2% in the X-Sub evaluation method and 0.1% in the X-View evaluation method. At the same time, it can also be seen that the accuracy rates on X-Sub and X-View have increased by 0.3% and 0.2% respectively after using DC-GCN.

Under the CV evaluation benchmark of the NTU-RGB + D dataset, the confusion matrix of the validation set is shown in Fig. 8. There are a total of 60 behaviors in the

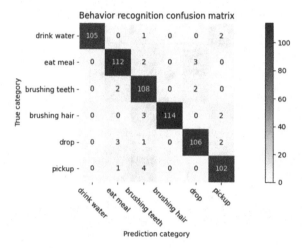

Fig. 8. Behavior recognition confusion matrix

data set. For the convenience of display, the recognition results of the first 6 behaviors are drawn as a confusion matrix for analysis. The recognition accuracy of these six behaviors is above 95%, confirming the effectiveness of our proposed two modules.

4.3 Two-Stream Fusion Experiment

In addition to the first-order information (coordinates, confidence), bone information, its second-order information (length and direction of the bone) is also very important [17]. We use Joint to extract the Bone information of the skeleton, and train the Joint flow and Bone flow information respectively. This is the meaning of 2S in 2S-AGCN. Finally, the results of the two-stream recognition are fused to obtain the recognition result of the final model. In the X-View evaluation mode of the NTU-RGB + D dataset, multiple experiments have shown that bone data can improve the performance of the method. As shown in Table 2.

Table 2. Dual-stream network performance under X-View

Modal	Accuracy(%)
J stream	94.72%
B stream	94.34%
2 stream	95.8%

4.4 Compared with Other Behavior Recognition Methods

In order to verify the performance level of the method proposed in this paper, we compared the recognition accuracy of the behavior recognition method proposed in this paper with several current research popular recognition technologies on the NTU-RGB + D dataset. The methods involved in the comparison include CNN-based methods and GCN-based methods. Table 3 below lists the recognition accuracy of these algorithms on the NTU-RGB + D dataset. It can be seen from Table 3 that the accuracy of 2S-AGCN under the new partition strategy and decoupled graph convolution is significantly higher than other behavior recognition methods. Compared with other methods based on CNNs or RNNs, the recognition accuracy of this method has been greatly improved.In the NTU-RGB + D dataset X-Sub division mode, the recognition rate is 0.6 percentage points higher than that of the 2S-AGCN model, and in its X-View division mode, the recognition rate is 0.7 percentage points higher than that of the 2s-AGCN model. This shows that the decoupled 2S-AGCN based on the new partition strategy proposed in this paper can better improve the performance of the model on large data sets.

Table 3. Comparison of recognition accuracy between the proposed method and other methods

Methods	X-Sub (%)	X-View (%)
Deep LSTM	60.7%	67.3%
Two-Stream 3DCNN	66.8%	72.6%
ST-LSTM	69.2%	77.7%
TCN	74.3%	83.1%
ST-GCN	81.5%	88.3%
2S-AGCN	88.5%	95.1%
Ours	**90.1%**	**95.8%**

5 Conclusion

The traditional graph convolutional network only uses three stable spatial configuration partitions and manually sets the connection relationship between the joint points of the bones, which cannot better adapt to the changing characteristics of different actions and ignores the information of non-adjacent nodes. A new division strategy is proposed, which can better extract the feature information of the neighbor nodes of the nodes in the skeleton graph and adaptively obtain the joint connection relationship. In addition, for the coupling aggregation phenomenon caused by using the same graph convolution kernel for all channels of the input X feature, by introducing decoupled graph convolution to each partition, the channel information of the feature is fully utilized to improve the network's modeling of human bone information. Ability. In order to verify the effectiveness of the method, extensive experiments are conducted on the NTU-RGB + D dataset. The results show that the method proposed in this paper can obtain higher action recognition accuracy than most current literatures, and the accuracy rates of 90.1% and 95.8% were respectively achieved under the X-Sub and X-View division methods of the NTU-RGB + D dataset. The next step of research will be to introduce the attention module to improve the ability of the network to model spatio-temporal features.

References

1. Xuanye, L., Xingwei, H., Jingong, J., et al.: Human action recognition method combining multi-attention mechanism and spatiotemporal graph convolutional network. J. Comput. Aided Des. Graph. **33**(07), 1055–1063 (2021)
2. Hualei, X., Yingqiang, D., Meng, G., et al.: Skeletal action recognition based on multi-partition spatiotemporal graph convolutional network. Signal Process. **38**(02), 241–249 (2022). https://doi.org/10.16798/j.issn.1003-0530.2022.02.003
3. 0036 L J,Shahroudy A,Xu D, et al. Spatio-Temporal LSTM with Trust Gates for 3D Human Action Recognition.[J]. CoRR,2016,abs/1607.07043
4. Yan, S., Xiong, Y., Lin, D.: Spatial temporal graph convolutional networks for skeleton-based action recognition. In: Thirty-Second AAAI Conference on Artificial Intelligence (AAAI-2018) and the Thirtieth Annual Conference on Innovative Applications of Artificial Intelligence (IAAI-2018) (2018)
5. Haoli, Z.: Action recognition based on spatial-temporal graph convolutional network with fusion of geometric features. Computer Syst. Appl. **31**(10), 261–269 (2022)
6. Shi, L., Zhang, Y., Cheng, J., Lu, H.: Two-stream adaptive graph convolutional networks for skeleton-based action recognition. In: 2019 IEEE/CVF Conference on Computer Vision and Pattern Recognition (CVPR) (2019)
7. Zhang, P., Lan, C., Zeng, W., Xing, J., Xue, J., Zheng, N.: Semantics-guided neural networks for efficient skeleton-based human action recognition. In:2020 IEEE/CVF Conference on Computer Vision and Pattern Recognition (CVPR) (2020)
8. Chen, W., Qiang, S., Hongyu, N., et al.: Abnormal behavior recognition based on skeleton sequence extraction. Comput. Syst. Appl. **31**(11),215–222 (2022).https://doi.org/10.15888/j.cnki.csa.008773
9. Mikolov T,0010 C K,Corrado G, et al. Efficient Estimation of Word Representations in Vector Space[J]. CoRR,2013,abs/1301.3781
10. Wang, Q., Zhang, K., Asghar, M.A.: Skeleton-based ST-GCN for human action recognition with extended skeleton graph and partitioning strategy. IEEE Access **10**, 41403–41410 (2022)
11. Wu, J., Wang, L., Chong, G., Feng, H.: 2S-AGCN human behavior recognition based on new partition strategy. In: 2022 Asia-Pacific Signal and Information Processing Association Annual Summit and Conference (APSIPA ASC) (2022)
12. Li, Q., Han, Z., Wu, X.M.: Deeper insights into graph convolutional networks for semi-supervised learning. In: Thirty-Second AAAI Conference on Artificial Intelligence (2018)
13. Shi, L., Zhang, Y., Cheng, J., Lu, H.: Skeleton-based action recognition with directed graph neural networks. In: The IEEE Conference on Computer Vision and Pattern Recognition (CVPR) (2019)
14. Molchanov, P., Tyree, S., Karras, T., Aila, T., Kautz, J.: Pruning convolutional neural networks for resource efficient inference. arXiv preprint arXiv:1611.06440(2016)
15. Cheng, K., Zhang, Y., Cao, C., Shi, L., Cheng, J., Lu, H.:GCN with dropgraph module for skeleton-based action recognition. In: Vedaldi, A., Bischof, H., Brox, T., Frahm, JM. (eds.) Computer Vision – ECCV 2020. ECCV 2020. LNCS, vol. 12369, 536–553. Springer, Cham (2020). https://doi.org/10.1007/978-3-030-58586-0_32
16. Fernando, B., Gavves, E., José Oramas, M., Ghodrati, A.,Tuytelaars, T: Modeling video evolution for action recognition(Conference Paper). In: Proceedings of the IEEE Computer Society Conference on Computer Vision and Pattern Recognition, vol.7, pp. 5378–5387 (2015)
17. Qixiang, S., Ning, H., Congcong, Z., Shengjie, L.: Human skeleton action recognition method based on lightweight graph convolution. Comput. Eng.. Eng. **48**(5), 306–313 (2022)

Image Processing and Computer Vision

Human Behavior Recognition Algorithm Based on HD-C3D Model

Zhihao Xie[1], Lei Yu[2], Qi Wang[1], and Ziji Ma[1($\boxtimes$)] (iD)

[1] College of Electrical and Information Engineering, Hunan University, Changsha 410082, China
zijima@hnu.edu.cn

[2] Information Institute of Ministry of Emergency Management of the People's Republic of China, Beijing 100029, China

Abstract. To address the problems of low recognition accuracy and long training time of the original C3D (Convolutional 3D) model, this paper proposes a modified method to improve its framework. Firstly, the Relu activation function in the hidden layer is replaced by the Hardswish function to allow more neurons to participate in parameter updating and to alleviate the problem of slow gradient convergence. Secondly, the dataset was optimised using the background difference method and the image scaling improvement respectively, and the optimised dataset was used for model training. The image scaling improvement combined with the activation function improvement results in a better HDs-C3D (Hardswish Data scaling - Convolutional 3D) model. Its accuracy on the training dataset reached 89.1%; meanwhile, the training time per round was reduced by about 25% when trained in the experimental environment of this paper.

Keywords: C3D model · activation function · background difference method · image scaling improvement

1 Introduction

The recognition of human behavior in video is one of the most popular aspects of video understanding. The scientific results generated by human behavior recognition technology are now being used in various aspects of life.

Nowadays, traditional human behavior recognition algorithms based on feature extraction are gradually replaced by algorithms based on deep learning. Tran et al. [1] proposed a C3D convolutional neural network, which differs from previous 2D convolutional neural networks in that both convolution and pooling operations are implemented using 3D kernels. Ye et al. [2] added DenseNet from the 3D convolutional layer to

This work is supported in part by the National Nature Science Foundation of China under Grant 61971182, in part by Nature Science Foundation of Hunan Province 2021JJ30145, in part by Hunan Province Enterprise Science and technology commis-sioner program 2021GK5021, in part by Guangxi key R&D plan project 2022AB41020

C. Wu et al. (Eds.): MONAMI 2023, LNICST 559, pp. 85–93, 2024.
https://doi.org/10.1007/978-3-031-55471-1_7

improve the feature utilization in the network, and finally verified its effectiveness in recognition. Niu et al. [3] combined the C3D model with an SVM classifier and L2 regularisation to improve the running speed of the algorithm and prevent model over-fitting. Liu et al. [4] proposed the CoDT method for dealing with domain sharing and target-specific feature co-clustering for cross-domain 3D action recognition. Si et al. [5] proposed adversarial self-supervised learning for 3D action recognition. Singh et al. [6] proposed a two-path temporal comparison model to address video behavior recognition with few labels. Yang et al. [7] proposed a temporal pyramid network to capture action instances at different tempos. Hong et al. [8] proposed Video Pose Distillation. (VPD) to improve the performance of few-shot, fine-grained action recognition, retrieval, and detection tasks. Li et al. [9] proposed a Channel Independent Directional Convolution (CIDC) structure that allows the network to focus on the more meaningful and behav-iorally relevant parts of the frame. Jiang et al. [10] proposed a new strategy of aggregated decentralized down-sampling to prevent the loss of feature information. Yuan et al. [11] proposed Dynamic Inference Network (DIN) network for group activity recognition, which reduces the computational overhead of the inference module. Sudhakaran et al. [12] proposed Gate Shift Module (GSM) module, which reduces the complexity of the model with the use of this network. Yang et al. [13] proposed the Recurrent Vision Trans-former (RViT) framework, which can correctly process video clips of various lengths without consuming large amounts of GPU memory. Li et al. [14] proposed the Dynamic Spatio-Temporal Specialization (DSTS) module, which yields advanced performance in fine-grained action recognition. Liu et al. [15] proposed cascade vision detection. Huang et al. [16] proposed the RoofSplit framework to enable efficient execution of deep learning models at the edge of the network.

In order to improve the recognition accuracy and shorten the training time of the C3D model, the improved method proposed in this paper has the following effects. Replacing the Relu function with the Hardswish function enables more neurons to be updated with parameters, while improving the gradient convergence speed to a certain extent. The use of background difference method can get the foreground action of changes in the dataset, there is easy feature extraction. Improvements to the image scaling operation during model training can shorten the training time as well as improve recognition accuracy.

2   Human Behavior Recognition Based on C3D Model

The convolution operation in the C3D model with a convolution kernel of $3 \times 3 \times 3$ size can get better experimental results. The $3 \times 3 \times 3$ sized convolution kernel in the model is sliding in $1 \times 1 \times 1$ steps throughout the convolution layer, while the 3D pooling kernel is not. In order to preserve the initial timing information at the time of video frame input, the pooling kernels and sliding steps of the first pooling layer are set to $1 \times 2 \times 2$, while the pooling kernels and sliding steps of the remaining pooling layers are set to $2 \times 2 \times 2$ (Fig. 1).

The network contains 8 convolutional layers, 5 pooling layers, 2 fully connected layers and a Softmax classifier. The data size is denoted as $c \times l \times h \times w$, where c is the number of channels of video frames, l is the number of video frames, h is the height

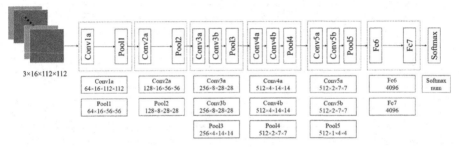

3×16×112×112

Conv1a 64×16×112×112	Conv2a 128×16×56×56	Conv3a 256×8×28×28	Conv4a 512×4×14×14	Conv5a 512×2×7×7	Fc6 4096	Softmax num
Pool1 64×16×56×56	Pool2 128×8×28×28	Conv3b 256×8×28×28	Conv4b 512×4×14×14	Conv5b 512×2×7×7	Fc7 4096	
		Pool3 256×4×14×14	Pool4 512×2×7×7	Pool5 512×1×4×4		

Fig. 1. Structure of C3D convolutional neural network. This structural diagram shows the size changes of the input data after passing through various parts of the model.

of video frames, and w is the width of video frames. The data size of the input network is $3 \times 16 \times 112 \times 112$ in size.

The 3D convolution kernel can be represented by $d \times k \times k$, with d being the time depth and k being the spatial size of the convolution kernel. The image data is processed with a quantity of n, kernel size $3 \times 3 \times 3$, and sliding step and padding of both $1 \times 1 \times 1$, and the output feature map size is $n \times l \times h \times w$. Optimizer uses SGD (Stochastic Gradient Descent) algorithm, Relu as the activation function in the hidden layer, and Dropout regularization to prevent overfitting.

3 Improvements to This Paper

3.1 Optimisation of Activation Functions

The activation function used in the original C3D convolutional neural network is Relu, which has the following drawbacks: (i) As the initial parameters are randomly assigned, when the parameter value is negative, then its output value and gradient are zero, resulting in a break in back propagation using chain derivation, and thus the corresponding parameters cannot continue to be updated down the line (ii) The function has no negative output, which can slow down the convergence speed of the gradient and easily enter local optima.

To relieve the above problem, the Hardswish [17] function is applied to this paper instead of the Relu function, which does not increase the computational complexity significantly. The expression for this function is shown in Eq. (1):

$$Hardwish(x) = \begin{cases} 0 & x \leq -3 \\ \frac{x \cdot (x+3)}{6} & -3 < x < 3 \\ x & x \geq 3 \end{cases} \quad (1)$$

The Hardswish function has the following advantages over the Relu function: (i) The function has an output value and gradient of 0 at $x < -3$, with a wider range of valid values than the Relu function, enabling more neurons to be involved in parameter updating; (ii) The function has negative values in the $(-3,0)$ interval, which can alleviate the problem that the gradient convergence rate becomes slower and easier to enter the local optimum (Fig. 2).

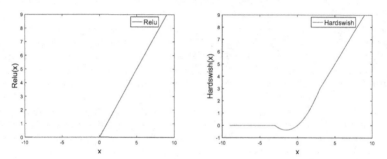

Fig. 2. Relu activation function and Hardswish activation function.

3.2 Background Difference Method Optimisation of Dataset

The background difference method [18] is commonly used in the field of target detection. The basic principle is that a frame is selected as the background frame and the current frame is subtracted from the background frame. The region where the pixel difference between the current frame and the background frame exceeds a certain threshold is used as the foreground to obtain the size contour of the moving body. The process of implementation is as follows (Table 1):

Table 1. Algorithm 1 the pseudocodes of background difference method.

Algorithm 1: Background Difference Method
Input: Current frame F_t , Background frame B, Binarization threshold T.
Output: Background differential frame D_t.
1: $F_t \leftarrow$ *Grayscale processing*
2: $B \leftarrow$ *Grayscale processing*
3: # Add *Gaussian blur* to F_t ,B
4: F_t , $B \leftarrow G(x,y) = \dfrac{1}{2\pi\sigma^2} e^{-\frac{(x^2+y^2)}{2\sigma^2}}$
5: $D_t = |F_t(x,y) - B(x,y)|$
6: # Add *Binarization process* to D_t
7: **if** $D_t(x,y) > T$
8:     $D_t(x,y) = 255$
9: **else**
10:    $D_t(x,y) = 25$
11: $D_t \leftarrow$ *Morphological Dilation*
12: **return** D_t

In this paper, the dataset is processed using the background difference method, and the new data after processing is uniformly cropped to a size of 106 × 106. The network structure is also modified for model training, and the data flow under the new structure is shown below (Fig. 3).

Table 2. Simulation environment

Hardware	Software environment
Operating system: Ubuntu 18.04.6 LTS CPU: Intel Core i7-10700K Disk: 512 GB GPU graphics card: RXT3080 GPU memory: 12G	Python version: 3.8 Pytorch version: 1.8 CUDA Version: 11.4 Torchvision version: 0.9.0 OpenCV version: 4.1.2

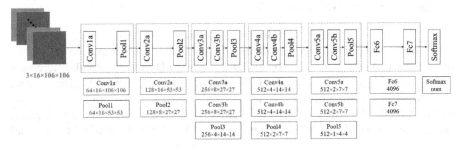

Fig. 3. Model structure and data flow under the background difference method

3.3 Image Scaling Improvements

The UCF-101 dataset is chosen for this experiment, and the video frames undergo two scale transformations before being trained. In this paper, the process is improved by first scaling the 171×128 size to 106×106 size before scaling to 112×112 size. This is shown in Fig. 4 below.

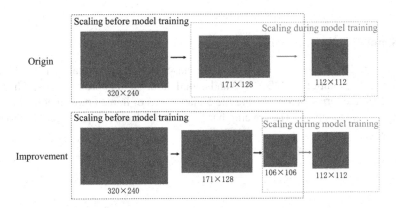

Fig. 4. Comparison of improved image scaling operations

As obtaining a certain size of image, equal scaling produces clearer images than non-equal scaling, resulting in less image data loss. Also, the scaling of the image from

171 × 128 to 112 × 112 size is done during the training of the model. When the image to be scaled is close to the target size, the time taken to run the image scaling function can be reduced. Therefore, this time, the image of 171 × 128 size is first scaled to 106 × 106 size to improve the image quality and shorten the model training time. The reason for using shrink then zoom for the images is that (i) it makes the dataset more lightweight (ii) scaling down and then scaling up allows for pixel filling of the images.

4   Experiments and Analysis of Results

4.1   Improved Model HD-C3D

In this paper, based on the original C3D model, the HD-C3D (Hardswish Data optimization - Convolutional 3D) model is proposed by combining three improvement points, which consists of two parts: the HDb-C3D (Hardswish Data background difference - Convolutional 3D) model and the HDs-C3D model. The HDb-C3D model is derived from the Hardswish activation function combined with the background difference method; the HDs-C3D model is derived from the Hardswish activation function combined with image scaling. We unify the HDb-C3D model and HDs-C3D model into HD-C3D model (Fig. 5).

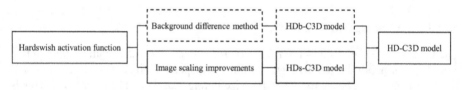

Fig. 5. Structure of the HD-C3D model.

4.2   Simulation Environment

(1) Data set: This paper uses the UCF-101 dataset, which has a total of 13,320 videos all with a resolution of 320 × 240 and a total duration of approximately 27 h. There are 101 categories encompassing the 5 main types of human movement.
(2) Experimental setting: The specific hardware and software environment is shown in Table 2.

4.3 Analysis of Results

In this experiment, the HDb-C3D model and HDs-C3D model are compared with the original C3D model for data comparison. For the experiments, the UCF-101 dataset is used for training, and the number of epochs is 50.

The accuracy curves and loss curves of the model training are shown in Figs. 6 and 7. As the number of training rounds increased, the accuracy of the model increased and the loss value decreased, and levelled off at around 25 rounds. Finally, the accuracy of HDb-C3D model in this training can reach 85.4%, and the accuracy of HDs-C3D model in this training can reach 89.1%, and the accuracy of the original C3D model in this experiment is 50.2%. The accuracy of HDb-C3D model is improved about 35% compared with the original model, and the accuracy of HDs-C3D model is improved about 39% compared with the original model. Meanwhile, the loss reduction of HDb-C3D and HDs-C3D over

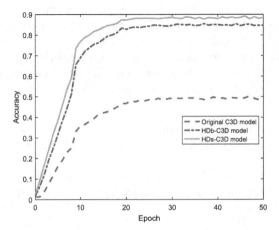

Fig. 6. Variation curve of model training accuracy.

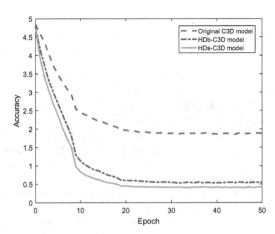

Fig. 7. Variation curve of model training loss.

the original C3D model is 1.3 and 1.4, respectively. It can be seen that both improved models have good results in improving accuracy and reducing loss.

In addition, the new dataset obtained using background difference method reduces the storage space by approximately 3.7 GB compared to the original dataset, while the detection time can be reduced by approximately half compared to the original detection time when using the new video set composed. Without the image scaling improvement, the training dataset takes about 8 min to train once, and with it the training takes about 6 min, a 25% reduction in training time.

5 Summary

In this paper, three C3D model improvement methods are proposed and combined into two improved models. The recognition accuracy of HDb-C3D model and HDs-C3D model are improved by about 35% and 39% respectively compared with the original C3D model; the loss is reduced by 1.3 and 1.4 respectively; meanwhile the training time per round of HDs-C3D model is shortened by about 25%.

Although this paper has improved the original C3D model, it has mostly improved the data pre-processing and the study is not comprehensive enough. For this reason, subsequent work could be directed towards improving the model architecture in the following directions:

(1) Adding an attention mechanism to the network. This mechanism allows the network to pay more attention to the behavioral actions of interest, thus improving recognition accuracy.
(2) The introduction of a residual network. The addition of this network allows the model to learn higher level features without gradient disappearance, thus improving the accuracy of recognition.

References

1. Tran, D., Bourdev, L., Fergus, R., et al.: Learning spatiotemporal features with 3D convolutional networks. In: 2015 IEEE International Conference on Computer Vision (ICCV), pp. 4489–4497 (2015)
2. Ye, Q., Yang, H.: Design of human behavior recognition network based on deep learning. China Sci. Technol. Inf. **10**(628), 91–94 (2020)
3. Niu, Y., Su, W., Yu, C., et al.: Real-time behavior recognition for intelligent surveillance based on TX2 environment. Inf. Technol. Informatization **4**(253), 243–245 (2021)
4. Liu, Q., Wang, Z.: collaborating domain-shared and target-specific feature clustering for cross-domain 3D action recognition. In: In: Avidan, S., Brostow, G., Cissé, M., Farinella, G.M., Hassner, T. (eds.) ECCV 2022. LNCS, vol. 13664, pp. 137–155. Springer, Cham (2022). https://doi.org/10.1007/978-3-031-19772-7_9
5. Si, C., Nie, X., Wang, W., et al.: Adversarial Self-Supervised Learning for Semi-Supervised 3D Action Recognition. In: Vedaldi, A., Bischof, H., Brox, T., Frahm, JM. (eds.) ECCV 2020. LNCS, vol. 12352, pp. 35–51. Springer, Cham (2020). https://doi.org/10.1007/978-3-030-58571-6_3

6. Singh, A., Chakraborty, O., Varshney, A., et al.: Semi-supervised action recognition with temporal contrastive learning. In: 2021 IEEE/CVF Conference on Computer Vision and Pattern Recognition (CVPR), pp. 10389–10399 (2021)

7. Yang, C., Xu, Y., Shi, J., et al.: Temporal pyramid network for action recognition 2020. In: 2020 IEEE/CVF Conference on Computer Vision and Pattern Recognition (CVPR), pp. 588–597 (2020)

8. Hong, J., Fisher, M., Gharbi, M., et al.: Video Pose Distillation for Few-Shot, Fine-Grained Sports Action Recognition. 2021, in 2021 IEEE/CVF International Conference on Computer Vision (ICCV), Oct. 2021, pp. 9234–9243

9. Li, X., Shuai, B., Tighe, J.: Directional temporal modeling for action recognition. In: Vedaldi, A., Bischof, H., Brox, T., Frahm, J.-M. (eds.) ECCV 2020. LNCS, vol. 12351, pp. 275–291. Springer, Cham (2020). https://doi.org/10.1007/978-3-030-58539-6_17

10. Jiang, Z., Ma, Z., Wang, Y., et al.: Aggregated decentralized down-sampling-based ResNet for smart healthcare systems. Neural Comput. Appl. **75**, 1–13 (2021)

11. Yuan, H., Ni, D., Wang, M.: Spatio-temporal dynamic inference network for group activity recognition. In: 2021 IEEE/CVF International Conference on Computer Vision (ICCV), pp. 7456–7465 (2021)

12. Sudhakaran, S., Escalera, S., Lanz, O.: Gate-shift networks for video action recognition. In: 2020 IEEE/CVF Conference on Computer Vision and Pattern Recognition (CVPR), pp. 1099–1108 (2020)

13. Yang, J., Dong, X., Liu, L., et al.: Recurring the transformer for video action recognition. In: 2022 IEEE/CVF Conference on Computer Vision and Pattern Recognition (CVPR), pp. 14043–14053 (2022)

14. Li, T., Foo, L., Ke, Q., et al.: Dynamic spatio-temporal specialization learning for fine-grained action recognition. In: Avidan, S., Brostow, G., Cissé, M., Farinella, G.M., Hassner, T. (eds.) ECCV 2022. LNCS, vol. 13664, pp. 386–403. Springer, Cham (2022). https://doi.org/10.1007/978-3-031-19772-7_23

15. Liu, J., Liu, H., Chakraborty, C., et al.: Cascade learning embedded vision inspection of rail fastener by using a fault detection IoT vehicle. IEEE Internet Things J. **10**(4), 3006–3017 (2021)

16. Huang, Y., Zhang, H., Shao, X., et al.: RoofSplit: an edge computing framework with heterogeneous nodes collaboration considering optimal CNN model splitting. Future Gener. Comput. Syst. **140**, 79–90 (2023)

17. Duta, I.C., Liu, L, Zhu F, et al.: Improved residual networks for image and video recognition. In: 2020 25th International Conference on Pattern Recognition (ICPR), pp. 9415–9422 (2021)

18. Rosin, P., Ellis, T.: Image difference threshold strategies and shadow detection. In: 1995 British Machine Vision Conference, pp. 347–356 (1995)

Inverse Pyramid Pooling Attention for Ultrasonic Image Signal Recognition

Zhiwen Jiang[1], Ziji Ma[1,2](✉), Xianglong Dong[1], Qi Wang[1,2], and Xun Shao[3]

[1] College of Electrical and Information Engineering, Hunan University, Changsha 410082, China
zijima@hnu.edu.cn
[2] Greater Bay Area Insititute for Innovation, Hunan University, Guangzhou 511340, China
[3] Department of Electrical and Electronic Information Engineering, Toyohashi University of Technology, Toyohashi 4418580, Japan

Abstract. Ultrasound is commonly used for diagnosis and detection in a variety of fields, and the analysis of ultrasound echo signals presents a significant challenge in terms of the amount of time required by professionals to make subjective judgements. With the advances made in artificial intelligence technology on computers, more and more fields are being aided by it, not only increasing efficiency but also improving overall accuracy. In this paper, an inverse pyramid pooling of attention (IPPA) mechanism is proposed for images transformed from ultrasound echo signals. IPPA performs different pooling operations at multiple scale levels for each channel of the feature matrix, obtaining rich regional feature associations and thus improving the representation of the channels. In addition, different probability factors were assigned for the different pooling, and domain channel information was extracted by adaptive 1D convolution to enhance the adaptation range of the network model. Experimental results on a 10-class ultrasound hyperdata set (consisting of three sub-datasets) show that the sensitivity and robustness of the ResNet integrated with IPPA are improved over the original ResNet, with an accuracy of up to 99.68%.

Keywords: Convolutional neural network · Inverse pyramid attention · Combinatorial pooling · Ultrasound signal recognition

1 Introduction

Detection using ultrasonic signals is an important non-destructive testing technique that is now used in a variety of fields and has played a significant role in

This work is supported in part by the National Nature Science Foundation of China under Grant 61971182, in part by Nature Science Foundation of Hunan Province 2021JJ30145, in part by Hunan Province Enterprise Science and technology commissioner program 2021GK5021, in part by Guangxi key R&D plan project 2022AB41020.

C. Wu et al. (Eds.): MONAMI 2023, LNICST 559, pp. 94–107, 2024.
https://doi.org/10.1007/978-3-031-55471-1_8

several areas. In agriculture, ultrasound is commonly used to treat seeds, activate dormant seeds, and improve seed quality prior to planting [1,2]. Ultrasonic flaw detection, as a common non-destructive testing method in industrial inspection, is very frequently used. It utilizes ultrasonic echoes to reflect the internal properties of materials and can identify potential hidden problems [3]. In the medical field, ultrasound is widely used and considered a mature technology. Its development time is also longer. Ultrasound is used as a routine examination technique in medicine to scan a wide range of tissues and organs in the human body, providing a great deal of valid diagnostic value while causing less harm to the body [4–6].

Recently, artificial intelligence techniques, including deep learning, have been developed with the arithmetic power, algorithms and data base of computer technology [7–9]. The technology in the use of ultrasonic signal detection is also becoming digital and intelligent. Typically, the ultrasonic echo signal is converted into an image, and the interpretation of the target is performed by a trained professional relying on the ultrasound image. However, this approach presents a significant challenge in terms of diminishing accuracy and efficiency.

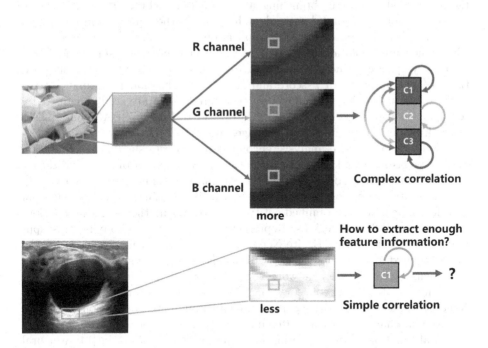

Fig. 1. Structural Disparities in Ultrasound and Optical Imaging Representations. In contrast to optical imaging, the ultrasound image (bottom left) has only a single channel and the pixel points can only contain neighbourhood relationships, lacking correlation information between channels and across channel neighbourhoods.

In addition, the image obtained after ultrasound imaging is a single-channel grayscale image, in contrast to the three-channel color image produced by conventional light imaging. Moreover, while natural light imaging captures multiple frequency bands of reflected light, ultrasound imaging operates at and around a single central frequency point during emission and reception. As a result, the ultrasound image contains significantly fewer informative features. Consequently, ordinary algorithms often struggle to perform effectively on both light images and ultrasound images. For a visual comparison, refer to Fig. 1. In this paper, we propose the Inverse Pyramid Pooling Attention (IPPA) algorithm to address this problem.

2   Related Works

Attention mechanisms have demonstrated remarkable efficacy across diverse domains within the realm of deep learning, captivating an ever-growing cohort of researchers. These attention mechanisms can be broadly categorized, based on their dimensions, into various types including channel attention, spatial attention, temporal attention, branching attention, and hybrid attention. Among these, one widely recognized network architecture is the Squeeze-and-Excitation Networks (SENet) [10]. In a notable application, Gao et al. [11] integrated SeNet within their implementation of YOLOv4 to detect microaneurysms, which serve as early symptomatic indicators of diabetes. This approach exhibited a substantial 13% enhancement in F-score and superior localization performance compared to the unmodified YOLOv4. Furthermore, a separate study conducted a comparative evaluation of SeNet, VGG6, ResNet50, ResNet-CBAM, and SKNet network models on liver pathology images across different stages of differentiation. The comprehensive analysis, encompassing metrics such as the confusion matrix, precision, recall, F1 score, and other relevant indicators, concluded that the SENet network model surpassed the others, establishing its superiority [12].

The spatial attention mechanism operates by treating the entire region of each feature channel as a unified entity and scrutinizing the weighting relationship between different regions. Representative networks embodying this approach include the Gather-Excite Net and Spatial Transformer Network (STN). In the context of cell imaging, some researchers have devised a deep learning auto-focus phase (DLFP) network to achieve rapid auto-focus. This method has demonstrated both efficiency and cost-effectiveness for cell imaging [13]. Nonetheless, the performance gains attained through the application of a single attention mechanism alone are often limited. Therefore, researchers often explore the amalgamation of two attention mechanisms. For instance, in [14], a neural network model that combines a BAM (Bottleneck Attention Module) module, a rectified linear unit (C.ReLU), and an initial module is proposed. This model was employed for the detection of human eye position and exhibited exceptional accuracy when evaluated across multiple datasets.

Recently, there has been a proliferation of different attention methods and there is room for different degrees of improvement in the different attention mechanisms respectively [15]. Different types of attentional mechanisms have different focuses and can be applied differently, and a combination of them can be used to obtain more attentional power in more dimensions and thus improve the results.

3   Inverse Pyramid Pooling Attention Module

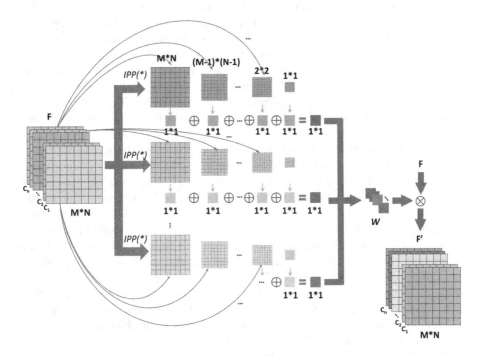

Fig. 2. The pipeline of IPPA. The input feature matrix F has C channels, each of which is subjected to an IPP operation. Multiple pooling operations are conducted on a single channel, where the size of the pooling decreases progressively from the outer regions to the center. Various pooling methods, corresponding to different sizes, are selected using a certain probability. The outcomes obtained from these multiple pooling operations are subsequently fused and summed to derive the original weight vector for the current channel.

The IPPA module offers the capability to integrate with arbitrary convolutional layers through adaptive transformations, thereby enhancing the representation of channel and spatial features. The module's comprehensive structure is depicted in Fig. 2. Within this structure, the initial adaptation vector $W \in R^{1*1*C}$ for each channel is constructed through pooling combinations with varying probabilities.

$$F' = F * \sigma(\sum_{k=1}^{N}(IPP(F_c))) \tag{1}$$

where F_i is the C_i-th channel of the feature map F, $IPP(*)$ is the inverse pyramiding process and the sigma function is calculated as $\sigma(x) = \frac{1}{(1+e^{(-x)})}$.

3.1   Inverse Pyramid Pooling

A series of sets of images of progressively smaller sizes obtained by downsampling the same image several times in succession is an image pyramid. The process can be described as generating multiple images from a single graph, which carry different scale information. Pooling is widely used in convolutional neural networks and has important effects. However, pooling also poses some problems, such as the loss of a large amount of detailed pixel information and the retention of only a small number of important features. Given that ultrasound images contain less information than optical imaging images, there are limitations to the performance of conventional networks on ultrasound images. To solve the above problems and extract sufficient effective information from the feature maps, we propose a new set of inverse pyramid pooling (IPP) methods. Firstly, multiple pooling is performed in the feature matrix. Secondly, the window of each pooling operation is reduced by the maximum length and width of the feature matrix, in turn by a certain step in, and different pooling methods are chosen with a certain probability. Finally, multiple results can be obtained after multiple pooling of a single channel. In order to make the final result consistent with the number of channels, the summation and fusion of these pooling results are considered as the initial adjustment weights for that channel. The fused weights contain more hierarchical and scaling information compared to a single pooling. The overall pipeline process for IPP is to apply multiple pooling operations to the same feature map with non-equivalent size windows to form a corresponding single conditioning factor, called IPP. The overall pipeline process for IPP can be described as a fusion from multiple feature matrices of different sizes into a single representative weight, hence the term IPP.

The IPP process does not use any down-sampling operations when reducing the size. We reduce the selected area directly from the outer circle to the centre and pool accordingly, without using upsampling to revert to the original size, further reducing the computational effort. The IPP process for a single channel feature map is shown in Fig. 3. The resolution of the channel is $M * N$, after pooling (pooling window of $M * N$) to obtain W_1, reduce the pooling window to $M_1 * N_1$ (yellow box) to obtain W_2, until the smallest pooling window is $M_n * N_n$, the result is W_n. Each step in the reduction process produces a layer of feature maps of the corresponding size, from L1 to Ln layers, each of which can be individually selected for a different pooling operation. The results of multiple pooling are summed to obtain the final pooling result of the jth channel as W_j. The different colours indicate different pooling methods, such as maximum pooling, average pooling, etc. The pooling is done in different colours, such as maximum pooling, average pooling and minimum pooling. The calculations associated with the IPP to produce the initial conditioning weights for each channel are described below. First, the total number of layers F of the atlas that can be generated from a feature map of a single channel is calculated by stepping down the pixel s by the size of the feature map to $M * N$.

$$F = \lceil (min(M, N) - 2)/(2 * S) + 1 \rceil \tag{2}$$

The size of the minimum layer map, M_n and N_n, is calculated as follows:

$$A = (min(M, N) - 2) \quad mod \quad 2 * S \tag{3}$$

$$M_n = \begin{cases} 2 * S, & A=0 \\ M - 2 - \lfloor (M-2)/2S \rfloor * 2S, & \text{otherwise.} \end{cases} \tag{4}$$

$$N_n = \begin{cases} 2 * S, & A=0 \\ N - 2 - \lfloor (N-2)/2S \rfloor * 2S, & \text{otherwise.} \end{cases} \tag{5}$$

To achieve adaptation for various scenes, we employ distinct step-reduction and feature map sizes. Furthermore, we calculate the total number of pixels, denoted as P_F, obtained through the IPP of the feature map for a single channel, using the aforementioned results F.

$$P_F = \sum_{i=1}^{F} (M - 2 * s * i)(N - 2 * s * i) \tag{6}$$

The detailed procedure steps are shown in Algorithm 1. The input feature map contains multiple channels (C), each of size M*N, which form a multilayer feature map after inverse pyramid. The inverse pyramid layers (F) discriminant factor of the channel is obtained after a 2-fold step-size residue calculation. The side with the smaller length and width of the feature map is used as the base for calculation to accommodate image features of different scales. The inverse pyramid layer (F) discriminant factor of the channel is obtained by 2-fold step residual calculation. When Min cannot divide T, the minimum feature map size is taken as the number of pixel points of the residual length and width, in which case the number of pyramid layers needs to be added one more layer. Finally traversal calculates the pooling result of each layer of the feature map, and the specific pooling method selection is determined by the random factor r. The summation result of the jth layer (F_j) of the ith channel is W_i, and the final channel weight matrix W is obtained from the weight contribution of each channel.

$$F = \lceil (min(M, N) - 2)/(2 * S) + 1 \rceil. \tag{7}$$

The size of the minimum layer map, M_n and N_n, is calculated as follows:

$$A = (min(M, N) - 2) \quad mod \quad 2 * S \tag{8}$$

$$M_n = \begin{cases} 2 * S, & A=0 \\ M - 2 - \lfloor (M-2)/2S \rfloor * 2S, & \text{otherwise.} \end{cases} \tag{9}$$

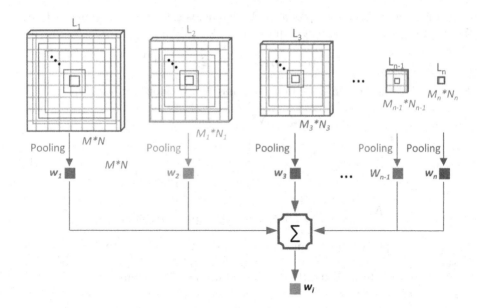

Fig. 3. Overview diagram of the single channel IPP operation.

Algorithm 1: Inverse Pyramid Pooling

Input: Standardised Channels Data C, step size T, random thresholdands
$0<r_1<r_2<r_3<1$, and feature map resolution data $M*N$

Output: Weighting of standardised channels W

1 $Min = min(M, N)$;

2 $A = Min \bmod 2T$;

3 **if** $A == 0$ **then**

4 $\quad\lfloor\; F = |Min/(2T) - 1/T|$;

5 **else**

6 $\quad\lfloor\; F = |Min/(2T) - 1/T + 1|$;

7 **for** $i : C$ **do**

8 $\quad\quad D = D + C_i/D_i$;

9 $\quad\quad$**for** $j : F$ **do**

10 $\quad\quad\quad r = random(0, 1)$;

11 $\quad\quad\quad$**if** $0<r<r_1$ **then**

12 $\quad\quad\quad\quad\lfloor\; W_j = MaxPooling(F_j)$;

13 $\quad\quad\quad$**else if** $r_1<r<r_2$ **then**

14 $\quad\quad\quad\quad\lfloor\; W_j = AveragePooling(F_j)$;

15 $\quad\quad\quad$**else**

16 $\quad\quad\quad\quad\lfloor\; W_j = StochatiscPooling(F_j)$;

17 $\quad\quad\lfloor\; W_i = \sum_{j=1}^{F} W_j$;

18 $W = |W_1, W_2, ..., W_i, ..., W_C|$;

$$N_n = \begin{cases} 2 * S, & A=0 \\ N - 2 - |(N - 2)/2S| * 2S, & \text{otherwise.} \end{cases} \tag{10}$$

Taking a 128*128 size image with a vertical and horizontal indentation of 2 pixels, the inverse pyramid atlas is 32 layers with a minimum layer image size of 2*2, using a combined pixel count of nearly 45,000. Within the network, the feature maps exhibit varying numbers of channels, which differ across convolutional layers. Consequently, in the case of feature maps with multiple channels, the total number of pixels after pyramidalization can be denoted as P_C:

$$P_C = C * P_F \tag{11}$$

where F is the number of feature map layers, C is the number of channels, and P_C is the sum of the C channel pixels.

3.2 Inverse Pyramid Pooling ResNet

Since its inception, residual networks have been widely used in a variety of industries. The jump connections in residual network blocks [16] have guided the depth of the network body structure into a new level of hierarchy and also facilitated the development of deep learning. The inverse pyramid Pooling attention (IPPA) module given in this paper can be coupled to the convolutional layers of different convolutional neural networks as channel importance adjustment weights for the feature matrix to enhance the performance of the network. We take the "bottleneck" building block of a residual network with 50 layers or more as an example (as shown in Fig. 4), and couples the IPPA module to the last convolutional layer of the residual block, with the weight vector multiplied by Activation is multiplied by the corresponding channel. The input X_i is coupled by the IPPA to the ResNet output X_o, called IPPA-ResNet.

4 Experiments and Analysis

4.1 Experimental Preparation

Data: We employed three open datasets as the training sample pool for our model, comprising a cumulative sample size of approximately 2000 ultrasound images. These datasets include: the Dataset of breast ultrasound images (hereinafter referred to as DBUI) authored by Walid AI-Dhabyani et al. from Cairo University, Egypt [17]; the FAscicle Lower ultrasound image dataset for the prevention of calf muscle injury outlined in Michard et al.'s Leg Muscle Ultrasound Dataset (hereinafter referred to as FALLMUD) [18]; and a publicly accessible abdominal organ ultrasound image dataset (hereinafter referred to as AOUI) [19]. Furthermore, we conducted data augmentation techniques on the dataset, resulting in the final training library of ultrasound images.

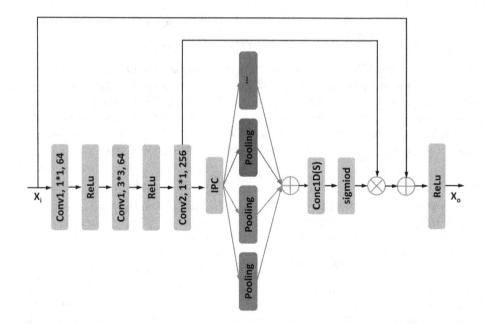

Fig. 4. The structure of IPPA-ResNet. The colored parts correspond to different pooling methods.

Devices and Parameters: We constructed an IPPA module and a 50-layer ResNet network based on the pyhton language and Pytorch's learning library. The IPP-ResNet was formed by embedding the IPPA module on the last convolutional layer of each residual block of the residual network. the training process was performed on a mobile configured with an Intel(R) Core(TM) i9-11900H @ 2.50 GHz CPU, 16G DDR4 RAM, and 8G RTX3070 GPU. The input to the network was a 64*64 sized ultrasound images with a bachsize of 48. The loss calculation was implemented by a cross-entropy loss function with 10 classifications, the optimizer was stochaastic gradient descent (SGD), and the learning rate used a thermal learning rate with an initial value of 0.005.

Assessment of Indicators: The performance of the network model is reflected by a number of metrics, namely accuracy (Acc), recall, precision, and F1 score, and the predicted sample types are classified as positive samples predicted by the model as positive class (TP), negative samples predicted by the model as negative class (TN), negative samples predicted by the model as positive class (FP), and positive samples predicted by the model as negative class (FN), which are calculated as follows:

$$Accuracy = \frac{TP + TN}{TP + TN + FP + FN} \tag{12}$$

Table 1. Comparison of multiple indicators on the same or similar data sets with the latest methods

	Mathonds	Dataset	Precision (%)	Sensitivity (%)	F1-score (%)	Acc (%)
Xu et al. [17](2020)	VGG6	muscle ultrasound images (1498)	/	/	/	95.20
Reddy et al. [20](2021)	CNN+ Transfer learning	abdomenultrasound images (1096)	/	/	/	98.77
Gheflati et al. [21](2022)	Vision Transformers	DBUI	/	/	/	79.00
		DBUI+UDITA	/	/	/	86.70
Joshi et al. [22](2022)	VGG 19/ Yolo v3	DUBI	88.22	90.32	89.07	90.00
		UDITA	91.72	91.16	91.43	95.25
		DUBI+UDITA	96.36	96.71	92.99	96.31
Xu et al. [23](2022)	MTL-COSA	UDITA	89.36	82.17	90.41	87.08
		DUBI	95.05	92.20	93.59	91.48
Alireza et al. [24](2022)	Decision Tree Integration	DUBI	94.00	93.00	93.00	91.00
Ours	**IPPA-ResNet**	**DUBI**	**99.48**	**98.67**	**99.06**	**99.28**

$$Precision = \frac{TP}{TP + FP} \qquad (13)$$

$$Sensitivity = \frac{TP}{TP + FN} \qquad (14)$$

$$F1 - score = \frac{2 * Precision * Sensitivity}{Precision + Sensitivity} \qquad (15)$$

4.2 Comparison with the Most Advanced Methods

We compare network models equipped with IPPA mechanisms with recent new results on the same dataset.

As can be seen from Table 1, our proposed IPPA-ResNet has better performance in terms of *Accuracy, Sensitivity, F1 − score* and *Prision* on the dataset compared to other recent methods, and is more adaptable to ultrasound images, which has better potential for development and contributes to the performance of the network on ultrasound images.

4.3 Comparison of Model Improvement Effects

The results of the experiments conducted on a dataset consisting of a combination of three datasets, AOUI, FALLMUD and DBUI, are represented in Fig. 5. The dataset contains 10 categories and we tested networks equipped with the IPPA mechanism and other attention mechanisms as well as some classical networks and their variants. SE-ResNet and ECA-ResNet are both ResNet with the attention mechanism inserted, ResNeXt is a variant of ResNet, and Inception-ResNetv2 also contains residual structures internally.

The diminishing fluctuation of the network's training results is observed as it approaches convergence. In order to provide a comprehensive evaluation of the network's performance, the mean value of $E\text{-}Acc$ was calculated by considering the Acc of the last 10 epochs across all networks. The Inception-ResNet-v2 network does not exhibit a notable advantage when applied to the ultrasound dataset, primarily due to its lack of channel focus. Moreover, the network possesses a significant number of parameters, rendering it less practical in real-world applications. On the other hand, the ResNet, as presented in this paper, lacks the incorporation of IPPA, which results in a less smooth convergence process. A more visually appealing representation of this outcome is illustrated in Fig. 5.

The analysis depicted in Fig. 5 reveals a noticeable disparity in the effectiveness of various attention methods applied to the ultrasound image dataset. When compared to the attention mechanisms employed in ResNet-based models such as ECA-ResNet and SE-ResNet, the approach presented in this paper (IPPA-ResNet) demonstrates superior performance and quicker convergence. ECA-ResNet and SE-ResNet exhibit a smoother progression at approximately the 120th and 90th epochs, respectively. However, ECA-ResNet tends to encounter challenges related to the accurate determination of channel weights during the extraction of ultrasound image channel interactions. Conversely, SE-ResNet lacks

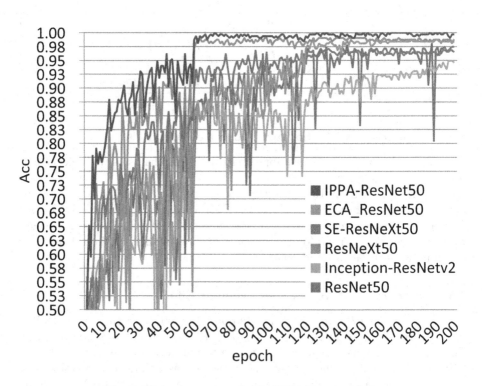

Fig. 5. Test set accuracy for six different networks.

the ability to extract multi-level weights for ultrasound image channels, resulting in an inadequate representation of channel differences.

In summary, the convolutional neural network incorporating the attention mechanism showcases enhanced performance in terms of Precision and F1-score compared to the original network. It demonstrates faster and smoother convergence. Moreover, our proposed IPPA further improves the network's generalization performance.

5   Conclusion

In the study in this paper, we developed a new attentional approach (IPPA) with 50 layers of ResNet as the core network to construct IPP-ResNet50. Extensive experiments were conducted on an ultrasound dataset (consisting of AOUI, DBUI together with FALLMUD), which included six classes of abdominal organs (gallbladder, bladder, liver, bowel, kidney, spleen), three types of breast (benign, malignant, normal) and calf muscles. The experimental results show that our proposed IPCPA-ResNet50 is superior in all metrics on the dataset compared to similar as well as the latest state-of-the-art methods. The integration of our proposed IPCPA onto a convolutional neural network enhances the extraction of the information density of each feature channel by the convolutional layer of the network. The fusion of multiple dimensional features of the extracted single channel obtains a better generalisation capability compared to single features. Moreover, probability factors are introduced into the feature extraction process of each individual channel to accentuate the differences between channels. Our approach embeds IPPA into a 50-layer ResNet network and introduces probabilistic elements, resulting in improved accuracy and convergence speed. The highest average accuracy (E-Acc) achieved is 99.68%, with a maximum sensitivity of 99.60%.

This work unveils the potential and application value of integrating IPPA into convolutional neural networks for ultrasound signal imaging classification. However, there is still room for improvement and refinement in the IPPA module, particularly in the inverse pyramid process, where smaller strides can generate more scales of feature maps compared to larger strides. The presence of a large number of feature maps results in increased computational overhead. Therefore, it is worth considering the possibility of retaining only the essential feature maps or adjusting the trade-offs for different scenarios. This approach can help reduce the computational burden without compromising accuracy. Lastly, we will endeavor to validate the performance of the proposed method by integrating it into more networks and evaluating it on diverse datasets.

References

1. Huang, S., Rao, G., Ashraf, U., et al.: Ultrasonic seed treatment improved morpho-physiological and yield traits and reduced grain Cd concentrations in rice. Ecotox. Environ. Safe. **214**, 112119 (2021)

2. Mo, Z., Liu, Q., Xie, W., et al.: Ultrasonic seed treatment and Cu application modulate photosynthesis, grain quality, and Cu concentrations in aromatic rice. Photosynthetica **58**(3), 682–691 (2020)

3. Kou, X., Pei, C., Liu, T., et al.: Noncontact testing and imaging of internal defects with a new Laser-ultrasonic SAFT method. Appl. Acoust. **178**, 107956 (2021). https://doi.org/10.1016/j.apacoust.2021.107956

4. Chen, X., Li, T., Dou, X., et al.: Reverse osmosis membrane combined with ultrasonic cleaning for flue gas desulfurization wastewater treatment. Water **14**(6), 875 (2022)

5. Chammas, M.C., Bordini, A.L.: Contrast-enhanced ultrasonography for the evaluation of malignant focal liver lesions. Ultrasonography **41**(1), 4–24 (2022)

6. Jiang, Z., Ma, Z., Wang, Y., et al.: Aggregated decentralized down-sampling-based ResNet for smart healthcare systems. Neural Comput. Appl. **75**, 1–13 (2021)

7. Shao, X., Asaeda, H., Dong, M., et al.: Cooperative inter-domain cache sharing for information-centric networking via a bargaining game approach. IEEE Trans. Netw. Sci. Eng. **6**(4), 698–710 (2019)

8. Liu, B., Fang, Z., Wang, W., et al.: A region-based collaborative management scheme for dynamic clustering in green vanet. IEEE Trans. Green Commun. Netw. **6**(3), 1276–1287 (2022)

9. Liu, J., Liu, H., Chakraborty, C., et al.: Cascade learning embedded vision inspection of rail fastener by using a fault detection IoT vehicle. IEEE Internet Things J. 1–12 (2021)

10. Li, X., Zhao, H., Ren, T., et al.: Inverted papilloma and nasal polyp classification using a deep convolutional network integrated with an attention mechanism. Comput. Biol. Med. **149**, 105976 (2022)

11. Gao, W., Shan, M., Song, N., et al.,: Detection of microaneurysms in fundus images based on improved YOLOv4 with SENet embedded. 2022, Sheng Wu Yi Xue Gong Cheng Xue Za Zhi, vol. 39, no. 4, pp. 713–720

12. Chen, C., et al.: Classification of multi-differentiated liver cancer pathological images based on deep learning attention mechanism. BMC Med. Inform. Decis. Mak. **22**(1), 176 (2022)

13. Liu, Y., Huaying, W., Zhao, D., et al.: Application of auto-focusing technology based on improved U-Net in cell imaging. China J. Lasers **49**(15), 1507302 (2022)

14. Nguyen, D.L., Putro, M.D., Vo, X.T., et al.: Convolutional neural network design for eye detection under low-illumination. In: Sumi, K., Na, I.S., Kaneko, N. (eds.) IW-FCV 2022. LNCS, vol. 1578, pp. 143–154. Springer, Cham (2022). https://doi.org/10.1007/978-3-031-06381-7_10

15. Zhu, X., Cheng, D., Zhang, Z., Lin, S., et al.: An Empirical study of spatial attention mechanisms in deep networks . In: 2019 IEEE/CVF International Conference on Computer Vision (ICCV), pp. 6687–6696 (2019)

16. He, K., Zhang, X., Ren, S., Sun, J.: Deep residual learning for image recognition. In: Proceedings of the IEEE Conference on Computer Vision and Pattern Recognition, pp. 770–778 (2016)

17. Xu, J., Xu, D., Wei, Q., et al.: Automatic classification of male and female skeletal muscles using ultrasound imaging. Biomed. Sig. Process. Control **57**, 101731 (2020)

18. Michard, H., Luvison, B., Pham, Q.C., et al.: AW-Net: automatic muscle structure analysis on b-mode ultrasound images for injury prevention. In: 12th ACM Conference on Bioinformatics, Computational Biology, and Health Informatics (ACM-BCB 2021), pp. 1–9 (2021)
19. Li, K., Xu, Y., Zhao, Z., et al.: Automatic recognition of abdominal organs in ultrasound images based on deep neural networks and k-nearest-neighbor classification. IEEE-Robio 2021, pp. 1980–1985 (2021)
20. Reddy, D.S., Rajalakshmi, P., Mateen, M.A.: A deep learning based approach for classification of abdominal organs using ultrasound images. Biocybern. Biomed. Eng. **41**(2), 779–791 (2021)
21. Gheflati, B., Rivaz, H.: Vision transformers for classification of breast ultrasound images. In: Annual International Conference of the IEEE Engineering in Medicine and Biology Society. IEEE Engineering in Medicine and Biology Society. Annual International Conference, vol. 2022, pp. 480–483 (2022)
22. Joshi, R.C., Singh, D., Tiwari, V., et al.: An efficient deep neural network based abnormality detection and multi-class breast tumor classification. Multimedia Tools Appl. **81**(10), 13691–13711 (2022)
23. Xu, M., Huang, K., Qi, X.: Multi-task learning with context-oriented self-attention for breast ultrasound image classification and segmentation. In: IEEE ISBI 2022, pp. 1–5 (2022)
24. Rezazadeh, A., Jafarian, Y., Kord, A.: Explainable ensemble machine learning for breast cancer diagnosis based on ultrasound image texture features. Forecasting **4**(1), 262–274 (2022)

An Improved 4D Convolutional Neural Network for Light Field Reconstruction

Qiuming Liu[1,2]([✉])[iD], Ruiqin Li[1][iD], Ke Yan[1][iD], Yichen Wang[1][iD],
and Yong Luo[3]

[1] School of Software Engineering, Jiangxi University of Science and Technology,
Nanchang 330013, China
liuqiuming@jxust.edu.cn, 6720210698@mail.jxust.edu.cn
[2] Nanchang Key laboratory of Virtual Digital Factory and Cultural
Communications, Nanchang 330013, People's Republic of China
[3] School of Software, Jiangxi Normal University, Nanchang 330022, China

Abstract. Light field (LF) camera sensors often face a trade-off between angular resolution and spatial resolution when shooting. High spatial resolution image arrays often result in lower angular resolution, and vice versa. In order to obtain high spatial resolution and at the same time have high angular resolution. In this paper, we propose an improved 4D convolutional neural network (CNN) algorithm for angular super-resolution (SR) to improve the quality of angular SR images. Firstly, to address the problem of low luminance of images captured by LF cameras, this paper uses block threshold square reinforcement (BTSR) for image luminance enhancement. Secondly, to make the reconstructed new view-points of higher quality, this paper improves the attention mechanism convolutional block attention module (CBAM). This paper incorporates it into a 4D dense residual network as high dimensional attention module (HDAM). HDAM generates images along two independent dimensions, spatial and channel. The HDAM generates attention maps along two independent dimensions, space and channel, which guide the network to focus on more important features for adaptive feature modification. Finally, this paper modifies the activation function to make the network perform better in the later stages of training and more suitable for LF reconstruction tasks. This paper evaluates the network on many LF data, including real-world scenes and synthetic data. The experimental results show that the improved network algorithm can achieve higher quality LF reconstruction.

Keywords: Light field reconstruction · 4D convolution · Convolutional neural network · Attention mechanism

1 Introduction

Light Field (LF) is often represented as the set of all light rays in a scene, and LF cameras can be used to record 3D information about the scene. Unlike

C. Wu et al. (Eds.): MONAMI 2023, LNICST 559, pp. 108–120, 2024.
https://doi.org/10.1007/978-3-031-55471-1_9

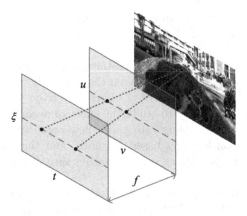

Fig. 1. 4D representation of the light field. Where (ξ, t) denotes the camera plane, (u, v) denotes the image plane, and f is the focal length of the camera.

traditional 2D imaging systems, LF cameras record the position and direction of each light $L(u, v, \xi, t)$ in the scene in two planes. This representation is shown in Fig. 1, where (ξ, t) denotes the camera plane, (u, v) denotes the imaging plane, and f is the focal length of the camera. A single exposure of the camera will result in a set of image arrays that record the light intensity of the scene as observed at different positions. Such a rich way of recording information makes many applications possible, such as depth estimation [1], refocusing [2], image segmentation [3], 3D reconstruction [4], etc. But there is a trade-off in this way of scene information capture. Because the product of spatial resolution and angular resolution cannot exceed the resolution of the sensor. A high spatial resolution necessarily makes the angular resolution lower, and vice versa.

To solve this problem, many researchers have proposed many methods to reconstruct dense LF views with sparse LF as input. The technique is called angular super-resolution (SR), also known as view synthesis. Wang *et al.* [5] used an algorithm of depth estimation to obtain an accurate depth map, and then warped the existing image into the new views. In [6], Pearson *et al.* layered the scene depth based on plenoptic function theory and rendered the new views using probabilistic interpolation. Zhang *et al.* [7] estimated the parallax information from the perspective of phase using parallax cues and phase synthesis methods, and then synthesized the new view using a parallax-based warping method. Paper [8] further developed the patched-based method, and Zhang et al. decomposed the central view into different depth layers and then performed the synthesis of the new views. On the other hand, Chai *et al.* [9] consider the rendering of new views as equivalent to the reconstruction of functions from the collected samples. They introduced plenoptic sampling into the Fourier framework for the first time by assuming an unobstructed Lambert scene, for which the effect of the maximum minimum depth on the plenoptic spectrum structure was derived. This assumption is extended to non-Lambertian scenes and obscured scenes of [10,11] in [10]. Similarly, Zhu *et al.* [12] investigated the effect of the surface curvature of the irregular geometry of the scene on the plenoptic spectrum and used it to design an efficient reconstruction filter for the rendering of new views.Vagharshakyan *et al.* [13] treat view synthesis as a restoration task on EPI and use a sparse representation of LF in the shearlet transform for view synthesis. In [14], Chen *et al.* build a mathematical model of self-obscuration by studying the slope relationship between the parabolic tangents and the light captured by the camera. They derive a closed spectrum formulation based on the established model as a way to study the effect of occlusion on the spectrum and to derive a specific sampling rate and a new reconstruction filter. All the above methods are non-learning based methods, and the rendered new views are prone to ghosting when facing complex scenes such as reflections, occlusions, and rich textures.

In recent years, many learning-based algorithms have emerged in the field of view synthesis due to the development of deep learning. Yoon *et al.* [15] designed a deep learning algorithm that uses two adjacent views to generate a new virtual view. Flynn *et al.* [16] synthesized novel views based on image sequences with wide baselines. Wu *et al.* [17] started with EPI to obtain richer angle and parallax information. They used the "blur-restoration-deblu" framework to achieve LF reconstruction. In order to reconstruct scenes with larger parallaxes, [18] proposed a method that incorporates sheared EPIs to continue the improvement of the previous method. With the improvement of Wu *et al.*, the algorithm is able to adapt to sparse LF data with larger parallax. Despite the increased parallax, they only considered 2D EPI, and there are still some deficiencies in the fusion of angular information. Wang *et al.* [19] proposed to combine EPI and EPI volume representation of 4D LF for LF angle reconstruction. They combine 2D convolutional operations and 3D convolutional operations to construct a pseudo-4D CNN. Yeung *et al.* [20] proposed an end-to-end network for densely sampled LF reconstruction. Exploring the relationship between subaperture images (SAI) and pseudo-4D filters, the method achieves state-of-the-art performance in a large number of real scenes captured by Lytro cameras. The above methods use 2D or pseudo-4D convolutional neural network (CNN) to extract features when training the network, instead of using a real 4D CNN. The complexity of 4D LF data may lead to less comprehensive information obtained by their algorithms, and can also lead to inefficiency of the algorithms. Meng *et al.* [21] proposed to use a high-dimensional dense residual CNN to recover LF. The method takes each SAI of LF as input and captures the association relationship between the views by 4D convolution. After experiments this paper founds that the algorithm [21] still has room for improvement in terms of training preprocessing, network modules, and activation functions. Therefore, this paper improves and adjust the structure and modules of the network to make it have better performance.

It is well known that the images obtained by LF cameras such as Lytro are of low brightness. The decoded images have more bad points and more noise in the edge SAI. Directly using the decoded images for training will greatly affect the training effect of the network. To solve this problem, this paper performs block threshold square reinforcement (BTSR) on the images before angle SR.

This method equalizes the grayscale values within each block and smoothes out the extreme pixel values in the image, making the texture more visible.

In order to keep the integrity and consistency of the reconstructed image with ground truth in terms of structure and pixels, respectively. 4D CNN can achieve better SR for LF images, but it is still not sufficient to grasp the importance of semantic information in the feature map. Many researchers keep increasing the sensory field to obtain the semantic information of the scene in order to extract the image global information more comprehensively. Although the semantic information of the network becomes rich, it is not differentiated and processed separately according to the importance of the information. This not only leads to the loss of low-level image texture information, but also makes the important information regions not better processed, which in turn affects the quality of the generated new views. Therefore, this paper first improves the attention mechanism CBAM by extending its input dimension to become a high dimensional attention module (HDAM). This module can adapt to high dimensional feature maps and infer the attention map along the high dimensional feature information. By introducing an attention mechanism, it focuses on the information that is more critical to the current task among the many input information. Reducing the attention to other information and even filtering out irrelevant information. This solves the information overload problem and improves the efficiency and accuracy of task processing. In addition, this paper also replaced the activation function from LeakyReLU to GELU, which suppresses the generation of pixels with large negative values in the prediction process and gives the network a higher reconstruction effect.

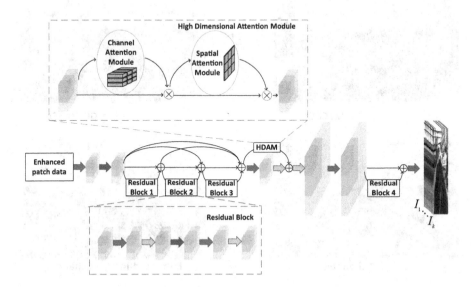

Fig. 2. The overview of the proposed model. Green arrows indicate convolution, blue arrows indicate activation functions, yellow arrows indicate normalization operations, and pink arrows indicate upsampling. (Color figure online)

In this paper, we propose an improved 4D convolutional angular SR network incorporating an attention mechanism. As shown in Fig. 2, the image is first preprocessed for enhancement, and the enhanced image needs to be converted from RGB to YCbCr format. The Y channel of the image is used as the input, and the 4D convolution is used to extract the image features, and the HDAM is used to guide the network to focus on the important regions. Finally, the feature map is upsampled to the same number of views as the ground truth to achieve angular SR.

2   Proposed Method

In this section, this paper will address three aspects of image enhancement preprocessing, attention mechanism, and GELU activation function in detail. The exposition includes the principle of the module and how the data operates in the module.

2.1   Image Enhancement Preprocessing

The LF subviews obtained by decoding the images captured by the LF camera have different luminance ranges from the edges to the center, and the edge

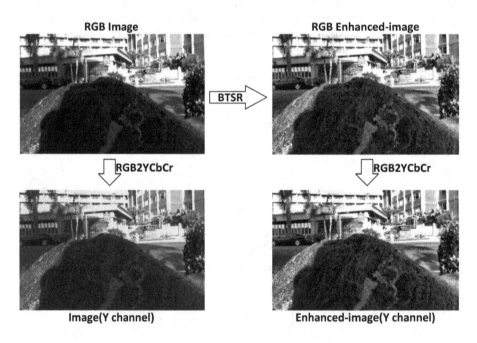

Fig. 3. The original image is compared with the enhanced image. The left side shows the RGB and Y channels of the original image, and the right side shows the RGB and Y channels of the enhanced image.

subviews will be dark. If the decoded image is directly used as the input, it will affect the reconstruction result of the network. This is because in the darker images, the texture information will be suppressed and it is difficult for the network to extract useful features from them. In particular, the high frequency parts of the image will become blurred due to the lower luminance. The boundaries between different objects become blurred, resulting in multiple objects being blended together. This causes distortion and ghosting in scene reconstruction in the presence of occlusion and complex textures. To avoid these problems, this paper uses BTSR to enhance the image, increasing the contrast between objects and making textures more visible.

In a single image, the correlation between pixels is inversely proportional to their distance in space. Therefore, the image $I(x, y)$ is first partitioned into k small blocks of $N \times N$ before image enhancement to obtain the set of local regions $R = \{R_1, R_2, ..., R_k\}$, where k is the number of local regions. Histogram equalization enhancement is applied to each block to obtain the enhanced local regions. The expression of enhancement as,

$$E_i(x, y) = T(R_i(x, y)), \tag{1}$$

where T is the mapping function that represents the mapping of the pixel value at position (x, y) in the local region R_i to the new pixel value $E_i(x, y)$. In order to avoid excessive increase in contrast, it is necessary to apply a contrast limit to each local area. The formula for the contrast limit is as follows:

$$CE_i(x, y) = \begin{cases} E_i(x, y), \text{if} \sigma_i \leq H \\ \frac{E_i(x,y)H}{\sigma_i}, \text{if} \sigma_i > H \end{cases}, \tag{2}$$

where σ_i is the standard deviation of the pixel values in the local region E_i and H is the specified threshold value. Finally this paper recombines the contrast-limited enhanced local region CE_i into the final enhanced image as,

$$F(x, y) = \begin{cases} CE_i(x, y), \text{if}(x, y) \in R_i \\ I(x, y), otherwise \end{cases}. \tag{3}$$

To simplify the training, this paper convert the enhanced RGB image into the format of YCbCr. Y denotes the intensity and brightness of the image, while Cb and Cr denote the blue chromaticity and red chromaticity of the image, respectively. The Y channel of the image has all the texture information of the original image, and this paper only need to use the Y channel image as the input during training. The effect of image enhancement is shown in Fig. 3, with the unenhanced image on the left and the enhanced image on the right. It can be clearly seen that the texture of the enhanced image is more obvious, both RGB and Y channel images.

2.2 HDAM

The core of the attention mechanism is resource allocation, which adjusts the allocation of resources according to the importance of the target in order to

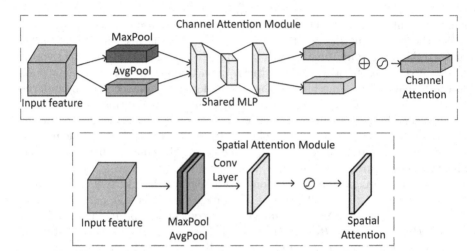

Fig. 4. Schematic diagram of each attention submodule. As shown in the figure, the channel attention utilizes the maximum pooled output and the average pooled output of the shared network. Spatial attention utilizes two similar outputs pooled along the channel axis and forwards them to the convolutional layer.

focus more on the important objects. In CNN, the attention mechanism adjusts the allocation of weight parameters. By allocating more weight parameters to the objects of attention, the representation of these objects is enhanced during feature extraction. Introducing the attention mechanism into the viewpoint synthesis task can improve the representation ability of the model and reduce the interference of irrelevant targets. Enhancing the reconstruction effect on the objects of attention and consequently improving the overall visual effect.

This paper introduces HDAM, an attention mechanism for CNN performance enhancement, into the network. It improves the expressive and perceptual capabilities of the model by introducing channel attention and spatial attention at different levels of the CNN.

As shown in the upper part of Fig. 4, channel attention is used to weight the feature maps of each channel to enhance the representation of important features. It converts each channel's feature map into a scalar by a global averaging pooling operation, and then learns it through two fully connected layers. Finally, the weighting factor is restricted between 0 and 1 using a Sigmoid function. In this way, the feature maps of each channel are multiplied by an attention weight to highlight the important features.

As shown in the lower part of Fig. 4, spatial attention is used to weight the different spatial locations of the feature maps to enhance the representation of important regions. It obtains two feature maps by performing maximum pooling and average pooling operations on each channel. Then they are connected and learned by a convolutional layer. Finally the weighting factor is restricted between 0 and 1 using a Sigmoid function. In this way, the features at each spatial location are multiplied by an attention weight to highlight the important regions.

HDAM invokes channel attention and spatial attention sequentially along the output of the 4D convolutional feature map. The network is instructed to assign different attention to each feature module. Note that we place HDAM before upsampling, which ensures that the network's receptive field is large enough. It also balances the weight ratio between the perceptual field and the number of channels to a certain extent. The adaptive modification of the feature modules by HDAM allows for better retention and processing of important scenes in the image during upsampling.

2.3   GELU

During the training process, some pixels may be predicted to have negative values. Since all pixel values in the image should be greater than or equal to 0, this paper need to deal with the negative values that appear in the prediction. Generally, we think that negative-valued pixels around 0 still contribute to the image and this paper should keep them. On the other hand, negative pixels far from 0 should be excluded because they do not contribute much. Therefore, this paper chooses to use GELU as the activation function of the network, and its expression as,

$$GELU(X) = 0.5 \cdot x \cdot (1 + \tanh(\sqrt{\frac{2}{\pi}}(x + 0.044715x^3))). \qquad (4)$$

Starting from the characteristics of the function itself, it treats pixel values in the way we expect. the GELU function is derivable throughout the real number domain and has continuous, smooth properties. This makes it easier to optimize in training and can provide faster convergence. Compared to LeakyReLU, GELU has a larger gradient in the region close to zero. This property makes GELU more advantageous in mitigating the gradient disappearance problem and facilitating gradient propagation. At the same time, the nonlinear property of GELU enables it to introduce more nonlinear transformations, thus providing stronger feature representation.

3   Experimental Results

Comprehensive experiments were conducted on real-world [22] and synthetic [23] scenes to verify the effectiveness of the proposed method. The 9 × 9 dense LF was reconstructed with 3 × 3 subviewpoint maps on the reconstruction task. the proposed method was compared with two LF angle reconstruction methods (HDDRNet and M-HDDRNet) proposed by Meng et al. [21]. This paper used the average PSNR and SSIM of the reconstructed SAI with its corresponding ground truth as performance criteria. For the proposed and compared methods, the positions of the input sparse 3 × 3 SAIs are shown in the red cells in the grid diagram.

3.1   Real-World Scenes

Table 1 shows the quantitative comparison results of our algorithm with HDDR-Net and M-HDDRNet on the real-world dataset. As can be seen from the table, our proposed LF perspective SR network performs better in terms of target quality. Our method shows significant improvement in both the average PSNR metrics and also obtains consistent results on the average SSIM for all tested LF datasets. This is mainly due to the attention module we introduced during the network training process to guide the network to focus the reconstruction on scene features useful for SR. By using a more targeted reconstruction approach, we are able to obtain better reconstruction quality, especially in some fine-texture regions.

Figure 5 shows the visual comparison results of three real-world scenes reconstructed by SAI using three different methods. Reflective_29 is occupied by some reflective surfaces, Occlusions_9 contains many occluded regions, and scene Cars_7 has complex textures and large chromatic aberrations. As can be observed in Fig. 5, our proposed method is able to achieve a better perceptual quality of SAI reconstruction than the other two methods. Since the quality is susceptible

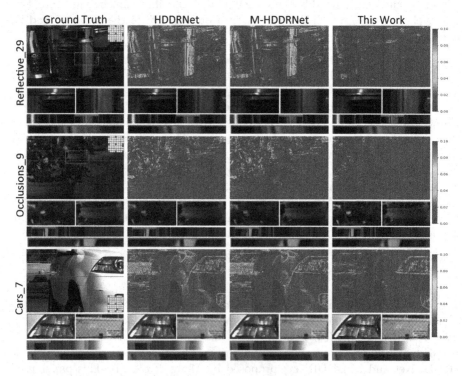

Fig. 5. A visual comparison of the three methods for the real-world perspective SR. The comparison shows the ground truth SAI, the error map of the Y-channel reconstructed SAI, the close-up version of the SAI part in the red and green boxes, and the EPI extracted at the blue line and its close-up. (Color figure online)

Table 1. Quantitative comparison of three algorithms for LF dataset Reflective, Occlusions and Cars reconstructions (PSNR/SSIM).

Algorithm	Reflective_29	Occlusions_9	Cars_7
HDDRNet	35.969/0.975	36.235/0.942	34.164/0.964
M-HDDRNet	36.021/0.976	36.276/0.943	34.219/0.964
This work	41.195/0.989	40.676/0.962	38.315/0.979

to parallax variations, it can be observed from the close-up images and error maps that HDDRNet and M-HDDRNet introduce blurring and ghosting artifacts. In contrast, our proposed method not only performs better in terms of reconstruction quality, but also has good results in processing and recovering details.

3.2 Synthetic Scenes

Table 2. Quantitative comparison of three algorithms for LF dataset Cotton, Dino and Tomb reconstruction (PSNR/SSIM).

Algorithm	Cotton_29	Dino_9	Tomb_7
HDDRNet	38.700/0.953	34.472/0.913	36.405/0.852
M-HDDRNet	38.822/0.955	34.615/0.916	36.468/0.855
This work	43.368/0.973	39.215/0.949	39.088/0.900

In order to verify the effectiveness of our proposed method in synthetic scenes, this paper conducted experiments and selected three synthetic scenes from the HCI dataset. These three scenes are Cotton, Dino and Tomb, which have different texture characteristics. The Cotton scene contains complex shadows and reflections, the Dino scene is rich in line textures, and the Tomb scene contains complex noise-like textures. We present the quantitative comparison results of the three methods in Table 2.

As can be observed from the table, our proposed method achieves higher PSNR than the other two methods in all scenes. Especially for Cotton scenes, our method achieves an average PSNR gain of up to 4.668 dB. This shows that our method performs well in LF synthetic scenes with smooth surfaces with self-obscuring shadows and reflections. For the Dino scene, this paper obtained consistent experimental results. This is due to the enhanced preprocessing we used during the network training process, which allows the network to perceive more texture details. In the Tomb scene, our method achieves a PSNR gain of 2.683 dB. This also indicates that our method has stronger resistance to interference for scenes with noisy textures.

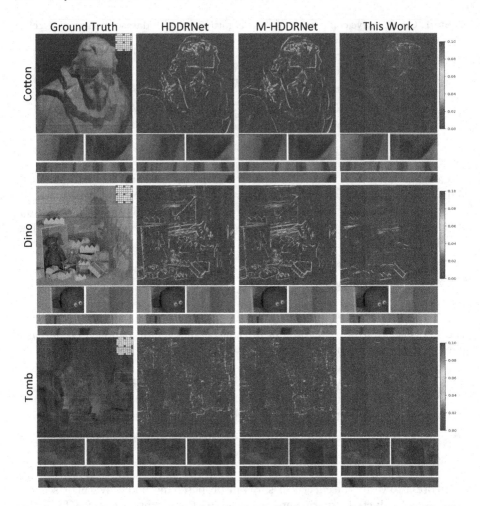

Fig. 6. A visual comparison of the three methods for the synthetic scene angle SR. The comparison shows the ground truth SAI, the error map of the Y-channel reconstructed SAI, the close-up version of the SAI part in the red and green boxes, and the EPI extracted at the blue line and its close-up. (Color figure online)

Figure 6 shows more visually the differences between the three methods in the reconstruction. Especially for the Tomb scene, this paper can clearly find that HDDRNet and M-HDDRNet do not reconstruct well at high frequencies and tend to lose high-frequency textures. And our proposed method achieves the recovery of many high-frequency detailed textures by exploring more texture information. Further observing the close-up images and error maps, we find that our method is also applicable to Dino and Cotton scenes, and especially performs well in the reconstruction of some textures and edge regions.

4   Conclusion

In this paper, we improve and replace some modules of 4D CNN in paper [21]. We enhance the image pre-processing in the pre-training stage, which enhances the image contrast and makes the texture clearer. The attention mechanism HDAM is introduced, and this module can be applied to 4D convolution to build the attention map along the direction of the original activation function is replaced to make the network converge faster. Finally, after an experimental comparison, our proposed method leads to a better performance of the network. In subsequent work we will consider lightweighting the model so that it can be applied to real-time tasks.

Acknowledgment. This work was supported in part by National Natural Science Foundation of China (No. 62067003), Culture and Art Science Planning Project of Jiangxi Province (No. YG2018042), Humanities and Social Science Project of Jiangxi Province (No.JC18224).

References

1. Shin, C., Jeon, H.-G., Yoon, Y., Kweon, I.S., Kim, S. J.: EPINET: a fully-convolutional neural network using epipolar geometry for depth from light field images. In Proceedings of IEEE Conference on Computer Vision Pattern Recognition, pp. 4748–4757 (2018)
2. Mitra, K., Veeraraghavan, A.: Light field denoising, light field superresolution and stereo camera based refocussing using a GMM light field patch prior. In: Proceedings of IEEE Conference on Computer Vision Pattern Recognition Workshops, pp. 22–28 (2012)
3. Yucer, K., Sorkine-Hornung, A., Wang, O., Sorkine-Hornung, O.: Efficient 3D object segmentation from densely sampled light fields with applications to 3D reconstruction. ACM Trans. Graph. **35**(3), 22:1–22:15 (2016)
4. Kim, C., Zimmer, H., Pritch, Y., Sorkine-Hornung, A., Gross, M.: Scene reconstruction from high spatio-angular resolution light fields. ACM Trans. Graph. **32**(4), 73:1–73:12 (2013)
5. Wang, T.-C., Efros, A.A., Ramamoorthi, R.: Occlusion-awaredepth estimation using light-field cameras. In: Proceedings of IEEE International Conference on Computer Vision, pp. 3487–3495 (2015)
6. Pearson, J., Brookes, M., Dragotti, P.L.: Plenoptic layer-based modeling for image based rendering. IEEE Trans. Image Process. **22**(9), 3405–3419 (2013)
7. Zhang, Z., Liu, Y., Dai, Q.: Light field from micro-baseline image pair. In: Proceedings of IEEE Conference on Computer Vision Pattern Recognition, pp. 3800–3809 (2015)
8. Zhang, F.-L., et al.: PlenoPatch: patch-based plenoptic image manipulation. IEEE Trans. Visualization Comput. Graph. **23**(5), 1561–1573 (2017). https://doi.org/10.1109/TVCG.2016.2532329
9. Chai, J.X., Tong, X., Chan, S.C., et al.: Plenoptic sampling. In: Proceedings of the 27th Annual Conference on Computer Graphics and Interactive Techniques, pp. 307–318 (2000)

10. Zhang, C., Chen, T.: Spectral analysis for sampling image-based rendering data. IEEE Trans. Circuits Syst. Video Technol. **13**(11), 1038–1050 (2003)
11. Do, M.N., Marchand-Maillet, D., Vetterli, M.: On the bandwidth of the plenoptic function. IEEE Trans. Image Process. **21**(2), 708–717 (2011)
12. Zhu, C.J., Yu, L.: Spectral analysis of image-based rendering data with scene geometry. Multimedia Syst. **23**, 627–644 (2017)
13. Vagharshakyan, S., Bregovic, R., Gotchev, A.: Light field reconstruction using shearlet transform. IEEE Trans. Pattern Anal. Mach. Intell. **40**(1), 133–147 (2018)
14. Chen, W., Zhu, C.: Spectral analysis of a surface occlusion model for image-based rendering sampling. Digital Signal Process. **130**, 103697 (2022)
15. Yoon, Y., Jeon, H.G., Yoo, D., Lee, J.Y., So Kweon, I.: Learning a deep convolutional network for light-field image superresolution. In: Proceedings of IEEE International Conference on Computer Vision Workshops, pp. 24–32 (2015)
16. Flynn, J., Neulander, I., Philbin, J., Snavely, N.: DeepStereo: learning to predict new views from the world's imagery. In: Proceedings of IEEE Conference on Computer Vision Pattern Recognition, pp. 5515–5524 (2016)
17. Wu, G., Liu, Y., Fang, L., Dai, Q., Chai, T.: Light field reconstruction using convolutional network on EPI and extended applications. IEEE Trans. Pattern Anal. Mach. Intell. **41**(7), 1681–1694 (2019)
18. Wu, G., Liu, Y., Dai, Q., Chai, T.: Learning sheared EPI structure for light field reconstruction. IEEE Trans. Image Process. **28**(7), 3261–3273 (2019)
19. Wang, Y., Liu, F., Wang, Z., Hou, G., Sun, Z., Tan, T.: End-to-end view synthesis for light field imaging with Pseudo 4DCNN. In: Proceedings of European Conference on Computer Vision, pp. 333–348 (2018)
20. Yeung, W.F.H., Hou, J., Chen, J., Chung, Y.Y., Chen, X.: Fast light field reconstruction with deep coarse-to-fine modeling of spatial-angular clues. In: Proceedings of European Conference on Computer Vision, pp. 137–152 (2018)
21. Meng, N., So, H.K.H., Sun, X., et al.: High-dimensional dense residual convolutional neural network for light field reconstruction. IEEE Trans. Pattern Anal. Mach. Intell. **43**(3), 873–886 (2019)
22. Raj, S., Lowney, M., Shah, R., Wetzstein, G.: Stanford lytro light field archive (2016). http://lightfields.stanford.edu/LF2016.html.
23. Honauer, K., Johannsen, O., Kondermann, D., Goldluecke, B.: A dataset and evaluation methodology for depth estimation on 4D light fields. In: Proceedings of Asian Conference on Computer Vision, pp. 19–34 (2016)

Fusing PSA to Improve YOLOv5s Detection algorithm for Electric Power Operation Wearable devices

Qiuming Liu[1,2]([🖂]), Wei Xu[1], Yang Zhou[3], Ruiqing Li[1], Dong Wu[3], Yong Luo[4], and Longping Chen[1]

[1] School of Software Engineering, Jiangxi University of Science and Technology, Nanchang 330013, China
`liuqiuming@jxust.edu.cn,6720210702@mail.jxust.edu.cn`
[2] Nanchang Key laboratory of Virtual Digital Factory and Cultural Communications, Nanchang 330013, China
[3] Information and Communication Branch, State Grid Jiangxi Electric Power Co, Nanchang 330095, China
`6720210698@mail.jxust.edu.cn`
[4] School of Software, Jiangxi Normal University, Nanchang 330022, China

Abstract. In order to determine whether the electric power workers wear safety equipment such as safety helmet, insulation boots, insulation gloves, insulation clothes, etc., to ensure the safety of the electric power construction site. We propose a electric power operation safety equipment detection algorithm incorporating PSA to improve YOLOv5s algorithm, using polarized self-attention mechanism to improve the feature extraction end of YOLOv5s algorithm, improving the channel resolution and spatial resolution of safety equipment images of electric power operation scenes, and preserving the information of key nodes of small targets that are obscured; GSConv is used to replace the ordinary convolution to reduce the complexity of the model, improve the calculation speed of the algorithm and improve the detection accuracy. The experimental results show that the average accuracy mean (IoU = 0.5) of the proposed algorithm reaches 0.961, which is 1.58% higher than that of the original network detection performance, and the model parameters are reduced from 7.03 to 5.48 millions. It effectively improves the detection speed and accuracy of the algorithm, and can effectively monitor whether the operator wears the safety equipment correctly when there are occlusions and missing safety equipment in the electric power operation scene, which has a excellent application effect.

Keywords: Improved YOLOv5s algorithm · Polarized self-attention · Power operation scenario · VoV-GSCSP · Safety wearable

ⓒ ICST Institute for Computer Sciences, Social Informatics and Telecommunications Engineering 2024
Published by Springer Nature Switzerland AG 2024. All Rights Reserved
C. Wu et al. (Eds.): MONAMI 2023, LNICST 559, pp. 121–135, 2024.
https://doi.org/10.1007/978-3-031-55471-1_10

1   Introduction

The safety of electric power operation is always one of the hot issues of social concern. From the investigation results of the causes of electric power operation accidents, most of the accidents are caused by the construction process is not standardized enough [1,2], and the workwear equipment is the basic equipment to ensure the safety of construction personnel. Staff wearing the operating equipment can not only effectively prevent the risk of electric shock during electrical operations and reduce personal injury caused by safety accidents, but also avoid serious safety accidents. Therefore, safety helmets, insulated boots, insulated gloves, insulated clothing and other safety equipment, etc. are the safety of electric power workers when operating [3].

For this reason, it is of great significance to test the wearing condition of the operating equipment for construction personnel in electric power operations. At present, many scholars have proposed methods for detecting construction personnel wearing equipment for electrical operations, such as the helmet wearing detection method proposed by Xin Liu et al. [4], which is to input construction scene images into a convolutional neural network, use this network to continuously iterate to extract construction personnel helmet features, and output helmet wearing classification results. However, this method is affected by the blurred images of the construction scenes and the existence of obscuring situations, and its monitoring results are not accurate enough; Zhang Mingyuan et al [5] explored the automatic real-time detection of construction workers wearing helmets at construction sites and proposed a Tensorflow-based framework, which uses a region based convolutional neural network (Faster R-CNN) method to monitor workers' helmet wearing condition in real time, but the evaluation indexes selected by the method are all expert voting results, which are subjective and lead to its poor final detection results; Wang Yusheng et al. [6] proposed a helmet wearing detection method based on human pose estimation (HPE) algorithm for the problem of difficult detection and low accuracy under complex posture of construction personnel.

Many scholars in China and abroad have used other deep learning and YOLO algorithms for the detection of electric power behavior. Such as, Qu Wenqian et al [7] proposed a YOLOv3-based helmet wearing detection method for electric power grid operation sites in order to effectively monitor the irregular helmet wearing behavior of electric power grid operators, and constructed image samples under three cases of correct, incorrect and un-wearing helmets, with 92.59% detection accuracy; Wang Jian et al. [8] proposed a separable convolution method to improve the YOLOv5 algorithm in order to identify the helmet wearing situation of the staff at the electric construction site, using the mosaic data enhancement method to improve the clarity of the visual image of the helmet and introducing the self-attention mechanism, which can effectively identify the helmet wearing situation; Fu Desu et al. [9] proposed an improved detection algorithm based on YOLOv5 for electric power operation helmet and insulated gloves wearing, adding a small target extraction mechanism and incorporating a weighted bidirectional feature pyramid network structure, the accuracy value of the detection of the target reached 93.3%.

In summary, although the YOLO series has made a breakthrough in target detection, its wearing equipment detection in a single case can achieve high detection accuracy, electric power wearing equipment including helmets, insulated boots, insulated gloves, insulated clothing, etc., obviously can not meet the requirements of the actual electric power operators multi-attribute wearing equipment. In order to ensure the life safety of electric power operators, the actual electric power operation also needs to detect and give feedback in real time to the danger and violation of wearing equipment in the complex environment of electric power operators, so the YOLO algorithm has high requirements for speed.

Therefore, in order to solve the requirement of single identification attribute of electric power operation wearer and the need for multiple wearer attributes to be detected simultaneously, and also the need for real-time detection and feedback of irregular and dangerous wearer behaviors in the shortest possible time, this paper proposes a electric power operation safety equipment detection algorithm incorporating PSA (Polarized self-attention mechanism) improvement of YOLOv5s algorithm, using polarized self-attention mechanism to improve the feature extraction end of YOLOv5s algorithm, and using orthogonal approach to ensure the low number of parameters while improving the channel resolution and spatial resolution of safety equipment images of electric power operation scenes; The K-mean clustering algorithm is used to obtain the candidate frame settings at the output of YOLOv5s algorithm; GSConv is used to replace the normal convolution to reduce the complexity of the model, improve the computational speed of the algorithm and increase the detection accuracy. It is able to detect the attributes of multiple wearable devices for electric power operation at the same time, and the detection speed has been greatly improved, solving the problems of single identification and slow detection speed of the attributes of wearable devices for electric power operation.

2 YOLOv5 Algorithm

After YOLOv1 appeared in 2015, a series of algorithms such as YOLOv2 [10]-YOLOv5 [11] emerged in order to continue improving its performance. YOLOv5 is more flexible and faster than YOLOv4, and it can also improve its accuracy. YOLOv5 has four models, YOLOv5s, YOLOv5m, YOLOv5l and YOLOv5x, with gradually increasing parameter size and accuracy. Distinguished by the number of Bottleneck, a control factor similar to that of EfficientNet [12] is used to achieve the variation of the version, enabling the selection of a suitable size model according to the application scenario. In this paper, version 6.0 of the YOLOv5s model is used, as shown in Fig. 1. The network structure of YOLOv5s includes 4 parts: Input side, Backbone model, Neck model, and Head side.

3 Improved YOLOv5s Algorithm

Although YOLOv5s is a fast and accurate algorithm, in the target detection task of the wearable device in this paper, the background image accounts for a relatively large portion of the image, and semantic segmentation of the image is needed to retain key points of small target information, such as insulated boots and insulated gloves in this paper. Therefore, it is necessary to maintain high resolution as much as possible, but also consider the computational volume, as well as try to connect global information to get the results, which is what YOLOv5s lacks at present. In the task of electric power operation equipment wear detection, real-time detection and feedback of detection results are needed to further improve the detection accuracy and speed, so it is necessary to lighten the YOLOv5s model while improving its accuracy. Based on the above factors, this paper proposes a fusion of PSA [13] to improve YOLOv5s algorithm for electric power operation wearable detection, and its main improvement points are as follows.

- Using the K-mean clustering algorithm mechanism to generate candidate boxes that match the data image, the boxes are divided into three categories of different size levels according to the size of the data image wearing device, and there are three types of boxes in each category to match the size of the power operation wearing device, which helps to improve the detection accuracy.
- The Polarized Self-Attention mechanism (PSA) is introduced with the aim of ensuring high channel resolution and high spatial resolution while effectively fusing global information to give different attention, thus improving the attention effect of the neural network on small target key node detection information; adding nonlinearity to the attention mechanism makes the fitted output more delicate and closer to the real output.
- The VoV-GSCSP method is introduced by replacing the normal convolution with the GSConv [14] structure, which lightens the model complexity while maintaining the accuracy and can improve the detection speed of wearable devices.

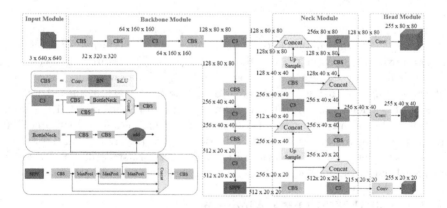

Fig. 1. YOLOv5s overall model structure diagram

3.1   Improvements of Backbone Module

Some of the key points in the image to be detected occupy fewer pixels but contain a lot of semantic information, and the prediction of their location information often has a large error, which can easily produce false detection or missed detection when detecting small targets such as insulated boots and insulated gloves in the image. Introducing attention mechanism in backbone net- works can better improve the detection of small targets. Attention mechanism is a widely used method in various target detection tasks. Attention mechanisms can be broadly classified into two categories according to the imposed dimensions: channel attention and spatial attention. For channel attention mechanisms, the representative mechanisms are effective channel attention (ECA) [15], and for spatial attention mechanisms, the representative mechanisms are squeeze and excitation (SE) [16]. With the proposal of spatial and channel attention mechanisms, it is natural that dual attention mechanisms combining both spatial and channel dimensions are also proposed, representing working convolutional block attention module (CBAM) [17], etc. The above self-attentive mechanisms usually use global pooling to write spatial information, but it is easy to cause the loss of position of the detected target. While PSA can maintain a relatively high resolution in channel and spatial dimensions (maintaining the dimensionality of C/2 in channel and [H,W] in space), this step can reduce the information loss caused by dimensionality reduction, thus improving the attention effect of the neural network on the detection information of small target critical nodes, and thus improving the accuracy of the YOLOv5s network on the detection of small target critical node information.

Therefore, the PSA module is introduced in the Backbone module. The PSA module is divided into two branches, one branch does the self-attention mechanism in channel dimension and the other branch does the self-attention mechanism in spatial dimension, and finally the results of these two branches are fused to get the output of the polarized self-attention structure. The PSA module architecture is shown in Fig. 2.

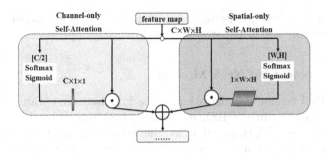

Fig. 2. PSA module architecture diagram

The PSA attention mechanism performs different degrees of compression in the spatial and feature map channel dimensions, respectively. The input feature map is first converted into two parts, the channel and spatial dimensions, using convolution, in which the information in the spatial dimension is completely compressed, while the information in the channel dimension remains at a relatively high level (i.e., C/2). Since the information in the spatial dimension is compressed, it needs to be augmented with information, so the authors augmented the information in the spatial dimension with Softmax and followed by convolution to raise the dimension of C/2 on the channel to C. Finally, the Sigmoid function is used to keep all the parameters between 0 and 1.

The formula for calculating the weights of channel branches is as follows:

$$A^{ch}(X) = F_{SG}[W_{z|\theta_1}(\sigma_1(W_v(X)) \bullet F_{SM}(\sigma_2(W_q(X))))] \tag{1}$$

where X represents the data in the feature map, W_q, W_v and W_z are 1×1 convolution layers respectively, σ_1 and σ_2 are two tensor reshape operators, $F_{SG}()$ is a SoftMax operator and "×" is the matrix dotproduct operation $F_{SM}(X) = \sum_{j=1}^{N_p} = \frac{e^{x_j}}{\sum_{m=1}^{N_p} e^{x_m}} x_j$. The internal number of channels, between $W_v|W_q$ and W_z, is C/2.

The formula for calculating the weights of spatial branches is as follows:

$$A^{sp}(X) = F_{SG}[\sigma_3(F_{SM}(\sigma_1(F_{GP}(W_q(X))))) \bullet \sigma_2(W_v(X))] \tag{2}$$

where W_q and W_v are standard 1×1 convolution layers respectively, σ_1, σ_2 and σ_3 are three tensor reshape operators, and $F_{SM}()$ is the SoftMax operator. $F_{GP}()$ is a global pooling operator $F_{SG}(X) = \frac{1}{H \times W} \sum_W^H \sum_{j=1}^W X(:, i, j)$, and × is the matrix dot-product operation.

For the calculation of the results of the two branches, two fusions were used: parallel (Formula 3) and series(Formula 4) (attention on the channel first, then on the spatial one):

$$PSA_p(X) = Z^{ch} + Z^{sp} = A^{ch}(X) \odot^{ch} X + A^{sp}(X) \odot^{sp} X \tag{3}$$

$$PSA_s(X) = Z^{sp}(Z^{ch}) = A^{sp}(A^{ch}(X) \odot^{ch} X) \odot^{sp} A^{ch}(X) \odot^{ch} X \tag{4}$$

where "+" is the element-wise addition operator, $\odot^{ch}$ is a channel-wise multiplication operator, $\odot^{sp}$ is a spatial-wise multiplication operator.

3.2 Improvements of Neck Module

In the YOLOv5 version 6.0 algorithm, three functions are encapsulated in the basic convolution module (CBS), including convolution (Conv2d), BN (Batch Normalization) and SiLU function as the activation function, as shown in Fig. 3(a). Meanwhile autopad(k, p) implements the effect of automatic padding calculation. Overall CBS implements the input features through the convolution layer, activation function, and normalization layer to obtain the output layer.

Improvement of Convolutional Networks. Target detection based on YOLOv5 series is a difficult downstream task in computer vision. On the one hand, for the detection of power operation safety wearable equipment in this paper, it is difficult for large models to meet the requirements of real-time detection; on the other hand, the lightweight model constructed by a large number of deep separable convolutional layers cannot achieve sufficient accuracy for multi-attribute wearable devices. Therefore, this paper introduces the latest method GSConv instead of CBS in YOLOv5s Neck module to reduce the complexity of the model and maintain accuracy. GSConv can better balance the accuracy and speed of the model, as shown in Fig. 3(b).

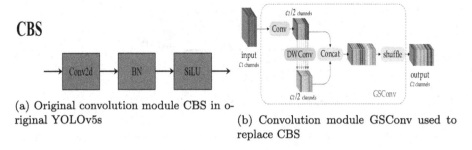

(a) Original convolution module CBS in o-
riginal YOLOv5s

(b) Convolution module GSConv used to replace CBS

Fig. 3. The structures of the (a) CBS module and the (b) GSConv modules

To accelerate the computation of predictions, the feed images in the CNN must undergo almost a similar transformation process in Backbone: the spatial information is gradually transferred to the channels. And each spatial compression and channel expansion of the feature map results in partial loss of semantic information. Dense convolution computation maximally preserves the hidden connections between each channel, while sparse convolution completely cuts off these connections. GSConv, on the other hand, preserves these connections as much as possible. But if it is used at all stages of the model, the network layers of the model will be deeper, and the deep layers will exacerbate the resistance to the data flow and significantly increase the inference time. By the time these feature maps go to Neck, they have become slender (channel dimension reaches its maximum and width-height dimension reaches its minimum) and no longer need to be transformed. Therefore, a better choice is to use them only at Neck. At this stage, using GSConv to process concatenated feature maps is just right: less redundant repetitive information, no need for compression, and better results for the attention module.

As can be seen from Fig. 3(b), GSConv firstly downsamples the input feature map with a normal convolution to obtain feature map_1, then obtains feature map_2 after DWConv (DSC) deep convolution operation, and then stitches the results of feature map_1 and feature map_2 together; finally, it performs shuffle operation, i.e., randomly disrupts the channel arrangement, so that the corresponding channel numbers of the previous two convolutions are combined to obtain the new feature map.

The purpose of the GSConv operation is to make the output of the DSC as close as possible to the CBS. The information generated by the CBS (dense convolution operation) is permeated into each part of the information generated by the DSC using shuffle. This method allows the information from the CBS to be completely mixed into the output of the DSC without increasing the number of parameters. This method makes the output of the convolutional computation as close as possible to the CBS, while reducing the computational cost.

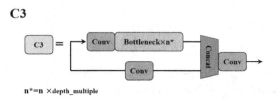

Fig. 4. C3 module structure diagram

VoV-GSCSP Replaces C3. The C3 module is transformed from the BottleneckCSP (bottleneck layer) module, whose structural roles are basically the same both for the CSP architecture, as shown in Fig. 4. This module is the main module for learning the residual features, and its structure is divided into two branches, one using the above specified multiple Bottleneck stacks and three standard convolutional layers, and the other only after a basic convolutional module, and finally the two branches are concat operation. Since C3 uses all base convolution, this necessarily results in a significant increase in the number of parameters.

To lighten the model, we chose to replace C3 with the latest VoV-GSCSP: First, the lightweight convolutional method GSConv is used instead of CBS. Its computational cost is about 60%–70% of that of CBS, and its contribution to the learning ability of wearable device detection in this paper is comparable to the latter. Then, GSbottleneck is continued to be introduced on top of GSConv. as shown in Fig. 5(a). Again, a one-time aggregation approach is used to design the cross-level partial network module VoV-GSCSP. The VoV-GSCSP module reduces the complexity of the computation and network structure, but maintains sufficient accuracy. Figure 5(b) shows the structure of VoV-GSCSP. It is noteworthy that if we use VoV-GSCSP instead of Neck's C3, where the C3 layer consists of standard convolution, the FLOPs (float operations per second) will be reduced by 15.72% on average compared to the latter, and the number of parametres decreases from 7.03M to 5.48 millions in the YOLOv5s model, which achieves the purpose of reducing the model and improving the detection speed of the model while ensuring the detection accuracy of the wearable device.

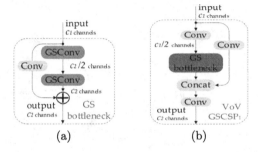

Fig. 5. The structures of the (a) GSbottleneck module and the (b) VoV-GSCSP modules

3.3   Improved YOLOv5s Network Structure

The PSA module was added to the Backbone module of the original YOLOv5s, and then the CBS of the Neck module is replaced with the latest GSConv, and C3 is replaced with VoV-GSCSP. Finally, an improved YOLOv5s model is generated, and its model structure is shown in Fig. 6. The model parameters are 5.48 millions, and the original YOLOv5s model parameters are 7.03 millions. The improved model is 30 % less than the original parameters, and the PAS module is added to the improved model, which can maintain a high resolution of the feature map in the space and channel dimensions, reduce the information loss caused by dimensionality reduction, and is more superior to the feature extraction of small targets such as insulating boots and insulating gloves. GSConv can lighten the convolution module. The VoV-GSCSP module with GSConv as the main body can ensure the detection accuracy and greatly reduce the parameters of the model. It is suitable for the requirements of fast detection speed and high precision for safe wearable devices in power operation.

4   Experimental Results and Analysis

The experimental computer operating system is Windows 10, CPU model is Intel(R) Xeon(R) Platinum8358P CPU@2.6 GHz, GPU model is GeForce RTX3090 with 24 GB memory size and 80 GB memory size. Python 3.8 and GPU acceleration using Cuda 11.8.

4.1   Data Set Production and Processing

In deep learning, the dataset largely influences the final experimental results. In this paper, the data is extracted from the simulated video frames of electric power operation scenes taken under surveillance as the dataset of the algorithm. Through YOLOv5s data cleaning, image enhancement (rotation, contrast change, flip, crop, zoom) and other methods, we finally obtained 2200 images of electric workers wearing protective equipment such as helmets, insulated boots,

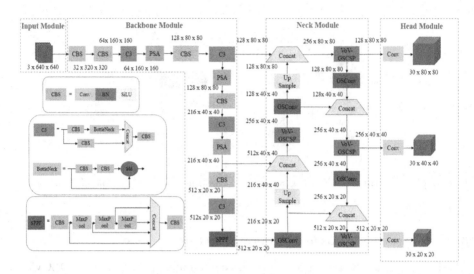

Fig. 6. YOLOv5s-VoVGSCSP-PSA overall model structure diagram

insulated gloves and insulated clothing during operation, including 1800 images in the training set, 250 images in the validation set and 150 images in the test set, and used the Labelimg tool to type The labels are divided into 5 types, namely "worker, shoes, glove, helmet, person". The target detection, the distribution of data samples and the candidate frame data after K-mean clustering are shown in Fig. 7.

From Fig. 8, it can be seen that most of the insulated gloves and insulated boots in the detection images belong to small targets. From the label distribution in Fig. 4(a), we can know that there are about 4,400 insulated gloves and 2,100 insulated boots. From the object size distribution in Fig. 4(b), it is known that the number of small target detection categories accounts for a large percentage.

4.2 Training Network

The hyperparameters of the model are configured before the network training. Initial learning rate $lr0 = 0.01$, final learning rate $lr0 \times lrf = 0.001$, weight decay coefficient weight_ decay $= 0.0005$, learning rate momentum momentum $= 0.937$, preheat initialization momentum is 0.8, its bias learning rate is 0.1. The effect of weight decay coefficient is to add a regularization term after the loss function with the purpose of reduce the problem of model overfitting; The learning rate momentum is mainly used to initialize the weights of the network when training the network. Using the adam [18] adaptive optimizer, the training period is set to 75 rounds, and then the K-means algorithm is used to re-cluster, and then the rectangular filling training is used to accelerate the model inference process. In the training process, the picture with bad training results in the previous round is also used. The training method of increasing the weight in the next

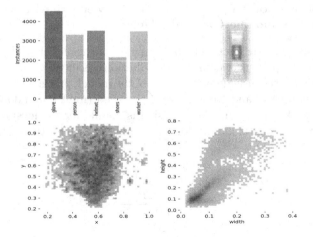

Fig. 7. Distribution of labels and data samples in target detection

round, and adjusting the cosine annealing function value in the hyperparameter and changing the picture shear ratio, flip direction, rotation angle, scaling size, learning rate momentum value, Mixup coefficient, etc. Finally, after repeated training, the best improved YOLOv5s network model is obtained. The improved model training process is shown in Fig. 8. The upper part of the picture is the training IOU loss, confidence loss and classification loss, accuracy and recall rate; the lower part of the picture is the verified IOU loss, confidence loss and classification loss, mAP value and mAP0.5: 0.95 value. It can be seen that the training process is stable and the model fitting ability is excellent.

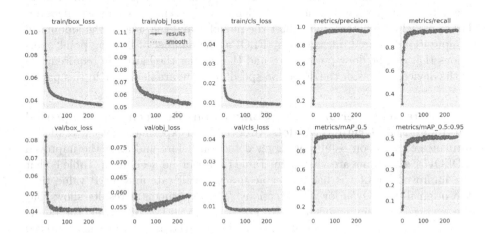

Fig. 8. Model Fitting Process

4.3   Comparison of Model Evaluation Between the Improved Algorithm and the Original Algorithm

Model Evaluation Metrics. The performance of the model needs a good evaluation. In order to prevent the uneven distribution of sample targets, which leads to failure to reflect the actual performance of the model, precision (P), recall (R), average precision (AP) and mean average precision (mAP) are adopted as evaluation indexes. Among them, the precision is mainly for the level of prediction results, while the recall is mainly for the sample itself, and the related formula is as follows:

$$P = \frac{TP}{TP + FP} \tag{5}$$

$$P = \frac{TP}{TP + FN} \tag{6}$$

$$AP = \int_0^1 P(R)dR \tag{7}$$

$$mAP = \frac{\sum\limits_{i=1}^{m} AP_i}{m} \tag{8}$$

where TP(true positives) denotes positive samples predicted by the model as positive classes; FP(false positives) denotes negative samples predicted by the model as positive classes; FN(false negatives) denotes positive samples predicted by the model as negative classes. AP is the area enclosed by the P-R curve (P is the vertical coordinate and R is the horizontal coordinate), mAP is the mean of the average precision AP of all categories, where m is the number of detected categories.

Second, the number of model parameters is also an important indicator to evaluate the performance of a model. Generally speaking, the smaller the number of model parameters, the lighter the model is and the smaller the amount of computation required, measured by FLOPs, the number of floating point operations that can be done per second, and the smaller the hardware requirements of the device, the faster the detection speed of the wearable device in this paper.

The Detection Performance Comparison Between the Improved Model and the Original Model. After repeated experiments, the overall performance comparison results of target detection before and after the improved YOLOv5s algorithm are shown in Table 1. It can be seen from Table 1 that the improved YOLOv5s has higher accuracy, recall rate and mAP value than the original YOLOv5s for all detections. The experimental results show that the average accuracy is increased by 1.58%, up to 96.1%. Moreover, the model parameters are reduced from 7.03 to 5.48 millions, the model size is also reduced from 13.7 MB to 10.7 MB, and the amount of calculation required per second is also reduced from 15.8 GFlops to 12.5 GFLOPs. The lightweight model ensures the accuracy of detection. On the whole, it not only improves the accuracy of detection, but also meets the requirements of real-time detection of power operation wearable devices in reality.

Table 1. Overall performance comparison results of target detection before and after YOLOv5s algorithm improvement

Model	Parameter	Model Size	P	R	mAP0.5	GFLOPs
YOLOv5s	7037095	13.7 MB	93.1%	94.43%	94.43%	15.8G
YOLOv5s-VoVGSCSP-PSA	5485661	10.7 MB	95.07%	96.01%	96.01%	12.5G

Ablation Experiments. In order to compare the advantages and disadvantages of the models more comprehensively, ablation experiments were also conducted to compare the effects of the added modules on the original models before and after the modules were added to YOLOv5s 6.0. The results of the ablation experiments are shown in Table 2. From Table 2, it can be seen that the PSA module can effectively increase the accuracy of the YOLOv5s model when adding a separate attention module. When adding VoV-GSCSP to the existing attention module, the experimental results of YOLOv5s+VoVGSCSP+PSA model are the best, i.e., the improved model is the highest in detection accuracy, recall, and mean accuracy mean.

Table 2. Results of ablation experiments

Model	no-K_mean	K_mean	PSA	VoVGSCSP	P/%	R/%	mAP0.5/%
YOLOv5s	✓				93.1	93.86	94.43
YOLOv5s-K		✓			94.19	93.77	95.04
YOLOv5s-PSA		✓	✓		95.25	94.24	95.37
YOLOv5s-VoVGSCSP		✓		✓	94.12	94.47	95.52
YOLOv5s-VoVGSCSP-PSA		✓	✓	✓	96.51	95.07	96.01

The Comparison of the Detection Effect Between the Improved Model and the Original Model. The differences of YOLOv5s under different detection conditions before and after the improvement are compared, some of which are shown in Fig. 9. It can be seen from Fig. 9 that the detected object may be affected by occlusion, position, distance and other factors during the detection process, resulting in missed detection or false detection. For example, the detection confidence of the improved YOLOv5s is much larger than that of the original YOLOv5s in the lower left corner insulation boots. As a whole, it can be seen that the improved YOLOv5s model has obvious advantages. By adding PSA and VoV-GSCSP modules, the network training enhances the feature extraction of key nodes of the object, so that the generated model is better and easier to detect. It not only reduces the missed detection rate and false detection rate of target detection, but also improves the accuracy and speed of detection while lightweighting the model. It has certain advancement in the target detection algorithm of power operation wearable equipment.

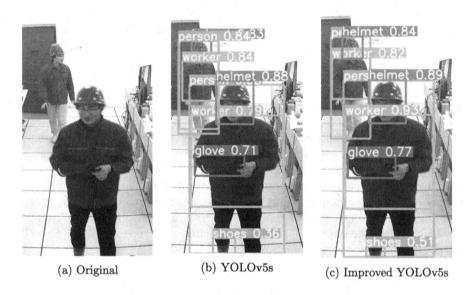

(a) Original   (b) YOLOv5s   (c) Improved YOLOv5s

Fig. 9. Comparison of detection results

5   Conclusion

Aiming at the problems of high missed detection rate, low recognition accuracy and slow detection speed of the traditional detection algorithm for power operation safety wearable devices, an improved YOLOv5s algorithm is proposed. By adding VoV-GSCSP structure and PSA module to lightweight the model, the accuracy and speed of detection are improved. In particular, the detection of partial occlusion of wearable devices has been greatly improved compared with traditional algorithms. The VoV-GSCSP structure added in provides a good help for the model to be lightweight while ensuring the detection accuracy, and the PSA module enables the network model to better extract the feature of the key nodes of the occluded small target, thereby improving the ability to detect the occluded small target. The experimental results show that the improved YOLOv5s network has higher final accuracy and recall rate and better detection effect on the basis of satisfying real-time detection, which greatly improves the robustness and generalization of the algorithm.

Acknowledgment. This work was supported in part by National Natural Science Foundation of China (No. 62067003), Culture and Art Science Planning Project of Jiangxi Province (No. YG2018042), Humanities and Social Science Project of Jiangxi Province (No. JC18224).

References

1. Zhang, Y., Wu, K., et al.: Research based on the improved yolov3 helmet detection method. Comput. Simul. (2021)
2. Liu, Z., Wang, X., et al.: An improved method for infrared image target detection based on yolo algorithm. Laser Infrared **50**(12), 9 (2020)
3. Han, K., Li, S., et al.: Yolov3-based helmet wearing status detection in construction scenarios. J. Rail. Sci. Eng. **018**(001), 268–276 (2021)
4. Liu Xin, Z.C.: Mining helmet wearing detection based on convolutional neural network. Electron. Technol. Appl. **46**(9), 6 (2020)
5. Zhang, M., Cao, Z., et al.: Deep learning based construction worker helmet wearing recognition research. J. Saf. Environ. (2), 7 (2019)
6. Wang, Y., Gu, Y., et al.: Research on helmet wearing detection method based on pose estimation. Comput. Appl. Res. (2021)
7. Qu, W.Q., Qiu, Z.B., et al.: Yolov3-based helmet wear detection for power grid operators. China Saf. Prod. Sci. Technol. **18**(2), 6 (2022)
8. Jian, W.: Visual image detection method of helmet for power construction scene based on improved yolov5 algorithm. Rob. Appl. **2**, 22–26 (2023)
9. Fu, D., Su, G., et al.: Improved yolov5 algorithm based on critical equipment detection for electrical workers' operational safety. J. Hubei Univ. National. Nat. Sci. Ed. **40**(3), 320–327 (2022)
10. Redmon, J., Farhadi, A.: Yolo9000: better, faster, stronger. In: IEEE Conference on Computer Vision & Pattern Recognition, pp. 6517–6525 (2017)
11. G.J.: Yolov5 (2021)
12. Tan, M., et al.: Efficientnet: rethinking model scaling for convolutional neural networks (2019)
13. Liu, H., Liu, F., Fan, X., Huang, D.: Polarized self-attention: towards high-quality pixel-wise regression (2021)
14. Li, H., et al.: Slim-neck by gsconv: a better design paradigm of detector architectures for autonomous vehicles (2022)
15. Wang, Q., Wu, B., Zhu, P., Li, P., Zuo, W., Hu, Q.: ECA-NET: efficient channel attention for deep convolutional neural networks (2019)
16. Hu, J., Shen, L., Sun, G.: Squeeze-and-excitation networks. In: 2018 IEEE/CVF Conference on Computer Vision and Pattern Recognition (CVPR) (2018)
17. Woo, S., Park, J., Lee, J.Y., Kweon, I.: CBAM: convolutional block attention module. In: Lecture Notes in Computer Science (Including Subseries Lecture Notes in Artificial Intelligence and Lecture Notes in Bioinformatics), pp. 3–19 (2018)
18. Kingma, D., Ba, J.: Adam: a method for stochastic optimization. Comput. Sci. (2014)

Image Deblurring Using Fusion Transformer-Based Generative Adversarial Networks

Jionghui Wang[1($\boxtimes$)], Zhilin Xiong[2], Xueyu Huang[2,3], Haoyu Shi[2], and Jiale Wu[2]

[1] Minmetals Exploration and Development Co. Ltd., Beijing 100010, China
wangjh@minmetals.com
[2] School of Software Engineering, Jiangxi University of Science and Technology,
Nanchang 330013, People's Republic of China
[3] Key Laboratory of Virtual Digital Factory and Cultural Communications, Nanchang 330013,
People's Republic of China

Abstract. Using the Transformer for motion deblurring enables a broader receptive field, and by stacking multiple Transformer modules, it captures global correlations in features. However, this increases network complexity and poses convergence challenges. To address this, a Generative Adversarial Network called XT-GAN, which combines multiple-scale Transformers, has been proposed.XT-GAN leverages pyramid features from a convolutional network as a lightweight substitute for multi-scale inputs. Within the output pyramid convolutional features, different-scale features are computed in parallel using multi-head self-attention. These features are combined with a proposed feature enhancement module to represent information at different scales. Finally, the network outputs from various modules are concatenated and restored to the original image size.In experiments conducted on the synthetic dataset GoPro, XT-GAN outperformed ordinary networks such as DeblurGAN, DeepDeblur, and SRN. It achieved a reduction in computational complexity of at least 70% while achieving PSNR and SSIM values of 29.13dB and 0.923, respectively. XT-GAN also demonstrated good robustness in the real dataset RealBlur-J, with PSNR and SSIM values of 28.40 and 0.852. It effectively handles motion blur in real-world scenarios, suppresses image artifacts, and restores natural and clear details.

Keywords: image deblurring · Transformer · multi-head attention · GAN · multi-scale fusion

1 Introduction

In the process of image capture, when the photographed object is in relative motion with the image capture device or is affected by factors such as defects in the capture device or the environment, it often leads to motion blur in the captured photos. This

This work is supported by the National Key Research and Development Program of China 2020YFC1909602.

C. Wu et al. (Eds.): MONAMI 2023, LNICST 559, pp. 136–153, 2024.
https://doi.org/10.1007/978-3-031-55471-1_11

blurring obscures the features of the photographed object, affecting identification, and the resulting low-quality images do not meet the requirements of advanced visual tasks such as object recognition and semantic segmentation. Therefore, conducting research on image deblurring is not only of practical significance but also holds important research value.

Traditional image processing techniques address various degrees of blur by estimating the point spread function (PSF). However, motion blur in the real world is more complex, and solving the PSF for each pixel becomes an ill-posed problem [1]. In traditional methods, errors in calculating the blur kernel directly impact the deblurring results, leading to poor restoration effects or even image distortion.

Deep learning methods have shown better adaptability to various blurry scenarios and possess stronger generalization capabilities, enabling them to handle more complex real-world blurs. Sun et al. [2] utilized a convolutional neural network (CNN) combined with a Markov random field to jointly estimate the motion blur kernel and perform restoration for a single image. However, this method still has limitations when dealing with computationally complex spatial blur kernels. To address this issue, Nah et al. [1] proposed the application of multi-scale information to provide a wide receptive field and avoid direct estimation of the blur kernel, achieving better results. Building upon the "coarse-to-fine" structure design of Nah et al. [1], Tao et al. [3] further introduced weight sharing of the feature extraction module across sub-networks at different scales, reducing the feature extraction burden in different parts of the model.

The stacking of multi-scale sub-networks unavoidably introduces greater model complexity and longer computation time. Cho et al. [4] proposed an asymmetric feature fusion network that uses a single encoder for inputting down-sampled or subsampled images and a single decoder for outputting deblurred images. This approach effectively fuses multi-scale features. Kupyn et al. [5] applied Generative Adversarial Networks (GANs) to image deblurring tasks and introduced the Feature Pyramid Network (FPN) into the deblurring task in their DeblurGANv2 [6]. The fusion of multi-scale pyramid features [7] achieved deblurring results similar to those obtained with multi-scale inputs but at a lower computational complexity. Zhang et al. [8] proposed using a GAN to learn blurring and guide another GAN to learn deblurring, aiming to enable the network to better recover images by learning the blurring process of the images.

Handling complex spatial motion blur requires a larger receptive field [3], and multi-scale fusion achieves the goal of information flow and sharing between different scale features. Existing networks [3, 9] increase model size and inference time by stacking multi-scale convolutions, changing the size of convolution kernels, or increasing network depth to expand the receptive field. However, interactions between features at the same scale are still limited by the distance of the convolution kernel. Transformers, with their global interaction and the ability to capture long-range dependencies, have been proposed in literature [10]. A cyclic network structure completely based on self-attention mechanisms has been introduced, utilizing multiple stacked self-attention modules to establish connections between every feature on the feature map, unrestricted by the size of convolution kernels. While Transformers can capture long-range dependencies for individual features, convolutions still possess the advantages of parameter sharing and translational invariance. Moreover, the computational complexity of pure attention networks grows quadratically with the length of the input sequence, which is not acceptable for computing-intensive tasks with high-resolution images.

Based on the analysis mentioned earlier, we propose a Fusion Transformer-based Generative Adversarial Network for Image Deblur (XT-GAN). The main contributions and work of XT-GAN are as follows:

1. XT-GAN utilizes pyramid features as a lightweight alternative to multi-scale inputs, resulting in lower complexity and faster processing of high-resolution images.
2. For the multi-scale features from the Feature Pyramid Network (FPN) [7], XT-GAN employs a Transformer-based cross-layer parallel computing structure. This approach extracts rich context while considering the locality of convolutions, thereby improving the deblurring performance of the model.
3. XT-GAN introduces Attention Enhancement Modules to enhance the information interaction between the self-transformer (ST) and low-level/high-level features. This special fusion structure enhances the flow of information within the network, improves the utilization of semantic information from different hierarchical features, and further enhances the network performance of XT-GAN.

2   Related Work

The XT-GAN network structure proposed in this paper is illustrated in Fig. 1.

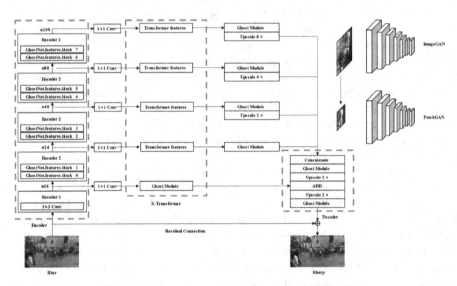

Fig. 1. Depicts the network architecture of XT-GAN.

The generator consists of an encoder feature extraction backbone called the Backbone, a cross-layer feature fusion module called X-Transformer (XT), and a decoder for image scale restoration. The discriminator network consists of two components: ImageGAN and PatchGAN, which are based on VGG19 [11] and a dual-scale discriminator network [12], respectively.

2.1 Design of the Generator

The generator of XT-GAN follows an Encoder-Decoder structure, which is commonly used for image super-resolution restoration and has been proven effective for image deblurring tasks as well [3].

In the Encoder part, the Backbone network performs spatial compression and transformation on the input image. The number of channels and the level of abstraction of the features increase progressively, while the network learns and separates the blurry features of the image. In recent years, various Backbone networks [13] have been proposed, each with different sensitivities to blurry image features and structural advantages [6].

GhostNet [14] achieves multiple groups of feature maps with similar information by stacking inexpensive linear transformations called Ghost-Modules. It effectively utilizes redundant feature information and has shown excellent performance in image processing tasks such as image classification and object detection. Furthermore, research [16] has demonstrated that using GhostNet [14] as the backbone network, along with the corresponding Ghost-Module modules, for image deblurring tasks yields superior deblurring performance and lower model complexity compared to lightweight networks like MobileNetV3 [13].

XT-GAN chooses GhostNet [14] as the backbone network for its generator. Following the approach described in [16], the first 8 feature extraction modules (Blocks) of the network are selected as the backbone output for the deblurring task. The output channel dimension of the last layer is set to 160.

The use of multi-scale image inputs in XT-GAN satisfies the network's requirement for different receptive fields and introduces correlation at different positions for the features. Instead of directly incorporating features from images of different scales during the feature extraction process [4], XT-GAN utilizes the structure of Feature Pyramid Network (FPN) [7] as a lightweight alternative for the multi-scale approach. The outputs of different levels of feature extraction modules from the Backbone are selected as the input feature maps of the XT modules. The convolutional layers of the Backbone network serve as connections between the features, ensuring the continuity of intercorrelation and semantic information among the extracted multi-scale features.

The input to the network is a 3-channel image with a size of 256×256. It undergoes initial processing through an enhancement module consisting of a 3×3 convolutional layer with a stride of 2, normalization, and activation function, which increases the number of channels to 16 and reduces the size to 128×128. This processed image serves as the input to the Backbone network. The outputs of different levels of the Encoder's Blocks are combined pairwise in a shallow-to-deep order to obtain multi-scale features. The output channel dimensions of the multi-scale features are 24, 40, 80, and 160, while the corresponding sizes of the feature maps are 64×64, 32×32, 16×16, and 8×8, respectively. This process can be represented by the following equation:

$$ED_0 = \text{relu}(\text{norm}(\text{conv3}(I_{\text{blur}}))) \tag{1}$$

$$ED_n = ED_n(ED_{n-1}) \tag{2}$$

I_{blur} represents the input blurry image. ED_0 is enhance represents the feature map output of the enhancement module, which is also the output of the first layer of the

Encoder. conv3 represents the 3×3 convolution operation. norm represents the normalization operation. relu represents the ReLU activation function. ED_n represents the scale feature output of the nth layer of the Encoder. Its input is the output of the previous layer of the Encoder ED_{n-1}.

The process of fusing the multi-scale feature maps as input to the XT module can be represented by the following equations:

$$F_n = XT(ED_1, ED_2, ED_3, ED_4,) \tag{3}$$

XT represents the XT feature fusion module, and F_n represents the output of the nth XT module.

In the Decoder, the high-dimensional, high-semantic feature maps F_1, F_2, F_3, F_4 from XT are first upsampled to the same size and concatenated along the channel dimension. Then, they are added element-wise with the low-semantic feature map ED_0, and mapped to the size of the original input image through a 1×1 convolution. The output is activated using Tanh. We employ residual connections in the network to propagate the input to the end, aiming to capture the relevant information from the original image. This process can be represented as follows:

$$D_{\text{out}} = \text{cat}(F_1, F_2, F_3, F_4) + ED_0 \tag{4}$$

$$I_{\text{sharp}} = \tanh(\text{resize}(D_{\text{out}})) + I_{\text{blur}} \tag{5}$$

D_{out} represents the output of the Decoder, I_{sharp} denotes the generated clear image, tanh represents the activation function used, resize indicates the upsampling operation for image scale restoration, and cat denotes the channel-based concatenation operation.

2.2 Design of the Discriminator

The discriminator in XT-GAN utilizes a dual-scale structure [12], consisting of a global information capture discriminator and a local information extraction discriminator.

Research [17] has shown that using a Markovian discriminator with patch size of 70×70 can better promote the generation of visually superior clear images compared to using the complete image size. However, Kupyn et al.[6] demonstrated that using a dual-scale discriminator, called DoubleGAN, can complement the scene background and object motion trajectory in the image, thereby enabling the network to handle complex and diverse blurry scenes in the real world.

During the training process, ImageGAN takes in the complete image size of 256×256 for discrimination. PatchGAN, on the other hand, divides the image into patches of size 70×70 and performs discrimination on each patch separately, taking the average of the corresponding scores. Therefore, the calculation formula for the overall confidence of the target image is as follows:

$$S_{\text{out}} = \frac{1}{2}(S_I + E(S_P)) \tag{6}$$

where S_{out} represents the average overall confidence of the DoubleGAN discriminator, S_I represents the confidence score outputted by ImageGAN, S_P represents the confidence scores for each patch and their summation, and E represents taking the average of the aggregated results.

2.3 XT Moudle

Pan et al. [18] pointed out that convolutional layers can provide good local information in the early stages, but in later stages, the network requires globally aware features provided by self-attention mechanisms. In XT-GAN, the Encoder's multi-scale features are fused across layers using Transformer-based XT modules, as shown in Fig. 2(a). The XT feature fusion module, illustrated in Fig. 2(b), consists of Shifted Window-based Multi-Head Self-Attention (W-MSA), and feature enhancement modules, namely Dot Transformer (DT) and Pool Transformer (PT), which collectively extract cross-scale correlation information. The output of XT, depicted in Fig. 2(c), comprises a set of pyramid features with richer semantics and more distinctive characteristics, reducing the overlap and redundancy of different scale feature information.

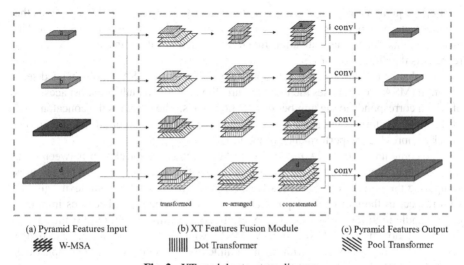

(a) Pyramid Features Input   (b) XT Features Fusion Module   (c) Pyramid Features Output

▨ W-MSA ||||| Dot Transformer   ▨ Pool Transformer

Fig. 2. XT module structure diagram.

Multi-scale structures have been proven effective in handling complex image blurring [19]. However, directly incorporating untreated multi-scale features can easily disrupt the correlation between features. In literature [20–22], stacking Transformer modules or adding convolutional layers to process the feature maps after feature fusion ensures that the information is preserved during semantic fusion. However, this approach increases the complexity of the network and introduces a large number of parameters, which can impact convergence. In XT-GAN, the Encoder extracts pure convolutional features at different stages from the GhostNet [14] network, which eliminates the need for additional convolutional processing when inputting locally spatially correlated scale features. XT utilizes parallel W-MSA and attention enhancement modules to complement global information, implicitly performing feature fusion on pyramid features. The following sections will describe the specific structure and function of XT.

ST Moudle. The Transformer was initially used in natural language processing (NLP) and relies on self-attention (SA) with a Key-Query-Value (KQV) mechanism to capture

long-range dependencies effectively. In this mechanism, K represents the key information, Q represents the query information, and V represents the corresponding values.
KQV matrices are obtained through matrix transformations of the original feature map,
providing different descriptions of the original features. The correlation matrix between
K and Q is computed through matrix multiplication and activated by Softmax. It is then
multiplied with the corresponding V. This process can be mathematically represented as
follows:

$$Q, K, V = MW_q, MW_k, MW_v \tag{7}$$

$$\text{Attention} = \text{Softmax}(\frac{QK^T}{\sqrt{d_k}})V \tag{8}$$

In the equations, W_q, W_k, W_v represent different weight matrices, M represents the
original feature map, Attention represents the output of the self-attention (SA) mechanism, Softmax denotes an activation function, K^T denotes the transpose of K, and d_k
represents the dimension of K.

To enhance the representational capacity of self-attention (SA), multi-headed self-
attention (MSA) decomposes the input feature dimension into multiple subspaces, each
of which corresponds to the number of attention heads. The output is the concatenation
of the value vectors from each head. Each head can learn different attention patterns,
thereby improving the performance of the model.

The computation of MSA involves calculating the cross-correlation between each
feature value in a feature map and every other position's feature value. This requires
computing the correlations of all features, resulting in a quadratic complexity growth
with respect to the size of the input feature map. Consequently, it becomes impracti-
cal to handle high-resolution blurry images. To address this, literature [23] introduces
Shifted Window based Self-Attention (W-MSA), which achieves good results in image
restoration or denoising tasks with linear complexity. The computational complexities
of MSA and W-MSA are as follows:

$$\Omega(\text{MSA}) = 4hwC^2 + 2(hw)^2C \tag{9}$$

$$\Omega(\text{W-MSA}) = 4hwC^2 + 2M^2hwC \tag{10}$$

h and w represent the height and width of the input feature map, respectively, while
C represents the dimension of the feature map. M represents the window size, which
is typically set to 8 by default. The computational complexity of W-MSA depends on
the number of windows into which the feature map is divided. The output is the linear
transformation of the Multi-head Self-Attention (MSA) within each window's subspace.
The calculation process is as follows:

$$\text{Attention}_{W-MSA} = \text{resize}(\text{Attention}_n) \tag{11}$$

Attention_{W-MSA} refers to the operation of applying Multi-head Self-Attention
(MSA) within each window's subspace. resize represents the merging or concatenation

of the outputs of MSA performed on each window. Attention$_n$ represents the summation or aggregation of the MSA outputs from all the divided windows. Attention$_n$ represents performing MSA calculation within the n divided windows.

To address the issue of limited communication between windows in different positions, the windows are shifted and another round of W-MSA calculation is performed. A mask is used to prevent the propagation of irrelevant features, allowing only the exchange of cross-correlation information between adjacent windows. Although performing W-MSA twice increases the overall computational complexity, it transforms the problem of global computation on the feature map into localized attention calculations within associated windows. This significantly reduces the computational resource requirements for restoring high-resolution images. Additionally, W-MSA provides local information similar to convolutional kernels, while the global context is controlled by the shifted windows. The combination of local information and global context contributes to significant improvements in the deblurring task.

Feature Enhancement Module. The FPN (Feature Pyramid Network) structure, as described in [7], provides an upward path based on upsampling, enabling lower-level information to access richer semantic feature maps from higher levels. Lower-level information may have less semantic information and may not directly serve as effective features. However, it contains global statistical information that can complement the high-level network in capturing fine details.

Inspired by Zhang et al. [24], the feature enhancement module in the XT-GAN network utilizes DT to map higher-level feature maps to the current scale feature map and PT to render lower-level features onto the current scale feature map. Unlike traditional attention mechanisms that enhance the original feature map by weighted summation of attention feature maps, this approach generates new feature maps. To avoid information confusion among different semantic feature maps, the new feature maps are concatenated with the original feature map. The expectation is that the network can use information from other scales to determine the relevance of different-scale features and the semantic representation range of features at the current scale. The combination of these feature maps strengthens the multidimensional expressive power of the current scale, emphasizing its semantic information and characteristics. It implicitly models the semantic information between upper and lower layers and achieves better multi-scale information fusion compared to the FPN structure [7].

DT achieves feature enhancement by treating higher-level features as keys (K) and the current scale as queries (Q) and values (V). It calculates the dot product between K and Q to obtain the correlation matrix of their feature vectors. This correlation matrix is then multiplied element-wise with V to obtain the correlation mapping of K on V. This process can be represented by the following equations:

$$Q_{dt}, K_{dt}, V_{dt} = M_{low}W_{dt\text{-}q}, M_{high}W_{dt\text{-}k}, M_{low}W_{dt\text{-}v} \tag{12}$$

$$\text{Out}_{dt} = \text{mat}(\frac{K_{dt}Q_{dt}^T}{hw}, V_{dt}) \tag{13}$$

$Q_{dt}, K_{dt}, V_{dt}, W_{dt\text{-}q}, W_{dt\text{-}k}, W_{dt\text{-}v}$ represents the matrices for K, Q, V, and their respective weight matrices in the DT operation. M_{low} represents the lower-level feature,

M_{high} represents the higher-level feature, Out_{dt} represents the output result of DT, Q_{dt}^T represents the transpose of Q_{dt}, and mat represents matrix multiplication.

PT achieves feature enhancement by using the lower-level feature as V, the global average pooling result of V as Q, and the current scale feature as K. It calculates the element-wise product of K and Q, and then adds this result to the downsampled V, resulting in rendered feature map of the lower-level feature at the current scale. This process can be represented by the following equations:

$$Q_{pt}, K_{pt}, V_{pt} = avg(M_{low})W_{pt\text{-}q}, M_{high}W_{pt\text{-}k}, down(M_{low}) \tag{14}$$

$$Out_{pt} = add(Q_{pt}K_{pt}, V_{pt}) \tag{15}$$

Q_{pt}, K_{pt}, V_{pt} represents the matrices for K, Q, and V in the PT operation. $W_{pt\text{-}q}$, $W_{pt\text{-}k}$ represents the weight matrix. avg represents the global average pooling operation. down represents the downsampling operation. Out_{pt} represents the output result of PT.

2.4 Data Normalization

In image restoration tasks, which often require high-resolution outputs, the computational demand is significant. Therefore, network training is typically performed using small batches (Mini-Batch). Instance Normalization (IN) and Layer Normalization (LN) are normalization techniques that have advantages when training on Mini-Batch data. They help overcome the drawbacks of using Batch Normalization (BN), which can result in significant variations in feature variance across different batches.

In XT-GAN, the W-MSA operation in the XT module utilizes LN for training. This choice is influenced by the findings mentioned in reference [25], which suggests that LN is beneficial for training Transformers. LN is used as a normalization method to stabilize the training process and improve the performance of the W-MSA operation.

Reference [26] introduces an improved version of Instance Normalization called the Half Instance Normalization Block (HIB). HIB normalizes only half of the channels, which helps to preserve more scale information from the original features while reducing complexity. In XT-GAN, HIB is combined with other modules of the network to perform data normalization.

2.5 Loss Function

XT-GAN uses a composite generator loss function, which consists of two components: the content loss of the generator and the adversarial loss from the multi-scale discriminator. It can be represented as follows:

$$L_G = L_{content} + \frac{1}{2}\lambda(L_{adv\text{-}full} + L_{adv\text{-}patch}) \tag{16}$$

The content loss $L_{content}$ is used to measure the semantic differences between the generated restoration image and the target image, capturing the discrepancy in semantic content. The adversarial loss $L_{adv\text{-}full}$ and $L_{adv\text{-}patch}$ are employed to train the model in generating more realistic and natural restoration images. The output result L_G represents the average value of the content loss and the adversarial loss multiplied by λ and added to $L_{content}$. The value of λ, as recommended in reference [6], is typically set to 0.01, determining the weight coefficient for balancing the importance of the content loss and the adversarial loss in the overall generator loss.

XT-GAN's discriminator loss is computed based on the results of the multi-scale discriminator. It can be represented as follows:

$$L_D = \frac{1}{2}(L_{D\text{-full}} + L_{D\text{-patch}}) \tag{17}$$

where $L_{D\text{-full}}$ represents the global discriminator loss value and $L_{D\text{-patch}}$ represents the local discriminator loss value. The output result L_D is the average value of both losses, representing the overall discriminator loss from the multi-scale discriminator.

Loss Function of Generator. In image restoration, commonly used loss functions include pixel-space losses such as Mean Squared Error (MSE) or Mean Absolute Error (MAE). Reference [6] suggests that MSE loss can better reflect the similarity between pixels, allowing for better correction of color errors and texture distortions. However, using only MAE or MSE can struggle to restore high-frequency image details and may introduce abnormal artifacts [27].To address the information loss caused by using pixel-space losses, reference [28] proposes defining and optimizing a perceptual distance loss based on high-level features as part of the content loss function. Compared to traditional pixel-space losses, the perceptual distance loss based on high-level features better reflects human perception of semantic similarity in images. It helps the model learn more accurate and semantically informed restoration images, leading to better visual results.The content loss function used in this paper is represented as follows:

$$L_{content} = \alpha L_{perc} + \beta L_{mse} \tag{18}$$

where L_{perc} represents the perceptual loss and L_{mse} represents the mean squared error (MSE). The values of α and β, as recommended by Kupyn et al.[6], are typically set to 0.006 and 0.5.

Loss Function Of Discriminator. GANs are widely used in image restoration and image super-resolution tasks, aiming to improve both the discriminator's ability to distinguish real samples and the generator's ability to generate realistic fake samples. However, training GANs often faces challenges such as training difficulties and loss convergence issues, resulting in a situation where the discriminator's capability surpasses that of the generator, leading to severe gradient vanishing for the generator. The Wasserstein GAN (WGAN) loss function is commonly used as the discriminator loss in GANs. The Wasserstein GAN with Gradient Penalty (WGAN-GP) loss function is an upgraded version that introduces a gradient penalty term, which computes the Wasserstein distance between real and fake samples, encouraging smooth gradients between the adversarial networks. This helps alleviate gradient vanishing and exploding issues, eliminates the need for manual parameter tuning during training, and accelerates network convergence. Reference [6] proposes the RaGAN-LS loss function, which further enhances stability, computational efficiency, and deblurring performance compared to using WGAN-GP.

In XT-GAN, the RaGAN-LS loss function is utilized by calculating the losses of two discriminator networks. The adversarial loss L_{adv} improves the generator's ability to generate fake samples, while the discriminator loss L_D enhances the discriminator's ability to detect fake samples. The discriminator loss L_D and the adversarial loss L_{adv} can be represented as follows:

$$L_D = E[(D(I_{real}) - E(D(I_{fake-p})) - 1)^2]$$
$$+E[(D(I_{fake}) - E(I_{real-p}) + 1)^2] \tag{19}$$

$$L_{adv} = E[(D(I_{real}) - E(D(I_{fake-p})) + 1)^2]$$
$$+E[(D(I_{fake}) - E(I_{real-p}) - 1)^2] \tag{20}$$

where D represents the discriminator network, I_{real} is the label image of the input image, I_{fake} is the fake sample generated by the generator from the input image. These samples are stored in the ImagePool [29] for future use. With a probability of 50%, the discriminator has a choice between directly receiving the new input label I_{real} or the generated I_{fake}, or randomly selecting an image stored in the ImagePool [29].

3 Experimental Evaluation

The experiment was conducted on a server with a 15 vCPU Intel(R) Xeon(R) Platinum 8358P CPU @ 2.60 GHz, 80 GB of memory, and a PTX A5000 GPU with 24 GB of VRAM. The operating system used was Ubuntu 18.04, and the CUDA version was 11.7. The deep learning framework used was PyTorch version 1.11.0. During training, the input image size was set to 256×256, and the number of heads (Head-Num) for W-MSA was set to 4. The batch size was set to 1, and Adam optimizer was used for training with an initial learning rate of 10^{-4}. The training process involved freezing the backbone network for the first 3 epochs and then proceeding with normal training. A linear decay learning rate schedule was applied starting from the 50th epoch, decaying the learning rate to 10^{-4} by the 2000th epoch. Data augmentation techniques used included random cropping, random motion blur, median blur, image compression, random sharpening, and random grayscale.The total training duration was 2000 epochs, which took approximately 160 h considering the hardware configuration. This duration was deemed sufficient for the model to fully converge.

3.1 Datasets

In this experiment, the synthetic GoPro dataset [1] and the real-world dataset RealBlur-J [30] were chosen to evaluate the robustness, generalization, and effectiveness of the proposed model. To reduce overfitting to specific datasets, incremental data created by Kupyn et al. [6] was used for the GoPro dataset [1]. Multiple datasets, including GoPro [6], were selected following the same data split [6], with 4400 pairs used for training and 2200 pairs for validation. This ensured that the model performed well when handling blurry images from different sources and could address a wider range of image restoration problems.For testing on real-world images, the model trained on the GoPro dataset [1] was tested on the test set of RealBlur-J [30], which contains 980 pairs of images. This was done to verify the robustness and generalization ability of the proposed model when dealing with real-world blurry images.

3.2 Comparative Experiment

In this paper, we will compare the proposed Cross-Layer Fusion Transform Generative Adversarial Network with recent and outstanding deblurring network models on the GoPro [1] and RealBlur-J [30] test sets. We will use commonly used image restoration performance metrics, such as Peak Signal-to-Noise Ratio (PSNR) and Structural Similarity Index (SSIM), as objective measures to evaluate the deblurring effectiveness of the networks. We will also consider the floating-point operations (FLOPs) and model parameters (Params) as indicators to assess the model complexity and size. Additionally, the runtime required for the model to restore a single image will serve as an objective measure of the model's computational speed. The input image size for testing is set to the standard 720 × 1280 dimensions in the GoPro dataset [1]. The results of the testing are presented in Table 1.

Table 1. Performance on the GoPro test dataset

Model	PSNR (dB)	SSIM	Runtimes (s)	Parms (MB)	FLOPs (G)
Sun et al. [2]	24.64	0.842	1200	54	–
Xu et al. [31]	25.10	0.890	13.41	37.1	–
DeblurGAN [5]	28.70	0.927	0.85	12.9	678.29
DeblurGAN-v2 [6]	29.55	0.934	0.35	23.8	411.34
Ghost-Deblur [16]	28.75	0.919	0.037	6.08	20.51
SRN [3]	30.10	0.932	1.6	6.8	1434.82
DeepDeblur [1]	29.23	0.916	4.33	11.7	1760.04
XT-GAN(ours)	29.13	0.923	0.068	8.5	120.4

Although the proposed model in this paper exhibits a lower PSNR compared to conventional models like SRN [3], it achieves a significant reduction of 70% in computational complexity. Moreover, it outperforms DeepDeblur [1] with an improved SSIM value by 0.007. When compared to the lightweight model Ghost-Deblur [16], which utilizes the same backbone network, the proposed XT structure enhances the collection of contextual information and improves the deblurring performance of the network. The PSNR and SSIM values are improved by 0.38 dB and 0.004, reaching 29.13 dB and 0.923, respectively.

To evaluate the generalization ability of the proposed network model, we test its effectiveness on real blurry scenes. After training on the GoPro [1] dataset, we perform testing and comparisons on the RealBlur-J [30] test set. The results are shown in Table 2.

Table 2. Performance on the RealBlur-J test dataset(trained on GoPro)

Model	PSNR (dB)	SSIM
Sun et al. [2]	–	–
Xu et al. [29]	27.14	0.8303
DeblurGAN [5]	29.97	0.834
DeblurGAN-v2 [6]	28.70	0.866
Ghost-Deblur [16]	28.25	0.846
SRN [3]	28.56	0.867
DeepDeblur [1]	27.87	0.827
XT-GAN(ours)	28.40	0.854

The XT-GAN model demonstrates good robustness in dealing with real-world blurry scenarios, surpassing the PSNR values of DeepDeblur [1], DeblurGAN [5], and Ghost-Deblur [16] by 0.53 dB, 0.43 dB, and 0.15 dB, respectively. It achieves a PSNR value of 28.40 dB and an SSIM value of 0.854, indicating stable and promising results. This indicates that the XT-GAN model is effective in handling real-world blur and can produce improved image restoration outcomes.

3.3 Subjective Deblurring Effect

Subjective Deblurring Effect of XT-GAN on Real Dataset, as shown in Fig. 3 and Fig. 4.

(a)Blur   (b)DeblurGAN   (c)GhostDelur   (d)DeepDeblur   (e)XT-GAN   (f)Sharp

Fig. 3. Performance on the GoPro test dataset

Among the compared models, DeepDeblur [1] achieves the highest objective deblurring metrics, as shown in Fig. 3(d). Its restored image exhibits thicker and more distinct edges, but it tends to remove or enhance certain details in the blurry regions, resulting in overall color or structural distortions. On the other hand, the image restored by XT-GAN in Fig. 3(e) appears more natural with even coloring. In Fig. 4, XT-GAN effectively suppresses blurry artifacts and restores the desired contours.

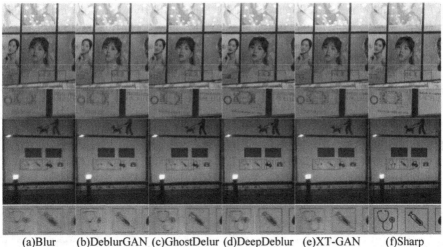

(a)Blur   (b)DeblurGAN (c)GhostDelur (d)DeepDeblur (e)XT-GAN   (f)Sharp

Fig. 4. Performance on the RealBlur-J test dataset

3.4 Ablation Experiment

To validate the effectiveness of the proposed XT module in different positions within the generator network, the combined effectiveness of the three module variations within the XT module, and the integration effect of the XT module's multi-head self-attention with the network, ablation experiments were conducted on the incremental GoPro dataset [1]. The input size for the images was set to 720×1280. Apart from the attention hyperparameter experiments, the Head-Num for W-MSA was uniformly set to 4.

Structural Validity. XT-v1 represents the XT structure using MSA. XT-v2 represents the optimized structure using W-MSA [23]. ADD-XT indicates the fusion of the XT structure with the output features of the FPN upsampling structure in an additive manner. FPN-XT indicates the computation of XT features within the FPN upsampling fusion structure. The effectiveness of the model structures is shown in Table 3.

Table 3. Effectiveness of Network Structures: Ablation Tests

Model	PSNR (dB)	SSIM
XT-v2	29.13	0.923
XT-v1	28.89	0.921
ADD-XT	28.59	0.920
FPN-XT	28.69	0.922
Ghost-Deblur [16]	28.75	0.919

From Table 3, it can be observed that XT can effectively serve as an independent structure for cross-scale feature fusion and provide richer deblurring information compared to using FPN upsampling fusion [16]. However, when XT is combined with the FPN structure features proposed in [16] either through addition (ADD-XT) or sequential combination (FPN-XT), redundant modules with similar functionality are introduced, leading to a decrease in deblurring performance with a PSNR reduction of 0.16dB and 0.06dB, respectively. XT-v2, on the other hand, achieves the best deblurring performance and further enhances the results obtained with XT-v1.

Module Validity. The effectiveness of the individual components of the additional Transformer introduced in this paper was evaluated through ablation experiments, and the results are presented in Table 4.

Table 4. Effectiveness of XT Structures: Ablation Tests

FPN	ST	DT	PT	PSNR	SSIM
√	–	–	–	28.75	0.919
–	√	√	√	29.13	0.923
–	√	√	–	29.06	0.924
–	√	–	√	28.83	0.921
–	–	√	√	27.79	0.921
–	√	–	–	29.02	0.921
–	–	√	–	28.89	0.922
–	–	–	√	28.61	0.917

According to the data in Table 4, it can be observed that using ST, DT, and PT individually resulted in changes in PSNR values of 0.27 dB, 0.14 dB, and −0.14 dB, respectively. The inclusion of ST alone provided a significant amount of informative content and achieved similar performance. Although the individual use of DT and PT did not yield satisfactory results, they contributed additional scale information to ST. The combination of ST, DT, and PT achieved the best overall performance. Compared to using interpolation-based upsampling fusion [16], the XT structure yielded an improvement of 0.38 dB in PSNR and 0.004 in SSIM, indicating enhanced deblurring performance.

Hyperparameters Setting. The difference between MSA (Multi-Head Self-Attention) and SA (Self-Attention) lies in the number of Head-Num, which determines the total number of feature maps output by MSA. Therefore, it is important to choose a reasonable number of Head-Num in MSA. Table 5 presents the effectiveness of different Head-Num values for the network.

It can be observed that the network achieves the best deblurring performance when the Head-Num value is set to 16. It achieves the highest PSNR and SSIM evaluation values of 29.20 dB and 0.925, respectively. However, considering the performance on

Table 5. Effectiveness of different Head-Num values in XT's multi-head attention

Model	PSNR (dB)	SSIM
1	29.02	0.923
2	29.08	0.924
4	29.13	0.923
8	29.01	0.922
16	29.20	0.925
32	29.18	0.924

the RealBlur-J [31] test set, where Head-Num = 4 performs the best, we selected it as the optimal value for the hyperparameter setting.

4 Conclusion

This paper proposes a multi-scale fusion generative adversarial network based on the Transformer architecture, which includes an Encoder-Decoder structure. The Encoder extracts the pyramid features from the GhostNet convolutional network as multi-scale feature inputs. The XT structure combines global and local information and the Decoder restores the image to the original scale. This structure has linear complexity, with a floating-point computation of 120.4G when processing high-resolution images of size 720×1280, and a runtime of only 0.068 s, outperforming conventional networks such as SRN [3] and DeblurGAN-v2 [6]. The effectiveness and robustness of the algorithm are verified on the GoPro and RealBlur-J datasets. The next steps will focus on further optimizing the structure of the XT module and developing backbone networks with higher computational efficiency and better performance tailored to different blurry scenarios.

References

1. Nah, S., Hyun Kim, T., Mu Lee, K.: Deep multi-scale convolutional neural network for dynamic scene deblurring. In: Proceedings of the IEEE Conference on Computer Vision and Pattern Recognition, pp. 3883–3891 (2017)
2. Sun, J., Cao, W., Xu, Z., et al.: Learning a convolutional neural network for non-uniform motion blur removal. In: Proceedings of the IEEE Conference on Computer Vision and Pattern Recognition, pp. 769–777 (2015)
3. Tao, X., Gao, H., Shen, X., et al.: Scale-recurrent network for deep image deblurring. In: Proceedings of the IEEE Conference on Computer Vision and Pattern Recognition, pp. 8174–8182 (2018)
4. Cho, S.J., Ji, S.W., Hong, J.P., et al.: Rethinking coarse-to-fine approach in single image deblurring. In: Proceedings of the IEEE/CVF International Conference on Computer Vision, pp. 4641–4650 (2021)
5. Kupyn, O., Budzan, V., Mykhailych, M., et al.: Deblurgan: blind motion deblurring using conditional adversarial networks. In: Proceedings of the IEEE Conference on Computer Vision and Pattern Recognition, pp. 8183–8192 (2018)

6. Kupyn, O., MaPTyniuk, T., Wu, J., et al.: Deblurgan-v2: deblurring (orders-of-magnitude) faster and better. In: Proceedings of the IEEE/CVF International Conference on Computer Vision, pp. 8878–8887 (2019)

7. Lin, T.Y., Dollár, P., Girshick, R., et al.: Feature pyramid networks for object detection. In: Proceedings of the IEEE Conference on Computer Vision and Pattern Recognition, pp. 2117–2125 (2017)

8. Zhang, K., Luo, W., Zhong, Y., et al.: Deblurring by realistic blurring. In: Proceedings of the IEEE/CVF Conference on Computer Vision and Pattern Recognition, pp. 2737–2746 (2020)

9. Zhang, H., Patel, V.M.: Density-aware single image de-raining using a multi-stream dense network. In: Proceedings of the IEEE Conference on Computer Vision and Pattern Recognition, pp. 695–704 (2018)

10. Vaswani, A., Shazeer, N., Parmar, N., et al.: Attention is all you need. Adv. Neural Inf. Process. Syst. **30** (2017)

11. Simonyan, K., Zisserman, A.: Very deep convolutional networks for large-scale image recognition. arXiv preprint arXiv:1409.1556 (2014)

12. Iizuka, S., Simo-Serra, E., Ishikawa, H.: Globally and locally consistent image completion[J]. ACM Trans. Graph. (ToG) **36**(4), 1–14 (2017)

13. Howard, A., Sandler, M., Chu, G., et al.: Searching for mobilenetv3. In: Proceedings of the IEEE/CVF International Conference on Computer Vision, pp. 1314–1324 (2019)

14. Han, K., Wang, Y., Tian, Q., et al.: Ghostnet: more features from cheap operations. In: Proceedings of the IEEE/CVF Conference on Computer Vision and Pattern Recognition, pp. 1580–1589 (2020)

15. Xia, X., Xu, C., Nan, B.: Inception-v3 for flower classification. In: 2017 2nd International Conference on Image, Vision and Computing (ICIVC), pp. 783–787. IEEE (2017)

16. Liu, Y., Haridevan, A., Schofield, H., et al.: Application of ghost-DeblurGAN to fiducial marker detection. In:2022 IEEE/RSJ International Conference on Intelligent Robots and Systems (IROS), pp. 6827–6832. IEEE (2022)

17. Isola, P., Zhu, J.Y., Zhou, T., et al.: Image-to-image translation with conditional adversarial networks. In: Proceedings of the IEEE Conference on Computer Vision and Pattern Recognition, pp. 1125–1134 (2017)

18. Pan, X., Ge, C., Lu, R., et al.: On the integration of self-attention and convolution. In: Proceedings of the IEEE/CVF Conference on Computer Vision and Pattern Recognition, pp. 815–825 (2022)

19. Liu, S., Wang, H., Wang, J., et al.: Blur-kernel bound estimation from pyramid statistics. IEEE Trans. Circuits Syst. Video Technol. **26**(5), 1012–1016 (2015)

20. 李现国,李滨.基于 Transformer 和多尺度 CNN 的图像去模糊[J/OL].计算机工程1–10 (2023).https://doi.org/10.19678/j.issn.1000-3428.0065513

21. 杨浩,周冬明,赵倩.结合梯度指导和局部增强 Transformer 的图像去模糊网络[J/OL].小型微型计算机系统 1–10 (2023).https://doi.org/10.20009/j.cnki.21-1106/TP.2022-0344

22. 刘婉春,景明利,王子昭等.基于 Transformer 和双残差网络的图像去模糊算法研究[J].信息技术与信息化 **274**(01), 217–220 (2023)

23. Liang, J., Cao, J., Sun, G., et al.: Swinir: image restoration using swin transformer. In: Proceedings of the IEEE/CVF International Conference on Computer Vision, pp. 1833–1844 (2021)

24. Zhang, D., Zhang, H., Tang, J., et al.: Feature pyramid transformer. In: Computer Vision–ECCV 2020: 16th European Conference, Glasgow, UK, August 23–28, 2020, Proceedings, PaPT XXVIII 16, pp. 323–339. Springer, Heidelberg (2020). https://doi.org/10.1007/978-3-030-58604-1_20

25. Dosovitskiy, A., Beyer, L., Kolesnikov, A., et al.: An image is woPTh 16x16 words: transformers for image recognition at scale. arXiv preprint arXiv:2010.11929 (2020)
26. Chen, L., Lu, X., Zhang, J., et al.: Hinet: half instance normalization network for image restoration. In: Proceedings of the IEEE/CVF Conference on Computer Vision and Pattern Recognition, pp. 182–192 (2021)
27. Ledig, C., Theis, L., Huszár, F., et al.: Photo-realistic single image super-resolution using a generative adversarial network. In: Proceedings of the IEEE Conference on Computer Vision and Pattern Recognition, pp. 4681–4690 (2017)
28. Johnson, J., Alahi, A., Fei-Fei, L.: Perceptual losses for real-time style transfer and super-resolution. In: Computer Vision–ECCV 2016: 14th European Conference, Amsterdam, The Netherlands, 11–14 October 2016, Proceedings, PaPT II, vol. 14, pp. 69–711. Springer, Heidelberg (2016). https://doi.org/10.1007/978-3-319-46475-6_43
29. Shrivastava, A., Pfister, T., Tuzel, O., et al.: Learning from simulated and unsupervised images through adversarial training. In: Proceedings of the IEEE Conference on Computer Vision and Pattern Recognition, pp. 2107–2116 (2017)
30. Rim, J., Lee, H., Won, J., et al.: Real-world blur dataset for learning and benchmarking deblurring algorithms. In: Computer Vision–ECCV 2020: 16th European Conference, Glasgow, UK, 23–28 August 2020, Proceedings, PaPT XXV, vol. 16, pp. 184–201. Springer, Heidelberg (2020). https://doi.org/10.1007/978-3-030-58595-2_12
31. Xu, L., Zheng, S., Jia, J.: Unnatural l0 sparse representation for natural image deblurring. In: Proceedings of the IEEE Conference on Computer Vision and Pattern Recognition, pp. 1107–1114 (2013)

Improved AODNet for Fast Image Dehazing

Shiyu Chen[1(✉)], Shumin Liu[1], Xingfeng Chen[1,2], Jiannan Dan[1], and Bingbing Wu[1]

[1] School of Software Engineering, Jiangxi University of Science and Technology,
Nanchang 330013, China
`6720210718@mail.jxust.edu.cn`
[2] Aerospace Information Research Institute, Chinese Academy of Sciences, Beijing 100101,
China

Abstract. Application scenarios such as unmanned driving and UAV reconnaissance have the requirements of high performance, low delay and small space occupation. Images taken in foggy days are easy to be affected by fog or haze, thus losing some important information. The purpose of image dehazing is to remove the influence of fog on image quality, which is of great significance to assist in solving high-level vision tasks. Aiming at the shortcomings of the current defogging method, such as slow defogging speed and poor defogging effect, this paper introduces the idea of FPCNet and the attention mechanism module, and proposes an improved AODNet fast defogging algorithm to ensure the defogging speed and defogging performance. The public dataset RESIDE was used for training and testing. Experimental results show that in terms of dehazing performance, the proposed algorithm achieves 25.78 and 0.992 in PSNR and SSIM respectively. In terms of dehazing speed, the proposed method is close to AODNet, with only 5 times more parameters than AODNet, but more than 100 times smaller than other methods.

Keywords: Fast image dehazing · AODNet · Attention mechanism · FPCNet

1 Introduction

In atmospheric fog or haze environment, large particulate matter absorbs object light and scatters atmospheric light, resulting in visual blur and low image quality, which reduces the processing performance of advanced computer vision tasks (image recognition, target detection, image segmentation, etc.). Therefore, it is of great significance to solve the visual blur in fog in the field of image processing. At present, according to the image dehazing technology, it can be divided into two categories: traditional dehazing methods and deep learning-based dehazing methods [1].

Traditional defogging methods include image enhancement based defogging methods and atmospheric model based image defogging [2]. Image dehazing methods based on image enhancement achieve dehazing through image denoising, improving brightness, contrast and other image indicators, mainly including histogram equalization [3],

C. Wu et al. (Eds.): MONAMI 2023, LNICST 559, pp. 154–165, 2024.
https://doi.org/10.1007/978-3-031-55471-1_12

Retinex algorithm [4], wavelet transform [5], homomorphic filtering [6] and other methods. The main principle of image dehazing methods based on atmospheric model is that the fog map model is constructed based on the atmospheric scattering mechanism, and the haze-free image is solved by statistically estimating the relevant parameter values. The main methods include dark channel dehazing algorithm, dark channel dehazing algorithm based on guided filtering, Bayesian dehazing algorithm, etc. Fattal et al. [7] achieved image dehazing by estimating atmospheric transmittance. He et al. [8] found that in the dark channel map data of more than 5000 haze-free images, about 75% of the pixels had a value of 0, and 90% of the pixels had a very low value, which was concentrated in, and thus proposed the dark channel prior theory. Meng et al. [9] regarded the dehazing problem as an optimization problem based on boundary contrast and regularization, and realized image dehazing based on this theory. The color of a haze-free image is approximately divided into hundreds of different colors, which can form a close cluster in RGB three-dimensional space, and the pixels contained in the cluster are distributed on the entire image plane. In the case of fog, different camera distances can be converted into different transmission coefficients. Therefore, Berman et al. [10] proposed a dehazing method. Zhong et al. [11] used support vector regression to learn a regression model so that it could accurately estimate the transmission map of hazy images. To solve the delay problem, Tarel et al. [12] proposed a dehazing method that makes its complexity linearly related to the number of image pixels. In addition, Zhang Di et al. [13] used the improved dark channel method to realize atmospheric light estimation, but the dehazing performance could not be guaranteed.

In recent years, deep learning technology has been applied to the field of image dehazing. The dehazing methods based on deep learning can be divided into indirect deep learning dehazing methods and direct deep learning dehazing methods. Among them, the indirect deep learning dehazing method constructs an estimation model based on the deep network, so that the network model learns various atmospheric parameters in the training samples, and inverts the haze-free image based on the atmospheric parameters. The basic principle of direct deep learning dehazing method is that the model is separated from the atmospheric scattering model through large sample learning. The input value is the fog map, and the output value is the dehazing map.

Cai et al. [14] constructed a DehazeNet network through convolutional neural network to learn the foggy images and predict the foggy media transmission map. Li et al. [15] proposed an end-to-end dehazing method to avoid large image dehazing errors caused by intermediate parameter estimation. On this basis, to realize image dehazing, Ren et al. [16] proposed a multi-scale convolutional neural network. Ju Qingqing et al. [17] constructed three convolution kernels of different scales to convolve the hazy image and obtain a rough transmittance map through feature learning of different scales, but the dehazing delay of this method is large. Mei et al. [18] proposed an end-to-end deep learning dehazing method based on the U-net model, which was composed of an encoding block, a feature extraction block and a decoding block. Qin et al. [19] proposed an end-to-end feature fusion attention network, which is composed of a basic block and a feature attention module, and the basic block is composed of a multi-level residual model and an attention module. In order to achieve effective feature extraction, the direct dehazing method based on deep learning needs to build a deeper network to ensure the image dehazing performance, but it will bring problems such as complex model, huge parameters and high calculation delay.

In summary, the current main dehazing methods only focus on the dehazing performance, and ignore the model footprint, dehazing speed and other indicators. Especially in the field of unmanned driving, UAV reconnaissance and other fields that rely on computer vision, the landing of such technology not only requires the algorithm to overcome all kinds of complex and adverse weather, but also needs to meet the advantages of low delay and small space occupation. Therefore, it is of great significance to propose an image dehazing algorithm with good dehazing performance, low dehazing delay and small space occupation.

In order to better balance the two aspects of dehazing speed and dehazing performance, this paper introduces the idea of FPCNet [20] and the attention mechanism module, and proposes an improved AODNet fast dehazing model, which improves the expression ability of the network and reduces the complexity of the network, and enhances the network's learning of the depth of field fog characteristics to a certain extent. Under the condition of ensuring the dehazing speed of AODNet, the performance of dehazing is improved.

2 AODNet Image Dehazing

2.1 Atmospheric Scattering Model

In foggy scenes, due to atmospheric occlusion, interference from large particulate matter and other reasons, the light of interfering objects enters the camera system through reflection and refraction, resulting in blurred vision and incomplete image information. The formation process of fog map is shown in Fig. 1.

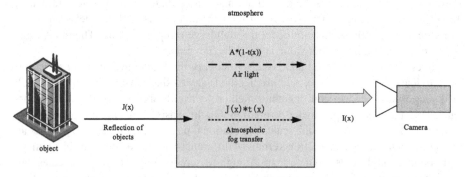

Fig. 1. Schematic diagram of the atmospheric scattering model

In Fig. 1, $I(x)$ is the hazy image taken by the camera, and $J(x)$ is the haze-free image of the corresponding scene. Based on the formation mechanism of atmospheric fog, the construction model of hazy image can be expressed as follows.

$$I(x) = J(x)t(x) + A(1 - t(x)) \qquad (1)$$

Where, A is the atmospheric light value, $t(x)$ is the atmospheric transmittance, and $t(x)$ is defined as, $t(x) = e^{-\beta d(x)}$, β is the scattering coefficient, and $d(x)$ represents the depth information of the pixel.

According to the atmospheric light value A and transmittance $t(x)$, the haze-free image $I(x)$ can be inverted from the hazy image $J(x)$, as shown in Eq. 2:

$$J(x) = \frac{I(x) - A}{t(x)} + A \qquad (2)$$

Equation 2 shows that the atmospheric light value and transmittance can be obtained by solving the haze-free image requirements. However, the obtained actual fog image cannot accurately estimate the value to obtain the optimal defogging effect, and the corresponding value can only be estimated by the atmospheric model and inversion to obtain the defogging image.

2.2 AODNet Dehazing

The dehazing algorithm based on convolutional neural network constructed by AODNet can realize end-to-end image dehazing. By estimating the atmospheric light value and transmittance at one time, that is, replacing A and t(x) with variable K(x) as a whole:

$$K(x) = \frac{(I(x) - A)/t + (A - 1)}{I(x) - 1} \qquad (3)$$

Thus, the fog image model shown in Eq. (3) can be re-expressed as follows:

$$J(x) = K(x)I(x) - K(x) + 1 \qquad (4)$$

The integrated variables $K(x)$ replace the transmittance and atmospheric light values after making the dependence on the fog map I(x) only. Based on the above single functional relationship, it can be obtained $K(x)$ by optimizing each weight parameter in the network through continuous iteration of deep learning, avoiding the empirical evaluation of transmittance and atmospheric light value. Compared with the traditional defogging methods, on the one hand, by constructing a convolutional neural network, the haze-free image is used as a label for training and learning, and then the value $K(x)$ is predicted and tends to the optimal value, so as to realize the image defogging function.On the other hand, simplifying the estimation of two different values into one value estimation can reduce the error accumulation, simplify the overall process, greatly reduce the processing delay compared with the traditional method, and improve the dehazing speed to a certain extent (Fig. 2).

Compared with the existing deep learning defogging algorithms, AODNet's defogging speed is a highlight. The design idea of network model and the core idea of defogging based on atmospheric model are worthy of reference. However, AODNet has the disadvantage of poor dehazing effect in removing fog images such as dark fog and thick fog [21]. Figure 3 shows the effect of AODNet to remove dark fog and thick fog, respectively.

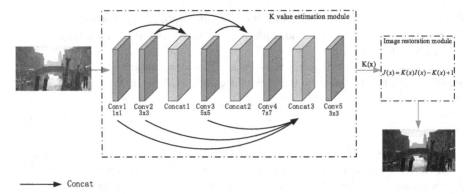

Fig. 2. Schematic diagram of AODNet network model

| Ground truth | Hazy image | AOD dehazing effect |

Fig. 3. Comparison of AODNet dehazing effect

3 Improved AODNet for Dehazing

Aiming at the problems of incomplete dehazing and loss of detailed information in AODNet dehazing algorithm, the idea and attention mechanism module of FPCNet are introduced into the dehazing algorithm proposed in this paper. Figure 4 is the overall network architecture of this paper. The network consists of two parts, k value estimation module and image restoration module. The part to the left of AB in the k value estimation module is called the feature extraction module. The feature extraction module is improved on the basis of the structure of the original AOD, and consists of four 1x1 convolution operations, three pooling operations of different sizes, and three feature concatenation operations. The AB and the right part of the k value estimation module are called feature enhancement module, which is composed of an attention mechanism and two layers of convolution. The attention mechanism can make the model realize self-attention of image features when dealing with local image information such as defogging brightness and dark, so as to solve problems such as dark local defogging. Finally, through the image restoration module, the value of k estimated by the model was substituted into the atmospheric scattering model to obtain the clear image J(x).

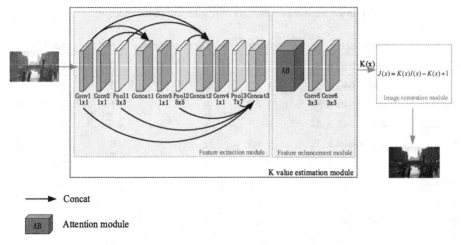

Concat

AB Attention module

Fig. 4. Schematic of the overall network model in this paper

3.1 Feature Extraction Module

In order to improve the feature representation ability of AOD-Net, inspired by the full pointwise convolution unit of FPC-Net, this paper uses pointwise convolution and different sizes of pooling to replace the large-scale convolution in AODNet. This improved method can not only effectively improve the expression ability of the network for features, make the network more compact, but also reduce the overfitting phenomenon during training to a certain extent [22]. In addition, this paper believes that it is necessary to fuse the features of Conv1 into the Concat2 fusion layer. It is found through experiments that such optimization can improve the network's ability to process the depth of field fog to a certain extent.

The network structure of the feature extraction module consists of four 1x1 convolution operations, three pooling operations of different sizes, and three feature concatenation operations. Among them, the size of the convolution kernel of each pointwise convolution is 1×1, the 1×1 pointwise convolution layer of the input layer is followed by no pooling layer and batch normalization layer, and the remaining pointwise convolution will connect the batch normalization layer, ReLU activation function and pooling layer. The first pooling layer has a kernel size of 3×3 and a padding value of 1, the second pooling layer has a kernel size of 5×5 and a padding value of 2, and the third pooling layer has a kernel size of 7×7 and a padding value of 3 with a step size of 1 for each convolution kernel and pooling layer. Concat1 is concatenated from conv1, conv2, concat2 is concatenated from conv1, pool1, pool2, and concat3 is concatenated from conv1, pool1, pool2, and pool3. The details of the network parameters of the feature extraction module are shown in Table 1.

Table 1. Network parameters of feature extraction module

	Input Size	Filter	Filter Number	Pad	Stride
Conv1	480 × 640 × 3	1 × 1	32	0	1
Conv2	480 × 640 × 32	1 × 1	32	0	1
Pool1	480 × 640 × 32	3 × 3	—	1	1
Concat1	480 × 640 × 64	—	—	—	—
Conv3	480 × 640 × 32	1 × 1	32	0	1
Pool2	480 × 640 × 32	5 × 5	—	2	1
Concat2	480 × 640 × 96	—	—	—	—
Conv4	480 × 640 × 32	1 × 1	32	0	1
Pool3	480 × 640 × 32	7 × 7	—	3	1
Concat3	480 × 640 × 128	—	—	—	—

3.2 Attention Mechanism Module

Image quality and details may be affected to different degrees when performing operations such as object classification, compression, and restoration on images, which may affect subsequent high-level vision tasks. In order to overcome the influence of image quality differences on the dehazing effect, this paper adds an attention mechanism module based on the improved AODNet model, so as to solve the shortcomings of dark image dehazing and low generalization of the model limited by samples. The fusion of channel attention mechanism and spatial attention mechanism enables the model to realize self-attention of image features when dealing with local image information such as defogging bright and dark, and ensures that the model solves problems such as local dark defogging (Fig. 5).

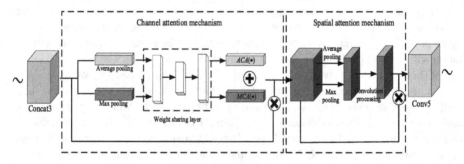

Fig. 5. Schematic of the attention mechanism module

The attention module adopted in this paper is jointly composed of a channel attention module and a spatial attention module. Firstly, the feature maps obtained by concat3 were processed by average pooling and maximum pooling respectively to realize the channel feature map processing from 3D feature map to 2D. Secondly, the channel feature maps after two processing are processed by a 1* 1 convolution kernel to realize adaptive channel weight calculation. The corresponding positions of the channel weights obtained by the two are added together, which is expressed as:

$$AMCA(K) = ACA(K) + MCA(K) \tag{5}$$

Thirdly, the added weights were normalized by the sigmoid function. Finally, the spatial attention weights are multiplied with the input feature map K to achieve the same dimension, and the channel self-attention is expressed as follows:

$$CA(K) = K * sig\text{mod}(AMCA(K)) \tag{6}$$

The feature maps $CA(K)$ obtained after processing by the channel attention mechanism are firstly used as the input values of the spatial attention module to undergo average pooling and maximum pooling operations respectively. Secondly, the results of the two pooling were concatenated together. Thirdly, the sigmoid function was used to normalize the weights to ensure that the weights were within a reasonable range. Finally, the weights are multiplied with the input values $CA(K)$ to achieve the corresponding position, and the feature map is output to conv5.

4 Experiment and Analysis

4.1 Experimental Scheme

Dataset. In this paper, the public Reside- β dataset is used as the data source. The training set is composed of 2061 clear outdoor images each generating 35 types of synthetic fog images, and the synthetic fog atmospheric light values A = [0.8,0.85,0.9,0.95, 1], β = [0.04,0.06,0.08,0. 1,0. 12,0.16,0.2] are obtained. A total of 72135 synthetic fog images are obtained. The test Set is selected from the outdoor data set of OTS (Objective Testing Set), which consists of 500 images.

Experimental Environment. The experimental environment of this paper is as follows: Win10 operating system, processor InterlCore i5-12400F CPU, GTX 3060TI GPU accelerated computing, python3.8 programming language, and Pytorch deep learning framework.

Parameter Setting. The clear image is taken as the true label, the MSE defines the model loss function, the Gaussian random variable is used to initialize the weight value of the network model, the initial learning rate is set to 0.0001, and the momentum and decay are set to. The Adam optimizer was used to realize the loss convergence to minimize, and the weight update optimization model of the network was trained, with a total of 50 iterations.

4.2 Comparative Analysis of Dehazing Performance

Because the synthetic fog image is synthesized from the clear image through the atmospheric scattering model, the corresponding clear image can be found when evaluating the defogging performance of the synthetic fog image. PSNR and SSIM are used as the classical image quality indicators to quantify the defogging performance of various algorithms, and the higher the value is, the better the image quality is. PSNR indicates how close the dehazed image is to the original image, and SSIM describes the structural similarity between the dehazed image and the haze-free image.

Table 2 lists the index results of the synthetic fog data set OTS (Outdoor) tested by each method. The data PSNR and SSIM in the table are obtained by taking the average value last. The algorithm in this paper performs better than other algorithms, reaching 25.78 and 0.992. The proposed algorithm improves the feature extraction ability of the original AODNet, so that the image restoration effect is more excellent.

As shown in Fig. 6, some dehazing maps are selected from OTS (Outdoor) test results for subjective evaluation. DCP dehazing is prone to color distortion and halo phenomenon, and the overall brightness is dark. Although the overall dehazing effect of FFA is good, the effect is often not very impressive in the case of low image contrast. Some of the results of PFF dehazing appear dark shadows, and there are a lot of fog residue. GCA needs to be improved in removing dark fog, and the color reproduction is not high. After AOD dehazing, there are some fog residues in the image, and the image details cannot be restored well. The defogging images obtained by the proposed algorithm have high color fidelity, obvious defogging effect, and satisfactory defogging quality.

Table 2. Comparison of synthetic fog dehazing performance of different algorithms

	PSNR	SSIM
DCP	16.57	0.941
FFANet	23.34	0.989
GCANet	20.94	0.960
PFFNet	19.96	0.982
AODNet	22.97	0.976
Our model	25.78	0.992

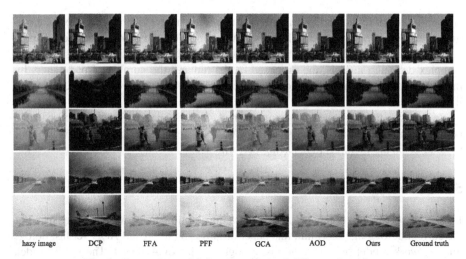

hazy image   DCP   FFA   PFF   GCA   AOD   Ours   Ground truth

Fig. 6. Comparison of defogging effects of different algorithms

4.3 Comparative Analysis of Dehazing Speed

In order to compare the dehazing speed of various dehazing algorithms, the dehazing speed of each algorithm is compared in the same experimental environment, and the time consumed by various dehazing algorithms to process 500 fog images of OTS dataset is counted. Table 3 lists the average dehazing time of a single image. Since the DCP dehazing method is the traditional dehazing method, there is no model parameter value, and the deep learning models are all calculated by GPU acceleration under the same conditions, as shown in the table.

Table 3. Dehazing time for different dehazing algorithms

	time (s)	Programming languages	Number of parameters
DCP	0.0754	Python	X
FFANet	0.4892	Python	16.998 MB
GCANet	0.0573	Python	2.681 MB
PFFNet	0.0223	Python	57.038 MB
AODNet	0.0258	Python	0.0067 MB
Our model	0.0392	Python	0.0269 MB

According to the table, in terms of dehazing speed, PFFNet has the fastest dehazing speed, followed by AODNet and FFANet has the slowest dehazing speed. Because FFANet and GCANet both construct a deeper dehazing model, the dehazing speed is slow. The proposed model is only slightly lower than AODNet, and the average dehazing time of a single image is 0.0392 s. Although the number of parameters can not reflect the operation time of the model, it can reflect whether the model is more complex. In terms of the number of parameters, PFFNet, GCANet and FFANet construct more complex dehazing models, while AODNet constructs a lightweight dehazing model. For more complex dehazing models, the proposed model reduces the number of parameters by more than 100 times, and only increases the number of parameters by 4 times than the lightweight AODNet.

In general, the improved dehazing method in this paper achieves a good balance between time and performance, is close to AODNet in dehazing speed, and is superior to other dehazing methods in dehazing performance.

5 Summary

In order to solve the problems of large space consumption and slow defogging speed of the current defogging algorithm, this paper proposes an improved AODNet fast defogging network model based on the fast defogging idea of AODNet. The FPCNet idea is introduced to replace the convolution of AODNet with point-wise convolution and pooling operation. The features of the second feature concatenation layer and the first convolutional layer are fused to form a dense connection structure, and the attention mechanism is introduced to make up for the shortcomings of AODNet in dehazing details. The experimental results on OTS synthetic fog data set show that the proposed dehazing algorithm is superior to the traditional algorithm and deep learning algorithm in the classic image quality indicators PSNR and SSIM. The parameter amount is reduced by more than 100 times, and the dehazing speed can reach an average of 0.0392 s per image. A good balance among performance, space and time is achieved.

References

1. Xie, Y., Jia, H., Wang, T., Lei, C., Xu, K., Chen, Q.: Review of image dehazing algorithms∗. Comput. Dig. Eng. **50**(12), 2765–2774 (2022)
2. Wu, D., Zhu, Q.: Research progress of image dehazing. Acta Automatica Sinica **41**(2), 221–239 (2015)
3. Jiang, H., Yang, Z., Zhang, X.: Research progress of image dehazing algorithm. J. Jilin Univ. Eng. Technol. Ed. **51**(4), 1169–1181 (2021)
4. Li, X.: Image enhancement algorithm Based on Retinex theory. Comput. Appl. Res. **22**(2), 235–237 (2005)
5. Chen, S., Cao, S., Cui, M.Y.: Blind image deblurring algorithm based on deep multilevel wavelet transform. J. Electron. Inf. Technol. **43**(1), 1–8 (2021)
6. Ma, X.: Ship image enhancement method based on homomorphic filtering. Ship Sci. Technol. **42**(6), 89–91 (2020)
7. Fattel, R.: Single image dehazing. ACM Trans. Graph. **27**(3), 721–728 (2008)
8. He, K., Sun, J., Tang, X.O.: Single image haze removal using dark channel prior. IEEE Trans. Pattern Anal. Mach. Intell. **33**(12), 2341–2353 (2011)
9. Meng, G.F., Wang, Y., Duan, J.H., et al.: Efficient image dehazing with boundary constraint and contextual regularization. In: IEEE International Conference on Computer Vision, pp. 617–624 (2013)
10. Berman, D., Treibitz, T., Avidan, S.: Non-local image dehazing. In: IEEE Conference on Computer Vision and Pattern Recognition (CVPR) (2016)

11. Zhong, L., Shang, Y., Zhou, X., et al.: Fast single image dehazing based on a regression model. Neurocomputing **245**, 10–22 (2017)
12. Tarel, J.-P., Hautiere, N.: Fast visibility restoration from a single color or gray level image. In: IEEE 12th International Conference on Computer Vision, pp. 2201–2208 (2009)
13. Zhang, D., Wu, P.: Fast dehazing algorithm for single image. Comput. Eng. Appl. **55**(10), 213–217 (2019)
14. Cai, B., Xu, X., Jia, K., et al.: DehazeNet: an end-to-end system for single image haze removal. IEEE Trans. Image Process. **25**(11), 5187–5198 (2016)
15. Li, B., Peng, X., Wang, Z., Xu, J., Feng, D.: Aod-net: all-in-one dehazing network. In: IEEE International Conference on Computer Vision, pp. 4770–4778 (2017)
16. Ren, W., Liu, S., Zhang, H., et al.: Single image dehazing via multi-scale convolutional neural networks. In: Leibe, B., Matas, J., Sebe, N., Welling, M. (eds.) Computer Vision-ECCV, pp. 154–169. Springer, Heidelberg (2016). https://doi.org/10.1007/978-3-319-46475-6_10
17. Ju, Q., Li, C., Sang, Q.: Single image dehazing method based on improved multi-scale convolutional Neural Network. Comput. Eng. Appl. **55**(10), 179–185 (2019)
18. Mei, K., Jiang, A., Li, J., et al.: Progressive feature fusion network for realistic image dehazing (2018)
19. Qin, X., Wang, Z., Bai, Y., et al.: FFA-net: feature fusion attention network for single image dehazing. In: Proceedings of the AAAI Conference on Artificial Intelligence (2020)
20. Zhang, J., Tao, D.: FAMED-net: a fast and accurate multi-scale end-to-end dehazing network. IEEE Trans. Image Process. **29**, 72–84 (2019)
21. Tran, L.-A., Moon, S., Park, D.-C.: A novel encoder-decoder network with guided transmission map for single image dehazing. Procedia Comput. Sci. **204**, 682–689 (2022)
22. Zhang, J., Cao, Y., Wang, Y., Zha, Z.J., Wen, C., Chen, C.W.: Fully point-wise convolutional neural network for modeling statistical regularities in natural images. ArXiv (2018)

Image Classification Algorithm for Graphite Ore Carbon Grade Based on Multi-scale Feature Fusion

Xueyu Huang[1,2], Haoyu Shi[1(✉)], Yaokun Liu[1], and Haoran Lu[1]

[1] School of Software Engineering, Jiangxi University of Science and Technology,
Nanchang 330013, China
qq437211826@163.com
[2] Key Laboratory of Virtual Digital Factory and Cultural Communication, Jiangxi University of
Science and Technology, Nanchang 330013, China

Abstract. Based on the tedious process of using a carbon-sulfur analyzer to detect the carbon grade of graphite in graphite mining production, this paper proposes a graphite carbon grade image recognition and classification method based on multi-scale feature fusion. The experiment preprocesses the images and constructs a residual network model that combines pyramid convolution (PyConv) and spatial attention mechanism (SAM). This model enhances the extraction of both global and local feature information from graphite images. Transfer learning is introduced by using pre-trained weights to accelerate the convergence of the model, achieving efficient and accurate recognition and classification of graphite carbon grade with an accuracy of 92.5%, surpassing traditional machine learning methods using single features. The experimental results demonstrate that the neural network model constructed in this paper effectively extracts texture and color features from graphite images, improving the accuracy of graphite image classification and recognition. The model exhibits good robustness and provides valuable insights for practical graphite mining production.

Keywords: Pyramid Convolution · Residual Network · Graphite Ore Carbon Grade · Image Classification · Attention Mechanism

1   Introduction

With the development of the new energy field, graphite has a wide range of applications as a negative electrode in the new energy industry. In the process of graphite mining and production, timely prediction of the carbon grade of graphite ore is particularly important. Traditionally, high-frequency infrared carbon-sulfur analyzers have been used for carbon grade determination in graphite mining [1, 2]. However, this method requires manual labor, time, and incurs costs such as machine wear and tear. With the advancement of industrial intelligence, mining production methods are gradually becoming more intelligent [3]. Therefore, proposing an efficient and convenient method for carbon grade detection in graphite mining is of significant practical importance.

© ICST Institute for Computer Sciences, Social Informatics and Telecommunications Engineering 2024
Published by Springer Nature Switzerland AG 2024. All Rights Reserved
C. Wu et al. (Eds.): MONAMI 2023, LNICST 559, pp. 166–177, 2024.
https://doi.org/10.1007/978-3-031-55471-1_13

Image recognition technology is one of the key areas in artificial intelligence. It aims to enable machines to mimic human image recognition systems and achieve recognition of complex images through processing information at different levels of the image. In traditional image recognition, the focus is on extracting features such as shape, texture, and color from the images [4–6]. Classification is typically performed using methods such as Support Vector Machine (SVM) [7], Random Forest (RF) [8], K-Nearest Neighbor (KNN) [9], and Back Propagation Neural Network (BPNN) [10]. However, traditional image recognition methods rely on manually extracting features and are limited in their ability to extract higher-dimensional features.

In recent years, with the continuous development of deep learning, its application in the field of image recognition has become increasingly widespread. Deep learning models, through multi-layer convolutional neural network structures, autonomously learn and extract more representative features [11, 12]. This enables various applications such as image recognition and classification, and has found extensive use in industrial domains. Chen Weihao et al. [13] proposed a deep residual neural network (ResNet) model that incorporates transfer learning methods for automatic classification of seven types of rock images. Cheng Guojian et al. [14] presented a deep learning-based automatic classification method for rock particle sizes using convolutional neural networks. Bai Lin et al. [15] utilized deep learning methods for rock identification and successfully extracted minerals from various types of rocks, demonstrating the effectiveness of deep learning in rock recognition. Bai Lin and Wei Xin [16] attempted to apply deep learning methods to thin section image classification and developed a VGG model for thin section classification of rocks. Liu Xiaobo et al. [17] employed a simplified VGG16 as the base feature extraction network within the Faster R-CNN deep learning object detection framework, creating a model for recognizing rock image categories.

Deep learning has achieved significant progress and development in the field of rock image recognition. However, most experiments have focused on distinguishing different types of rocks, while there has been limited research on identifying the content of a specific substance within the same type of rock.

To address the aforementioned situation and problem, this paper proposes an image recognition and classification method for graphite ore carbon grade based on multiscale feature fusion. In the feature extraction stage of this approach, a pyramid structure neural network is employed, which consists of filters with different types, sizes, and depths, as well as grouped convolutions. This network extracts texture features and color features at different levels of the image. Furthermore, a spatial attention mechanism is introduced to localize the regions of interest, reducing the receptive field and improving context modeling. The extracted feature information is then fused. The fused features comprehensively capture the texture and color information of graphite ore images from multiple scales and levels. This enables more accurate identification and classification of graphite ore carbon grade.

The main contributions of this paper are as follows:

1) In the process of graphite ore image classification, the introduction of transfer learning allows for the full utilization of the generic features learned by a pre-trained model on a large-scale dataset. By fine-tuning the model for the specific task of graphite

ore image classification, the performance and generalization ability of the model are significantly improved, accelerating the training process.

2) To address the challenges of diverse textures and complex feature extraction in graphite ore images, a residual network based on pyramid convolution is utilized. By stacking convolutions with different sizes, this network can effectively capture multi-scale features.

3) To capture the differences and importance among different regions in graphite ore images, a spatial attention mechanism is incorporated. This mechanism automatically learns the significance of different regions and focuses on the most informative areas, enabling more accurate feature extraction, improving classification performance, and enhancing the robustness of the model.

In Sect. 2, the structure and details of the multi-scale feature fusion method for graphite ore carbon grade image classification are presented. Section 3 discusses the experimental setup, result analysis, and method comparisons. Finally, Sect. 4 concludes the paper.

2   Multi-scale Feature Fusion Method for Graphite Ore Carbon Grade Image Classification

This paper proposes a multi-scale feature fusion method for graphite ore carbon grade image classification, as illustrated in Fig. 1. Firstly, the graphite ore images are pre-processed. Secondly, the pyramid convolutional network, combined with the spatial attention mechanism, extracts multi-dimensional features from the preprocessed images and integrates them. Lastly, the features from different levels are fused, and the classification is performed using a classifier, resulting in a robust and high-accuracy model. This approach achieves the classification and recognition of various grades of graphite ore.

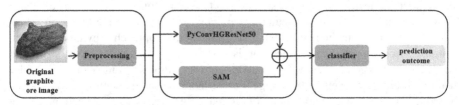

Fig. 1. Flowchart of the Proposed Method

2.1   Experimental Raw Data

Currently, there is a scarcity of publicly available graphite ore image datasets. The image data used in this experiment were collected from graphite mines by experienced professionals. The data were captured and annotated by professional personnel and equipment. To increase the size of the experimental dataset, multiple angles of the same sample were photographed to capture different regions. The accurate carbon grade data for each sample was determined using a conventional carbon-sulfur analyzer, which was then matched with the corresponding images to create the final graphite ore carbon grade dataset. The overall carbon grade of the image dataset ranges from 0% to 20% and can be categorized into four classes: low-grade graphite ore (0% to 5%), relatively low-grade graphite ore (5% to 10%), relatively high-grade graphite ore (10% to 15%), and high-grade graphite ore (15% to 20%). Some original images from the experiment are shown in Fig. 2.

(a)0%~5%   (b)5%~10%   (c)10%~15%   (d)15%~20%

Fig. 2. Examples of Graphite Ore Samples with Different Carbon Grades

Each image has a resolution of 6000x4000 pixels, and a total of 8159 images were used in this study. All images are in.JPG format. The dataset was randomly divided into training and testing sets in an 8:2 ratio for each class of images. The training set consists of 6529 images, while the testing set consists of 1630 images. The distribution of the graphite ore image dataset for each class is shown in Table 1.

Table 1. Distribution of Graphite Ore Image Dataset

Dataset Type	Different Carbon Grade Graphite Ores				Total Count
	0%–5%	5% ~ 10%	10%–15%	15%–20%	
Total Count	1207	1729	3286	1937	8159
Training Set	966	1383	2629	1550	6529
Testing Set	241	346	657	387	1630

2.2 Graphite Ore Image Feature Extraction

Multi-scale Feature Extraction Based on Pyramid Convolution

Pyramid Convolution Structure (PyConv)

Graphite ore surfaces exhibit high complexity in terms of texture features, and the diverse texture distribution resulting from multi-angle image acquisition further increases the complexity. To capture the variability of different categories and their scale variations, using a single type of convolutional kernel (e.g., standard convolution) and a single spatial size may not be the optimal solution for addressing this complexity. Therefore, the conventional convolutional neural networks (e.g., ResNet50) for image feature extraction have limitations.

The pyramid convolution structure consists of convolutional kernels of different levels, sizes, and depths. In addition to enlarging the receptive field, PyConv can process inputs in parallel using different-sized convolutional kernels to capture details at different levels. Apart from these advantages, after designing its structure, PyConv can maintain a similar number of parameters and computational costs as standard convolution. Therefore, we adopt pyramid convolution to replace traditional convolution and construct a pyramid convolutional neural network.

The pyramid convolution, as shown in Fig. 3, consists of n layers of convolutional kernels with different types, without increasing computational cost or model complexity. At each level of PyConv, the spatial size of the convolutional kernels varies, starting from the bottom of the pyramid (Level 1 of PyConv) and gradually increasing towards the top (Level n of PyConv). Simultaneously, as the spatial size increases, the depth of the convolutional kernels decreases from Level 1 to Level n. At each level of PyConv, convolutional kernels of different depths are used, and the input feature maps are divided into different groups. The convolutional kernels are independently applied to each group of input feature maps, which is known as grouped convolution.

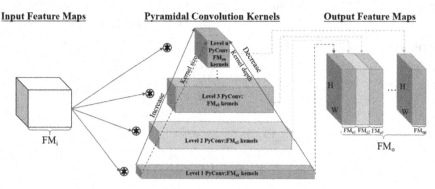

Fig. 3. Proposed Pyramidal Convolution Structure Model

As shown in Fig. 3, for the input feature map FM_i, at each level $\{1, 2, 3, \ldots, n\}$ of PyConv, different convolutional kernels $\{K_1^2, K_2^2, K_3^2, \ldots, K_n^2\}$ with different spatial sizes and different convolutional kernel depths $\{FM_i, \frac{FM_i}{\left(\frac{K_2^2}{K_1^2}\right)}, \frac{FM_i}{\left(\frac{K_2^2}{K_1^2}\right)}, \ldots, \frac{FM_i}{\left(\frac{K_n^2}{K_1^2}\right)}\}$ are applied. This results in different numbers of output feature maps $\{FM_{o1}, FM_{o2}, FM_{o3}, \ldots, FM_{on}\}$ (with height H and width W). Therefore, the number of parameters and computational cost (in terms of FLOPs) of PyConv are given by:

$$
\begin{vmatrix}
parameters = \\
K_n^2 \cdot \frac{FM_i}{\left(\frac{K_n^2}{K_1^2}\right)} \cdot FM_{o_n} + \\
\vdots \\
K_2^2 \cdot \frac{FM_i}{\left(\frac{K_2^2}{K_1^2}\right)} \cdot FM_{o2} + \\
K_1^2 \cdot FM_i \cdot FM_{o1};
\end{vmatrix}
\begin{vmatrix}
FLOPs = \\
K_n^2 \cdot \frac{FM_i}{\left(\frac{K_n^2}{K_1^2}\right)} \cdot FM_{o_n} \cdot (W \cdot H) + \\
\vdots \\
K_2^2 \cdot \frac{FM_i}{\left(\frac{K_2^2}{K_1^2}\right)} \cdot FM_{o2} \cdot (W \cdot H) + \\
K_1^2 \cdot FM_i \cdot FM_{o1} \cdot (W \cdot H),
\end{vmatrix}
\tag{1}
$$

In the Eq. (1), each row represents the parameter count and computational cost of one level of PyConv. If each level of PyConv outputs an equal number of feature maps, then the parameter count and computational cost of PyConv will be evenly distributed across each level of the pyramid. From the equation, it can be observed that regardless of the number of levels in PyConv and the spatial size of the convolutional kernels, its computational cost and parameter count are similar to that of a standard convolution with a single kernel size $K_1{}^2$.

Pyramid Residual Network Structure
Based on the ResNet residual module, the pyramid convolution is incorporated. Table 2 presents a comparison between PyConvResNet and the baseline architecture ResNet, showcasing a 50-layer deep network scenario. It also demonstrates a higher group number architecture of PyConv, called PyConvHGResNet, where the group number is set to a minimum of 32 and a maximum of 64. The feature map quantity for spatial convolution is doubled to provide better spatial filtering capability, which slightly increases the number of FLOPs.

Table 2. Comparison of PyConvResNet and PyConvHGResNet

Stage	output	ResNet-50	PyConvResNet-50	PyConvHGResNet-50
	112 × 112	7 × 7,64, stride 2	7 × 7,64,stride 2	7 × 7,64,stride 2
		3 × 3max pool, stride 2		

(continued)

Table 2. (*continued*)

Stage	output	ResNet-50	PyConvResNet-50	PyConvHGResNet-50
Stage1	56 × 56	$\begin{bmatrix} 1 \times 1, 64 \\ 3 \times 3, 64 \\ 1 \times 1, 256 \end{bmatrix} \times 3$	$\begin{bmatrix} 1 \times 1, 64 \\ \text{PyConv4, 64 :} \\ \begin{bmatrix} 9 \times 9, 16, G = 16 \\ 7 \times 7, 16, G = 8 \\ 5 \times 5, 16, G = 4 \\ 3 \times 3, 16, G = 1 \end{bmatrix} \\ 1 \times 1, 256 \end{bmatrix} \times 3$	$\begin{bmatrix} 1 \times 1, 128 \\ \text{PyConv4, 128 :} \\ \begin{bmatrix} 9 \times 9, 32, G = 32 \\ 7 \times 7, 32, G = 32 \\ 5 \times 5, 32, G = 32 \\ 3 \times 3, 32, G = 32 \end{bmatrix} \\ 1 \times 1, 256 \end{bmatrix} \times 3$
Stage2	28 × 28	$\begin{bmatrix} 1 \times 1, 128 \\ 3 \times 3, 128 \\ 1 \times 1, 512 \end{bmatrix} \times 4$	$\begin{bmatrix} 1 \times 1, 128 \\ \text{PyConv3, 128 :} \\ \begin{bmatrix} 7 \times 7, 64, G = 8 \\ 5 \times 5, 32, G = 4 \\ 3 \times 3, 32, G = 1 \end{bmatrix} \\ 1 \times 1, 512 \end{bmatrix} \times 4$	$\begin{bmatrix} 1 \times 1, 256 \\ \text{PyConv3, 256 :} \\ \begin{bmatrix} 7 \times 7, 128, G = 64 \\ 5 \times 5, 64, G = 64 \\ 3 \times 3, 64, G = 32 \end{bmatrix} \\ 1 \times 1, 512 \end{bmatrix} \times 4$
Stage3	14 × 14	$\begin{bmatrix} 1 \times 1, 256 \\ 3 \times 3, 256 \\ 1 \times 1, 1024 \end{bmatrix} \times 6$	$\begin{bmatrix} 1 \times 1, 256 \\ \text{PyConv2, 256 :} \\ \begin{bmatrix} 5 \times 5, 128, G = 4 \\ 3 \times 3, 128, G = 1 \end{bmatrix} \\ 1 \times 1, 1024 \end{bmatrix} \times 6$	$\begin{bmatrix} 1 \times 1, 512 \\ \text{PyConv2, 512 :} \\ \begin{bmatrix} 5 \times 5, 256, G = 64 \\ 3 \times 3, 256, G = 32 \end{bmatrix} \\ 1 \times 1, 1024 \end{bmatrix} \times 6$
Stage4	7 × 7	$\begin{bmatrix} 1 \times 1, 512 \\ 3 \times 3, 512 \\ 1 \times 1, 2048 \end{bmatrix} \times 3$	$\begin{bmatrix} 1 \times 1, 512 \\ \text{PyConv1, 512 :} \\ [3 \times 3, 512, G = 1] \\ 1 \times 1, 2048 \end{bmatrix} \times 3$	$\begin{bmatrix} 1 \times 1, 1024 \\ \text{PyConv1, 1024 :} \\ [3 \times 3, 1024, G = 32] \\ 1 \times 1, 2048 \end{bmatrix} \times 3$
	1 × 1	global avg pool 1000-d fc	global avg pool 1000-d fc	global avg pool 1000-d fc
FLOPs		4.14×10^9	3.88×10^9	4.61×10^9
#params		25.56×10^6	24.85×10^6	25.23×10^6

Spatial Attention Mechanism (SAM)

Introducing the spatial attention mechanism into the model enables adaptive allocation of attention weights, focusing on the most informative and important regions in the image. This enhances the model's ability to capture and understand key features, improving the accuracy and robustness of image processing tasks. In this study, the spatial attention module is placed before the first residual structure and after the last residual structure. Figure 4 illustrates the structure of the spatial attention mechanism.

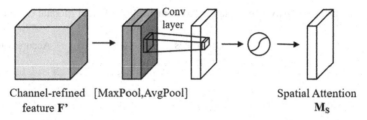

Channel-refined   [MaxPool,AvgPool]   Spatial Attention
feature **F'**   **M**$_S$

Fig. 4. Spatial Attention Module

3 Experimental Results and Analysis

3.1 Experimental Setup

The hardware environment for this study consisted of the following specifications: operating system: Windows 10, GPU: Nvidia GeForce RTX 3080 (10 GB), CPU: 12-core Intel(R) Xeon(R) Platinum 8255C CPU @ 2.50 GHz. The software environment included PyTorch 1.9.0, Python 3.8, and CUDA 11.3.

3.2 Network Model Ablation Experiments

In this study, a series of ablation experiments were conducted on a professionally collected graphite ore image dataset to verify the effectiveness of various improvement modules in the task of graphite ore image classification. The purpose was to gain a deeper understanding of the impact of different modules on graphite ore image classification and their role in the overall network performance. The specific combinations are described as follows (as shown in Table 3):

Baseline: The Baseline model is a conventional ResNet50 residual network model.

Baseline + PyConv: This combination replaces the 3 × 3 convolutional layers in the ResNet50 residual structure with Pyramid Convolution (PyConv). By using convolutional kernels of different sizes and depths, it extracts more multidimensional feature information from graphite ore images, captures spatial context dependencies, and improves model performance.

Baseline + PyConv + HG: This combination builds upon Baseline + PyConv by using a higher number of groups, doubling the spatial convolution feature quantity. This enhances spatial filtering capability and improves feature extraction, thereby enhancing the network's ability to represent and express input data.

Baseline + PyConv + HG + SAM: This combination incorporates the Spatial Attention Mechanism (SAM) into the entire residual structure network before and after Baseline + PyConv + HG. By adaptively allocating attention weights, it improves the model's ability to capture key features in graphite ore images, thereby enhancing the accuracy and robustness of image classification.

Table 3. Comparative Analysis of Ablation Experiments for Different Module Combinations.

Model Variants	Modules			Accuracy (%)
	PyConv	HG	SAM	
Baseline				90.2%
Baseline + PyConv	✓			91.5%
Baseline + PyConv + HG	✓	✓		92.2%
Baseline + PyConv + HG + SAM	✓	✓	✓	92.5%

3.3 Comparative Experiments with Other Methods

This section compares the performance of the PyConvHGResNet50-SAM, a pyramid convolutional neural network, with other popular convolutional neural networks in the field of graphite mineral image classification. The comparison includes the ResNet series of residual networks, specifically ResNet50 and ResNet101, the lightweight neural network MobileNet series, specifically MobileNet_V2, the dense convolutional network DenseNet series, specifically DenseNet121, and the PyConvResNet101, which is based on the deeper pyramid convolutional layers proposed in this paper.

In the training process of each model, the same parameter settings were selected to ensure a fair and objective comparison between different models. The image resolution was uniformly adjusted to 224 × 224 before inputting into the network. The batch size was set to 32, meaning that 32 images were selected for training in each iteration. The maximum number of training epochs was set to 400. The SGD optimizer was used to update the model parameters, with an initial learning rate of 0.01, a decay parameter of 0.005, and a momentum parameter of 0.9. The training was stopped when the model converged. Figure 5 shows the accuracy of the six models on the test set as a function of the number of training epochs, and Fig. 6 shows the corresponding loss values as a function of the number of epochs.

From Fig. 5, it can be observed that, under the same batch size, all models benefit from the introduction of transfer learning and the use of pre-trained weights, resulting in a rapid improvement in accuracy during the initial stages of training. The DenseNet121 model reaches an accuracy of 80% after 50 epochs and shows a slow but steady increase. It converges at around 350 epochs with accuracy fluctuating around 87%. The MobileNet_V2 model reaches 78% accuracy after 50 epochs but experiences more significant fluctuations during the training process. It converges at around 330 epochs with accuracy fluctuating around 87%. The ResNet50 model, based on the conventional residual network, converges after approximately 300 epochs with accuracy fluctuating around 89%. The ResNet101 model also converges after 300 epochs with accuracy fluctuating around 88%. The PyConvResNet101 model, with its higher depth and multi-size convolutional kernels, starts to converge at around 270 epochs with accuracy fluctuating around 89%. On the other hand, the PyConvHGResNet50-SAM model reaches its highest accuracy of 85% relative to other models after approximately 50 epochs, and then converges at around 300 epochs with accuracy fluctuating around 91%.

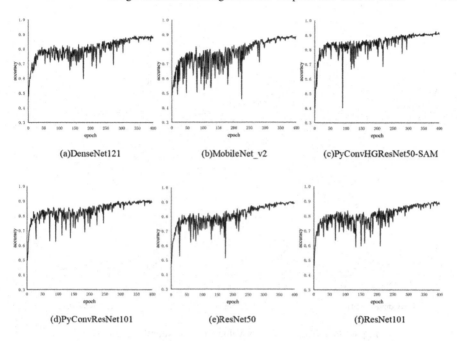

Fig. 5. Compares the accuracy of the six neural network models.

According to the comparison of loss values in Fig. 6, the DenseNet121 model shows a rapid decrease in loss to around 0.28 after 50 epochs, and it converges around 350 epochs with fluctuations around 0.07. The MobileNet_V2 model exhibits a similar trend, with the loss dropping to 0.37 after 50 epochs and converging around 0.08 after 350 epochs. The loss curves of ResNet50 and ResNet101 are similar, converging around 360 epochs with fluctuations around 0.055. Both the PyConvResNet101 and PyConvHGResNet50-SAM models show similar patterns, with the loss decreasing to below 0.2 after 50 epochs and converging around 0.045 after 350 epochs. Considering both accuracy and loss, it can be concluded that the PyConvHGResNet50-SAM model achieves the highest accuracy while maintaining a fast convergence speed, making it the most effective among the compared models.

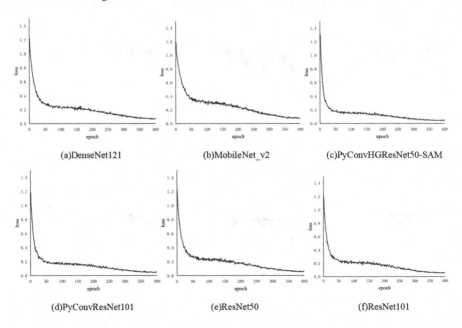

Fig. 6. Comparison of Loss Values for Six Neural Networks

4 Conclusion

In this study, we proposed a method for graphite ore carbon grade image classification based on multi-scale feature fusion. We replaced the convolutional layers in the traditional residual structure with a newly designed pyramid convolutional layer, which consists of convolutional kernels with different sizes and depths. This enables the extraction of complex texture features from multiple dimensions on the surface of graphite ore. We introduced transfer learning to accelerate model convergence and incorporated spatial attention mechanism to focus on important information in the regions of interest, thus improving the accuracy of the model. Experimental results demonstrated that our method outperforms other existing methods in terms of classification accuracy. Moreover, compared to traditional carbon-sulfur analyzers used for detecting graphite ore carbon grade, our method offers advantages such as higher efficiency, accuracy, and convenience. It is feasible and of significant importance for the construction of smart mines.

References

1. Xie, J.: Exploration of the method for determining the fixed carbon content in carbonate graphite ore based on high-frequency infrared. Gansu Sci. Technol. **39**(01), 18–20 (2023)
2. Liu, Y., Xiang, L., Dong, A., et al.: Study on the method of measuring fixed carbon in graphite by high-frequency infrared carbon-sulfur analyzer. Chem. Eng. Des. Commun. **47**(11), 44–45 (2021)

3. Chai, F.: Exploration and practice of intelligent mine construction in Zhengzhuang coal mine. Shandong Coal Sci. Technol. **40**(12), 25–27+34 (2022)
4. Pinto, D.L., et al. Image feature extraction via local binary patterns for marbling score classification in beef cattle using tree-based algorithms. Livestock Sci. 267 (2023)
5. Baigts, A.D., Ramírez, RM., Rosas, R.R.: Monitoring of the dehydration process of apple snacks with visual feature extraction and image processing techniques. Appl. Sci. **12**(21), 11269–11269 (2022)
6. Singh, N., Singh, T.N., Tiwary, A., Sarkar, K.: Textural identification of basaltic rock mass using image processing and neural network. Comput. Geosci. **14**, 301–310 (2010)
7. Deepa, S., Umarani, R.: Steganalysis on images using SVM with selected hybrid features of Gini index feature selection algorithm. Int. J. Adv. Res. Comput. Sci. **8**(5), 1503–1509 (2017)
8. Yang, L., Bai, Z., Kou, Y.G.: Analysis of the loss of civil aviation customers by random forest algorithm based on RFM model. Comput. Modernization **1**, 100–104 (2021)
9. Guettari, N., Capelle-Laizé, A.S., Carr, P.: Blind image steganalysis based on evidential K-Nearest neighbors. In: Proceedings of the 2016 IEEE International Conference on Image Processing, 2742–2746 (2016)
10. Dong, W.K., Min, S.K., Lee, J., et al.: Adaptive learning rate backpropagation neural network algorithm based on the minimization of mean square deviation for impulsive noises. IEEE Access **8**, 98018–98026 (2020)
11. Zhou, N., Ouyang, X.Y.: Development of convolutional neural networks. J. Liaoning Univ. Sci. Technol. **44**(05), 349–356 (2021)
12. Yan, C., Wang, C.: Development and application of convolutional neural network models. J. Comput. Sci. Explor. **15**(01), 27–46 (2021)
13. Chen, W., et al.: Rock image classification using deep residual neural network with transfer learning. Front. Earth Sci. (2023)
14. Cheng, G., Guo, W., Fan, P.: Rock image classification based on convolutional neural network. J. Xi'an Shiyou Univ. (Nat. Sci. Edit.) **32**(04), 116–122 (2017)
15. Bai, L., Yao, Y., Li, S., Xu, D., Wei, X.: Mineral composition analysis of rock images based on deep learning feature extraction. China Min. **27**(07), 178–182 (2018)
16. Bai, L., Wei, X., Liu, Y., Wu, C., Chen, L.: Rock thin section image recognition based on VGG model. Geol. Bull. **38**(12), 2053–2058 (2019)
17. Liu, X., Wang, H., Wang, L.: Intelligent recognition of rock types based on Faster R-CNN method. Mod. Min. **35**(05), 60–64 (2019)

Graphite Ore Grade Classification Algorithm Based on Multi-scale Fused Image Features

Jionghui Wang[1(✉)], Yaokun Liu[2], Xueyu Huang[2,3], and Shaopeng Chang[2]

[1] Minmetals Exploration & Development Co. Ltd., Beijing 100010, People's Republic of China
wangjh@minmetals.com
[2] School of Software Engineering, Jiangxi University of Science and Technology,
Nanchang 330013, People's Republic of China
[3] Nanchang Key Laboratory of Virtual Digital Factory and Cultural Communications,
Nanchang 330013, People's Republic of China

Abstract. Aiming at the problems of complex pre-processing and expensive equipment in chemical detection of graphite ore grade, a graphite ore identification and classification method based on fusing multi-scale image features is proposed. In the feature extraction stage, a deep convolutional neural network and a residual network model based on spatial attention mechanism are constructed to improve the learning ability of local and global features of graphite ore images; in the feature aggregation stage, a global response normalization technique is introduced to achieve more accurate graphite ore grade recognition, and the accuracy of the model reaches 93.401% and the macro F1 reaches 93.086%, which is better than the single The accuracy of the model reaches 93.401% and the macro F1 reaches 93.086%, which is better than the traditional machine learning methods with single feature. The experimental results show that the features extracted by different methods can describe the texture and edge information of graphite ore, and the proposed method has better extraction ability in terms of local features and global features of graphite ore images, and achieves more accurate graphite ore grade recognition with good robustness.

Keywords: feature aggregation · texture features · depthwise convolution · residual network · attention mechanism · global response normalization (GRN) · graphite ore

1 Introduction

Timely prediction of ore grade is crucial in the mining and processing of graphite ore. It not only improves production efficiency but also helps enterprises save costs in subsequent intelligent blending and scientific ore selection processes. Currently, two traditional methods are commonly used to determine the grade of graphite ore: sulfur-carbon

This work is supported by the National Key Research and Development Program of China 2020YFC1909602.

C. Wu et al. (Eds.): MONAMI 2023, LNICST 559, pp. 178–198, 2024.
https://doi.org/10.1007/978-3-031-55471-1_14

analysis and high-frequency infrared methods. However, these methods have complex pre-processing requirements, expensive equipment, and are difficult to operate in mining environments. Moreover, delays in determining the grade of graphite ore can occur when faced with a heavy workload. Resolving this time delay issue is crucial for improving production efficiency and aligns with the trend of industrial production becoming more intelligent. Therefore, constructing an automated ore identification model is beneficial for unleashing productivity and assisting industrial enterprises in enhancing the accuracy and efficiency of classification, thereby holding significant practical implications.

In recent years, computer vision techniques have gained significant attention in the industrial field and mineral classification due to the advancements in deep learning and image processing technologies. Su et al. [1] optimized the network structure of LeNet-5, one of the earliest convolutional neural network-based image classification algorithms. They trained the model on a dataset of 20,000 images to successfully perform binary classification of coal and gangue. The experimental results exhibited an impressive accuracy of 95.88% on the validation set. For smaller datasets comprising 240 images each for coal and gangue, Pu et al. [2] utilized transfer learning by freezing the convolutional layers of VGG16 and customizing the fully connected layers. Their trained model achieved a classification accuracy of 82.5% on the test set. Wang et al. adopted the Wu-VGG19 transfer learning network structure to accomplish binary classification of surrounding rocks and black tungsten ore, resulting in an outstanding recognition rate of 97.51%. These findings highlight the effectiveness of utilizing advanced deep learning techniques for accurate and efficient mineral classification in various scenarios.

Efficiently identifying the grade of graphite ore through image recognition, by building a relationship model between mineral texture features, color features, and mineral types, is a valuable research topic. Deep learning has contributed to significant advancements in various fields, including computer vision, in recent years. In the domain of mineral image classification and recognition, researchers from both domestic and international backgrounds have gradually incorporated deep learning techniques. Notably, Zhang et al. [3] successfully employed the Inception-v3 network to intelligently classify granite, quartz diorite, and gabbro. Similarly, Baraboshkin et al. and Bai et al. utilized the same network to classify 5 and 7 different types of minerals, respectively. Li et al. [4] further developed a comprehensive intelligent coupled classification method for minerals using Inception-v3. Their approach effectively differentiated 19 distinct minerals by leveraging texture and color features derived from mineral images through K-means. Building on this foundation, Liu et al. [5] validated the effectiveness of combining deep learning with clustering algorithms. Zeng et al. employed a two-layer fully connected neural network to enhance the scalar Mohs hardness. They utilized EfficientNet-b4 [6] for extracting mineral image features and successfully achieved the classification of 36 different types of minerals by integrating the results and feeding them into a fully connected layer. To address overfitting, Liang et al. [7] employed CutMix and image cutting as data augmentation methods. Notably, they pioneered the use of ViT, an evolution of Transformer, for classifying 7 different types of minerals.

Expanding problem-solving approaches and flexibly applying deep learning techniques are valuable for mineral type recognition tasks. These tasks extend beyond natural scene images and can incorporate additional data types, such as microscopic images [8–11] and spectral images [12]. Polarized microscopic images extract fine-grained features of minerals. Iglesias et al. [8] utilized the ResNet18 model to classify polarized microscopic images of five minerals: biotite, quartz, garnet, muscovite, and olivine, achieving an accuracy of 89%. Spectral images also play a significant role in mineral classification tasks. Han et al. [13] acquired spectral images of minerals using a visible-infrared reflectance spectrometer and trained a custom hollow convolutional neural network with these images. This approach successfully classified hematite, magnetite, granite, quartz diorite, and greenstone.

Comparing neural network characteristics, developing deep learning models suitable for mineral type classification, and optimizing conventional algorithms are important topics among researchers in the field. One technique of interest is the dual-task processing capability of object detection networks, which effectively classify multiple mineral blocks within the same image. In a study referenced as [14], an object detection dataset with around 800 mineral samples was constructed. Faster R-CNN was trained on this dataset to classify eight types of minerals, including olivine, basalt, marble, slate, conglomerate, limestone, granite, and magnetite quartzite. In contrast, another study referenced as [15] revealed that Faster R-CNN outperformed YOLOv4 [16] in classifying three categories (volcanic rock, sedimentary rock, and metamorphic rock) and 32 subcategories of minerals. Additionally, in a study mentioned as [17], Faster R-CNN was optimized using multiscale feature fusion techniques and the particle swarm optimization algorithm, achieving an impressive 98% classification accuracy for minerals such as biotite, hematite, turquoise, and quartz.

Additionally, semantic segmentation networks have the capability to classify multiple mineral blocks within the same image at the pixel level. In Reference [18], an improved U-Net was utilized to segment minerals in images, resulting in the classification of red rocks, green hematite, yellow siderite, blue greenstone, and purple pyrite. In Reference, the instance segmentation network Mask RCNN [19] was employed, which combines the functionalities of object detection and semantic segmentation. This approach achieved a comprehensive accuracy of 97.6% in both mineral identification and localization.

In the classification of graphite ore images, the texture features and global image correlations present in the ore images receive more attention compared to other image classification tasks. Additionally, the recognition of ore itself is highly sensitive to positional information. Traditional convolutional neural networks (CNNs) gradually capture image characteristics by extracting features through multiple convolutional layers [20]. CNNs inherently possess a strong inductive bias due to their design characteristics of locality and weight sharing mechanisms. Moreover, CNNs demonstrate sample and parameter efficiency due to their translational equivariance properties. On the other hand, Visual Transformers excel in modeling long-range dependencies through self-attention mechanisms, making them dominant in natural language processing (NLP) research. Transformers have recently been successfully applied to various computer vision tasks, showcasing impressive performance. Consequently, some researchers have explored the direct incorporation of convolutional operations into visual Transformers to introduce the inductive bias. However, forcibly modifying the structure may compromise the integrity of the Transformer and reduce model capacity.

To address these issues, this paper presents a novel pretraining-driven approach for graphite ore classification and recognition, utilizing multiscale image feature fusion. In the feature extraction stage, deep convolutional layers are employed to extract local texture features of the image in the channel dimension. Additionally, a spatial attention mechanism is introduced to extract global contextual feature information. The two sets of extracted features are then normalized and fused together in a cascaded manner. The resulting fused features provide a comprehensive description of the texture information present in graphite ore images, encompassing both channel and spatial dimensions. This progressive fusion approach enables the model to capture the correlations between different spatial regions and channels, effectively guiding the network to focus on the target region. As a result, the recognition accuracy of graphite ore images is significantly improved.

The main contributions of this paper are as follows:

(1) In the classification of graphite ore images, transfer learning methods are employed to pre-train the backbone network using existing large-scale publicly available image datasets. This approach ensures full optimization of the model parameters and effectively addresses the problem of limited training data.
(2) To enhance the recognition and classification of graphite ore images, this paper proposes a residual network structure with a spatial attention mechanism. This novel approach improves the model's capability to learn long-range dependencies within the images.
(3) To enhance the accuracy of recognition and classification tasks, we propose the addition of a global response normalization layer to each convolutional neural network module. This layer normalizes the features in the channel dimension, allowing for better control of feature proportions during training. As a result, the model exhibits improved generalization and performance.

In the second section of this paper, we present the overall structure and specific details of the graphite ore recognition and classification method that integrates multiscale image features. The third section covers the experimental process and results. By comparing the macro precision, macro recall, macro F1 score, accuracy, and confusion matrix with other methods, we analyze the performance of the proposed method. Finally, in the fourth section, we provide the main conclusions of this article.

2 Graphite Ore Image Classification and Recognition Method by Fusing Multi-scale Features

This paper proposes a graphite ore image classification and recognition method based on fused multiscale features, firstly, the input image is preprocessed by better initialization improvement; secondly, a deep convolutional layer performs feature extraction on the incoming preprocessed data, and the deep convolutional will run on a per-channel basis and mix the information of spatial dimensions; after that, an independent downsampling layer integrates the data; finally, the fused feature data is global level pooling to obtain a highly informative feature subset, and complete the classification by the classifier. The overall model has strong generalization ability, high accuracy and robustness. To achieve classification and recognition of different types of graphite ores. The framework of the classification method is shown in Fig. 1 below.

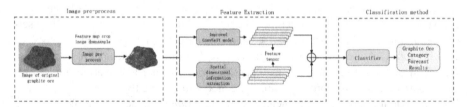

Fig. 1. Graphite ore image classification method framework based on multi-scale feature fusion

2.1 Migration Learning and Graphite Ore Image Data Situation

Image Pre-training. In addition to designing the model architecture, the effective utilization of large-scale datasets plays a crucial role in training an excellent network model with high accuracy and strong robustness. However, the availability of publicly accessible data for graphite ore image classification is limited. On the other hand, ImageNet, a comprehensive dataset containing diverse images with rich colors and textures, is extensively employed for image classification tasks. Transfer learning, widely adopted in the field of deep learning, has become a conventional strategy for classification tasks. Convolutional neural networks have achieved remarkable advancements in recognition accuracy, with the emergence of deep models such as ResNet, EfficientNet, and Patch-Convnet, which comprise millions or even tens of millions of parameters. To address the challenge of limited training data, this paper proposes an enhanced ConvNeXt model that pretrains parameters on ImageNet and initializes the backbone network. This approach optimizes model parameters and alleviates the adverse impact of insufficient training data.

Experimental Dataset Description. The availability of publicly accessible graphite ore image data is limited. To address this, rock samples were meticulously collected by professional personnel to obtain comprehensive image data, which were then carefully labeled. Furthermore, highly accurate chemical methods were employed to determine the carbon content in the ore, and these results were annotated using a carbon-sulfur analyzer. Consequently, a dataset of graphite ore images was constructed. There are four categories of graphite ores included in the dataset, from low to high according to the carbon grade values contained in the minerals: waste rock (for comparison reference only, not involved in training 0%~1%) 1126 sheets of low grade ores (1%~5%), 2170 sheets of lower grade ores (6%~10%), 3476 sheets of higher grade ores (11%~15%) and 1567 sheets of high grade ores (16%~20%), as shown in Fig. 2.

In order to mitigate the impact of image quality on recognition performance, we employed professional equipment to capture high-quality images with a resolution of 6000×4000 pixels during the data collection process. To ensure optimal feature learning

(a) low grade ore (1%~5%)   (b) lower grade ores (6%~10%)

(c) higher grade ores (11%~15%)   (d) high grade ores (16%~20%)

Fig. 2. Image samples of ore with different grades in the dataset

during training and reliable evaluation, the image data for each category was randomly divided into training, validation, and test sets using a ratio of 6:2:2. The table below illustrates the categories of graphite ore rocks as an example (Table 1).

Table 1. Distribution of graphite ore image dataset after preprocessing

Data set type	Different grades of graphite ore			
	1%~5%	6%~10%	11%~15%	16%~20%
train set	676	1302	2086	941
validation set	225	434	695	313
test set	225	434	695	313

Preprocessing the Dataset. In convolutional neural networks, the stem layer plays a crucial role in processing input images at the network's outset. In natural environments, redundant information is present, and the stem layer efficiently downsamples input images to meet the feature map size requirements of standard convolutional networks and visual Transformers. In the standard ResNet, the stem layer comprises a 7 × 7 convolutional layer with a stride of 2 and a MaxPooling layer, resulting in a 4x downsampling of input images. Visual Transformers employ a more direct "Patchify" strategy in their stem layer, utilizing larger kernel sizes and non-overlapping convolutions. To accommodate the multi-stage design of the Swin Transformer, a similar "Patchify" layer with smaller convolutions is employed. Inspired by visual Transformers, we replace the stem layer in ResNet with a Patchify layer implemented using a 4×4 convolutional layer with a stride of 1. This modification yields a slight improvement in accuracy while reducing computational complexity. Experimental results affirm the positive impact of enhanced initialization on graphite ore image classification tasks.

2.2 Graphite Ore Image Feature Extraction

During the feature extraction stage, we addressed the challenge of capturing long-range dependencies in global features extracted from graphite ore images by enhancing the ResNet-50 model. Inspired by the capabilities of visual Transformers in modeling long-range dependencies, we developed a hierarchical convolutional neural network similar to Swin Transformer. Figure 3 illustrates the architecture. Initially, we trained the base model using a training strategy similar to that of visual Transformers, resulting in improved performance compared to the original ResNet-50. Subsequently, we made several enhancements, including: 1) improved initialization, 2) deeper convolutions, 3) preactivation bottleneck blocks, and 4) normalization and activation functions. In the following sections, we will delve into these enhancements made to the convolutional neural network for graphite ore image classification. Given the close relationship between network complexity and model performance, we carefully controlled the size of floating-point operations (FLOPs) during the enhancement process.

Feature Extraction Based on Deep Convolution in the Channel Dimension. The texture features of graphite ore images exhibit a random spatial distribution on the image, and they are typically composed of multiple layers and angles of textures, resulting in high complexity. Conventional convolutional networks often lack sufficient attention to the same region and fail to achieve sufficient depth in feature extraction.In this part, we attempt to draw inspiration from the design principles of ResNeXt [21]. Compared to conventional ResNet, ResNeXt offers better depth in feature extraction and can achieve higher accuracy. Its core component is the grouped convolution, where the convolutional filters are divided into different groups. From a macro perspective, ResNeXt aims to increase the number of groups to expand the convolutional width. This is reflected in the specific ResNeXt module, where the 3×3 convolutional layer adopts the grouped convolution method.By incorporating the ResNeXt design, we can effectively capture the complex texture features of graphite ore images. The grouped convolution allows for the exploration of different perspectives and variations within the texture, leading to more comprehensive feature representations. The experimental results demonstrate the effectiveness of this approach in improving accuracy and enhancing the model's ability to capture fine-grained texture information.

Drawing inspiration from the idea of grouped convolution, in our structural design, we employ a form of deep grouped convolution, as illustrated in Fig. 4. It is achieved by dividing the channels into equal-sized groups. The deep convolution applies a separate convolutional kernel to each input channel (input depth), followed by a simple 1 × 1 convolutional layer for pointwise convolution to create a linear combination of the outputs from the deep convolutional layer.

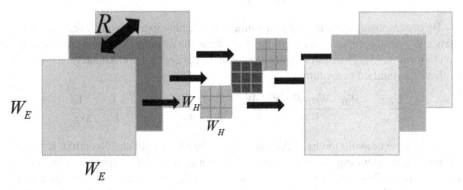

Fig. 3. Depthwise convolution with separate kernels applied

The formula expression for each input channel in the deep convolution is as follows:

$$\hat{Z}_{k,l,p} = \sum_{i,j} \hat{H}_{i,j,q} \cdot E_{k+i-1,l+j-1,p} \tag{1}$$

In the above formula, $\hat{H}$ is a depth convolutional kernel with a size of $W_H \cdot W_H \cdot R$. Each of the p th convolutional kernels in $\hat{H}$ is applied to the p th channel of the feature map E, resulting in the p th channel of the output feature map $\hat{Z}$ corresponding to that convolutional kernel.

The computational cost of deep convolution is:

$$C_{H1} = W_H \cdot W_H \cdot R \cdot W_E \cdot W_E \tag{2}$$

The computational cost in the above formula depends on the product of the number of input channels M, the size of the convolutional kernel $W_H \cdot W_H$, and the size of the feature map $W_E \cdot W_E$.

Compared to standard convolution operations, depth-wise convolution is highly effective in improving overall performance. However, it only extracts features from input data without combining the learned features to create new ones. Therefore, an additional layer is needed to combine the output of depth-wise convolution through a 1 × 1 convolution, resulting in the generation of new features. At this point, the computational cost of depth-wise convolution is given by:

$$C_{H2} = W_H \cdot W_H \cdot R \cdot W_E \cdot W_E + R \cdot U \cdot W_E \cdot W_E \qquad (3)$$

where U is the number of output channels, the computational cost of standard convolution is given by:

$$C_n = W_H \cdot W_H \cdot R \cdot U \cdot W_E \cdot W_E \qquad (4)$$

By decomposing the standard convolution into feature extraction and feature fusion parts, the overall computational cost is reduced from the formula (4) of standard convolution to formula (3). Therefore, the total computational cost is approximately one-eighth of that of a standard convolution.

$$\frac{C_{H2}}{C_n} = \frac{W_H \cdot W_H \cdot R \cdot W_E \cdot W_E + R \cdot U \cdot W_E \cdot W_E}{W_H \cdot W_H \cdot R \cdot U \cdot W_E \cdot W_E} = \frac{1}{U} + \frac{1}{W_H^2} \qquad (5)$$

Depthwise convolution has been popularized by MobileNet and Xception. It can be observed that operating on each channel is a characteristic of weighted operations in self-attention. This similarity to depthwise convolution lies in the fact that each convolution kernel individually processes a channel, just like the self-attention mechanism that performs spatial information fusion and weighting within a single channel. In this regard, we refer to the design logic of Swin Transformer and increase the spatial network width from 64 to 96.

Spatial Attention Mechanism. In convolutional neural networks, the spatial attention mechanism enhances the network's ability to extract features by selectively focusing on specific spatial positions of the input [22]. This mechanism allows the net-work to allocate its attention resources more effectively, leading to improved feature extraction performance.

Spatial Attention Module

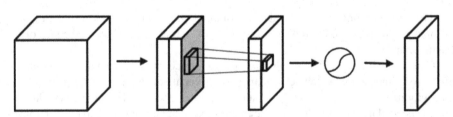

Fig. 4. Spatial Attention Module

In the spatial attention mechanism, a 2D attention weight matrix is commonly employed to indicate the importance of different positions. Each element of this matrix corresponds to a specific position in the input feature map, reflecting its significance.

During each convolutional operation, the neural network calculates a weighted average of the input feature map, with the weight for each position determined by the attention weight matrix. This enables the neural network to assign distinct weights to various spatial positions, facilitating more effective feature extraction.

Bottleneck Pre-activation. In standard ResNet, the bottleneck structure is employed as (large-dimension-small-dimension-large-dimension) to minimize computational complexity. Subsequently, the inverted bottleneck structure was introduced in Mo-bileNetV2, which follows the pattern of (small-dimension-large-dimension-small-dimension). This design enables seamless information transfer between different-dimensional feature spaces, avoiding information loss caused by dimension com-pression. A similar structure was also adopted in the MLP (Multi-Layer Perceptron) of Transformers, where the dimensionality of the middle layer and the fully connected layer is four times that of the two endpoints (Fig. 5).

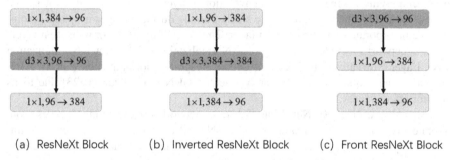

(a) ResNeXt Block   (b) Inverted ResNeXt Block   (c) Front ResNeXt Block

Fig. 5. Inversion and front improvement based on ResNeXt

The design order of convolutional blocks plays a crucial role in the sequence of targeted feature maps. In the context of mineral rock classification, it is advantageous to place the bottleneck layer in the front as it enables earlier learning of feature maps by the convolutional layers. Inspired by a significant design aspect of each Transformer block, an inverted residual bottleneck module was developed. In this module, the hidden dimension of the MLP block is expanded by a factor of four compared to the input dimension. Remarkably, this Transformer design exhibits a connection to the inverted residual bottleneck module utilized in ConvNets with an expansion rate of 4. This concept gained prominence through MobileNetV2 and has since been further adopted in various advanced convolutional architectures.

Therefore, in networks utilizing the inverted residual module, the FLOPs (floating-point operations) of deep convolutional layers demonstrate a notable increase. However, this is offset by a substantial reduction in FLOPs within the shortcut layers of subsequent downsampling residual blocks. Consequently, the overall network experiences a slight decrease in FLOPs while concurrently achieving improved performance.

Activation Function and Normalization Layer Optimization. To achieve performance on par with Vision Transformers in graphite ore image classification, we leverage the advantages of microarchitecture design. An important consideration that distinguishes natural language processing from vision architectures is the choice of activation function. In the field of computer vision, several activation functions have been proposed. While Rectified Linear Unit (ReLU) has been widely used in convolu-tional neural networks due to its simplicity and efficiency, recent models have in-creasingly adopted Gaussian Error Linear Unit (GELU) as the activation function. Notably, GELU has been employed in models such as BERT (by Google), GPT-2 (by OpenAI), and Transform-ers. GELU can be viewed as a smooth variant of ReLU. In this context, for the sake of alignment with other metrics, we have selected GELU as our activation function.

In standard ResNet, downsampling of spatial dimensions is typically achieved through 3×3 convolutions with a stride of 2. For convolutional blocks with resid-ual connections, downsampling is performed in the shortcut connection using 1×1 convolutions with a stride of 2. This ensures that the downsampling layers in the CNN maintain a similar computational strategy as the other layers. However, Swin Trans-former introduces an additional dedicated downsampling layer between stages. To align with the design principles of Swin Transformer, we experimented with a different app-roach, employing a separate 2×2 convolutional layer with a stride of 2 for spatial downsampling. Furthermore, to ensure stable training during changes in spatial resolu-tion, we incorporated a normalization layer. The commonly used normalization layers in neural networks include Local Response Normalization (LRN), Batch Normalization (BN), Layer Normalization (LN), and Global Response Normalization (GRN). After comparing these options, we ultimately selected GRN normalization [23] due to its superior effectiveness.

This study utilizes ResNet-50 as the main network for extracting features from graphite ore images. The parameters of ResNet-50 are initialized through pretrain-ing techniques. To capture long-range spatial context dependencies during the feature extraction stage in the convolutional layers, we incorporate the design logic of Swin Transformer. Additionally, the output of the local-global features is further normalized and serves as the output of the convolutional operation, leading to the generation of a multi-scale feature map.

The ConvNeXt-G model comprises five stages. The initial stage, known as "stem," employs a single convolutional layer for input data preprocessing. Subsequently, four bottleneck pre-activated deep convolutional layers follow, characterized by progressively increasing parameters. To ensure stable feature extraction within the convolutional lay-ers, Layer Normalization (LN) is incorporated into each downsampling layer, enhancing training stability. Additionally, the two 1×1 convolutions within each block are imple-mented using fully connected layers, offering a slight speed advantage over convolutional layers. Normalization layers are applied before downsampling, after the stem, and after the Global Average Pooling (GAP) layer. Finally, the hyperparameters related to data augmentation, preprocessing, and optimizer are harmonized to achieve the enhanced network structure of ConvNeXt-G (Figs. 6 and 7, Table 2).

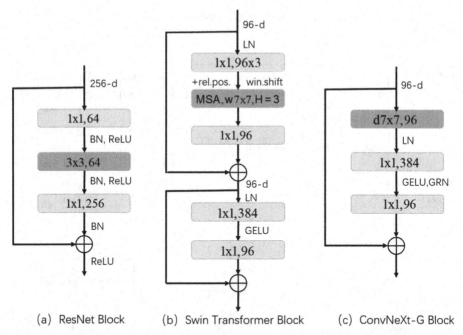

(a) ResNet Block   (b) Swin Transformer Block   (c) ConvNeXt-G Block

Fig. 6. Comparison between ConvNeXt-G based on ResNet fusion Swin Transformer design logic and the former two

Table 2. Swin Transformer, ResNet-50 and ConvNeXt-G network parameters

	output size	Swin-T	ResNet-50	ConvNeXt-G
Stem	56 × 56	4 × 4, 96, stride 4	7 × 7, 64, stride 2	4 × 4, 96, stride 4
Stage1	56 × 56	$\begin{bmatrix} 1 \times 1, 96 \times 3 \\ \text{MSA, w7} \times 7, \text{H} = 3, \text{rel.pos.} \\ 1 \times 1, 96 \end{bmatrix} \times 2$ $\begin{bmatrix} 1 \times 1, 384 \\ 1 \times 1, 96 \end{bmatrix}$	$\begin{bmatrix} 1 \times 1, 64 \\ 3 \times 3, 64 \\ 1 \times 1, 256 \end{bmatrix} \times 3$	$\begin{bmatrix} d7 \times 7, 96 \\ 1 \times 1, 384 \\ 1 \times 1, 96 \end{bmatrix} \times 3$
Stage2	28 × 28	$\begin{bmatrix} 1 \times 1, 192 \times 3 \\ \text{MSA, w7} \times 7, \text{H} = 6, \text{rel.pos.} \\ 1 \times 1, 192 \end{bmatrix} \times 2$ $\begin{bmatrix} 1 \times 1, 768 \\ 1 \times 1, 192 \end{bmatrix}$	$\begin{bmatrix} 1 \times 1, 128 \\ 3 \times 3, 128 \\ 1 \times 1, 512 \end{bmatrix} \times 4$	$\begin{bmatrix} d7 \times 7, 192 \\ 1 \times 1, 768 \\ 1 \times 1, 192 \end{bmatrix} \times 3$

(continued)

Table 2. (*continued*)

	output size	Swin-T			ResNet-50	ConvNeXt-G
Stage3	14×14	$\begin{bmatrix} 1 \times 1, 384 \times 3 \\ \text{MSA, w7} \times 7, \text{H} = 12, \text{rel.pos.} \\ 1 \times 1, 384 \end{bmatrix} \times 6$	$\begin{bmatrix} 1 \times 1, 1536 \\ 1 \times 1, 384 \end{bmatrix}$		$\begin{bmatrix} 1 \times 1, 256 \\ 3 \times 3, 256 \\ 1 \times 1, 1024 \end{bmatrix} \times 6$	$\begin{bmatrix} d7 \times 7, 384 \\ 1 \times 1, 1536 \\ 1 \times 1, 384 \end{bmatrix} \times 9$
Stage4	7×7	$\begin{bmatrix} 1 \times 1, 768 \times 3 \\ \text{MSA, w7} \times 7, \text{H} = 24, \text{rel.pos.} \\ 1 \times 1, 768 \end{bmatrix} \times 2$	$\begin{bmatrix} 1 \times 1, 3072 \\ 1 \times 1, 768 \end{bmatrix}$		$\begin{bmatrix} 1 \times 1, 512 \\ 3 \times 3, 512 \\ 1 \times 1, 2048 \end{bmatrix} \times 3$	$\begin{bmatrix} d7 \times 7, 768 \\ 1 \times 1, 3072 \\ 1 \times 1, 768 \end{bmatrix} \times 3$
FLOPs		4.5×10^9			4.1×10^9	4.5×10^9
#params.		28.3×10^6			25.6×10^6	28.6×10^6

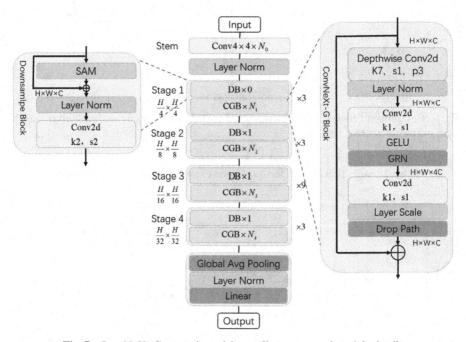

Fig. 7. ConvNeXt-G network model overall structure and module details

3 Experimental Analysis

3.1 Experimental Setup

The hardware environment used in this study includes: GPU: RTX 3080*1 with 10 GB VRAM, CPU: 12-core Intel(R) Xeon(R) Platinum 8255C CPU @ 2.50 GHz. The software environment consists of Python 3.8, PyTorch 1.8, Torchvision 0.9, CUDA 11.1, and others.

3.2 Evaluation Metrics

The implemented task in this paper is graphite ore image classification, which is a multi-class problem. Common evaluation metrics used in image classification tasks are employed to assess the algorithm's performance. These metrics include confusion matrix, macro-precision, macro-recall, macro-F1 score, and accuracy.

3.3 Network Model Effectiveness Ablation Experiment

This study primarily conducted ablation experiments on a dataset of graphite ore images collected by professionals working in graphite mines. The purpose was to validate the effectiveness of the pretraining strategy and various module components used in this study. We evaluated the contribution and detection capabilities of each module by constructing different combinations of modules. The specific combinations are described as follows:

Baseline: The baseline model in this study consists of a ResNet50 backbone network based on the RPG image modality and an image recognition classification module. The main component is a mask generation block with a sequential structure of Conv-ReLU-Conv-Sigmoid. Additionally, this model does not include any pretraining strategy.

Baseline + P: This combination builds upon the baseline model by incorporating a ResNet50 backbone encoding network that is pretrained (P) on the ImageNet dataset. By replacing the traditional random initialization approach with a pretrained model, it allows for better learning of image feature information.

Baseline + P + PAT: This combination builds upon the Baseline + P model by introducing an improved initialization method. It replaces the downsampling layer (stem) after the original input layer with a patchify layer (PAT), which ensures non-overlapping sliding windows and processes information from one patch window at a time. This approach allows for better learning and capturing of image feature information from a more optimal initialization perspective.

Baseline + P + PAT + DEPTH: This combination extends the Baseline + P + PAT model by introducing the concept of grouped convolution. It replaces the original residual convolutional layers with depthwise convolution (DEPTH) layers. By increasing the base channel number and performing operations on a per-channel basis, this approach enhances the computational speed of the model while further extracting spatial context dependencies.

Baseline + P + PAT + DEPTH + IB: This combination builds upon the Baseline + P + PAT + DEPTH model by repositioning the bottleneck layer within the convolutional feature extraction block (Inverted Bottleneck, IB). By placing the bottleneck layer earlier in the feature extraction stage, the model is enhanced to focus more on capturing long-range dependencies in the graphite ore images.

Baseline + P + PAT + DEPTH + IB + SAM: This combination extends the Baseline + P + PAT + DEPTH + IB model by incorporating micro-level adjustments to the architecture for the task of graphite ore image classification. Firstly, a spatial attention mechanism (SAM) is introduced in the downsampling layers. This mechanism pools the feature maps along the channel dimension, compressing the channel size and facilitating the learning of spatial features. The compressed feature maps are then concatenated along the channel dimension and subjected to convolutional operations and activation functions. Additionally, the more advanced and stable GELU activation function is used instead of ReLU to enhance the overall robustness of the model.

Baseline + P + PAT + DEPTH + IB + SAM + GRN: This combination represents the proposed network architecture in this paper, designed for the task of graphite ore image classification. Firstly, a Global Response Normalization (GRN) is introduced between the two 1 × 1 convolutional layers in the feature extraction module. This includes three steps: global feature aggregation, feature normalization, and feature recalibration, which enhances the contrast and selectivity among channels. Additionally, a separate downsampling layer is added between each stage. The purpose of this layer is to apply Layer Normalization (LN) to normalize all data in the samples, effectively alleviating the issue of feature collapse and preserving the diversity of graphite ore image features during the propagation of the network layers (Table 3).

3.4 Quantitative Experimental Results Compared with Other Methods Are Presented in This Section

This subsection provides a comparative analysis of popular convolutional neural network architectures for graphite ore image classification. The evaluated models include the ResNet series (ResNet-50, ResNet-101, ResNet-152), the EfficientNet series (EfficientNet-B0, EfficientNet-B2), and the Vision Transformer series (ViT-S, ViT-B, ViT-L). Their performance in the task of graphite ore image classification and recognition is analyzed.

During model training, a consistent set of hyperparameters was employed to ensure a fair and unbiased comparison among different convolutional neural network experiments. Images underwent preprocessing, with their resolution adjusted to 224 × 224 before being fed into the network. The participating convolutional neural networks were initialized with an initial learning rate of 5e-5, utilizing AdamW as the chosen optimizer. Each epoch involved a batch size of 512, indicating that 512 images were used for training in each iteration. The maximum number of epochs was set to 200. To decay the learning rate, a cosine decay learning rate schedule was implemented. This strategy gradually reduces the learning rate as the model approaches the global minimum of the loss function, facilitating closer convergence to this point. The cosine decay training method follows a pattern of initially slow descent in the cosine function value, followed by accelerated descent, and finally, decelerated descent. Hence, cosine decay was chosen to effectively reduce the learning rate. Figure 10 depicts the distribution of the confusion matrix on the test set, while Fig. 8 displays the accuracy curve of the four models on the

Table 3. Comparison results of ablation experiments of each module combination on the graphite ore dataset

Model Variants	Modules						Accuracy (%)	Convergent Epoch
	Pre-trained	PAT	DEPTH	IB	SAM	GRN		
Baseline							73.965	203
Baseline + P	✓						86.683	179
Baseline + P + PAT	✓	✓					86.803	172
Baseline + P + PAT + DEPTH	✓	✓	✓				91.542	174
Baseline + P + PAT + DEPTH + IB	✓	✓	✓	✓			91.662	171
Baseline + P + PAT + DEPTH + IB + SAM	✓	✓	✓	✓	✓		92.442	145
Baseline + P + PAT + DEPTH + IB + SD + GRN	✓	✓	✓	✓	✓	✓	93.401	136

validation set. Furthermore, Fig. 9 illustrates the loss curve in relation to the number of epochs.

Based on Fig. 8, the ResNet-101 model, a benchmark in the ResNet series of convolutional neural networks, achieves convergence at approximately 180 epochs. Following convergence, the accuracy remains steady around 88%. The Vision Transformer, originally developed for natural language processing and later adapted for image classification, demonstrates convergence within roughly 60 epochs, aided by transfer learning, and maintains an accuracy of around 88.6%. Despite its greater computational complexity and resource requirements, the EfficientNet-B3 model from the acclaimed EfficientNet series converges in 120 epochs, with the final accuracy fluctuating around 92.8%. In contrast, the ConvNeXt-G model reaches convergence at approximately 160 epochs, positioning it between the ResNet and Vision Transformer models, with an accuracy fluctuating around 93.4%. These findings highlight the similar performance of these four models in the multi-classification recognition of graphite mineral images.

Based on the comparison of loss values in Fig. 9, several key findings emerge. When using the same batch size, the Vision Transformer demonstrates slower convergence within the first 50 epochs compared to neural network models with residual connections. Its loss value fluctuates between 0.7 and 1.5, gradually stabilizing around 1.25 after 60 epochs. In contrast, ResNet-101 exhibits faster convergence, with the loss value approaching stability after 50 epochs and fluctuating around 0.8. However, larger fluctuations occur around 80, 120, and 160 epochs, eventually converging to approximately 0.8.ConvNeXt-G, a hybrid model combining ResNet-50 and Vision Transformer concepts, shows a gradual reduction in loss values from an initial 2.5. Due to appropriate initialization, the loss value stabilizes after approximately 45 epochs, gradually converging around 0.7. EfficientNet demonstrates a gradual decrease in loss values from an initial 3.5. By the 40th epoch, the loss value reaches 1.0 and further diminishes to around 0.6 at the 120th epoch, where convergence is achieved.In summary, these results indicate that ConvNeXt-G achieves significantly faster convergence compared to Vision Transformer and deeper EfficientNet models, while performing at a similar speed to ResNet models utilizing residual connections.

Based on the confusion matrix distribution shown in Fig. 10, the attention-based improved convolutional neural network model demonstrates high accuracy in recognizing mineral images when the actual grade distribution is within the ranges of 6%~10% and 11%~15%. By integrating spatial information and image features, the model effectively extracts and classifies features in graphite mineral images. Additionally, the introduction of the Global Response Normalization (GRN) layer enhances the error adjacency property of the improved neural network model during confusion matrix performance evaluation. This implies that misclassified samples often have grades that are close to each other. Leveraging this property can help minimize resource wastage resulting from recognition errors.

Based on the hyperparameter settings described in Sect. 2.4, the quantitative analysis of the four models and their variants, following the same training strategy, is presented in Table 4. ConvNeXt-G achieves an accuracy of 93.401%, macro precision of 93.317%, macro recall of 92.856%, and macro F1 score of 93.086%. Notably, ConvNeXt-G demonstrates significant improvement compared to ResNet-50 and slightly outperforms Vision Transformer across all evaluated parameters. EfficientNet-B3 attains an accuracy of 92.718%, macro precision of 92.261%, macro recall of 92.488%, and macro F1 score of 92.802%, placing its performance on par with that of the ConvNeXt-G model in terms of evaluation metrics.

Table 4. Quantitative analysis and comparison results of evaluation indexes of different convolutional neural networks on the test set

Model	macro-P	macro-R	macro-F1	accuracy/%
ResNet-50	86.784	86.355	86.569	86.862
ResNet-101	86.845	88.957	87.888	88.002
ResNet-152	89.002	88.562	88.782	89.082
EfficientNet-B0	87.623	87.191	87.406	87.702
EfficientNet-B3	**93.001**	**91.105**	**92.043**	**92.802**
Vision Transformer-S	88.762	88.324	88.542	88.842
Vision Transformer-B	87.951	88.903	88.424	88.602
Vision Transformer-L	86.905	86.475	86.691	86.983
ConvNeXt-G	**93.317**	**92.856**	**93.086**	**93.401**

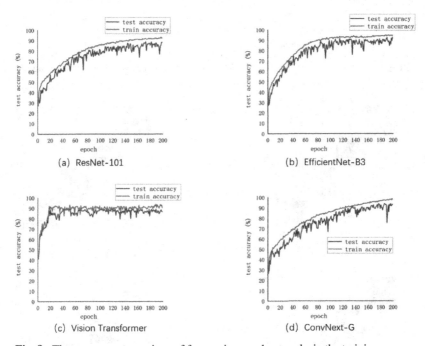

Fig. 8. The accuracy comparison of four main neural networks in the training process

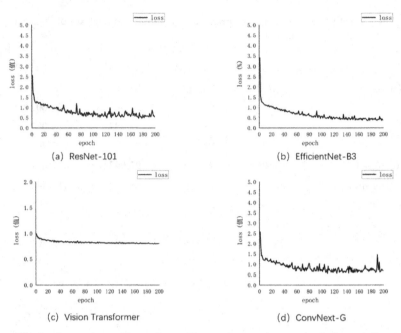

Fig. 9. Comparison of loss values of four main neural networks during training

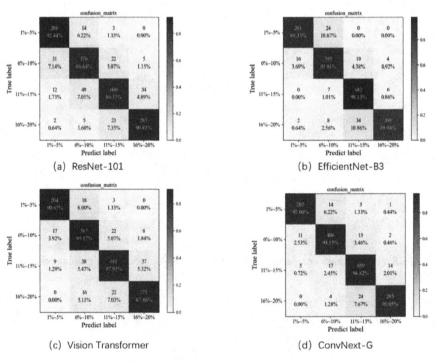

Fig. 10. The confusion matrix comparison of four main neural networks in the training process

4 Conclusion

This study proposes a convolutional neural network model that combines transfer learning and multi-scale fused image features to automatically recognize and classify graphite ore images, addressing the recognition and classification problem in this domain. Through experimental comparative analysis, we explore the application of deep learning techniques in classifying graphite ore grades, achieving improved accuracy by incorporating the ResNet-50 backbone network. To further enhance classification accuracy, we introduce spatial attention mechanisms to capture long-range dependencies more effectively. Additionally, Global Response Normalization (GRN) techniques are incorporated to enhance the precision of recognizing graphite ore grades. Our method demonstrates superior classification accuracy compared to other approaches through practical experiments. This demonstrates the effectiveness of our deep learning-based classification approach, utilizing the ResNet backbone network, in graphite ore grade classification tasks. Furthermore, compared to carbon-sulfur analysis methods that suffer from significant time delays, our approach of utilizing texture features from graphite ore images for ore grade recognition offers advantages in terms of speed, accuracy, and portability, making it a feasible solution. Through our experiments, we illustrate the complementary nature of long-range dependency learning and global response normalization in the context of graphite ore image classification. By integrating multi-scale features, we effectively improve the accuracy of graphite ore image recognition.

References

1. Su, L., Cao, X., Ma, H., et al.: Research on coal gangue identification by using convolutional neural network. In: 2018 2nd IEEE Advanced Information Management, Communicates, Electronic and Automation Control Conference (IMCEC), pp. 810–814. IEEE (2018)
2. Pu, Y., Apel, D.B., Szmigiel, A., et al.: Image recognition of coal and coal gangue using a convolutional neural network and transfer learning. Energies 12(9), 1735 (2019)
3. Szegedy, C., Vanhoucke, V., Ioffe, S., et al.: Rethinking the inception architecture for computer vision. In: Proceedings of the IEEE Conference on Computer Vision and Pattern Recognition, pp. 2818–2826 (2016)
4. Baraboshkin, E.E., Ismailova, L.S., Orlov, D.M., et al.: Deep convolutions for in-depth automated rock typing. Comput. Geosci. 135, 104330 (2020)
5. Lloyd, S.: Least squares quantization in PCM. IEEE Trans. Inf. Theory 28(2), 129–137 (1982)
6. Liu, C., Li, M., Zhang, Y., et al.: An enhanced rock mineral recognition method integrating a deep learning model and clustering algorithm. Minerals 9(9), 516 (2019)
7. Zeng, X., Xiao, Y., Ji, X., et al.: Mineral identification based on deep learning that combines image and mohs hardness. Minerals 11(5), 506 (2021)
8. Tan, M., Le, Q.: Efficientnet: rethinking model scaling for convolutional neural networks. In: International Conference on Machine Learning, pp. 6105–6114. PMLR (2019)
9. Yun, S., Han, D., Oh, S.J., et al.: Cutmix: regularization strategy to train strong classifiers with localizable features. In: Proceedings of the IEEE/CVF International Conference on Computer Vision, pp. 6023–6032 (2019)
10. Liang, Y., Cui, Q., Luo, X., et al.: Research on classification of fine-grained rock images based on deep learning. Comput. Intell. Neurosci. 2021 (2021)
11. Iglesias, J.C.Á., Santos, R.B.M., Paciornik, S.: Deep learning discrimination of quartz and resin in optical microscopy images of minerals. Miner. Eng. 138, 79–85 (2019)

12. Han, S., Li, H., Li, M., et al.: Measuring rock surface strength based on spectrograms with deep convolutional networks. Comput. Geosci. **133**, 104312 (2019)
13. Ran, X., Xue, L., Zhang, Y., et al.: Rock classification from field image patches analyzed using a deep convolutional neural network. Mathematics **7**(8), 755 (2019)
14. de Lima, R.P., Bonar, A., Coronado, D.D., et al.: Deep convolutional neural networks as a geological image classification tool. Sediment. Rec. **17**(2), 4–9 (2019)
15. Xiao, D., Le, B.T., Ha, T.T.L.: Iron ore identification method using reflectance spectrometer and a deep neural network framework. Spectrochim. Acta Part A Mol. Biomol. Spectrosc. **248**, 119168 (2021)
16. Liu, X., Wang, H., Jing, H., et al.: Research on intelligent identification of rock types based on faster R-CNN method. IEEE Access **8**, 21804–21812 (2020)
17. Xu, Z., Ma, W., Lin, P., et al.: Deep learning of rock images for intelligent lithology identification. Comput. Geosci. **154**, 104799 (2021)
18. Bochkovskiy, A., Wang, C.Y., Liao, H.Y.M.: YOLOV4: optimal speed and accuracy of object detection. arXiv preprint arXiv:2004.10934 (2020)
19. He, K., Gkioxari, G., Dollár, P., et al.: Mask R-CNN. In: Proceedings of the IEEE International Conference on Computer Vision, pp. 2961–2969 (2017)
20. Chen, Z., Yang, J., Chen, L., et al.: Garbage classification system based on improved ShuffleNet v2. Resources Conserv. Recycl. **178**, 106090 (2022)
21. Xie, S., Girshick, R., Dollár, P., et al.: Aggregated residual transformations for deep neural networks. In: Proceedings of the IEEE Conference on Computer Vision and Pattern Recognition, pp. 1492–1500 (2017)
22. Woo, S., Park, J., Lee, J.Y., et al.: CBAM: convolutional block attention module. In: Proceedings of the European Conference on Computer Vision (ECCV), pp. 3–19 (2018)
23. Woo, S., Debnath, S., Hu, R., et al.: ConvNeXt V2: co-designing and Scaling convnets with masked autoencoders. arXiv preprint arXiv:2301.00808 (2023)

Improved WGAN for Image Generation Methods

Jionghui Wang[1]([✉]), Jiale Wu[2], Xueyu Huang[2,3], and Zhilin Xiong[2]

[1] Minmetals Exploration and Development Co. Ltd., Beijing 100010, China
wangjh@minmetals.com
[2] School of Software Engineering, Jiangxi University of Science and Technology,
Nanchang 330013, People's Republic of China
[3] Nanchang Key Laboratory of Virtual Digital Factory and Cultural Communications,
Nanchang 330013, People's Republic of China

Abstract. For the problem of generating high-quality and diverse images, an image generation method combining residual module, spectral parametric normalization, and self-attention mechanism is proposed to be applied in WGAN networks. The specific improvement of the method is to introduce the residual module into the generator and discriminator networks to better capture the deep image information. The spectral parametric normalization technique is also applied to each convolutional layer of the residual block to improve the stability of the image generation process. The self-attention mechanism is introduced into the generator to enable the network to learn in a targeted manner and generate higher-quality images. The experimental results demonstrate that the combined application of these techniques can effectively solve the challenge of generating image samples, obtain stable and diverse data samples, generate better results than the original WGAN method and DCGAN method, and use the generated data samples as the dataset for expanding the classification experiments, which improves the recognition accuracy of the image classification network to a certain extent.

Keywords: Image generation · Generative adversarial network · Residual network · Self-attention mechanism · Spectral parametric normalization

1 Introduction

At present, deep learning has made great progress in the field of image recognition, including real-time object detection, semantic segmentation, face recognition, and image generation, but the implementation of these tasks requires a large dataset for training support, and the dataset collection workload is large, time-consuming, and requires professional equipment for operation, so it has limitations.

In response to the difficulty of collecting sample data in the field of image classification, we want to expand the data set by data augmentation with small samples. Currently, traditional data enhancement and adversarial methods are commonly used to expand data. Traditional data augmentation mainly consists of panning, rotating,

C. Wu et al. (Eds.): MONAMI 2023, LNICST 559, pp. 199–211, 2024.
https://doi.org/10.1007/978-3-031-55471-1_15

and scaling of images, but the diversity of images obtained in this way is insufficient. The generative adversarial approach, which generates images by training a generative adversarial network, was used by Wang et al. [1] used WGAN method for data enhancement to solve the problem of insufficient and unbalanced sample data for tomato leaf disease identification, and Guo et al. [2] proposed a conditional Wasserstein generative adversarial network model for image generation, which not only can effectively improve the accuracy of image generation, but also can improve the convergence speed of the network, although some experiments show that the quality of images generated by generative adversarial networks is better than traditional enhancement methods to some extent, but the training process will be unstable and pattern collapse during the training of generative adversarial networks [3]. However, during the training process of generative adversarial networks, problems such as unstable training process and pattern collapse can occur, which can also lead to poor quality of the generated images or failure to generate normal images [4]. However, during the training process of generative adversarial networks, problems such as stability of the training process and collapse of the model may occur, which may also lead to low quality or failure to generate normal images. Qiu et al. [5] proposed a DCGAN method combining spectral normalization and self-attention mechanism to address the problems of instability and poor generation effect in the training process, and Liu et al. [6] propose an algorithmic model of feature graph connectivity generation adversarial network to alleviate the problem of gradient disappearance.

An improved WGAN image generation method is proposed in response to the above analysis. The method replaces the network structure of the generator and discriminator with the residual structure to avoid problems such as pattern collapse during training; introduces spectral parametric normalization in the residual structure to improve the stability of overall network training; and introduces a self-attention mechanism in the generator to enhance the extraction of deep-level image features. The quality of the images generated by the improved WGAN method is experimentally demonstrated to be improved, and the accuracy in classification recognition is also improved to a certain extent.

2 Related Content

2.1 Generative Adversarial Networks

Generative Adversarial Networks [7] is a framework consisting of a deep learning model for generating realistic synthetic data. Its structure consists of a generator, which receives a random noise vector as input and generates as realistic a sample of synthetic data as possible, and a discriminator, which is a binary classifier whose goal is to distinguish the samples generated by the generator from the real samples. Through adversarial training, the generator strives to deceive the discriminator so that it cannot accurately discriminate between synthetic and real data, while the discriminator improves its accuracy by learning features of both real and synthetic data.

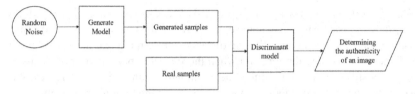

Fig.1. Generating an adversarial network model

The principle is shown in Fig. 1. The generator generates samples by mapping the true samples to a new data space and generating them. The discriminator takes the real sample and the generated sample as input and outputs a probability value indicating the probability of the real sample. The generator gradually improves the quality of the generated samples based on the feedback from the discriminator and eventually reaches a "Nash equilibrium" state, i.e., the generated samples are indistinguishable from the discriminator. This adversarial process motivates the generator to generate more realistic samples.

Generate the optimization objective function for the adversarial network:

$$\min_{G} \max_{D} V(D, G) = E_{x \sim p_{data}(x)}\big[logD(X)\big] + E_{z \sim p_z(z)}\big[log(1 - D(G(z)))\big] \quad (1)$$

In the expression (1), the D represents the discriminator, the G represents the generator, the x represents the real sample, and z represents the random noise, and $P_{data}(x)$ represents the distribution of the real sample, and $P_Z(z)$ denotes the distribution of the generated samples. The discriminator is trained to make its prediction value of the real data $lg\, D(x)$. The discriminator is trained to make its prediction of the real data as large as possible in order to improve the discriminator's ability to determine true and false. The generator is trained so that the generated samples are discriminated as true, even if they are $1 - D[G(z)]$ as small as possible, in order to achieve the effect of falsehood.

2.2 WGAN

WGAN7 is an improved method based on GAN proposed in 2017, with some improvements mainly in the original GAN to generate stable and high-quality images:

1) remove the sigmoid from the last layer of the discriminator, which is a regression problem rather than a classification problem since the discriminator is to fit the Wasserstein distance, so the values are not limited to 0–1;
2) the loss of generators and discriminators does not take log;
3) truncate the absolute values of the discriminator parameters to no more than a fixed constant c after each update of them;
4) Use non-momentum-based optimization algorithms.

WGAN introduces Wasserstein distance [9] instead of JS distance, it avoids the problem of gradient disappearance to some extent. Wasserstein distance has good continuity and convex property, it can quantify the distance between the real data distribution and the generator output distribution, and when the two distributions overlap, Wasserstein distance can still give a meaningful value. Compared with traditional metrics, Wasserstein distance can provide smoother gradients, making the training more stable. The loss functions of the generator and discriminator in WGAN are defined as follows:

Loss functions of generators:

$$L_G = -\frac{1}{N} \sum_{i=1}^{N} D(G(z^{(i)})) \tag{2}$$

Loss function of the discriminator:

$$L_D = \frac{1}{N} \sum_{i=1}^{N} D(G(z^{(i)})) - \frac{1}{N} \sum_{i=1}^{N} D(x^{(i)}) \tag{3}$$

where $D(G(z^{(i)}))$ denotes the degree to which the generated samples are discriminated as true samples by the discriminator. $D(x^{(i)})$ that is, the degree to which the true samples are discriminated as true samples by the discriminator. The loss function of the generator is the opposite of the mean of the discriminator's output of the generated samples, while the loss function of the discriminator is the difference between the mean of the output of the true samples and the generated samples.

3   Methods

3.1   Residual Network

Traditional deep neural networks suffer from the problem of gradient disappearance when the number of network layers increases, i.e., the gradient gradually becomes smaller with backpropagation leading to training difficulties [10]. This problem is solved by introducing residual connections. Residual connections build a "shortcut" by directly skipping one or more layers of network output and adding the skipped portion to the subsequent network output, allowing the gradient to propagate more easily. This structure allows the network to learn the difference between the input and the output, rather than learning the entire mapping directly.

An important variant of residual networks is the residual block, which is a module consisting of multiple residual connections with the same dimensionality. Each residual block is usually composed of two convolutional layers and one residual connection inside. By stacking multiple residual blocks, a deeper network structure can be constructed. The basic structure of a residual network is shown in Fig. 2.

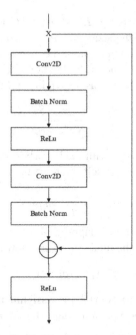

Fig. 2. Residual structure diagram

3.2 Self-attention Mechanism

Traditional GAN models for generating high-resolution images are usually generated by learning texture features from low-resolution images with fixed spatially localized points. This approach makes it relatively easy to learn texture features, such as subtle texture and color variations. However, traditional GAN models have difficulties in capturing specific structural and geometric features in images. This is because traditional GAN models do not explicitly model or constrain the structural and geometric features in the image during generation, but only focus on how to generate the whole image by learning the relationship between local pixels [11]. Therefore, when generating high-resolution images, these models may produce some results that do not match the structure and geometry of the real image.

To solve this problem, the structural and geometric features in the images are better captured by introducing a self-attention mechanism. Such a model is able to better generate high-resolution images and more accurately represent the structure and geometry of the image while maintaining the texture features.

Self-attention mechanism [12] is a mechanism to calculate the relationship between each element in a sequence and other elements. In the self-attention mechanism, each element in the input sequence calculates a relationship score with all other elements in the sequence, and then a weighted average is applied to all elements based on the score to obtain a contextual representation of each element. The specific calculation process is:

1) Suppose the input feature map is $X \in R^{C \times N}$, where C denotes the number of channels and N denotes the length of the sequence. After two 1×1 convolutions for linear transformation and channel compression, the two tensors are converted to matrix form, transposed, and then do the multiplication operation to get S_{ij} The attention map $\beta_{j,i}$ is normalized by Softmax, as shown in Eq. (4):

$$\beta_{j,i} = \frac{exp(S_{ij})}{\sum_{i=1}^{N} exp(S_{ij})} \tag{4}$$

2) Combine the attentional map $\beta_{j,i}$ with the linearly transformed original feature map $h(X_i)$ point by point, and obtain the self-attention feature map o_j, as shown in Eq. (5):

$$o_j = \sum_{i=1}^{N} \beta_{j,i} h(X_i) \tag{5}$$

3) Finally, the self-attention feature mapping and the original feature mapping are weighted and summed up as the final output, as shown in Eq. (6):

$$y_i = r o_i + X_i \tag{6}$$

r is a transition parameter to control the assignment of weights, which can be interpreted as a scaling factor with an initial value of 0.

3.3 Spectral Parametric Normalization

Traditional weight normalization methods, such as weight decay or batch normalization, can prevent problems such as overfitting or gradient disappearance to some extent, but they do not directly limit the spectral parametric number of the weight matrix. And the spectral parametric normalization [13]. The core idea is to ensure that the parameters of each layer of the network satisfy the condition that Lipschitz is equal to 1 by imposing a Lipschitz constraint on the discriminator parameters. This constraint is achieved by dividing the weight matrix of each layer by the spectral norm of the weight matrix of that layer, i.e., by applying Eq. (7) to the weights W

$$W_{normalized} = \frac{W}{\sigma} \tag{7}$$

where σ denotes the two-parametric number of weights W. By spectrally normalizing the weights of each layer of the discriminator, the discriminator can be considered as a function mapping and its Lipschitz constraint to be less than 1 to improve the stability of model training.

4   Network Structure

In this section, a residual module with embedded spectral parametric normalization is designed to replace some network layers of the discriminator and generator, and a self-attention mechanism is introduced in the intermediate layer of the generator to alleviate the problems of pattern collapse and poor quality and diversity of the generated images that occur during the training process. The specific flow of the generative adversarial network model is shown in Fig. 3.

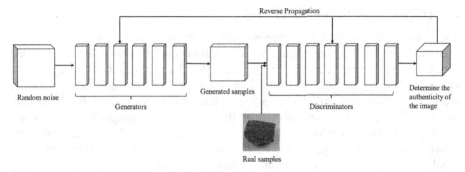

Fig. 3. Overall structure diagram

4.1 Generator Network

First, the input 100-dimensional noise is converted into a tensor with a size of $64 \times 2 \times 2$ by a linear layer. Then, this tensor is rearranged into a 64-channel, 2×2-sized feature map. Next, the feature map is gradually increased in size through a series of layers and blocks, including BasicBlock, UpsamplingNearest2d, and self-attention, while the features are processed and corrected. These layers and blocks are divided into 4 stages (layer1–layer4), where layer2–laye4 have the same network layer structure. Finally, the feature map is converted into the final generated image through a series of layers, including Conv2d, Tanh, etc., and the generated image is made flatter in terms of tonal distribution, as shown in Fig. 4.

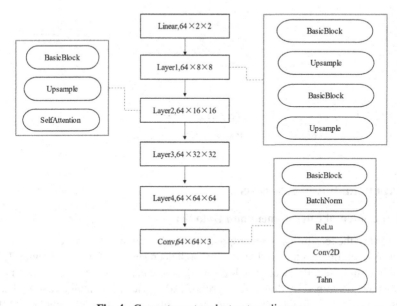

Fig. 4. Generator network structure diagram

4.2 Discriminator Network

The discriminator network has seven network layers. First, a 64 × 64 RGB image is used as the input of the discriminator network, and a convolution operation is performed by a Conv2d layer with a convolution kernel of 3 × 3 size to transform the number of channels of the input image from 3 to 64 and keep the size of the input image constant. Next, a series of layers and blocks, including BasicBlock, AvgPool2d, BatchNorm2d, and ReLU, are passed to gradually extract the features of the image. These layers and blocks are divided into 5 stages (layer1–layer5), where layer2–layer4 have the same network layer structure, and the feature map size of each stage is halved by AvgPool2d. Finally, a single value is an output after a fully connected layer, which represents the probability that the input image is a real image, and finally, the output value is converted to a probability value between 0 and 1 by a Sigmoid function. The specific structure is shown in Fig. 5.

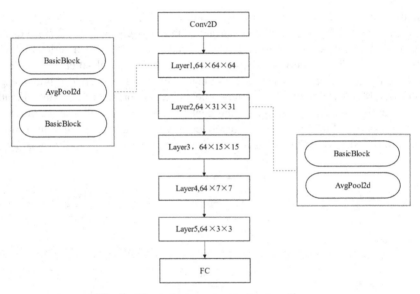

Fig. 5. Discriminator network structure diagram

5 Experiment and Analysis

5.1 Experimental Environment and Data Set

In order to test the feasibility of the proposed method, the experiments were run under the Windows operating system based on the PyTorch deep learning framework, with Python version 3.7, and the GPU used was RTX3060. The dataset used for the experiment is the ore images obtained by this project group. 1207 concentrate images and 664 waste images are selected from the dataset, and the size of the original data sample is 6000 × 4000, which is scaled equally to 64 × 64 in order to save computational resources, as shown in Fig. 6.

Fig. 6. Concentrate and waste ore images

5.2 Experimental Setup

The learning rate of both the generator and discriminator is 0.00005, the batch size is 32, the size of the generated image is 64 × 64 × 3, and the training is stopped after 10,000 epochs of iterations. The FID metric is used to evaluate the quality of the generated images, and the recognition accuracy is used as a further evaluation metric on MobileNet V2. Each class is expanded with 2000 data sets as the input data of MobileNet V2 network, and the recognition accuracy is obtained after 500 epochs of training.

5.3 Experimental Results

Generating Images for Display. Figure 7 shows the generated images of the original WGAN, DCGAN, and the improved WGAN methods, (a) is the real image, (b) is the image generated by DCGAN, (c) is the image generated by the original WGAN, and (d) is the image generated by the improved WGAN. From the figure, it can be seen that the images generated by DCGAN under the same training environment are still blurred and the features are not obvious, and the quality of the images generated by the original WGAN is improved compared with DCGAN, but the edge lines are not very clear yet, while the images generated by the improved WGAN are closer to the real images in terms of surface features and outperform DCGAN and the original WGAN in terms of quality and diversity method.

(a) Real image   (b) DCGAN   (c) Original WGAN   (d) Improved WGAN

Fig. 7. Generating images

Generating Image Evaluation Metrics. In this paper, FID (Fréchet Inception Distance [14] FID is a widely used metric for generative adversarial networks to quantify the quality of generated images by comparing the statistical information of the features of the real image distribution and the generated image distribution.

The computational process of FID consists of two key steps: feature extraction and feature statistics. First, the features are extracted from the real and generated images using a pre-trained convolutional neural network. These feature vectors capture the abstract features of the image and map the image to a high-dimensional feature space.

FID is the distribution distance between the real image and the generated image in the feature space [15]. Specifically, it calculates the Fréchet distance between the mean and covariance matrices of the feature vectors of the real and generated images. This distance measures the similarity between the two distributions, and a smaller value indicates that the generated image is closer to the real image. However, the FID value can only be used as an objective criterion to judge the quality problem of the generated images, because when encountering the pattern collapse problem, the generator tends to generate very similar samples, ignoring the diversity in the real data, which may lead to a lower FID value, thus making it easier for the classifier to find patterns for correct classification.

In the experiments of this paper, the two types of images generated by the original WGAN, DCGAN and the improved WGAN are compared. From the table of experimental results, it can be seen that the FID values of the improved WGAN are much lower than those of the original WGAN and DCGAN, which indicates that the improved WGAN outperforms the other methods in terms of quality and diversity of the generated images (Table 1).

Table 1. FID values

Generating method	Concentrate sample FID values	FID value of waste ore sample
DCGAN	148	183
WGAN	144	202
Improved WGAN	86	102

5.4 Comparison Experiments

To demonstrate the effectiveness of the improved WGAN method in generating ore images, the improved WGAN was experimentally compared with the original WGAN, traditional enhancement methods, and DCGAN, and the images generated by these four different data enhancement methods were expanded to the original dataset as the data input for the classification experiments, and the experiments and tests were conducted on the MobileNet V2 classification network, and the experimental results are shown in Table. As shown in the table, where the original data set is 1207 concentrate images and 665 waste images without any data enhancement methods, and this is used as the training set of each method for image enhancement experiments to obtain the recognition accuracy of different methods, as shown in Fig. 8.

The specific values are shown in Table 2. The traditional data enhancement method can improve the accuracy of ore binary classification to a certain extent, but this improvement is limited because using the traditional data enhancement method only changes the position of the ore in the image by rotation, translation, and other operations, and the generated image is relatively single, while the DCGAN method improves the accuracy by about 4% compared with the traditional enhancement method, but in the training process The effect of the original WGAN is better than the above methods, but there is still room for improvement in generating high-quality images.

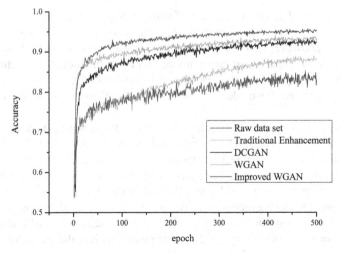

Fig.8. Recognition accuracy of different methods

In contrast, the improved WGAN method is stronger than the above methods. Replacing the original network structure with the residual structure in the original WGAN can improve the network performance and generate images with distinct features, so the recognition rate of ore images generated using the improved WGAN is higher than that of the traditional enhancement method, the original WGAN method and the DCGAN method on the classification network.

Table 2. Comparison of experimental results

Experimental method	MobileNet V2
Raw data set	83.01%
Traditional Enhancement	88.27%
DCGAN	92.38%
WGAN	93.19%
Improved WGAN	95.39%

5.5 Ablation Experiments

To demonstrate that the various improvements of the network are effective in improving the performance of the model, ablation experiments are conducted. In the ablation experiments, the accuracy of the classification network Mobilenet V2 is used as the main indicator, and the ablation experiments include the introduction of residual blocks, the introduction of spectral parametric normalization, and the introduction of a self-attentive mechanism.

To demonstrate that the introduction of residual blocks in the original WGAN can improve the model accuracy, comparative experiments are designed to replace the original network layers of the generator and discriminator with residual blocks; to demonstrate the contribution of spectral parametric normalization to the model, it is embedded on each convolutional layer of the residual blocks; and to demonstrate that the self-attentive mechanism is effective for model improvement, it is embedded in the middle layer of the generator.

The experimental results are shown in the Table 3. It can be seen that after replacing the original network layers of the generator and discriminator with residual blocks, the recognition accuracy of the model is improved by 2% and the phenomenon of gradient disappearance during training is moderated; after introducing spectral parametric normalization on each convolutional layer of the residual blocks, the stability of the model training is improved and the recognition accuracy of the model is also improved by 0.5%; after embedding the self-attention mechanism in the second, third, fourth and fifth layers of the generator After embedding the self-attention mechanism, the recognition accuracy of the model is improved by 1.9%, and the generated images are of higher quality and richer in features.

Overall, by introducing residual blocks, spectral parametric normalization, and self-attentiveness mechanisms, the algorithm proposed in this study is applied to ore classification recognition with 2.2% higher accuracy than the pre-improvement model and improves the quality and diversity of the generated images.

Table 3. Results of ablation experiments

Experimental method	MobileNet V2
WGAN	93.19%
WGAN + spectral parametric normalization	93.67%
WGAN + Self-Attention Mechanism	94.94%
WGAN + Residuals Module	95.08%
Improved WGAN	95.39%

6   Conclusion

In this paper, we propose a generative adversarial network model incorporating residual blocks, spectral parametric normalization, and self-attentive mechanism. Introducing residual blocks into the network can extract deeper features and generate better images, applying the weight normalization technique of spectral parametric normalization to each convolutional layer of the residual blocks can slow down the convergence of the discriminator more effectively, stabilize the training process, and ensure that the generator is fully trained training process and ensure that the generator is fully trained, and introducing the self-attention mechanism into the generator is more attentive to the structural and geometric features in the image and can generate images with richer diversity.

The images generated by the improved WGAN method were used to expand the sample dataset, and the newly generated images were tested by FID to show that the stability of the training process and the generation quality of the method were improved. Compared with the original WGAN method, the accuracy of the images generated by the improved WGAN method for classification and recognition is also improved. However, the method still faces some challenges in generating some other high-resolution images, which will be improved and optimized in the future.

References

1. Wang, Z.Q., Yu, X., Yang, X.J., et al.: Tomato leaf disease identification based on WGAN and MCA-MobileNet. J. Agric. Mach. **54**(05), 244–252 (2023)
2. Guo, M., Yang, Q., Zhao, L.: Image generation based on conditional Wassertein generative adversarial network. Comput. Appl. **41**(05), 1432–1437 (2021)
3. Heusel, M., Ramsauer, H., Unterthiner, T., et al.: Gans trained by a two time-scale update rule converge to a local nash equilibrium. In: Proceedings of the Advances in Neural Information Processing Systems, pp. 6626–6637. Curran Associates, Long Beach (2017)
4. Wu, S., Li, X.: A review of research progress in generative adversarial networks. Comput. Sci. Explor. **14**(03), 377–388 (2020)
5. Li, Q.-L., Ma, L.: A study of DCGAN combining spectrum normalization and self-attentive mechanism. Comput. Appl. Softw. **38**(02), 227–232+290 (2021)
6. Liu, J., Ma, S.H.: Data enhancement of colon cancer glandular cells based on feature map gradient connection generative adversarial network. Comput. Digital Eng. **50**(11), 2557–2561+2573 (2022)
7. Liang, J., Wei, S.J., Jiang, C.F.: A review on generative adversarial networks GAN. Comput. Sci. Explor. **14**(01), 1–17 (2020)
8. Gulrajani, I., Ahmed, F., Arjovsky, M., et al.: Improved training of wasserstein GANs. arXiv: 1704.00028 (2017)
9. Wang, Y., Han, J., Fan, L.: Research on speech enhancement algorithm based on WGAN[J]. J. Chongqing Univ. Posts Telecommun. (Nat. Sci. Ed.) **31**(01), 136–142 (2019)
10. Guo, Y., et al.: A review of residual network research. Comput. Appl. Res. **37**(05) (2020)
11. Wang, X.L., Girshick, R., Gupta, A., et al.: Non-local neural networks. Comput. Vision Pattern Recogn. **2**, 7794–7780 (2017)
12. Zhu, Z., Rao, Y., Wu, Y., et al.: Research progress of attentional mechanism in deep learning. Chin. J. Inf. **33**(06), 1–11 (2019)
13. Miyato, T., Kataoka, T., Koyama, M., et al.: Spectral normalization for generative adversarial networks. In: International Conference on Learning Representations (2018)
14. Hu, L.-M., Zhang, Y.: Short-wave infrared-visible face image translation based on generative adversarial networks. J. Opt. **40**(5), 75–84 (2020)
15. Chen, X., Huang, X., Xie, L.: A multiscale conditional generation adversarial network-based approach for blood cell image classification and detection. J. Zhejiang Univ. (Eng. Ed.) **55**(09), 1772–1781 (2021)

Distributed Computing

Research on Multi-scale Pedestrian Attribute Recognition Based on Dual Self-attention Mechanism

He Xiao[1,2(✉)], Wenbiao Xie[1], Yang Zhou[3], Yong Luo[4], Ruoni Zhang[1], and Xiao Xu[1]

[1] School of Software Engineering, Jiangxi University of Science and Technology, NanChang 330013, Jiangxi, People's Republic of China
`xiaohe804@gmail.com, vebrun@jxust.edu.cn`
[2] Nanchang Key laboratory of Virtual Digital Factory and Cultural Communications, Nanchang 330013, People's Republic of China
[3] Information and Communication Branch, State Grid Jiangxi Electric Power Co, Nanchang 330095, China
[4] School of Software, Jiangxi Normal University, Nanchang 330022, China
`luoyong1020@jxnu.edu.cn`

Abstract. As one of the important fields of computer vision research, pedestrian attribute recognition has gained increasing attention from domestic and foreign researchers due to its huge potential applications. However, obtaining long-distance pedestrian information in actual scenes poses challenges such as lack of information, incomplete feature extraction, and low attribute recognition accuracy. To address these issues, we propose a multi-scale feature fusion network based on a dual self-attention mechanism. The fusion module merges multi-scale features to enable more complete attribute extraction, while the dual self-attention module focuses the network on important regions. Experimental results on PA-100K, RAP, and PETA datasets achieved mean accuracies of 81.97%, 81.53%, and 86.37%, respectively. Extensive experiments demonstrate that the proposed method is highly competitive in pedestrian attribute recognition.

Keywords: incomplete feature · dual self-attention · multi-scale fusion · pedestrian attribute recognition

1 Introduction

As computer vision technology continues to evolve, pedestrian attribute recognition has emerged as a vital research focus, garnering extensive interest. Pedestrian attribute recognition refers to the recognition and classification of a range of pedestrian attributes in images (such as clothing, hairstyle, gender, age, etc.),

The Jiangxi Province Office of Education provided funding support for this research.

C. Wu et al. (Eds.): MONAMI 2023, LNICST 559, pp. 215–226, 2024.
https://doi.org/10.1007/978-3-031-55471-1_16

which enables quick recognition and judgment of pedestrian identities [1–4]. The technology of pedestrian attribute recognition holds extensive applicability in areas like intelligent monitoring, security detection, and intelligent transportation. Its deployment carries substantial importance for enhancing societal security and safeguarding individuals' lives and assets [5,6].

Over recent years, as deep learning technology has steadily evolved, models for pedestrian attribute recognition based on deep neural networks have made significant advancements. In the realm of existing research, some academics have put forward pioneering modules like multi-scale feature fusion [7,8] and self-attention mechanism [9,10], effectively enhancing the accuracy and stability of pedestrian attribute recognition. However, existing pedestrian attribute recognition models still have some problems, such as poor attribute recognition performance in complex scenes and insufficient processing of the mutual influence relationship between different attributes.

Pedestrian attribute recognition stands as a critical research focus within the computer vision domain and carries substantial importance across a multitude of applications. However, it also faces several challenges, including **viewpoint variations, illumination variations, occlusions, imbalanced attribute distributions, low resolution, and blurriness** [11].

Viewpoint variations occur due to different angles and distances between the shooting device and pedestrians, which cause changes in the viewpoint and size of pedestrians in the image. This can affect the recognition of pedestrian attributes. Illumination variations occur due to different lighting conditions that cause changes in the brightness, contrast, color, and other aspects of pedestrian images, making the recognition of pedestrian attributes more difficult. Occlusions occur when other objects such as pedestrians, vehicles, and buildings obstruct parts of the pedestrian's body or clothing, which can affect the recognition of pedestrian attributes. Imbalanced attribute distributions occur because the distribution of pedestrians with different attributes in the dataset is uneven, which can lead to poor recognition performance for certain attributes. Low resolution occurs owing to the substandard resolution of pedestrian images, making it difficult to capture the details of pedestrian attributes and thus affecting the recognition of pedestrian attributes. Blurriness occurs due to image blur or motion blur, making the recognition of pedestrian attributes more difficult.

2   Related Work

Global-based models. Li [13] et al. put forward two significant models: Deep-SAR and DeepMAR. The former, DeepSAR, operates without considering any correlation between attributes while the latter, DeepMAR, is built specifically to consider such correlations. Recognizing a prevalent issue in the field, Li et al. also made strides in addressing the problem of imbalanced attribute distribution. They did this by proposing a novel loss function, a solution that is designed to specifically tackle this imbalance. In an innovative approach, Sudowe [12] et al. incorporated AlexNet, a pre-existing, influential model, as the backbone for feature extraction in their global-based model. This model stands out due to its unique multi-branch classification layer designed for each attribute. Abdulnabi [14] et al. made a noteworthy contribution to the field by proposing a joint multi-task learning algorithm. This algorithm, used for attribute estimation, is based on Convolutional Neural Networks (CNN), a popular and effective tool in the realm of machine learning.

Part-based models. Tang [7] et al. developed a complex yet efficient approach to attribute analysis. They fused deep semantic features and low-level detail features into the attribute localization module and used an element-by-element voting mechanism to select the optimal value, ensuring a comprehensive and accurate process. Diba [17] et al. proposed an inventive CNN which is specifically engineered for mining mid-level image information. This tool is especially useful for fine-grained pedestrian attribute recognition, enhancing the detail and accuracy of such analyses. In a progressive move, YangDiba [16] et al. employed an end-to-end learning framework. This framework is uniquely tailored for the joint part localization and multi-label classification, thus serving dual purposes in an integrated manner. Li [18] et al. implemented a pose estimation algorithm with a specific purpose in mind - to accurately locate local bodies. This application of the algorithm demonstrates its utility in precise localization tasks. Zhu [15] et al. brought forth a novel approach in the form of a multi-label convolutional neural network. This innovative network is designed to jointly predict multiple attributes, showcasing the potential for simultaneous analysis.

Attention-based models. Guo [22] et al. suggested a path to enhance attribute recognition performance - by improving the attention map. This proposal highlights the critical role of attention maps in attribute recognition, and how their enhancement can potentially lead to superior performance outcomes. Sarfraz [21] et al. put forth a compelling argument for considering viewpoint cues in attribute analysis. They advocated that this consideration would significantly improve the estimation of the correlation between attributes, leading to more accurate and insightful results. Liu [20] et al. introduced a notable proposal to utilize the multi-directional attention (MDA) module. This innovative approach aims to maximize the potential of attention mechanisms in processing and analysing data.

This paper aims to propose a multi-scale pedestrian attribute recognition model based on a dual self-attention mechanism to address the aforementioned challenges and improve the accuracy and robustness of pedestrian attribute recognition. Specifically, this paper first designs a multi-scale feature fusion module to effectively extract multi-scale features from pedestrian images. Then, a dual self-attention mechanism is introduced to model the mutual relationships between different attributes in pedestrian images, thereby improving the accuracy and robustness of pedestrian attribute recognition.

The primary advancements presented in this study can be summarized as follows: 1. An innovative multi-scale feature fusion module has been proposed. The primary function of this module is to effectively extract the correlation between pedestrian attributes from multi-scale features. This approach aims to leverage the potential of multi-scale features and their correlation for in-depth analysis.

2. A dual self-attention mechanism module has been put forward. This module processes features using parallel channel self-attention and spatial self-attention, a unique approach that enables the network to focus more on significant feature regions. As a result, this module significantly improves the accuracy of attribute recognition, marking a step forward in this field. 3. To validate the effectiveness of the proposed methods, extensive experiments were conducted on three public datasets, namely PA-100K [20], RAP [23], and PETA [24]. These experiments included ablation experiments and comparison experiments with classical algorithms. The results demonstrated the superiority of the proposed network framework in the specific task of pedestrian attribute recognition, thereby endorsing its potential for practical application and further research.

3   Methods

This paper proposes an end-to-end multi-scale pedestrian attribute recognition framework. In this method, features with multi-level receptive fields are obtained through a fusion module, and the network focuses on important feature regions through a dual self-attention mechanism. The entire network learns end-to-end in a multi-task setting, with attribute recognition as the primary task. The network framework is illustrated in Fig. 1.

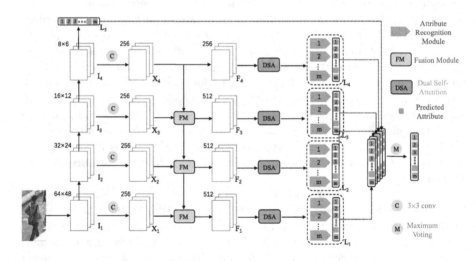

Fig. 1. The comprehensive structure of the framework.

3.1   Network Architecture

The fundamental concept of this study revolves around the use of the dual self-attention module to zero in on the essential details within multi-scale features. As it is well-known, shallow networks have larger receptive fields, which allow them to capture more details, but they lack contextual information. Deep features and shallow features complement each other. To address this, we employ a feature pyramid structure to glean features across varied scales, thereby making the information more complete.

We adopt ResNeXt50 [25] as the backbone to extract features of four stages, and the specifics of the features are depicted in the far left column of Fig. 1. The feature information of the four scales is represented as $I_i = R^{C_i \times H_i \times W_i}$, $i \in \{4, 3, 2, 1\}$. The spatial dimensions $H_i \times W_i$ of I_i stand at 8×6, 16×12, 32×24, 64×48. And the dimensions of the channels C_i correspondingly measure 2048, 1024, 512, and 256.

The backbone's pathway can be interpreted as a bottom-up approach, whereas the feature fusion module can be viewed as a top-down strategy. The lateral connections between them play a crucial role in adjusting the feature dimension to a unified d dimension, which is accomplished through convolution. In our experiments, d is set to 256. Then, features from adjacent stages are concatenated by fusion module, which can be articulated as:

$$F_i = FM(C(I_{i+1}), C(I_i)), i \in \{3, 2, 1\} \tag{1}$$

where C represents a 1×1 convolution, FM represents the feature fusion module, and F_i is the fused feature. Since the features of the fourth stage are not fused with other features, they are represented as:

$$F_i = X_i = C(I_i), i \in \{4\} \tag{2}$$

The channel dimension of F_i is $2d$, except for F_4, which has a dimension of d. This is because $F_i(i \in \{3, 2, 1\})$ merge features from two stages, as mentioned earlier, and in our experiments, d is set to 256.

3.2 Fusion Module

Shallow networks with larger receptive fields can capture rich details, while deep networks with smaller receptive fields can capture rich semantic features. To integrate neighboring features and apprehend the attribute correlation amid multi-scale features, we proposed a fusion module, which illustrated in Fig. 2.

For the deep-level feature information, we first upsample it and then perform a sigmoid activation operation. For the shallow-level feature information, we perform a four-layer convolution operation on it. Then, We perform an element-wise addition of the two features. The corresponding formula is articulated as:

$$s' = f(X_i) + \sigma\left(up(X_{i+1})\right), i \in \{3, 2, 1\} \tag{3}$$

where f represents a four-layer convolution, up represents upsampling, and σ represents sigmoid activation operation. Finally, the shallow-level feature $f(X_i)$ and s' are concatenated along the channel dimension to obtain F_i, whose dimension is $2d$. The formula is as follows:

$$F_i = cat(f(X_i), s'), i \in \{3, 2, 1\} \tag{4}$$

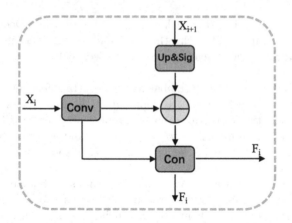

Fig. 2. Fusion Module.

3.3 Dual Self-Attention

In order to glean crucial data from the combined features, we introduce a dual self-attention module that simultaneously employs channel attention and spatial attention. We have termed this the Dual Self-Attention module, and comprehensive details about this module can be seen in Fig. 3.

For the channel self-attention, the feature F_i is split into three branches, each of which undergoes a convolution operation. In branch one, the feature is first average pooled, then softmax activated, and then dot producted with branch two. After being pooled again, the result is dot producted with branch three to obtain $F_{out}^{c_i}$. The equation can be articulated as follows:

$$F_{out}^{c_i} = p\left[\sigma(p(f(F_i))) \cdot f(F_i)\right] \cdot r(f(F_i)), i \in \{1, 2, 3\} \tag{5}$$

For the spatial self-attention, similarly, the feature F is split into three branches, each of which undergoes a convolution operation. However, unlike channel self-attention, branch one does not have a pooling operation, but an additional convolution operation after the first dot product, which is expressed in the formula below:

$$F_{out}^{s_i} = f\left[\sigma(f(F_i)) \cdot f(F_i)\right] \cdot r(f(F_i)), i \in \{1, 2, 3\} \tag{6}$$

where f represents convolution operation, p represents pooling operation, σ represents Sigmoid activation, and r represents ReLU activation. Finally, $F_{out}^{c_i}$ and $F_{out}^{s_i}$ are element-wise added together:

$$F_{out}^i = F_{out}^{c_i} + F_{out}^{s_i}, i \in \{1, 2, 3\} \tag{7}$$

4   Experiments

This chapter conducts experiments on the proposed method, which includes datasets, evaluation metrics, experimental equipment and settings, and comparison experiments.

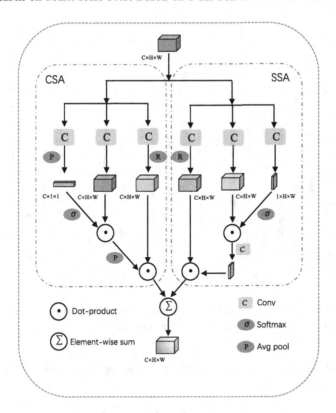

Fig. 3. Dual Self-Attention. The left CSA is Channel Self-Attention, the right SSA is Spatial Self-Attention, and both of them are used in parallel to form the Dual Self-Attention.

4.1 Datasets

The PA-100K [20] dataset, currently the most extensive one utilized for pedestrian attribute recognition, comprises 100,000 pedestrian images. Each of these images is annotated with 26 binary attributes.

The RAP [23] dataset comprises 41,585 images, with each pedestrian being marked with 69 binary attributes that cover both pedestrian characteristics and actions.

The PETA [24] dataset comprises 19,000 images, with their resolutions varying between 17×39 and 169×365. Every pedestrian in the dataset is marked with 61 binary attributes and 4 multi-class attributes.

4.2 Evaluation Metrics

We implement a **label-based** method to determine the mean accuracy (**mA**) of each attribute. This involves computing the classification accuracy for both

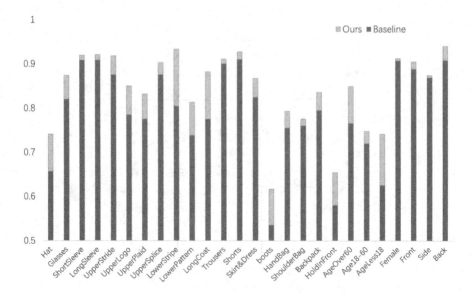

Fig. 4. Attribute comparison on PA-100K. The orange bars represent ours, while the blue bars represent the baseline. (Color figure online)

positive and negative samples and then averaging these results. The formula used for this calculation is

$$mA = \frac{1}{2N} \sum_{i=1}^{M} \left(\frac{TP_i}{P_i} + \frac{TN_i}{N_i} \right) \tag{8}$$

We employ a **sample-based** approach and evaluate our method using four commonly used metrics: **accuracy, recall, precision,** and **F1** score. Given the familiarity of these metrics, we omit their formulas and detail information.

Table 1. The Comparative Analysis on the PA-100K dataset

Method	mA	Rec	Prec	Acc	F1
ALM [7]	80.68	88.84	84.21	77.08	86.46
HPNet [20]	74.21	82.09	82.97	72.19	82.53
PGDM [18]	74.95	82.24	84.36	73.08	83.29
LGNet [26]	76.96	83.17	86.99	75.55	85.04
VeSPA [21]	76.32	81.49	84.99	73.00	83.20
DeepMar [13]	72.70	80.42	82.24	70.39	81.32
CoCNN [27]	80.56	84.36	**89.49**	78.30	86.85
StrongBaseline [29]	80.50	87.12	87.24	78.84	86.78
ours	**81.97**	**90.74**	85.69	**78.88**	**86.89**

Table 2. The Comparative Analysis on the RAP dataset

Method	mA	Rec	Prec	Acc	F1
ALM [7]	**81.87**	86.48	74.71	**68.17**	**80.16**
PGDM [18]	74.31	75.90	78.86	64.57	77.35
LGNet [26]	78.68	79.82	**80.36**	68.00	80.09
HPNet [20]	76.12	78.79	77.33	65.39	78.05
VeSPA [21]	77.70	79.67	79.51	67.35	79.59
DeepMar [13]	73.79	76.21	74.92	62.02	75.56
ours	81.53	**87.85**	76.78	67.96	79.69

Table 3. The Comparative Analysis on the PETA dataset

Method	mA	Rec	Prec	Acc	F1
MTA-Net [28]	84.62	86.42	85.67	78.80	86.04
WPAL [19]	85.50	85.78	84.07	76.98	84.90
ALM [7]	86.30	88.09	85.65	79.52	**86.85**
PGDM [18]	82.97	84.68	**86.86**	78.08	85.76
HPNet [20]	81.77	83.24	84.92	76.13	84.07
VeSPA [21]	83.45	84.81	86.18	77.73	85.49
DeepMar [13]	82.89	83.14	83.68	75.07	83.41
ours	**86.37**	**89.39**	85.62	**79.56**	86.77

4.3 Experimental Equipment and Settings

Our experimental process takes place on the Ubuntu 18.04 operating system, making use of Python 3.8. The network architecture we propose is brought to life using the PyTorch framework, and the training process occurs on a pair of 2080Ti devices. We establish the batch size at 48 and run the model training for a comprehensive 60 epochs.

4.4 Comparison Experiments

Attribute Comparison. Label-based mA is a crucial metric for assessing model performance. In this section, we present a visual representation of the mA values for every attribute present in the PA-100K dataset and compare them with the Baseline [29] in an intuitive manner. As evident from the visualization, our proposed model outperforms the Baseline for all attributes in terms of mA values.

Methods Comparison. There are many classic models that have been experimented on the RAP, PETA,PA-100K and datasets, including DeepMar(Deep

Multi-Attribute Recognition model) [13], VeSPA [21], HPNet(Hydra Plus Net) [20], LGNet (Location Guided Network) [26], CoCNN [27], ALM [7], PGDM(Posed Guided Deep Model) [18], WPAL [19], MTA-Net [28], Strong-Baseline [29], etc. The performance comparison of our model with others on the mentioned three datasets is displayed in Table 1, Table 2, and Table 3. It's clear that our approach outperforms others, especially on the PA-100K dataset, with a recall rate improvement of 1.8 over the second place, breaking through 90. The performance on the RAP dataset is slightly inferior, but still has the highest recall rate. There is also good performance on the PETA dataset, with a chance to break through a recall rate of over 90.

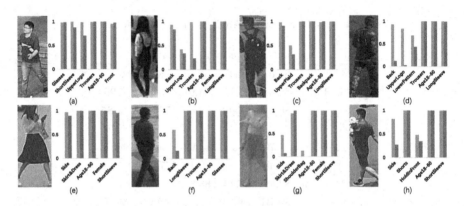

Fig. 5. Sample comparison. The orange bars represent ours, while the blue bars represent the baseline. (Color figure online)

Sample Comparison. Figure 6 displays eight pedestrian images labeled from 'a' to 'h', along with their true labels. The histogram on the right side illustrates the prediction outcomes from our model and the StrongBaseline [29] model. The x-axis of the histogram signifies the predicted attribute, whereas the y-axis denotes the probability of that predicted attribute. It's noticeable that our model outperforms the Baseline model in predicting both coarse-grained and fine-grained attributes. When it comes to attributes associated with blurry and obscured samples, such as the 'ShoulderBag' attribute of sample 'g' which is obscured by the body, the Baseline's prediction probabilities are incredibly low, registering at only 0.0027, which appears as zero on the histogram. In contrast, our model predicts a probability of 0.1258.

5   Conclusion

In this study, we initially employ the feature pyramid structure to extract feature information across multiple scales. Subsequently, our proposed Fusion Module is applied to enhance the completeness of the feature information. Additionally, we introduce a dual self-attention module that extracts information from both the channel and spatial dimensions of features. Comprehensive experiments carried out on RAP, PETA, and PA-100K datasets serve to underscore the superior performance of our model compared to preceding models.

Acknowledgment. This research received partial support from the National Natural Science Foundation of China(No. 62067003) and the Foundation of Jiangxi Educational Committee (No. GJJ200824).

References

1. Feris, R., Bobbitt, R., Brown, L., Pankanti, S.: Attribute-based people search: lessons learnt from a practical surveillance system. In: Proceedings of the ACM International Conference on Multimedia Retrieval 2014, Glasgow, United Kingdom, pp. 153–160, April 2014
2. Lin, Y., Zheng, L., Zheng, Z., Wu, Y., Hu, Z., Yan, C., et al.: Improving person re-identification by attribute and identity learning. Pattern Recognit. **95**, 151–161 (2019)
3. Di, X., Zhang, H., Patel, V.M.: Polarimetric thermal to visible face verification via attribute preserved synthesis. In: 2018 IEEE 9th International Conference on Biometrics Theory, Applications and Systems, United states, October 2018
4. Di, X., Riggan, B.S., Hu, S., Short, N.J., Patel, V.M.: Multi-scale thermal to visible face verification via attribute guided synthesis. IEEE Trans. Biom. Behav. Identity Sci. 266–280 (2021)
5. Shi, Y., Ling, H., Wu, L., Shen, J., Li, P.: Learning refined attribute-aligned network with attribute selection for person re-identification. Neurocomputing **402**, 124–133 (2020)
6. Li, H., Chen, Y., Tao, D., Yu, Z., Qi, G.: Attribute-aligned domain-invariant feature learning for unsupervised domain adaptation person re-identification. IEEE Trans. Inf. Forensics Secur. **16**, 1480–1494 (2021)
7. Tang, C., Sheng, L., Zhang, Z.-X., Hu, X.: Improving pedestrian attribute recognition with weakly-supervised multi-scale attribute-specific localization. In: 2019 IEEE/CVF International Conference on Computer Vision (ICCV), Seoul, Korea (South), pp. 4996–5005, October2019
8. Zhong, J., Qiao, H., Chen, L., Shang, M., Liu, Q.: Improving pedestrian attribute recognition with multi-scale spatial calibration. In: International Joint Conference on Neural Networks (IJCNN) 2021, pp. 1–8 (2021)
9. Liu, Z., Zhang, Z., Li, D., Zhang, P., Shan, C.: Dual-branch self-attention network for pedestrian attribute recognition. Pattern Recognit. Lett. **163**, 112–120 (2022)
10. Fan, Z., Guan, Y.: Pedestrian attribute recognition based on dual self-attention mechanism. Comput. Sci. Inf. Syst. **20**, 793–812 (2023)
11. Wang, X., Zheng, S., Yang, R., Luo, B., Chen, Z., Tang, J.: Pedestrian Attribute Recognition: A (2019)
12. Sudowe, P., Spitzer, H., Leibe, B.: Person attribute recognition with a jointly-trained holistic CNN model. In: 2015 IEEE International Conference on Computer Vision Workshop (ICCVW), Santiago, Chile, pp. 329–337, December 2015. Survey. Pattern Recognit., 121, 108220

13. Li, D., Chen, X., Huang, K.: Multi-attribute learning for pedestrian attribute recognition in surveillance scenarios. In: 2015 3rd IAPR Asian Conference on Pattern Recognition (ACPR), Kuala Lumpur, Malaysia, pp. 111–115, November 2015

14. Abdulnabi, A.H., Wang, G., Lu, J., Jia, K.: Multi-Task CNN model for attribute prediction. IEEE Trans. Multimed. **17**, 1949–1959 (2015)

15. Zhu, J., Liao, S., Yi, D., Lei, Z.: Multi-label CNN based pedestrian attribute learning for soft biometrics. In: 2015 International Conference on Biometrics (ICB), pp. 535–540 (2015)

16. Yang, L., Zhu, L., Wei, Y., Liang, S., Tan, P.: Attribute Recognition from Adaptive Parts (2016). ArXiv, abs/1607.01437

17. Diba, A., Pazandeh, A.M., Pirsiavash, H., Gool, L.V.: DeepCAMP: deep convolutional action & attribute mid-level patterns. In: IEEE Conference on Computer Vision and Pattern Recognition (CVPR) 2016, pp. 3557–3565 (2016)

18. Li, D., Chen, X., Zhang, Z., Huang, K.: Pose guided deep model for pedestrian attribute recognition in surveillance scenarios. In: IEEE International Conference on Multimedia and Expo (ICME) 2018, pp. 1–6 (2018)

19. Yu, K., Leng, B., Zhang, Z., Li, D., Huang, K.: Weakly-supervised Learning of Mid-level Features for Pedestrian Attribute Recognition and Localization (2016). ArXiv, abs/1611.05603

20. Liu, X., et al.: HydraPlus-Net: attentive deep features for pedestrian analysis. In: IEEE International Conference on Computer Vision (ICCV) 2017, pp. 350–359 (2017)

21. Sarfraz, M.S., Schumann, A., Wang, Y.: Deep View-Sensitive Pedestrian Attribute Inference in an end-to-end Model (2017). ArXiv, abs/1707.06089

22. Guo, H., Fan, X., Wang, S.: Human attribute recognition by refining attention heat map. Pattern Recognit. Lett. **94**, 38–45 (2017)

23. Li, D., Zhang, Z., Chen, X., Ling, H., Huang, K.: A Richly Annotated Dataset for Pedestrian Attribute Recognition (2016). ArXiv, abs/1603.07054

24. Deng, Y., Luo, P., Loy, C.C.: Pedestrian attribute recognition at far distance. In: Proceedings of the 22nd ACM International Conference on Multimedia (2014)

25. Xie, S., Girshick, R.B., Dollár, P., Tu, Z., He, K.: Aggregated residual transformations for deep neural networks. In: IEEE Conference on Computer Vision and Pattern Recognition (CVPR) 2017, pp. 5987–5995 (2016)

26. Liu, P., Liu, X., Yan, J., Shao, J.: Localization Guided Learning for Pedestrian Attribute Recognition (2018). ArXiv, abs/1808.09102

27. Han, K., Wang, Y., Shu, H., Liu, C., Xu, C., Xu, C.: Attribute Aware Pooling for Pedestrian Attribute Recognition (2019). ArXiv, abs/1907.11837

28. Ji, Z., Hu, Z., He, E., Han, J., Pang, Y.: Pedestrian attribute recognition based on multiple time steps attention. Pattern Recognit. Lett. **138**, 170–176 (2020)

29. Jia, J., Huang, H., Yang, W., Chen, X., Huang, K.: Rethinking of Pedestrian Attribute Recognition: Realistic Datasets with Efficient Method (2020). ArXiv, abs/2005.11909

Improving Pedestrian Attribute Recognition with Dense Feature Pyramid and Mixed Pooling

He Xiao[1,2(✉)], Chen Zou[1], Yaosheng Chen[1], Sujia Gong[1], and Siwen Dong[1]

[1] School of Software Engineering, Jiangxi University of Science and Technology, Nanchang 330013, Jiangxi, People's Republic of China
xiaohe804@gmail.com, chen@jxust.edu.cn, adsw@mail.jxust.edu.cn
[2] Nanchang Key Laboratory of Virtual Digital Factory and Cultural Communications, Nanchang 330013, People's Republic of China

Abstract. In the field of computer vision, pedestrian attribute recognition plays a crucial role in pedestrian detection and pedestrian re-identification. However, this task faces challenges such as blurry images, difficulty in recognizing fine-grained features, and overlooking relationships between pedestrian attributes. To address these challenges, we propose a novel method for pedestrian attribute recognition. Our method is based on convolutional neural networks and incorporates a feature pyramid structure that is specifically designed for the task of pedestrian attribute recognition (PAR). Additionally, we enhance feature information by employing multi-scale feature fusion. Furthermore, our proposed AIIM module facilitates interactions between different attributes by establishing both remote dependencies and short-range dependencies. Through comprehensive experimentation, we have validated the effectiveness of our method and achieved state-of-the-art results. Specifically, our method has achieved impressive average accuracies (mA) of 86.27%, 83.45%, and 81.56% on well-known datasets such as PETA, RAP, and PA100k, respectively.

Keywords: Convolutional neural network · Feature pyramid · Multi-scale fusion · Mixed pooling · Pedestrian attribute recognition

1 Introduction

Pedestrian attribute recognition [1] is a significant area of research in computer vision, with practical applications in video surveillance. This field focuses on identifying semantic descriptions that can be used as soft biometric features for purposes such as pedestrian detection, re-identification, and retrieval. The goal of pedestrian attribute recognition is to predict a set of attributes from a predefined list for a given person image. These attributes provide valuable semantic information to describe and understand pedestrians in images. Incorporating attribute information into computer vision algorithms for tasks like re-identification [2–4], pedestrian detection [5, 6], and retrieval [7, 8] can enhance performance. However, real-world surveillance scenarios present challenges due to factors such as camera angles, lighting conditions, and complexities in pedestrian attributes like pose, occlusion, and blur.

© ICST Institute for Computer Sciences, Social Informatics and Telecommunications Engineering 2024
Published by Springer Nature Switzerland AG 2024. All Rights Reserved
C. Wu et al. (Eds.): MONAMI 2023, LNICST 559, pp. 227–239, 2024.
https://doi.org/10.1007/978-3-031-55471-1_17

The initial approach to pedestrian attribute recognition involved manual feature extraction and separate classification models for each attribute. However, with the emergence of Convolutional Neural Networks (CNN), researchers started exploring multi-task training where all attributes are integrated into a single network, thereby sharing network parameters. This approach proved to be more effective in achieving improved results.

At present, the fundamental methods for pedestrian attribute recognition can be categorized into several groups:

Global image-based models such as DeepSAR [9] and DeepMAR [9] are simpler, more intuitive, and efficient in the context of pedestrian attribute recognition (PAR). However, their performance is constrained by the lack of fine-grained recognition and consideration of correlations between pedestrian attributes. Models that incorporate localization, such as PGDM [10] and LGNet [11], leverage both local and global information to achieve more precise performance. Yet, these models suffer from their heavy reliance on accurate localization, which increases training and inference time and cost. Attention-based models like HydraPlus-Net [12], VeSPA [13], and others selectively focus on specific information but overlook other relevant behavioral and cognitive processes. While these models showcase the effectiveness of attention mechanisms, they shift the research focus towards local features and attention-based features, neglecting the study of attribute correlations.

In recent years, several models have been proposed to address pedestrian attribute identification. These models, including JRL [15], RCRA [16], and other sequence prediction-based models, employ recurrent learning to capture correlations between attributes. Furthermore, some models, such as WPAL [17] and other loss function-based models, have improved upon the optimized loss function for PAR to achieve more precise predictions.

By incorporating multi-scale features into the feature pyramid architecture, convolutional neural networks (CNNs) have proven effective in utilizing the advantages of different feature levels. However, the conventional method of constructing the feature pyramid may not fully capture the intricate characteristics present in natural scenarios, such as pedestrian attribute recognition. In order to address this limitation, we propose an innovative and more dense feature pyramid model.

Our approach aims to enhance the feature pyramid architecture by incorporating additional scales and adding finer details to the feature hierarchy. This allows us to extract and analyze features at multiple levels of granularity, thereby enriching the representation of the input data. By doing so, we can better capture the distinctive attributes and characteristics of pedestrians in real-world scenarios.

Modeling contextual relationships among different regions in an image is advantageous for image recognition. However, previous methods may struggle to capture global context and identify distance dependencies between regions, resulting in high computational complexity. Our proposal introduces hybrid pooling to acquire context information. This approach involves a strip pooling sub-module that establishes long-range dependencies and a lightweight pyramidal pooling sub-module that creates short-range dependencies.

To gain a clearer understanding of the effectiveness and focus of our model, we randomly selected samples from the PETA dataset and conducted a sample heat map analysis. Figure 1 presents four sets of images arranged from left to right as follows: the sample map, the heat representation map of the backbone network output, and the heat map of the final model output.

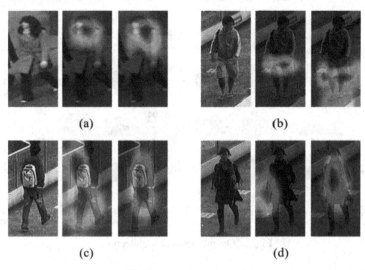

(a)   (b)

(c)   (d)

Fig. 1. Sample heat map

To achieve our goal, we present a novel model architecture that utilizes dense feature pyramids to extract and combine features at various scales. Furthermore, we enhance the model's performance by incorporating global contextual information to learn the relationships between different attributes in the attribute set and identifying long-range dependencies in diverse regions. We evaluate our approach on three publicly available datasets (PETA, PA100k, and RAP) to demonstrate its effectiveness. Our paper makes the following contributions:

- We propose an improved feature pyramid structure with a dense information encoding module and feature fusion module for the PAR task.
- We introduce a new PAR network model architecture that employs mixed pooling as our AIIM module, enabling the capture of remote dependencies and the learning of correlations between attributes.
- Through extensive ablation experiments on the PETA, PA100k, and RAP datasets, we validate the effectiveness of our proposed network framework.

2 Methods

2.1 Network Architecture

The paper presents a network architecture, as depicted in Fig. 2. Firstly, we feed images into the ResNeXt50 [23] backbone network and utilize a feature pyramid concept to construct a four-layer network model with a feature pyramid structure. The input image is resized to 256×192, and the output features in the main network are represented as $I_i = R^{C_i \times H_i \times W_i}$, where i ranges from 1 to 4, representing stages from shallow to deep. The output feature I_i are 64×48, 32×24, 16×12 and 8×6, respectively. The number of channels for each stage is 256, 512, 1024, and 2048.

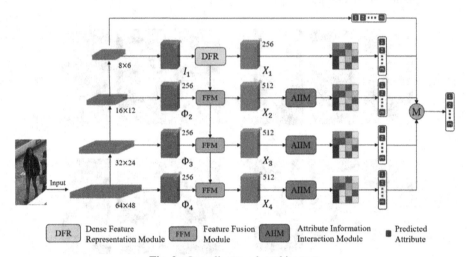

Fig. 2. Overall network architecture

In the construction of feature pyramids [24], existing approaches have primarily focused on inter-layer feature interactions, overlooking intra-layer feature relationships. However, taking inspiration from prior research on dense prediction tasks [25], we propose a denser approach to intra-layer feature conditioning. To accomplish this, we introduce a DFR module to the top layer of the feature pyramid and fuse it with other shallow features. Compared to conventional feature pyramids, our pyramid structure [26] captures global long-range dependencies both within and between layers, thereby producing a comprehensive and distinctive feature representation.

In order to minimize redundant information within the network and prepare for subsequent feature fusion across different scales, we compress the channel number of the previously acquired feature maps I_1, I_2, and I_3 to 256 channels each, denoted as Φ_i, where $i \in \{1, 2, 3\}$. Considering that deeper features typically encompass more abstract representations compared to shallower features, we propose a global concentration rule utilizing a top-down approach. This rule employs the spatial display visual center obtained from the deepest features to simultaneously condition all preceding shallow features. For I_4, we input it into the DFR module to obtain Φ_4, which also has 256 channels.

In order to acquire global information from each feature map, establish correlations between different attributes, we employ the attribute information interaction module. This module facilitates the establishment of correlations and dependencies among global information. Ultimately, the attribute identification module generates multiple prediction outputs, and the final PAR prediction results are obtained through a multi-branch voting mechanism.

2.2 Dense Feature Representation Module

The focus of this module is to propose a lightweight MLP architecture that captures the global long-range dependence of I_4. Instead of using the multi-headed self-attentive module from the standard transformer encoder, we replace it with an MLP layer. Compared to the transformer encoder that relies on the multi-headed attention mechanism, our lightweight MLP architecture is simpler in structure, has a smaller size, and offers higher computational efficiency. Additionally, we incorporate a learnable vision-centric mechanism to aggregate the local corner regions of the input image along with the lightweight MLP. This parallel structured network, which we refer to as spatial DFR (Dense Feature Representation), is placed in the processing of top-level features. Based on the proposed DFR, we construct the feature pyramid using a top-down approach and introduce a feature fusion technique that optimally combines the shallow features of the pyramid with the visually focused information from the deepest features (Fig. 3).

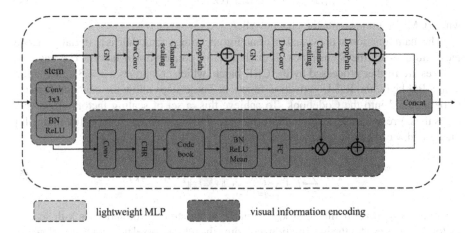

Fig. 3. Dense feature representation module

Our proposed Dense Feature Representation (DFR) module consists of two parallel connected blocks, as depicted in the upper part of Fig. 2. To capture global long-range dependencies, i.e., the global information of the image, we utilize a lightweight MLP. Furthermore, we incorporate a visual information encoding submodule in the lower part of the figure to preserve features in local corner regions, i.e., the local information of the image. This module is applied to the top-level features produced by the backbone network. Instead of directly processing the original feature map, we employ a stem block for feature smoothing between the top-level features and this module. The stem block comprises a 3×3 convolution with an output channel size of 256, a batch normalization layer, followed by a batch normalization layer and an activation function layer. The process can be mathematically expressed using Eq:

$$X = cat(MLP(X_{in}); VIE(X_{in})) \tag{1}$$

where X is the output of DFR. X_{in} refers to the output of the Stem block, which is obtained through the following steps:

$$X_{in} = \sigma(BN(conv_{3\times3}(I_4)))\qquad(2)$$

The lightweight MLP incorporates two primary residual modules: the depthwise convolution-based module and the channel MLP-based module. Each module incorporates a channel scaling layer and DropPath operation to enhance the generalization and robustness of features. The utilization of depthwise convolution, rather than traditional convolution, in this segment enhances the capability of feature representation while simultaneously reducing computational costs.

$$X'_{in} = DConv(GN(X_{in})) + X_{in}\qquad(3)$$

where X'_{in} represents the output of depthwise convolution-based module.

$$MLP(X_{in}) = CMLP\big(GN\big(X'_{in}\big)\big) + X'_{in}\qquad(4)$$

where CMLP($\cdot$) represents the channel MLP.

The main function of the visual information encoding submodule is to initially encode the features from the Stem block through a set of convolutional layers. The encoded features are further processed by the CBR block, which comprises a 3×3 convolution with a BN layer and ReLU activation function. These steps allow the encoded features to be inputted into the Codebook. To achieve this, a set of scaling factors effectively maps the corresponding positional information. The information of the entire image for the k_{th} codeword can be calculated as follows:

$$e_k = \sum_{i=1}^{N} \frac{e^{-s_k\|X'_i - b_k\|^2}}{\sum_{j=1}^{k} e^{-s_k\|X'_i - b_k\|^2}}\left(X'_i - b_k\right)\qquad(5)$$

where X'_i is i_{th} pixel point, b_k is k_{th} learnable visual codeword, and s_k is k-th scaling factor. $X'_i - b_k$ denotes the information regarding the relative pixel position to a codeword.

$$e = \sum_{k=1}^{K} \varnothing(e_k)\qquad(6)$$

The process involves incorporating a BN layer with ReLU and mean layer in $\varnothing$. Once the codebook output is obtained, we utilize a fully connected layer and a 1×1 convolution layer to forecast features that accentuate crucial classes. Subsequently, we apply channel-wise multiplication between the input features from the Stem block Xin and the scaling factor coefficient $\delta(\cdot)$. The aforementioned procedures can be represented as:

$$Z = X_{in} \otimes (\delta(Conv_{1\times1}(e)))\qquad(7)$$

The sigmoid function $\delta(\cdot)$ is utilized, and channel-wise multiplication $\otimes$ is applied. Afterwards, the features Xin generated from the Stem block are combined with the local corner region features Z via a channel-wise addition. This process is expressed as:

$$VIE(X_{in}) = X_{in} \oplus Z\qquad(8)$$

2.3 Feature Fusion Module

We use the concept of a feature pyramid to combine features from different scales, taking advantage of their unique levels. The deep layer network has a strong representation of semantic information and is capable of obtaining abundant semantic information. Shallow networks have the ability to capture intricate details due to their neurons having a narrower view of the input. This is a result of the smaller receptive fields that arise from fewer layers of processing. By merging the features of adjacent layers, we can capture the correlation between attributes of features at different scales.

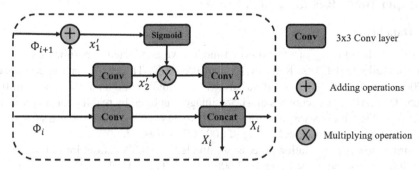

Fig. 4. Feature fusion module

Figure 4 illustrates the Flow-based Feature Module (FFM). Within adjacent layers of scaled features, the deeper feature maps are added and combined with the shallow features, followed by activation through the sigmoid function. The nearby shallow features undergo further processing via a convolutional block to extract information. This block consists of a 3×3 convolution layer, followed by normalization using Batch-Norm2d, and activation using ReLU. Finally, the newly obtained features, denoted as X', are integrated with the features extracted from the original shallow feature map in the channel dimension to yield the desired final feature output, denoted as X_i.

2.4 Attribute Information Interaction Module

The methods currently being researched to enhance the remote dependency modeling capability of CNN include introducing attention mechanisms [28–30], using dilation convolution or depthwise separable convolution [31], among others. However, some of these methods require significant memory consumption to compute large affinity matrices for each space, while others may not effectively analyze natural scenes such as pedestrian attribute recognition.

An important characteristic of natural images is that their features typically appear in a non-uniform manner. Previous research [32] has shown that strip pooling can effectively resolve some natural scenes and reduce computational complexity, while maintaining the ability for global modeling.

The pyramid pooling module [23] (PPM) is effective in enhancing scenario resolution networks, but it relies too heavily on standard spatial pooling operations. To address this, we propose a hybrid pooling approach that combines standard spatial pooling and strip pooling. This approach aggregates different pooling operations with different types of contextual information to create a more discriminative feature representation for pedestrian attribute recognition tasks.

In this paper, we propose using a hybrid pooling approach to establish attribute information correlations for pedestrians. The module consists of two sub-modules: a strip pooling module for establishing long-range dependencies and a sub-module for collecting short-range dependencies using lightweight pyramidal pooling.

3 Experiment Results and Analysis

3.1 Data Set

To evaluate the efficacy of our proposed model, we conducted experiments on three publicly available datasets: RAP, PETA, and PA-100K. The PETA dataset comprises 19,000 images featuring 8,705 pedestrians, with resolutions ranging from 17×39 to 169×365. The RAP dataset consists of 41,585 images captured by real indoor surveillance cameras, and resolutions varying from 36×92 to 344×554. PA-100K is a substantial pedestrian attribute dataset, consisting of 100,000 images.

During the experimentation process, we divided the PETA dataset into a training set of 11,400 images and a testing set of 7,600 images. The RAP dataset's 33,268 images were utilized for training, while 8,317 images were allocated for testing. As for the PA-100K dataset, we employed 90,000 images for training purposes and 10,000 images for testing purposes.

3.2 Evaluation Metrics

To evaluate the chosen datasets RAP, PETA, and PA100k, two evaluation metrics were employed: label-based and sample-based. In regard to label-based evaluation, we employed the mean accuracy (mA). We computed the accuracy for each attribute across all samples, and subsequently obtained the average of all attributes to derive mA. The mA evaluation metric is defined as follows:

$$mA = \frac{1}{2N} \sum_{i=1}^{m} \left(\frac{TP_i}{P_i} + \frac{TN_i}{N_i} \right) \tag{9}$$

For evaluating samples, we use four commonly used metrics: accuracy, precision, recall, and F1 value, which are defined as follows.

$$accuracy = \frac{1}{N} \sum_{i=1}^{N} \frac{|Y_i \cap f(x_i)|}{|Y_i \cup f(x_i)|} \tag{10}$$

$$precision = \frac{1}{2N} \sum_{i=1}^{N} \frac{|Y_i \cap f(x_i)|}{|f(x_i)|} \tag{11}$$

$$recall = \frac{1}{2N} \sum_{i=1}^{N} \frac{|Y_i \cap f(x_i)|}{|Y_i|} \tag{12}$$

$$F1 = \frac{2 * precision * recall}{precision + recall} \tag{13}$$

3.3 Comparison Experiments

Comparison with State-of-the-Arts

To demonstrate the effectiveness of our proposed method, we compared the performance of our proposed network with several state-of-the-art networks, such as DeepMar, PGDM, LG-Net, HPNet, VeSPA, JRL, MT-CAS, MTA-Net, and WPAL. Our experiments were conducted on three publicly available datasets: PETA, PA-100K, and RAP datasets. The results of these experiments are presented in Table 1, which includes evaluation metrics such as mA, accuracy, precision, recall, and F1. Upon analyzing the Table 1, it becomes apparent that our model exhibits clear advantages over the other networks.

Table 1. Comparison of our network with state-of-the-arts on PETA and RAP datasets

Methods	PETA					RAP				
	mA	Accu	Prec	Recall	F1	mA	Accu	Prec	Recall	F1
ACN	81.15	73.66	84.06	81.26	82.64	69.66	62.61	80.12	72.26	75.98
DeepMar	82.89	75.07	83.68	83.14	83.41	73.79	62.06	74.92	76.21	75.56
PGDM	82.97	78.08	86.86	84.68	85.76	74.31	64.57	78.86	75.90	77.35
LG-Net	–	–	–	–	–	78.68	68.00	**80.36**	79.82	80.09
HPNet	81.77	76.13	84.92	83.24	84.07	76.12	65.39	77.33	78.79	78.05
VeSPA	83.45	77.73	86.18	84.81	85.49	77.70	67.35	79.51	79.67	79.59
JRL	85.67	-	86.03	85.34	85.42	77.81	–	78.11	78.98	78.58
MT-CAS	83.17	78.78	**87.49**	85.35	86.41	–	–	–	–	–
MTA-Net	84.62	78.80	85.67	86.42	86.04	77.62	67.17	79.72	78.44	79.07
WPAL	85.50	76.98	84.07	85.78	84.90	81.25	50.30	57.17	78.39	66.12
ours	**86.27**	**79.34**	84.96	**88.86**	**86.59**	**83.45**	**68.94**	77.47	**85.09**	**80.80**

As depicted in the Table 1, our proposed model exhibits superior performance on all three datasets: PETA, RAP, and PA100k. In comparison to other models, our model ranks first in four evaluation metrics on both PETA and RAP datasets, and also ranks first in three evaluation metrics on the PA100k dataset. This indicates that our proposed model has better generalization ability. In addition, the PA100k dataset stands out due to its extensive image collection and relatively low resolution, making it a more representative portrayal of image diversity and motion blur in real-world scenarios. The impressive performance of RMFA module on the PA100k, as demonstrated in Table 2, highlights the effectiveness of integrating multi-scale information. Despite the PETA and RAP datasets having a larger number of labeled attributes compared to PA100k, the results presented in the table further underscore the importance and effectiveness of mining contextual information and attribute correlation.

Table 2. Comparison of our network with state-of-the-arts on PA100k datasets

Methods	PA100k				
	mA	Accu	Prec	Recall	F1
DeepMar	72.70	70.39	82.24	80.42	81.32
PGDM	74.95	73.08	84.36	82.24	83.29
LG-Net	79.96	75.55	86.99	83.17	85.04
HPNet	74.21	72.19	82.97	82.09	82.53
VeSPA	76.32	73.00	84.99	81.49	83.20
MT-CAS	77.20	78.09	**88.46**	84.86	**86.62**
ours	**81.60**	**78.40**	85.16	**88.85**	86.55

Attribute Recognition Comparison

As mA is one of the important metrics for evaluating the effectiveness of a model among all evaluation metrics, we plotted the mA values of 35 attributes in the PETA dataset based on the test results of our model compared to StrongBaseline [38].

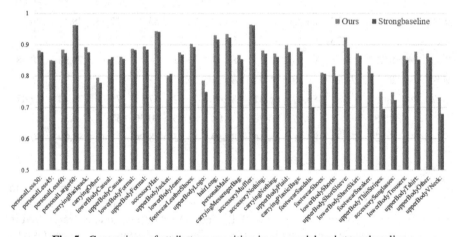

Fig. 5. Comparison of attribute recognition in our model and strongbaseline

The results, as shown in the Fig. 5, indicate that our model improves the identification of almost all attributes, including "upper Body Thin Stripes," "footwear Sandals," and "accessory Sunglasses." This improvement can be attributed to the DFR module, which allows for the construction of a dense feature pyramid and the fusion of multi-scale information. For pedestrian attributes such as "Age," "personal Male," and "upper Body Short Sleeve," the enhancement in high-resolution attributes like "lower Body Short Skirt" can be credited to attribute correlation and contextual information mining.

3.4 Ablation Experiments

In order to assess the effectiveness of the key components in our proposed network architecture and the influence of other factors, we conducted ablation experiments. The data set used in ablation experiments was PETA. The evaluation metrics employed for this experiment encompass mean average precision, accuracy, precision, recall, and F1. Table 3 shows two architectures: one without the DFR module and one without the AIIM module. Analyzing the data, our proposed complete architecture outperforms in four out of five evaluation indicators. This supports the importance and effectiveness of both the DFR and AIIM modules in the overall network architecture.

Table 3. Results of ablation experiments

	mA	Accu	Prec	Recall	F1
-DFR	84.74	76.70	81.34	89.51	84.81
-AIIM	85.24	76.79	81.33	**89.96**	85.00
ours	**86.27**	**79.34**	**84.96**	88.86	**86.59**

4 Conclusion

In this paper, we propose a dense feature pyramid structure for natural scenarios, such as pedestrian attribute recognition. We optimize the feature pyramid using the dense information encoding module and the proposed feature fusion method. Additionally, we propose a novel architecture for pedestrian attribute recognition that leverages the correlation between contextual information and pedestrian attributes, combined with the hybrid pooling-based AIIM module. We conducted extensive experiments on three datasets, namely PEAT, RAP, and PA100k, and concluded that our proposed architecture significantly improves performance while achieving excellent results. Furthermore, we demonstrate the effectiveness of key blocks in our proposed architecture through ablation experiments. However, the performance shown on the PA100K dataset is not satisfactory, indicating that the recognition performance of the model decreases when the dataset becomes larger. This result is possibly due to the increase of disturbing factors in the images caused by the increase of the dataset, which can be investigated in the future to improve the performance of the pedestrian attribute recognition model.

Acknowledgment. This work received support from the Foundation of Jiangxi Educational Committee under grant No. GJJ200824.

References

1. Liu, W., Liao, S., Ren, W., Hu, W., Yu, Y.: High-level semantic feature detection: a new perspective for pedestrian detection. In: Proceedings of the IEEE/CVF Conference on Computer Vision and Pattern Recognition, pp. 5187–5196 (2019)

2. Lin, Y., et al.: Improving person re-identification by attribute and identity learning. Pattern Recognit. **95**, 151–161 (2019)

3. Shi, Y., Ling, H., Wu, L., Shen, J., Li, P.: Learning refined attribute-aligned network with attribute selection for person re-identification. Neurocomputing **402**, 124–133 (2020)

4. Li, D., Zhang, Z., Chen, X., Huang, K.: A richly annotated pedestrian dataset for person retrieval in real surveillance scenarios. IEEE Trans. Image Process. **28**(4), 1575–1590 (2018)

5. Brunetti, A., Buongiorno, D., Trotta, G.F., Bevilacqua, V.: Computer vision and deep learning techniques for pedestrian detection and tracking: a survey. Neurocomputing **300**, 17–33 (2018)

6. Tay, C.P., Roy, S., Yap, K.H.: AANet: attribute attention network for person re-identifications. In: Proceedings of the IEEE/CVF Conference on Computer Vision and Pattern Recognition, pp. 7134–7143 (2019)

7. Sun, Y., Zheng, L., Deng, W., Wang, S.: SVDNet for pedestrian retrieval. In: Proceedings of the IEEE International Conference on Computer Vision, pp. 3800–3808 (2017)

8. Li, D., Chen, X., Huang, K.: Multi-attribute learning for pedestrian attribute recognition in surveillance scenarios. In: 2015 3rd IAPR Asian Conference on Pattern Recognition (ACPR), pp. 111–115. IEEE, November 2015

9. Li, D., Chen, X., Zhang, Z., Huang, K.: Pose guided deep model for pedestrian attribute recognition in surveillance scenarios. In: 2018 IEEE International Conference on Multimedia and Expo (ICME), pp. 1–6. IEEE, July 2018

10. Liu, P., Liu, X., Yan, J., Shao, J.: Localization guided learning for pedestrian attribute recognition (2018). arXiv preprint arXiv:1808.09102

11. Liu, X., et al.: HydraPlus-Net: attentive deep features for pedestrian analysis. In: Proceedings of the IEEE International Conference on Computer Vision, pp. 350–359 (2017)

12. Sarfraz, M.S., Schumann, A., Wang, Y., Stiefelhagen, R.: Deep view-sensitive pedestrian attribute inference in an end-to-end model (2017). arXiv preprint arXiv:1707.06089

13. Guo, H., Fan, X., Wang, S.: Human attribute recognition by refining attention heat map. Pattern Recognit. Lett. **94**, 38–45 (2017)

14. Wang, J., Zhu, X., Gong, S., Li, W.: Attribute recognition by joint recurrent learning of context and correlation. In: Proceedings of the IEEE International Conference on Computer Vision, pp. 531–540 (2017)

15. Zhao, X., Sang, L., Ding, G., Han, J., Di, N., Yan, C.: Recurrent attention model for pedestrian attribute recognition. In: Proceedings of the AAAI Conference on Artificial Intelligence, vol. 33, no. 01, pp. 9275–9282, July 2019

16. Yu, K., Leng, B., Zhang, Z., Li, D., Huang, K.: Weakly-supervised learning of mid-level features for pedestrian attribute recognition and localization (2016). arXiv preprint arXiv: 1611.05603

17. Luo, W., Li, Y., Urtasun, R., Zemel, R.: Understanding the effective receptive field in deep convolutional neural networks. Adv. Neural Inf. Process. Syst. **29** (2016)

18. Lin, T.Y., Dollár, P., Girshick, R., He, K., Hariharan, B., Belongie, S.: Feature pyramid networks for object detection. In: Proceedings of the IEEE Conference on Computer Vision and Pattern Recognition, pp. 2117–2125 (2017)

19. Honari, S., Yosinski, J., Vincent, P., Pal, C.: Recombinator networks: learning coarse-to-fine feature aggregation. In: Proceedings of the IEEE Conference on Computer Vision and Pattern Recognition, pp. 5743–5752 (2016)

20. Deng, Y., Luo, P., Loy, C.C., Tang, X.: Pedestrian attribute recognition at far distance. In: Proceedings of the 22nd ACM International Conference on Multimedia, pp. 789–792, November 2014

21. Li, D., Zhang, Z., Chen, X., Ling, H., Huang, K.: A richly annotated dataset for pedestrian attribute recognition (2016). arXiv preprint arXiv:1603.07054

22. Xie, S., Girshick, R., Dollár, P., Tu, Z., He, K.: Aggregated residual transformations for deep neural networks. In: Proceedings of the IEEE Conference on Computer Vision and Pattern Recognition, pp. 1492–1500 (2017)
23. Zhao, H., Shi, J., Qi, X., Wang, X., Jia, J.: Pyramid scene parsing network. In: Proceedings of the IEEE Conference on Computer Vision and Pattern Recognition, pp. 2881–2890 (2017)
24. Yang, M., Yu, K., Zhang, C., Li, Z., Yang, K.: DenseASPP for semantic segmentation in street scenes. In: Proceedings of the IEEE Conference on Computer Vision and Pattern Recognition, pp. 3684–3692 (2018)
25. Quan, Y., Zhang, D., Zhang, L., Tang, J.: Centralized Feature Pyramid for Object Detection (2022). arXiv preprint arXiv:2210.02093
26. Chen, L.C., Papandreou, G., Schroff, F., Adam, H.: Rethinking atrous convolution for semantic image segmentation (2017). arXiv preprint arXiv:1706.05587
27. Chen, L.C., Papandreou, G., Kokkinos, I., Murphy, K., Yuille, A.L.: Deeplab: semantic image segmentation with deep convolutional nets, atrous convolution, and fully connected CRFs (2016). arXiv preprint arXiv:1606.00915
28. Zhao, H., Jia, J., Koltun, V.: Exploring self-attention for image recognition. In: Proceedings of the IEEE/CVF Conference on Computer Vision and Pattern Recognition, pp. 10076–10085 (2020)
29. Wang, X., Girshick, R., Gupta, A., He, K.: Non-local neural networks. In: Proceedings of the IEEE Conference on Computer Vision and Pattern Recognition, pp. 7794–7803 (2018)
30. Huang, Z., Wang, X., Huang, L., Huang, C., Wei, Y., Liu, W.: CCNET: criss-cross attention for semantic segmentation. In: Proceedings of the IEEE/CVF International Conference on Computer Vision, pp. 603–612 (2019)
31. Guo, Y., Li, Y., Wang, L., Rosing, T.: Depthwise convolution is all you need for learning multiple visual domains. In: Proceedings of the AAAI Conference on Artificial Intelligence, vol. 33, no. 01, pp. 8368–8375, July 2019
32. Hou, Q., Zhang, L., Cheng, M.M., Feng, J.: Strip pooling: rethinking spatial pooling for scene parsing. In: Proceedings of the IEEE/CVF Conference on Computer Vision and Pattern Recognition, pp. 4003–4012 (2020)
33. Sudowe, P., Spitzer, H., Leibe, B.: Person attribute recognition with a jointly-trained holistic CNN model. In: Proceedings of the IEEE International Conference on Computer Vision Workshops, pp. 87–95 (2015)
34. Zeng, H., Ai, H., Zhuang, Z., Chen, L.: Multi-task learning via co-attentive sharing for pedestrian attribute recognition. In: 2020 IEEE International Conference on Multimedia and Expo (ICME), pp. 1–6. IEEE, July 2020
35. Di, X., Zhang, H., Patel, V.M.: Polarimetric thermal to visible face verification via attribute preserved synthesis. In: 2018 IEEE 9th International Conference on Biometrics Theory, Applications and Systems (BTAS), pp. 1–10. IEEE, October 2018
36. Tang, C., Sheng, L., Zhang, Z., Hu, X.: Improving pedestrian attribute recognition with weakly-supervised multi-scale attribute-specific localization. In: Proceedings of the IEEE/CVF International Conference on Computer Vision, pp. 4997–5006 (2019)
37. Ioffe, S., Szegedy, C.: Batch normalization: accelerating deep network training by reducing internal covariate shift. In: International Conference on Machine Learning, pp. 448–456. PMLR, June 2015
38. Zhong, J., Qiao, H., Chen, L., Shang, M., Liu, Q.: Improving pedestrian attribute recognition with multi-scale spatial calibration. In: 2021 International Joint Conference on Neural Networks (IJCNN), pp. 1–8. IEEE, July 2021
39. Jia, J., Huang, H., Yang, W., Chen, X., Huang, K.: Rethinking of pedestrian attribute recognition: Realistic datasets with efficient method (2020). arXiv preprint arXiv:2005.11909
40. Zou, C., Xie, W., Xie, X., Zhao, K., Liu, Q., Xiao, H.: Pedestrian Attribute Recognition Based on Multi-Scale Feature Fusion Over a Larger Receptive Field and Strip Pooling (2022)

Double DQN Reinforcement Learning-Based Computational Offloading and Resource Allocation for MEC

Chen Zhang[1], Chunrong Peng[2], Min Lin[1], Zhaoyang Du[3], and Celimuge Wu[3(✉)]

[1] College of Computer Science and Technology, Inner Mongolia Normal University, Saihan District, Hohhot, Inner Mongolia Autonomous Region, People's Republic of China
[2] Library, Inner Mongolia University of Finance and Economics, Xincheng District, Hohhot, Inner Mongolia Autonomous Region, People's Republic of China
[3] Graduate School of Informatics and Engineering, The University of Electro-Communications, 1-5-1 Chofugaoka, Chofu, Tokyo 182-8585, Japan
celimuge@uec.ac.jp

Abstract. In recent years, numerous Deep Reinforcement Learning (DRL) neural network models have been proposed to optimize computational offloading and resource allocation in Mobile Edge Computing (MEC). However, the diversity of computational tasks and the complexity of 5G networks pose significant challenges for current DRL algorithms apply to MEC scenarios. This research focuses on a single MEC server-multi-user scenario and develops a realistic small-scale MEC offloading system. In order to alleviate the problem of overestimation of action value in current Deep Q-learning Network (DQN), we propose a normalized model of Complex network based on Double DQN (DDQN) algorithm to determine the optimal computational offloading and resource allocation strategy. Simulation results demonstrate that DDQN outperforms conventional approaches such as fixed parameter policies and DQN regarding convergence speed, energy consumption and latency. This research showcases the potential of DDQN for achieving efficient optimization in MEC environments.

Keywords: mobile edge computing · computational offloading · resource allocation · single MEC server-multi-user · DDQN algorithm

1 Introduction

Currently, most of IoT applications have increasingly high demands for latency and transmission reliability. Achieving Ultra-Reliable and Low-Latency Communication (URLLC) is one of the major challenges for 5G networks, Fig. 1 illustrates the communication requirements for IoT-related applications in terms of latency and reliability [1], with latency varying between 1 ms (ultra-low) and 100 ms (low) and reliability varying between $1-10^{-2}$ (high) and $1-10^{-9}$ (ultra-high). With the exponential growth of IoT devices, Mobile Edge Computing (MEC) undoubtedly provides an efficient solution for

C. Wu et al. (Eds.): MONAMI 2023, LNICST 559, pp. 240–253, 2024.
https://doi.org/10.1007/978-3-031-55471-1_18

computationally intensive programs [2]. MEC sinks computing services to the edge of the network by deploying cloud servers at the Base Station (BS), thus bringing computing resources closer to the users to provide more efficient services. Due to the limited computational resources of end-user devices, they can offload latency-sensitive computing tasks to MEC servers via wireless channels to acquire additional computational resources.

Therefore, with the advent of 5G and 6G networks, MEC has attracted considerable interest. Nowadays, DRL has gained significant attention for successful perception-based decision making in complex scenarios [3]. This has prompted researchers to explore the integration of RL with conventional MEC algorithm models, resulting in notable advancements in this domain [4].

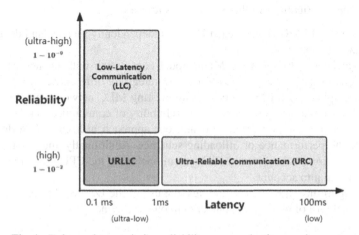

Fig. 1. Delay and transmission reliability communication requirements.

Liu et al. [5] implemented edge node selection and offloading sequence through heuristic algorithm and reconstruction linearization technology in a single-user multi-MEC server scenario to achieve a balance of delay performance and reliability performance in MEC. Liu et al. [6] studied the single MEC and muti-users in high reliability and low latency scenarios, then they introduce probability and extreme value theory to analyze the user's task queue and use Lyapunov theory to solve the problem of minimizing calculation and transmission energy. Huang et al. [7] proposed a DQN based task offloading and resource allocation algorithm for MEC, motivated by the concomitant need for proper resource allocation for computational offloading via MEC. Liang et al. [8] proposed a combination of DQN and Deep Deterministic Policy Gradient (DDPG) to optimize the total cost of UE transmission delay and energy consumption. Liang et al. [9] investigated the problem of computational offloading of interference perception in single MEC server and multi-user scenarios. Wu et al. [10] formulated the offloading decision and resource allocation problem. Li et al. [11] proposed method that users' tasks can be offloaded to multiple computing access points (CAPs). Gan et al. proposed an offloading strategy to jointly minimize latency [12], energy consumption of ES, and task loss rate while preserving privacy (PP). The above works have designed strategies from different perspectives and methods, but they lack consideration in terms of convergence speed and learning stability. Furthermore, in certain stochastic environments, the widely recognized reinforcement learning algorithm Q-learning exhibits significant performance deficiencies. The inadequate performance arises from the overestimation of action values, which is a consequence of Q-learning's utilization of the maximum action value as an estimate for the maximum expected action value, thereby introducing a positive bias [13].

We combine the DDQN algorithm with the principle of partial offloading to alleviate the problem of overestimation of action values. As shown in Fig. 2, in the simulated single MEC server-multi-user edge computing scenario, a group of N mobile User Equipment (UE) offloads their computational tasks to MEC server over a wireless link, each end-user device offloads computing tasks and acquires computing resources at minimal total task cost. The contributions of this study are as follows:

- In the proposed MEC system, each UE can independently make sound decisions to minimize total consumption costs.
- We apply DDQN to solve the MDP model considering both latency and energy consumption, and give a generic offloading strategy for different scenarios.
- We contemplate establishing a physically existing MEC network environment that captures dynamic network structure and reliability of communication. Unlike most studies that rely on simulation software, our approach utilizes real-world data to estimate the performance of offloading schemes. Additionally, the impact of each offload decision on the overall MEC system, including the CPU utilization of other UEs, is taken into account.
- According to the experimental findings, the use of the DDQN algorithm yields the lowest total cost of ownership compared to other baselines.

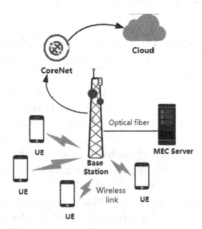

Fig. 2. The model of MEC server-multi-user edge computing scenario

The paper is structured as follows. In Sect. 2, we define the network environment and proposed computational offloading and resource allocation optimization. Section 3 presents our algorithm to address the problem mentioned above. Subsequently, in Sect. 4 conducts simulations of the proposed algorithm and discusses the obtained results. Section 5 provides the conclusions of this study.

2 System Overview

In this section, a system model for the optimization of computational offloading and resource allocation strategy is given. Initially, we present the network infrastructure of the real-life scenario of the MEC being simulated. On top of this it is analyzed and the optimization problems studied are presented in detail.

2.1 Network Module

To better emulate the heterogeneity and flexibility of MEC networks, we simulated a real MEC system using Raspberry Pi 4B and personal laptops. Raspberry Pi serves as an intelligent mobile device, incorporating computation, communication, and storage modules. As shown in Fig. 3, the laptop simulates the MEC server that provides computing resources for the entire MEC system. Raspberry Pi-1 simulates the base station connected to the MEC server and acts as an Access Point (AP). All Raspberry Pi devices (Pi-1, Pi-2, Pi-3, Pi-4) are part of an Ad hoc network environment. Ad hoc networks are characterized by self-organization, temporariness, and decentralization. In a self-organizing network, devices communicate through temporary connections to form an ad hoc network, independent of traditional infrastructure such as routers or base stations [14]. The MEC server linked to the AP via a network cable serves the n UEs in the ad hoc network. The system's main task is real-time object detection using the YOLO algorithm [15] on fixed-size images captured by the surveillance system. Due to the resource limitations of the Raspberry Pi devices, partial or binary offloading to the MEC server or other UEs [16] is required to handle computationally intensive tasks.

The Fig. 3 illustrates the network environment in which the experiments take place. We regard the simulated scenario as a fundamental network entity and portray it through the collective attributes of all UEs. Subsequently, the underlying network entity in the network scenario provide observations for the environment. M is the maximum workload of the MEC server, while C represents the maximum computational resources provided by the MEC server. Within the network entity, let $U_i(i \in \{1, 2, ..., N\})$ denote the set of UE in the network. Each UE can be defined as $UE_i = \{m_i, f_i, t_i, r_i, s_i\}$, for $\forall i \in U_i$ where mi represents the computation load of the user's task. If mi = 0, it implies that the terminal does not exist. f_i denotes the required computational resources for the user's task, while t_i represents the maximum waiting time of the UE. The variable r_i indicates the current state of the computation, when $r_i = 1$ indicating that the task is being computed. In the case where $m_i = 0$ and $r_i = 1$, the resources occupied by the terminal are still reserved and only the consumption of the other UEs is computed. The variable $s_i \in \{1, 2, 3\}$ represents the set of system offloading decisions, representing different offloading strategies. $s_i = 1$ denotes local computation, $s_i = 2$, represents task offloading, and $s_i = 3$ indicates task migration to another MEC server.

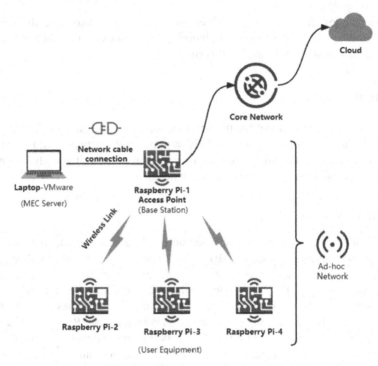

Fig. 3. MEC system network model

2.2 Computational Module

1. Local computing: We assume that the CPU in UE_i operates at a frequency f_i, representing the local computational power in terms of CPU cycles. Therefore, the local computation time can be calculated as follows:

$$t_i^{local} = \frac{f_i}{c_i^{local}}, \ \forall i \in U_i \tag{1}$$

Based on the findings presented in reference [17], the local energy consumption can be mathematically represented as:

$$E_i^{local} = k f_i (c_i^{lcoal})^2, \forall i \in U_i \tag{2}$$

Incorporating the influence of chip architecture [18], the effective switching capacitance κ is introduced in the equation. The total energy consumption is given by the expression (α, β is Loss factors):

$$C_i^{local} = \alpha t_i^{local} + \beta E_i^{local} \tag{3}$$

2. Edge computing: Delays and energy losses are introduced when tasks are offloaded to the MEC server. Assuming a constant transmission power for the MEC, denoted as pi and utilizing the standard path loss propagation index θ, di is the distance between

UE_i and the base station, the $UE_j's$ signal-to-noise ratio (SNR) can be formulated as follows:

$$SNR_i = \frac{p_i h_i d_i^{-\theta}}{\sigma^2}, \forall i \in U_i \qquad (4)$$

The SNR of UE_i is determined by the power of additive Gaussian white noise (σ^2) and the channel gain (h_i). Based on this, the upload transmission rate of UE_i can be described as:

$$R_i = W_0 \log_2(1 + SNR_i) \qquad (5)$$

Thus, transmission delay is:

$$t_i^{tran} = \frac{m_i}{R_i}, \forall i \in U_i \qquad (6)$$

Transmission energy loss denotes as:

$$E_i^{tran} = p_i t_i^{tran}, \forall i \in U_i \qquad (7)$$

The time requirement of edge computing is:

$$t_i^{edge} = \frac{f_i}{c_i}, \forall i \in U_i \qquad (8)$$

The total consumption including time loss and energy consumption gives:

$$C_i^{edge} = a(t_i^{tran} + t_i^{edge}) + \beta E_i^{tran}, \forall i \in U_i \qquad (9)$$

3. Migrating the computation: When the MEC server experiences excessive workload or when neighboring servers have available resources, the UE can migrate its computational tasks to the adjacent servers. This migration incurs additional transmission overhead for the UE, which involves transferring data between MEC servers. The magnitude of the transmission overhead is determined based on the allocated computational resources provided by the target server in response to the migration request from the UE, and therefore the transmission delay is:

$$t_i^{mig} = \frac{m_i}{R_i^{mig}} + Z_i^{mig}, \forall i \in U_i \qquad (10)$$

Assuming that the migration cost only depends on the task size which denoted as $Z_i^{mig} = \delta m$, the transmission energy loss is:

$$E_i^{mig} = p_i t_i^{mig}, \forall i \in U_i \qquad (11)$$

The computational delay and energy consumption of the UE is computed based on the resource allocation strategy of the migration server, with the computational formula remaining unchanged. Consequently, the total cost of the migration computation is expressed as:

$$C_i^{mig} = a(t_i^{mig} + t_i^{edge}) + \beta E_i^{mig}, \forall i \in U_i \qquad (12)$$

Due to the limited computational capacity of the MEC server, the allocated computational resources to the UE may not be sufficient to complete the task within the maximum duration. Therefore, we assign a very low reward to such allocation strategies, allowing them to be excluded from the model iteration. Combining 1, 2, 3 we can get the expression as:

$$C_i^{ue} = \begin{cases} C_i^{local} s_i = 0 \\ C_i^{local} s_i = 0, \quad \forall i \in U_i \\ C_i^{mig} s_i = 0 \end{cases} \quad (13)$$

2.3 Problem Formulation

On the basis of the above theory, C_{all} is expressed as the sum of the total cost of local computing, edge computing, and migration computing on each UE, computation offloading and resource allocation. Our purpose is to minimize the computing overhead cost of each UE, then it can be expressed for:

$$C_{all} = \sum_{n=i}^{N} C_i^{ue}, \forall i \in U_i \quad (14)$$

$$C_{all} = \sum_{n=i}^{N} C_i^{ue} = \sum_{n=i}^{N} (C_i^{local} + C_i^{edge} + C_i^{mig}), \forall i \in U_i \quad (15)$$

Under the premise of minimizing C_{all}, the problem can be described as:

$$MinC_{all}$$

$$s.t.\ C1 : \sum_{n=1}^{N} C_i \leq C,\ \forall i \in U_i;$$

$$C2 : a_i \in 0, 1, 2,\ \forall i \in U_i;$$

$$C3 : t_i^{tran} + t_i^{edge} < t_i,\ \forall i \in U_i \quad (16)$$

3 Algorithm Application

In this section we discuss the application of the algorithm within the model in detail.

3.1 Key Elements in RL

Reinforcement learning methods involve three key elements: state, action, and reward.

- State: We utilize an observation tensor as the state, which includes information about MEC Server and UE in the environment.
- Action: Since each UE is responsible for three computation tasks, there will be 3N possible offloading decisions for N UEs. Using the variable v to express the offloading policy, which simplifies the output of the decision network.
- Reward: A reward is provided at each training step. Considering the objective of minimizing the transmission time and energy consumption for UEs, the defined reward should be negatively correlated with the objective. It can be expressed as follows:

$$R(s, a) = \sum_{n=i}^{N} \gamma(C_i^{local} - C_i^{edge}), \forall i \in U_i \quad (17)$$

3.2 DDQN Algorithm Application

In the code implementation of DDQN-based computational offloading decision, we decouple the environment module from the neural network. On one hand, it enables us to test different RL algorithms and explore various hyperparameter settings without the need to reimplement the entire environment for each test. This approach facilitates performance optimization, code maintenance and feature expansion, significantly enhancing development efficiency. On the other hand, it enhances the generality of the DDQN algorithm for computing offloading decisions in different network environments [19]. This allows the environment module to be specifically responsible for generating environment feedback and computing rewards, which are then provided to the neural network module for training, as illustrated in Fig. 4.

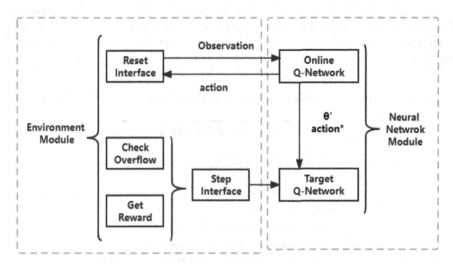

Fig. 4. The module of environment and neural network.

In the following sections, we will present the detailed implementation, functionality, and interaction process of these two modules. The environment module provides two crucial interfaces of reset and step to the neural network. The reset interface generates the network environment based on the observation tensor provided by the environment. The step interface calculates rewards based on the neural network's input actions and provides the next observation and reward for training the neural network. The environment obtains rewards for each step using the algorithm of Table 1 and 2. In the neural network module, we employ the DDQN method to train the online Q-network and target Q-network. DDQN's network update mechanism is based on the principles of Q-learning, but it mitigates the problem of overestimation bias by using two neural networks. Here are the key Eqs. (18) for DDQN network update:

$$Q_{target(s,a)} = r + \gamma Q_{current}\left(s', \underset{a}{argmax}\, Q_{current}\left(s', a\right)\right) \qquad (18)$$

where Q_{target} is the target Q-value, which represents the expected reward for performing action 'a' in state 's'. 'r' is the reward obtained after performing action 'a'. 'γ' is a discount factor to balance the importance of the current and future rewards. $Q_{current}$ represents the current Q-value for selecting the best action 'a'' for the current Q-value.

In the current Q-value calculation, the current state 's' and action 'a' are used to calculate the current Q-value. The mathematical representation of this process is:

$$Q_{current}(s, a) = Q_{current}(s, a) + \alpha[Q_{t\,arg\,et}(s, a) - Q_{current}(s, a)] \tag{19}$$

$Q_{current}$ refers to the current Q-value, which serves as an estimate of the expected reward when taking action 'a' in state 's'. Q_{target} represents the Q-value that has been previously calculated and acts as the target value for the update process. The parameter 'α', often referred to as the learning rate, α's principal purpose is twofold: it regulates the extent of adaptation to the Q-value while playing a pivotal role in determining the convergence and stability of the reinforcement learning algorithm. This fine-tuning mechanism ensures the Q-values converge towards an optimal policy without the risk of overshooting.

Table 1. The neural network module

Algorithm 1 DDQN Based Computational Offloading strategy algorithm
Initialize *Online network Q_θ, replay buffer D,* *Target network $Q_{\theta'}$, $\gamma \ll 1$,* *Observation_*
for each episode **do**
for each environment step **do**
Observe state s_t and select $a_t \sim \pi(s_t, a_t)$
Execute a_t and observe next state s_{t+1} *and reward $r_t = R(s_t, a_t)$*
Store (s_t, a_t, r_t, s_{t+1}) in replay buffer D
end for
for each update step **do**
Sample $e_t = (s_t, a_t, r_t, s_{t+1}) \sim D$
Compute target Q-value:
$Q^*(s_t, a_t)$ $\approx r_t + \gamma Q_\theta(s_{t+1}, argmax_{a'}Q_{\theta'}(s_{t+1}, a'))$
Perform gradient descent step with loss: $\|Q^*(s_t, a_t) - Q_\theta(s_t, a_t)\|^2$
Update target network parameters: $\theta' \leftarrow \tau * \theta + (1 - \tau) * \theta'$
end for
return *Observation_*
end for

These two equations form the update mechanism of the DDQN network. By alternating between the two neural networks to estimate and optimize the Q-value, DDQN can mitigate the over-estimation problem in Q-learning and thus improve the stability and performance of training. This updating process will be iterated several times during training to gradually improve the estimation of Q-values.

Table 1 and 2 show the pseudo-code of the algorithm for the two modules.

Table 2. The environment module

Algorithm 2 The environment module algorithm

---

require: *action*

return *reward, done, Observation*

Initialize *Observation, UE, loop*

get *action*

if overflow **then**

  reward = 0

  done = True

  *Observation ← Observation_*

  return *reward, done, Observation_*

  else

  get *consume (action)*

  get *consume (local)*

  get *reward*

  done = False

  update *Observation*

  end if

---

4 Simulation Result

In this section, we deploy a realistic MEC system for experimentation purposes. The network model consisted of a single Base Station, three additional UE, and a single MEC server. We use Raspberry Pi 4b as the UE, with a power consumption of 6.4 W during normal operation and 2.7 W in idle mode [20]. The MEC server is equipped with a GTX 3050 GPU. All UE are placed in a distributed communication mobile self-organizing network (Ad-hoc) environment with a radius of approximately 1 m. We introduce a real-time surveillance recognition system as a computational task that can generate 20 unprocessed 256×256 images per second in the UE as a batch for a pending task. Tests are carried out to verify that all UE and MEC servers met the requirements for running the YOLOv5 algorithm for object detection.

Subsequently, we conduct an analysis of the practical performance of the DDQN-based computation offloading and resource allocation strategy in edge computing and compare it with the simple DQN offloading strategy and the fixed-parameter strategy. The user devices are uniformly distributed in an area with a radius of approximately 1 m. The architecture of deep neural network consists of an input layer, a hidden layer with 256 neurons and an output layer with 3 neurons. Besides, the activation function is ReLU, and during the weight updating process, the experience replay method and the Adam optimizer are employed.

As shown in Fig. 5, the graph demonstrates the optimal approach of the DDQN-based computation offloading and resource allocation strategy in a MEC system under long-term dynamic and complex network environments. The expected reward of the system converges to approximately -0.24 after around 460 training episodes, which outperforms the other two baseline models. As depicted, the fixed-parameter strategy experiences significant disturbances during the training process from episodes 165 to 464, exhibiting poor robustness in practical network environments. Moreover, it lacks the memory function for the environment, making it unsuitable for complex and dynamic network environments.

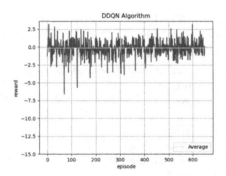

Fig. 5. The performance of DDQN method

As shown in Fig. 6 and Fig. 7 the DQN strategy starts to converge at around 570 episodes, reaching a stable and satisfactory reward value under the optimal policy. This indicates that the UE achieves relatively good performance in the environment and is less susceptible to environmental disturbances compared to the fixed-parameter strategy. However, there are still notable differences compared to the DDQN method in terms of convergence speed and action value estimation.

The Fig. 8 illustrates the dynamic changes in the average reward value during the training process. The DDQN method, without preset parameters, could select appropriate offloading actions based on the MEC system's state in the shortest possible time after a sufficient number of work events. Furthermore, it alleviates the problem of overestimating action values in the DQN method, thus improving training stability to some extent. The overall performance remains relatively stable.

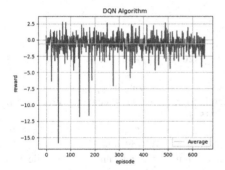

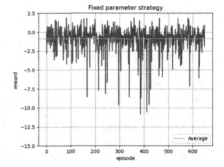

Fig. 6. The performance of DQN method   **Fig. 7.** The performance of Fixed-parameter method

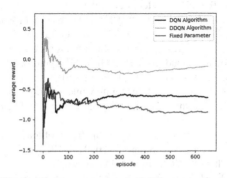

Fig. 8. The average reward of different methods

5 Conclusion

In this paper, we investigate a computational offloading strategy framework based on Double DQN, which maximizes the overall energy efficiency under transmission power and transmission delay constraints for each UE. Our approach builds upon the conventional method where the reward function is derived solely from immediate action without considering its impact on the future. Next, we employ the DQN algorithm, which leverages past learning experiences and takes into account future influences in the current action decision. However, the issue of overestimation of action values hampers the overall convergence performance and sum of rewards. Thanks to the framework of DQN, the Double DQN separates the selected actions from the target Q-value generation, thereby achieving more efficient edge computing offloading in the Mobile Edge Computing system. Extensive simulation results confirm the effectiveness of the computational offloading strategy based on DDQN. In future work, we will extend this model to networks with multiple MEC servers while experimenting with policy-based reinforcement learning algorithms to consider resource allocation.

Acknowledgments. This research was supported in part by the Inner Mongolia Science and Technology Key Project No. 2021GG0218, ROIS NII Open Collaborative Research 23S0601, and in part by JSPS KAKENHI Grant No. 21H03424.

References

1. Liu, J., Zhang, Q.: Offloading schemes in mobile edge computing for ultra-reliable low latency communications. IEEE Access **6**, 12825–12837 (2018). https://doi.org/10.1109/ACCESS.2018.2800032
2. Yang, J., Shah, A.A., Pezaros, D.: A survey of energy optimization approaches for computational task offloading and resource allocation in MEC networks. Electronics **12**(17), 3548 (2023). https://doi.org/10.3390/electronics12173548
3. Landers, M., Doryab, A.: Deep reinforcement learning verification: a survey. ACM Comput. Surv. **55**(14s), Article 330, 31 (2023). https://doi.org/10.1145/3596444
4. Kumaran, K., Sasikala, E.: Learning based latency minimization techniques in mobile edge computing (MEC) systems: a comprehensive survey. In: 2021 International Conference on System, Computation, Automation and Networking (ICSCAN), Puducherry, India, pp. 1–6 (2021). https://doi.org/10.1109/ICSCAN53069.2021.9526410
5. Liu, C.-F., Bennis, M., Poor, H.V.: Latency and reliability-aware task offloading and resource allocation for mobile edge computing. In: 2017 IEEE Globe com Workshops (GC Wkshps), Singapore, pp. 1–7 (2017). https://doi.org/10.1109/GLOCOMW.2017.8269175
6. Dab, B., Aitsaadi, N., Langar, R.: Q-learning algorithm for joint computation offloading and resource allocation in edge cloud. In: 2019 IFIP/IEEE Symposium on Integrated Network and Service Management (IM), pp. 45–52. IEEE (2019)
7. Huang, L., Feng, X., Zhang, C., et al.: Deep reinforcement learning-based joint task offloading and bandwidth allocation for multi-user mobile edge computing. Digit. Commun. Netw. **5**(1), 10–17 (2019)
8. Liang, Y., He, Y., Zhong, X.: Decentralized computation offloading and resource allocation in MEC by deep reinforcement learning. In: 2020 IEEE/CIC International Conference on Communications in China (ICCC), pp. 244–249. IEEE (2020)
9. Liang, S., Wan, H., Qin, T., et al.: Multi-user computation offloading for mobile edge computing: A deep reinforcement learning and game theory approach. In: 2020 IEEE 20th International Conference on Communication Technology (ICCT), pp. 1534–1539. IEEE (2020)
10. Wu, Y.C., Dinh, T.Q., Fu, Y., et al.: A hybrid DQN and optimization approach for strategy and resource allocation in MEC networks. IEEE Trans. Wireless Commun. **20**(7), 4282–4295 (2021)
11. Li, C., Xia, J., Liu, F., et al.: Dynamic offloading for multiuser muti-CAP MEC networks: a deep reinforcement learning approach. IEEE Trans. Veh. Technol. **70**(3), 2922–2927 (2021)
12. Gan, S., Siew, M., Xu, C., et al.: Differentially Private Deep Q-Learning for Pattern Privacy Preservation in MEC Offloading (2023). arXiv preprint arXiv:2302.04608
13. Silver, D., Huang, A., Maddison, C.J., et al.: Mastering the game of go with deep neural networks and tree search. Nature **529**(7587), 484–489 (2016)
14. Al-Absi, M.A., Al-Absi, A.A., Sain, M., et al.: Moving ad hoc networks—a comparative study. Sustainability **13**(11), 6187 (2021)
15. Jiang, P., Ergu, D., Liu, F., et al.: A review of Yolo algorithm developments. Procedia Comput. Sci. **199**, 1066–1073 (2022)
16. Nath, S., Li, Y., Wu, J., et al.: Multi-user multi-channel computation offloading and resource allocation for mobile edge computing. In: ICC 2020–2020 IEEE International Conference on Communications (ICC), pp. 1–6. IEEE (2020)
17. Silver, D., et al.: Mastering the game of go with deep neural networks and tree search. Nature **529**(7587), 484–489 (2016)
18. Hao, W., Yang, S.: Small cell cluster-based resource allocation for wireless backhaul in two-tier heterogeneous networks with massive MIMO. IEEE Trans. Veh. Technol. **67**(1), 509–523 (2017)

19. Zeng, H., Zhang, M., Xia, Y., et al.: Decoupling the depth and scope of graph neural networks. Adv. Neural. Inf. Process. Syst. **34**, 19665–19679 (2021)
20. Dennis, A.K.: Raspberry Pi Computer Architecture Essentials. Packt Publishing Ltd., Birmingham (2016)

Content Prediction for Proactive Tile-Based VR Video Streaming in Mobile Edge Caching System

Qiuming Liu[1,2(✉)], Hao Chen[1], Yang Zhou[3], Dong Wu[3], Zihui Li[1], and Yaxin Bai[1]

[1] School of Software Engineering, Jiangxi University of Science and Technology, Nanchang 330013, China
liuqiuming@jxust.edu.cn, 6720210688@mail.jxust.edu.cn
[2] Nanchang Key Laboratory of Virtual Digital Factory and Cultural Communications, Nanchang 330013, China
[3] Information and Communication Branch, State Grid Jiangxi Electric Power Co., Nanchang 330095, China

Abstract. Content prediction can avoid VR video streaming delay in mobile edge caching system. To reduce request delay, popular content should be cached on edge server. Existing work either focuses on content prediction or on caching algorithms. However, in the end-edge-cloud system, prediction and caching should be considered together. In this paper, we jointly optimize the four stages of prediction, caching, computing and transmission in mobile edge caching system, aimed to maximize the user's quality of experience. We propose a progressive policy to optimize the four steps of VR video streaming. Since the user's QoE is determined by the performance of the resource allocation and caching algorithm, we design a caching algorithm with unknown future request content, which can efficiently improve the content hit rate, as well as the durations for prediction, computing and transmission. We optimize the four stages under arbitrary resource allocation and simulate the proposed algorithm according to the degree of overlap, as well as completion rate. Finally, under the real scenario, the proposed algorithm is verified by comparing with several other caching algorithms, simulation results show that the user's QoE is improved under the progressive policy and the proposed algorithm.

Keywords: VR video streaming · Content prediction · Caching algorithm · Quality of experience · Edge computing

1 Introduction

VR video has ultra-high resolution (e.g. 16K), which requires high computing rate and transmission rate to ensure low delay. Nowadays, computing and transmission resources cannot support the rapid transmission of ultra-high resolution

C. Wu et al. (Eds.): MONAMI 2023, LNICST 559, pp. 254–265, 2024.
https://doi.org/10.1007/978-3-031-55471-1_19

VR video. In view of the above VR transmission difficulties, researchers have proposed some technical methods to improve the quality of VR transmission. At each moment, the area that a human sees is only a part of the VR video, which called the field of view (FoV) [1]. Dividing the video into tiles and focusing on the parts in the FoV can reduce the amount of content transmitted. The motion to photon (MTP) delay causes dizziness for users watching VR videos. Proactive tile-based VR video streaming can avoid the MTP delay [2], which sends the predicted content to the user's head mounted display (HMD) in advance. Caching popular content on the edge server and providing VR content directly to users at the edge can reduce backhaul link pressure and request delay. The above technical methods improve the quality of VR video transmission from three perspectives: reducing transmission content, prediction and caching. Next, we discuss the current research status of VR transmission.

In the existing works, VR video streaming research almost always divides VR video into tiles and system mainly transmits the content in FoV [3–12]. There are also many articles study caching algorithm that can cache popular content on the edge server to reduce remote request delay [4–7]. In the prediction study of FoV, researchers prefer to use machine learning to design predictors [8–12]. However, the above work either only designs the cache algorithm, or only designs the predictor, or only jointly optimizes the prediction, computation and transmission in end-edge system. These works do not jointly optimize prediction, computing and transmission under delay constraints in end-edge-cloud system (EECS) to improve user's quality of experience (QoE).

In this paper, we study the impact of prediction, computing, transmission on QoE under delay constraints. The main contributions are summarized as follows.

– We jointly optimize prediction, computing, and transmission under delay constraints in EECS. The relationship between four steps is analyzed and QoE is maximized under different resource allocations. We propose a progressive policy to balance the four steps to make QoE as big as possible. The use of the progressive policy makes 93.178% of the experimental segments achieve the maximum QoE. In the remaining experimental segments where the maximum value is not obtained, the maximum difference rate between the QoE obtained by the progressive strategy and the maximum value is 0.406298%, which is very close to the maximum value.
– We design a caching algorithm to improve the efficiency of caching and thus improve the overall QoE, which can effectively reduce the request delay. The time saved is used for prediction, computing, transmission to improve prediction performance and completion rate. Then, our algorithm provides better QoE among the six algorithms simulated.

2 Model System

In the EECS, each VR video V_i consists S segments, and each segment is composed by M tiles. We assume that the storage size of the MEC buffer is denoted by B, which means that the MEC can cache B tiles. User's HMD can record data

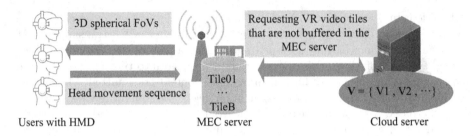

Fig. 1. End-Edge-Cloud System

of head movement sequence, and send the recorded data to the MEC server. The head motion sequence is used to predict FoV. Both HMD and the MEC server can render the VR videos. We only consider the rendering on the MEC server, since it would cause delay in HMD. The VR video stream is rendered to 3D spherical FoV by MEC and then sent to the user.

We consider an EECS with a proactive tile-based VR video streaming as shown in Fig. 1. The EECS includes some users with HMD, a MEC server co-located with base station (BS), and a back-end cloud. Clients request VR videos according to unpredictable patterns. If the edge sever holds the contents, it will response the request immediately. Otherwise, the edge server would resort to the cloud server, where holds the entire VR videos $V = \{V_1, V_2, \cdots\}$. Forwarding content requests to the back-end cloud incurs request delay.

In order to avoid MTP delay, the content required by the $(s + 1)$th segment should be sent to the user's HMD before t^e as shown in Fig. 2. Therefore, when the user's HMD plays (s)th segment, the MEC server is processing the tiles needed for $(s + 1)$th segment. The request delay t_{req} can be determined after the prediction is completed. Within the time delay t_{req}, the progressive policy allocates the duration of each task according to the optimization results. The predicted FoV tiles must be rendered as 3D spherical FoV to start transmission, so the runtime of the four-step task is serial. Each segment contains four steps: prediction, request delay, computing and transmission, which are processed serially in each segment. Next, we illustrate the processing of $(s + 1)$th segment as an example.

We use $[t^b, t^e]$ to represent the playback time of (s)th segment. The $(s+1)$th segment VR video streaming is serially processed as follows. Prediction stage: The MEC server observes in the observation window t_{pdc} and maps the recorded data into predicted tiles. Request delay: Predicted tiles that are not in the MEC server buffer should be requested from the back-end cloud with a request delay t_{req}, and the MEC server caches popular tiles. Computing stage: On the MEC server, predicted tiles are rendered into 3D spherical FoV in duration t_{cpt}. Transmission stage: The processed tiles are transmitted to the HMD with the duration t_{tra}. One segment duration denoted as T_{seg}, which is the total proactive streaming time available for prediction, caching, computing, and transmission, i.e. $t_{pdc} + t_{req} + t_{cpt} + t_{tra} \leq T_{seg}$.

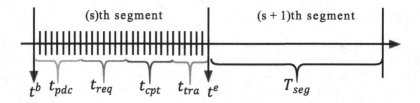

Fig. 2. Four processing steps within a segment

2.1 Delay Model

Due to the limited edge buffer size, the MEC server cannot cache all VR videos. Therefore, the content that is not at the edge needs MEC server to forward the request to the cloud for acquisition. The delay of requesting tiles to the cloud is related to the number of tiles being requested remotely. Then, the request delay is expressed as:

$$t_{req} = n_0 \cdot (T_e \cdot d_0),\qquad(1)$$

where T_e is the average transmission time of per tile at the edge. The number of remote request tiles is expressed as n_0. For the same data, the delay of remote cloud request is d_0 times of edge transmission time [13].

2.2 Computing Model

Rendering the predicted tiles within the computing duration t_{cpt}. The computing resources of rendering VR video on the MEC server are equally allocated to each user. Then, the computing rate for one user is expressed as:

$$C_{cpt} \triangleq \frac{C_{all}}{K \cdot U_0}(bits/s),\qquad(2)$$

where C_{all} is the total computing resource (FLOPS), which should be equally allocated to K users. The FLOPs required to render one bit is expressed as U_0.

2.3 Transmission Model

The proactive tile-based VR video streaming in one segment has undergone three-step processing, which should be transmitted to HMD with duration t_{tra}. Then the duration t_{tra} is expressed as:

$$t_{tra} \triangleq \frac{(R_w \cdot R_h \cdot b) \cdot N_{fov}}{C_e \cdot \gamma}(s),\qquad(3)$$

where γ is the Lossless compression ratio, and the transmission rate from MEC server to the user's HMD is expressed as C_e. The number of tiles in the FoV is expressed as N_{fov}. The corresponding transmission rate is expressed as C_{tra}. R_h and R_w are the pixels in high and wide of a tile, respectively. b is the number of bits per pixel.

3   Problem Formulation

The goal of this paper is to improve the quality of user experience, and the user's QoE is closely related to prediction, request delay, computing, and transmission. Prediction determines the accuracy of the content received by the user's HMD. We use the degree of overlap (DoO) to represent the predicted performance. DoO represents the proportion of correctly predicted tiles in FoV. We use completion rate to represent the performance of computing and transmission. DoO and completion rate affect user's QoE in content quality and content quantity respectively. The caching algorithm affects request delay. This section formulates the problem of maximizing QoE through completion rate and DoO.

3.1   Performance Metric of QoE

We use an existing predictor, and mainly analyze the effect of the observation window on the quality of the prediction. The larger the observation window, the better the prediction results [3]. We need to optimize the three-step task under delay constraints before the next segment request arrival, so we use the fitting function to represent DoO, which is expressed as:

$$DoO(t_{pdc}) = a_3 \cdot t_{pdc}^3 + a_2 \cdot t_{pdc}^2 + a_1 \cdot t_{pdc} + a_0, \tag{4}$$

where $\{a_0, a_1, a_2, a_3\}$ are the fitted coefficients. We only need to know the size of the observation window t_{pdc} to get the $DoO(t_{pdc})$.

The performance of computing and transmission is expressed by the completion rate, which can be expressed as:

$$R(t_{cpt}, t_{tra}) \triangleq min\left\{1, \frac{C_{cpt} \cdot t_{cpt}}{s_{cpt} \cdot N_{fov}}, \frac{C_{tra} \cdot t_{tra}}{s_{tra} \cdot N_{fov}}\right\}, \tag{5}$$

where s_{cpt} and s_{tra} are the number of bits to compute and transmit in one tile respectively.

The user's QoE is determined by the VR content quality and VR content integrity. QoE can be expressed by completion rate and DoO [3], which is defined as:

$$QoE(t_{pdc}, t_{cpt}, t_{tra}) \triangleq DoO(t_{pdc}) \cdot R(t_{cpt}, t_{tra}), \tag{6}$$

where $t_{pdc} + t_{req} + t_{cpt} + t_{tra} \leq T_{seg}$.

3.2   Joint Optimization

Under the known conditions of predictor, computing rate C_{cpt} and transmission rate C_{tra}, we optimize the duration of prediction, computing and transmission under delay constraints to maximize QoE, which can be expressed as:

$$\mathbf{P1}: \quad \max_{t_{pdc}, t_{cpt}, t_{tra}} \quad DoO(t_{pdc}) \cdot R(t_{cpt}, t_{tra}) \tag{7a}$$

$$s.t. \quad t_{pdc} + t_{req} + t_{cpt} + t_{tra} \leq T_{seg} \tag{7b}$$

$$t_{pdc} \geq \tau, \quad t_{req}, t_{cpt}, t_{tra} \geq 0 \tag{7c}$$

The total duration of the four steps should be less than or equal to one segment duration T_{seg}. τ is the minimum value of the observation window. Next section, we solve the **P1** problem, propose progressive policy and VIE online caching algorithm.

4 Optimal Durations and Progressive Policy and VIE Online Caching Algorithm

4.1 Optimal Durations

We solve the **P1** problem to obtain t_{pdc}^*, t_{cpt}^* and t_{tra}^*, where t_{pdc}^*, t_{cpt}^* and t_{tra}^* maximize the objective problem **P1**. The solution process is: we decompose the **P1** problem into optimizing the completion rate first and then solving the **P1** problem. The sum of computing and transmission duration is expressed as t_{ct}, i.e. $t_{ct} = t_{cpt} + t_{tra}$. According to the KKT condition, the first step optimization completion rate $\max\limits_{t_{cpt},t_{tra}} R(t_{cpt}, t_{tra})$ can be solved:

$$
t_{cpt}^*(t_{ct}) = \begin{cases} \frac{C_{tra}s_{cpt}}{C_{tra}s_{cpt}+C_{cpt}s_{tra}}t_{ct}, & t_{ct} \leq T_{ct}^{max} \\ \alpha, \alpha \in (\frac{s_{cpt}N_{fov}}{C_{cpt}}, \infty), & t_{ct} > T_{ct}^{max} \end{cases}
$$

$$
t_{tra}^*(t_{ct}) = \begin{cases} \frac{C_{cpt}s_{tra}}{C_{tra}s_{cpt}+C_{cpt}s_{tra}}t_{ct}, & t_{ct} \leq T_{ct}^{max} \\ \beta, \beta \in (\frac{s_{tra}N_{fov}}{C_{tra}}, \infty), & t_{ct} > T_{ct}^{max} \end{cases} \tag{8}
$$

$$
R_{(t_{cpt},t_{tra})}^*(t_{ct}) = \begin{cases} \frac{t_{ct}}{T_{ct}^{max}}, & t_{ct} \leq T_{ct}^{max} \\ 1, & t_{ct} > T_{ct}^{max} \end{cases},
$$

where only t_{ct} is a variable, we get the solution related to t_{ct}. In the above formula, $T_{ct}^{max} \triangleq \frac{s_{tra}N_{fov}}{C_{tra}} + \frac{s_{cpt}N_{fov}}{C_{cpt}}$. T_{ct}^{max} is the minimum value required for t_{ct} when the completion rate up to 100%, so t_{ct} does not need to exceed T_{ct}^{max}. T_{cr}^{max} represents the configuration of computing resources and transmission resources, which is a known value. In the case of $t_{ct} \leq T_{ct}^{max}$, problem **P1** can be re-writte as:

$$\textbf{P2}: \max\limits_{t_{pdc},t_{ct}} \quad DoO(t_{pdc}) \cdot \frac{t_{ct}}{T_{ct}^{max}} \tag{9a}$$

$$s.t. \quad t_{pdc} + t_{ct} + t_{req} \leq T_{seg} \tag{9b}$$

$$t_{pdc} \geq \tau, \quad 0 \leq t_{ct} \leq T_{ct}^{max} \tag{9c}$$

According to the KKT condition, the available result of **P2** is :

$$t_{pdc}^*(t_{req}) = \max\{(T_{seg} - t_{req}) - T_{cr}^{max}, \tau\}$$

$$t_{ct}^*(t_{req}) = \min\{T_{cr}^{max}, (T_{seg} - t_{req}) - \tau\} \tag{10}$$

Finally, we get $t_{pdc}^*(t_{req})$ and $t_{ct}^*(t_{req})$. Through $t_{ct}^*(t_{req})$, we can also get $t_{cpt}^*(t_{ct})$, $t_{tra}^*(t_{ct})$ and $R_{(t_{cpt},t_{tra})}^*(t_{ct})$, and QoE is expressed as $DoO(t_{pdc}^*(t_{req})) \cdot \frac{t_{ct}^*(t_{req})}{T_{ct}^{max}}$. The optimization result still has a variable t_{req}. Next, we design a progressive strategy to maximize QoE as much as possible in the case of t_{req} uncertainty, and design an online caching algorithm to reduce t_{req}.

4.2   Progressive Policy

Because t_{req} cannot be known before prediction, progressive policy is designed to make the QoE of each segment as close as possible to the optimal value. The prediction window expands step by step from the smallest τ is the progressive meaning. Each prediction window can get the corresponding request delay t_{req}, then the t_{ct} is obtained through the optimization results, and the QoE value under this prediction window is calculated.

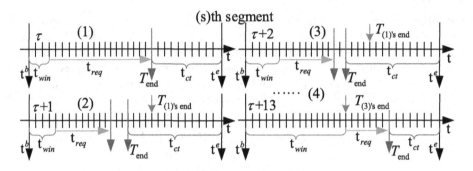

Fig. 3. An example of progressive policy operation

Figure 3 shows the process of progressive policy implementation. In (1) state, The observation starts from t^b, and the current observation window size is $t_{win} = \tau$. After observation, the request delay t_{req} corresponding to the predicted data is obtained, and t^*_{ct} is calculated according to the optimization result formula (10). According to the above information, if we want to select the durations allocation in (1), we can determine that the observation window can be extended to T_{end} at most. The observation window expands one step to state (2), where $t_{win} = \tau + 1$. In state (2), t^*_{ct} reaches t^{max}_{ct}, so the extensible space of state (2) is larger than t_{req}. We compare the QoE values of state (2) and state (1), and assume that the QoE of state (1) is larger. Therefore, we discard all the information of state (2) and only record the durations allocation and maximum extension time $T_{(1)'send}$ of state (1). The observation window expands one step to state (3), where $t_{win} = \tau + 2$. We assume that the QoE of state (3) is larger than that of state (1). So we only keep the information of state (3). Next, we omit the multi-step extension processing and assume that the QoE of state (3) is the largest, directly to the last state (4). The observation window has been extended to the maximum extension time $T_{(3)'send}$, and the QoE is less than the QoE of state (3), so we use the durations allocation of state (3).

The progressive policy is adopted in each segment, which pseudo code is shown in Algorithm 1.

Algorithm 1. Progressive Policy

1: $t_{win} \leftarrow \tau$, $Data \leftarrow None$
2: **do** {
3:      $N_{fov} = \text{predict}(t_{win})$
4:      $n_0 = N_{fov} - N_{inB}$, $t_{req} = n_0 \cdot T_e \cdot d_0$
5:      $t_{ct} = \min\{T_{ct}^{max}, (T_{seg} - t_{req}) - \tau\}$
6:      $QoE = DoO(t_{win}) \cdot \frac{t_{ct}}{T_{ct}^{max}}$
7:      **if** (this QoE is bigger)
8:           $T_{end} = 1 - min(T_{ct}^{max}, 1 - t_{win} - t_{req})$
9:           $Data \leftarrow \{T_{end}, QoE\}$
10:      $t_{win} \leftarrow t_{win} + 1$
11: }**while** $(t_{win} < T_{end})$
12: **Output:** QoE

4.3 The VIE Online Caching Algorithm

Our online caching algorithm consists of two parts: Caching popular tiles to the MEC buffer and removing unpopular tiles from the MEC buffer. We propose the *recent victor download and recent failure deletion* (VIE) online caching algorithm, which assumes the future request content is unknown.

Definition 1. *Recent victor download:* *Each tile is recorded when it was requested. Tile te_j is not in the MEC server buffer, and te_i is in the buffer. $te_i(t)$ represents whether tile te_i is requested at time t. $te_i(t) = 1$ indicates that the tile te_i is requested at t. $te_i(t) = 0$ indicates that the tile te_i is not requested at time t. At time t_0, if there exists a positive integer λ and a boundary η such that te_i and te_j satisfies:*

$$\sum_{t=t_0-\lambda}^{t_0} te_j(t) \geq \sum_{t=t_0-\lambda}^{t_0} te_i(t) + \eta \tag{11}$$

Then te_j will be cached in the MEC server buffer.

According to Definition 1, *recent victor download* algorithm judge the situation in the recent period according to the boundary parameter η. If a tile te_j that has not been cached in the MEC buffer in the recent period of time is requested more times than the tile cached in the MEC buffer, then we cache te_j. We call te_j the victor.

Definition 2. *Recent failure deletion:* *Tile te_i cached in the buffer corresponds to a positive integer ζ_i as small as possible. te_i satisfies the requested number at time $t_0 - \zeta_i \leq t \leq t_0$ is greater than or equal to η, that is, $\sum_{t=t_0-\zeta_i}^{t_0} te_i(t) \geq \eta$. Selecting the tile te_i with the biggest ζ_i to remove from MEC server.*

According to Definition 2, algorithm selects the te_i corresponding to the largest ζ_i to delete. ζ_i represents the size of the time range. In the experiment, we set $\eta = 2d_0$.

5   Simulation

We refer to the real scenario in [14], which includes 50 users and 10 VR videos. Each VR video is 1 minute long and divided into 60 segments. d_0 is set to 12 [13]. The pixel of the tile is 192×192, i.e. $R_w = 192$ and $R_h = 192$, and the number of bits per pixel is 12, i.e. $b = 12$. Lossless Coding Compression Rate Set to 2.41, i.e. $\gamma = 2.41$. T_{cr}^{max} is set to { 0.2s, 0.25s, 0.3s, $\cdots$,50s }. We use the existing RL predictor for simulation. Users requests VR video with Zipfian distribution [5], so the probability that the VR video $v \in V$ is selected for viewing is:

$$P_v = \frac{1/v^{\eta_v}}{\sum_{v \in V} 1/v^{\eta_v}} \tag{12}$$

We verified the performance of the VIE algorithm in terms of user's QoE and completion rate. The proposed algorithm is compared with five caching algorithms, which are:

- Static Offline: The most popular tiles are cached on edge server, which contains all future request information, and the cached content is not updated.
- LFU [4,5]: The number of times each tile has been requested is recorded, and caching newly arrived tiles by removing the least frequently used tiles.
- LRU [4,5]: The last requested time of each tile is recorded, and caching newly arrived tiles by removing least recently used tiles.
- FIFO [5]: Each requested tile is queued, and newly arriving tiles are cached by dequeuing.
- Randomized: Tiles are randomly cached in the buffer.

We first simulate the progressive policy. We use randomized algorithm and set the edge buffer to be 10% of the total data to conduct experiments on 1764690 segments. The experimental results show that 1644308 segments have achieved the maximum QoE, which accounts for 93.178% of the total experiments. In the remaining 6.822% results, the QoE obtained by the progressive policy is very close to the maximum value, the difference rate in the range of [0.227357%, 0.406298%]. Six examples of the progressive policy that did not achieve the maximum value in one segment are shown in Table 1.

Table 1. Six examples that do not reach the maximum QoE.

Minimum QoE	Maximum QoE	QoE of Progressive Policy	Difference Rate
0.149304	0.415359	0.413940	0.341632%
0.109049	0.465753	0.464640	0.238968%
0.090175	0.385383	0.383946	0.372876%
0.125859	0.352531	0.351507	0.290471%
0.079028	0.257461	0.256875	0.227607%
0.092893	0.396753	0.395804	0.239192%

In Fig. 4, we use boxplots to evaluate the performance of the six algorithms on QoE. Information can be obtained from the figure: a) The VIE algorithm achieves the highest QoE among the six algorithms. b) The baseline randomized algorithm is significantly lower than the other five algorithms. c) The overall QoE of LFU [4,5], LRU [4,5] and FIFO [5] is lower than the VIE algorithm.

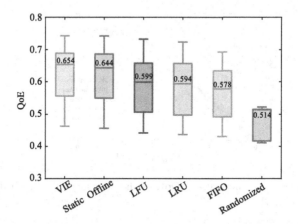

Fig. 4. Comparison of the VIE caching algorithm and other five algorithms on QoE. The cache size is 15% of total data and T_{cr}^{max} is 0.8 s.

In Fig. 5, we use boxplots to evaluate the performance of the six algorithms on completion rate. The buffer size is set to 15% of total data, and T_{cr}^{max} is set to 0.8 s. The completion rate of the VIE algorithm is the highest and random algorithm is the lowest. The completion rates of LFU [4,5], LRU [4,5], and FIFO [5] are significantly smaller than the VIE algorithm.

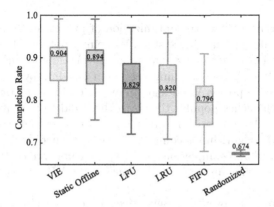

Fig. 5. Comparison of the VIE caching algorithm and other five algorithms on completion rate. The cache size is 15% of total data and T_{cr}^{max} is 0.8 s.

In Fig. 6, The graph illustrates that the average QoE increases as resources increase. The smaller the T_{cr}^{max}, the stronger the computing and transmission capabilities, and the higher the average QoE. Five different colored lines represent different edge buffer size. The edge cache size is proportional to the average QoE.

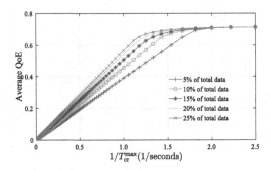

Fig. 6. The variation of the average QoE of the VIE algorithm with different cache sizes and different T_{cr}^{max}.

Under the duration allocation of the progressive policy, 93.178% of the data achieves the maximum QoE, and the maximum difference rate in QoE that does not reach the maximum value is 0.406298%. The experimental results show that the VIE algorithm significantly outperforms the other five caching algorithms in terms of user's QoE and completion rate. The static offline algorithm is only a little worse than the VIE algorithm, but the static offline algorithm needs to know all the request information in advance, which is unrealistic.

6   Conclusion

In this paper, we investigate the optimization of proactive tile-based VR video streaming in mobile edge caching system. We jointly optimized prediction, computing, transmission under delay constraints to maximize QoE, and proposed a progressive policy. A good caching algorithm can improve the optimization results of progressive policy. We design an online caching algorithm to improve user's QoE, which caches popular tiles by a threshold to improve cache performance. The six caching algorithms are simulated in real scenario using existing predictor. The VIE algorithm is compared with five other caching algorithms in terms of user's QoE and completion rate. Experiments verified the performance of the progressive policy and the performance of the VIE algorithm.

Acknowledgment. This work was supported in part by Culture and Art Science Planning Project of Jiangxi Province (No. YG2018042), Humanities and Social Science Project of Jiangxi Province (No. JC18224).

References

1. Kattadige, C.: PhD forum: encrypted traffic analysis & content awareness of 360-degree video streaming optimization. In: 2021 IEEE 22nd International Symposium on a World of Wireless, Mobile and Multimedia Networks (WoWMoM) (2021)
2. Fan, C.L., Lo, W.C., Pai, Y.T., Hsu, C.H.: A survey on 360° video streaming: acquisition, transmission, and display. ACM Comput. Surv. (CSUR) **52**(4), 1–36 (2019)
3. Wei, X., Yang, C., Han, S.: Prediction, communication, and computing duration optimization for VR video streaming. IEEE Trans. Commun. **69**(3), 1947–1959 (2021)
4. Mahzari, A., Nasrabadi, A.T., Samiei, A., Prakash, R.: FOV-aware edge caching for adaptive 360° video streaming. In: 2018 ACM Multimedia Conference (2018)
5. Maniotis, P., Thomos, N.: Viewport-aware deep reinforcement learning approach for 360° video caching. IEEE Trans. Multimedia **24**, 386–399 (2022). https://doi.org/10.1109/TMM.2021.3052339
6. Ji, S., Lee, S., Park, G., Song, H.: Head movement-aware mpeg-dash SRD-based 360° video VR streaming system over wireless network. In: 2022 IEEE 23rd International Symposium on a World of Wireless, Mobile and Multimedia Networks (WoWMoM), pp. 281–287 (2022). https://doi.org/10.1109/WoWMoM54355.2022.00054
7. Xiao, H., et al.: A transcoding-enabled 360° VR video caching and delivery framework for edge-enhanced next-generation wireless networks. IEEE J. Sel. Areas Commun. **40**(5), 1615–1631 (2022). https://doi.org/10.1109/JSAC.2022.3145813
8. Rondon, M., Sassatelli, L., Aparicio-Pardo, R., Precioso, F.: TRACK: a new method from a re-examination of deep architectures for head motion prediction in 360-degree videos. IEEE Trans. Pattern Anal. Mach. Intell. **44**(9), 5681–5699 (2021)
9. Zhang, R., et al.: Buffer-aware virtual reality video streaming with personalized and private viewport prediction. IEEE J. Sel. Areas Commun. **40**(2), 694–709 (2022). https://doi.org/10.1109/JSAC.2021.3119144
10. Cheng, Q., Shan, H., Zhuang, W., Yu, L., Zhang, Z., Quek, T.Q.: Design and analysis of MEC- and proactive caching-based 360° mobile VR video streaming. IEEE Trans. Multimedia **24**, 1529–1544 (2022). https://doi.org/10.1109/TMM.2021.3067205
11. Liu, X., Deng, Y., Han, C., Renzo, M.D.: Learning-based prediction, rendering and transmission for interactive virtual reality in RIS-assisted terahertz networks. IEEE J. Sel. Areas Commun. **40**(2), 710–724 (2022). https://doi.org/10.1109/JSAC.2021.3118405
12. Zhu, Y., Zhai, G., Yang, Y., Duan, H., Min, X., Yang, X.: Viewing behavior supported visual saliency predictor for 360 degree videos. IEEE Trans. Circuits Syst. Video Technol. **32**(7), 4188–4201 (2022). https://doi.org/10.1109/TCSVT.2021.3126590
13. Song, Y., Wo, T., Yang, R., Shen, Q., Xu, J.: Joint optimization of cache placement and request routing in unreliable networks. J. Parallel Distrib. Comput. **157**, 168–178 (2021)
14. Lo, W.C., Fan, C.L., Lee, J., Huang, C.Y., Chen, K.T., Hsu, C.H.: 360° video viewing dataset in head-mounted virtual reality. In: The 8th ACM, pp. 211–216 (2017)

Emerging Applications

Research on Latent Semantic Relationship Search Engine Based on Knowledge Graph

Minqin Mao[✉] and Jielan Zhang

Jiangxi Teachers College, Yingtan 335000, Jiangxi, China
maominqin@126.com

Abstract. Knowledge graph is a large database composed of entities, relationships and attributes, which can provide rich semantic information for search engines. The potential semantic relation search engine based on Knowledge graph is a novel search engine. It obtains potential semantic relationships from the Knowledge graph, and then uses these potential semantic relationships to search for data sources such as web pages and documents. This paper first analyzes the characteristics of the Knowledge graph, then lists the construction process of the Knowledge graph based on WordNet, and finally proposes the potential semantic relationship search engine architecture based on the Knowledge graph.

Keywords: Knowledge graph · Potential semantic relationships · Search Engines

1 Introduction

At present, search engines lack in-depth semantic analysis and understanding of massive text data. In the search process, it is often only possible to obtain corresponding data from the text, rather than extracting potential semantic relationships from it. Using this method of retrieval, it is not only difficult to meet user needs, but also leads to inaccurate query results.

The related search technology based on the potential semantic relationship of the Knowledge graph emerged in this environment. This technology extracts potential semantic relationships from the Knowledge graph to facilitate semantic related retrieval by users.

2 Definition and Characteristics of Knowledge Graph

The Knowledge graph is a knowledge base that forms a structured model based on logical abstraction of massive amounts of information from the real world. It is a large database consisting of entities, relationships, and attributes, which can describe an entity and its associated information. Knowledge graph is essentially a semantic network. The nodes represent entities, the vertices represent attributes, and the edges represent various semantic relationships between the entity attributes. The process of constructing Knowledge graph involves three stages: entity extraction, attribute extraction, and relationship extraction.

© ICST Institute for Computer Sciences, Social Informatics and Telecommunications Engineering 2024
Published by Springer Nature Switzerland AG 2024. All Rights Reserved
C. Wu et al. (Eds.): MONAMI 2023, LNICST 559, pp. 269–274, 2024.
https://doi.org/10.1007/978-3-031-55471-1_20

The Knowledge graph has the following characteristics.

1. The Knowledge graph uses the form of graphs to represent various elements and the relationships between them in the real world. It is an abstract expression of the real world.
2. Knowledge graph is a knowledge base that is made up of entities, relations, attributes, and more. It is based on facts and describes the objective world in a dynamic way and with a large amount of information. It is highly scalable and can transform human knowledge and experience into a form that can be understood by computers, making it highly versatile.
3. There are a lot of potential semantic relations in Knowledge graph, and different entities may have some connections. The connection may be subjective or objective. For example, the relationships among entities include hierarchical relationships, sibling relationships, adjacency relationships, inclusion relationships, and so on. These potential semantic relationships can be modeled to help us better understand the relationships between data and make more effective and accurate decisions.

3   Construction Process of Knowledge Graph

Building a Knowledge graph with WordNet dictionary can reduce the number of steps required to structure data. The construction process based on WordNet Knowledge graph includes the following steps:

1. **Clarify the purpose and scope of the Knowledge graph**: Before building a Knowledge graph, you need to clarify its purpose and scope, so as to better organize and manage information.
2. **Data collection:** Take the data source in WordNet as the original data, and determine the core concepts of sub domains by manually dividing the identified knowledge domains.
3. **Knowledge Extraction:** Extract knowledge entities, relationships, and attributes related to core domain concepts from structured, semi-structured, and unstructured data of WordNet. The acquired data are integrated to form a preliminary knowledge representation.
4. **Building Relational Networks:** Using the synonymous, antonymous, hypernymy, and partial overall relationship in WordNet2. Knowledge entities and relationships are gradually built into an entity relationship network through deep learning algorithms and natural language and other technologies.
5. **Storage and Management:** The extracted information is stored in the database, and the information in the database is regularly updated to ensure its accuracy, integrity and reliability.
6. **Update and maintenance:** We need to update and maintain the Knowledge graph regularly, and integrate the extracted structured data and new data to generate a more complete and accurate Knowledge graph.

4 The Architecture of Latent Semantic Search Engine Based on Knowledge Graph

Potential semantic search module traditional search engines retrieve web pages or documents by keyword matching. For example, search engines match search websites based on keywords and return web pages related to the search keywords. However, for many different web pages, traditional search engines will return multiple results. Traditional search engines are just a simple resource retrieval tool, which cannot effectively discover potential semantic relationships in data resources. In order to solve these problems, the author proposes a potential semantic relationship search engine architecture based on Knowledge graph. The search engine is a new type of search engine based on Knowledge graph. It extracts valuable information from a large amount of data and transforms it into a form that users can understand. The basic process of this framework system is as follows (Fig. 1).

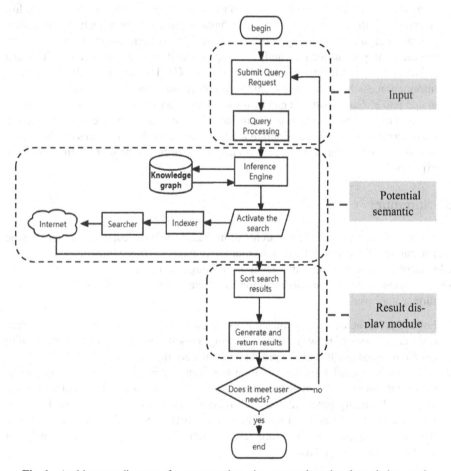

Fig. 1. Architecture diagram of a new search engine system based on knowledge graph

1. **Input module:** The user submits the query request through the query interface of the search engine, performs query processing, and submits the results of query processing to the inference engine.

2. **Knowledge graph building module:** This module uses natural language processing technology and machine learning algorithm to build a Knowledge graph, uses existing domain knowledge, domain model, etc. Through training and optimization of features, converts them into meaningful semantics, and realizes effective understanding and application of knowledge. It can contain a large amount of entity and relationship data, such as entities, attributes, relationships between attributes, etc. Then these data and relationships are transformed into structured representation, stored in the database, and the information in the database is regularly updated to ensure its accuracy, integrity and reliability.

3. **Potential semantic search module:** This module uses inference rules, statistical methods or machine learning algorithms in inference engine to extract entities and relationships from Knowledge graph, and classify and interpret them. The inference results from the inference engine are sent to the searcher, which provides high quality search results through various retrieval techniques and algorithms, such as information retrieval and rule-based query optimization, to provide high-quality retrieval results.

4. **Result display module:** The module is implemented using graphical a user interface (GUI) or a natural language generation tool (NLG). The search results and related information, such as text, image, audio and other multi-modal information, are integrated into a visual form that can be browsed and queried. Index and sort algorithms are used to sort the retrieved results in order. The sorted results are submitted to the page generation module to generate a result page, and the user accesses the generated search results through the access interface to improve the search effect and user experience.

5   Summary

The potential semantic relation search engine based on knowledge graph can provide rich semantic information for users. Its main advantage lies in the integration of Knowledge graph and potential semantic relation. Although the potential semantic relationship search engine based on Knowledge graph has made some achievements, it still needs to be further improved.

1. For example, the existing Knowledge graph cannot meet the requirements of large-scale data retrieval. How to add more entity, relationship a attribute information to the Knowledge graph is also a problem worth studying.

2. Although the potential semantic relation search engine based on Knowledge graph can use the information in knowledge atlas to some extent, it still needs manual annotation to get high quality potential semantic relation. There are three reasons. First, the Knowledge graph contains a lot of noise information. Second, some knowledge in the Knowledge graph is not completely accurate. Third, some data sources may not exist in the knowledge base.

3. How to use existing technology to improve search performance is also a challenge. There is currently no unified and clear answer on how to use existing technologies to improve the performance of latent semantic relationship search engines, and further research and exploration are needed.

References

1. Investigators at Nanyang Technological University Detail Findings in Neural Networks and Learning Systems (Brain-inspired Search Engine Assistant Based On Knowledge Graph). 2022(Jan.17), 13–14
2. Greg, R.: Notess. Search engine to knowledge engine? Online Search. **37**(4), 61–63 (2013)
3. Mayank, K., Pedro, S.: Knowledge graph for social good: an entity-centric search engine for the human trafficking domain. IEEE Trans. Big Data **8**(3), 592–606 (2022). https://doi.org/10.1109/TBDATA.2017.2763164
4. Uyar, A., Aliyu, F.M.: Evaluating search features of Google Knowledge Graph and Bing Satori Entity types, list searches and query interfaces. Online Inf. Rev. **39**(2), 197–213 (2015). https://doi.org/10.1108/OIR-10-2014-0257
5. Asgari-Bidhendi, M., Hadian, A., Minaei-Bidgoli, B.: FarsBase: the Persian knowledge graph. Semant. Web **10**(6), 1169–1196 (2019). https://doi.org/10.3233/SW-190369
6. Du, Y., Li, C., Hu, Q., et al.: Ranking webpages using a path trust Knowledge graph. Neurocomputing **269**(Dec.20), 58–72 (2017). https://doi.org/10.1016/j.neucom.2016.08.142
7. MICROSOFT TECHNOLOGY LICENSING, LLC. Knowledge graph for conversational semantic search:US15664124. 2022-09-06
8. Ma, C., Zhang, B.: A New query recommendation method supporting exploratory search based on search goal shift graphs. IEEE Trans. Knowl. Data Eng. **30**(11), 2024–2036 (2018). https://doi.org/10.1109/TKDE.2018.2815544
9. Berners-Lee, T., Hendler, J., Lassila, O.: The Semantic Web. Scientific American (2001)
10. Gruber, T.H.: A translation approach to portable ontology specifications. Knowl. Acquis. **2**, 199–220 (1993)
11. Han, L., Finin, T., Joshi, A.: GoRelations: an intuitive query system for DBpedia. Semant. Web **04**, 674–693 (2012)
12. Li, Q., Yang, W., Ye, X., Ma, X.: Research on knowledge base of device test training system based on rough set data mining. In: Proceedings of the 2013 International Conference on Intelligent System, Applied Materials and Control Technology (GSAMCT 2013) (2013)
13. Bordes, A, Usunier, N., Garcia-Duran, A., Weston, J., Yakhnenko, O.: Translating embeddings for modeling multi-relational data. In: Proceedings of the NIPS (2015)
14. Momtchev, V., Peychev, D., Primov, T.: Expanding the pathway and interaction knowledge in linked life data. In: Proceedings of International Semantic Web Challenge (2015)
15. Meng, Z.: Research on Construction of Course Knowledge Graph and Search Technology. Dissertation for Doctor Degree of Wuhan University (2016)
16. Xiangqian, L.: A method of searching entities based on wordnet noun network. Dissertation for Master Degree of Nanjing University (2015)
17. Yuncheng, G.: Research on Chinese-English-Mongolian Term Knowledge Graph of Computer Field Based on WordNet. Dissertation for Master Degree of Inner Mongolia Normal University (2021)
18. Berthold, M.R.: Towards bisociative knowledge discovery. Bisociative Knowledge Discovery. Springer-Verlag, Berlin, Heidelberg (2012)

19. Tom, H., Christian, B.: Linked Data. Morgan & Claypool., San Rafael (2011)
20. Berasaluce, S., Laurenço, C., Napoli, A., Niel, G.: An experiment on knowledge discovery in chemical databases. In: Boulicaut, J.F., Esposito, F., Giannotti, F., Pedreschi, D. (eds.) Knowledge Discovery in Databases: PKDD 2004. PKDD 2004. LNCS, vol. 3202. Springer, Berlin, Heidelberg (2004). https://doi.org/10.1007/978-3-540-30116-5_7

Promoting Animation Synthesis Through Dual-Channel Fusion

XiaoHong Qiu[1,2] ⓘ, ChaoChao Guo[1(✉)] ⓘ, and Cong Xu[1]

[1] Jiangxi University of Science and Technology, Nanchang 330013, China
1936452531@qq.com
[2] Nanchang Key Laboratory of Virtual Digital Factory and Cultural Communications, Nanchang 330013, People's Republic of China

Abstract. Although animation synthesis technology is widely applied, it also imposes higher demands on the precision of the synthesized animation. This paper employs a more lightweight channel attention module for image feature extraction. Compared to previous channel attention module, this approach utilizes fewer parameters, thereby assisting the network in achieving improved precision. Additionally, it replaces the sigmoid function with the more suitable output function tanh for image generation. Three evaluation metrics show improvements: a 1.3% increase in L1, an 18.9% increase in AED, and a 2.6% increase in AKD. To facilitate better image generation by the generator, improvements are made to the discriminator. Spectral normalization and instance normalization are combined to form a multi-normalization module for normalization during the image down sampling process. Additionally, an adaptive Dual-Channel Fusion output module is employed for the discriminator output, aiding in the rapid convergence of the network. The quality metrics of the generated images demonstrate improvements, with a 4.3% increase in L1, a 23.8% increase in AED, and a 5.5% increase in AKD.

Keywords: Animation Synthesis · Channel Attention · Dual-Channel Fusion

1 Introduction

Animation synthesis finds extensive applications in social platforms, virtual try-on, virtual character generation, and game sprite production [1]. On social platforms, individuals can showcase their positive aspects through videos, but some complex dance moves are challenging for the average person to perform. Traditional methods for animation compositing primarily rely on manually selecting existing actions through video or image editing software for composition. Although this approach can generate new action videos, it is difficult to synthesize previously non-existent body movements, and the synthesis process can be slow. The development of deep learning, convolutional neural networks, and generative adversarial networks have provided effective solutions. The integration of convolutional neural networks and generative adversarial networks in motion transfer has significantly alleviated the aforementioned issues. It not only speeds

C. Wu et al. (Eds.): MONAMI 2023, LNICST 559, pp. 275–285, 2024.
https://doi.org/10.1007/978-3-031-55471-1_21

up the animation compositing process and saves human resources but also generates entirely new actions.

Based on the maturation of generative adversarial network (GAN)-based image synthesis techniques [2], the "Everybody Dance Now" [3] algorithm in 2017 employed a two-stage approach to achieve motion transfer between images and generate animations. The first stage involved extracting key point information from the characters in the images, while the second stage utilized the key point information from the first stage to generate new animations. In 2018, Wiles [4] and Siarohin [5] respectively proposed the single-stage animation synthesis models "x2face" and "Monkey-Net". "x2face" primarily focused on facial expressions of the characters and could not handle other complex movements. "Monkey-Net" employed a self-supervised approach for key point localization and motion information learning but had limited representation capability for intense actions. In 2019, Siarohin [6] introduced the "First Order Motion Model" (FOMM), which used a set of self-learned key points and local affine transformations to describe complex motion processes. Compared to previous methods, this approach not only generated high-quality images and more natural movements but also required less training data, reducing training time and device requirements. However, challenges still exist regarding insufficient feature utilization and the need for further improvement in image quality. The introduction of channel attention, along with new activation functions and network architecture combinations, helps the network capture weighted features and generate higher-quality images.

2   Relate Work

FOMM not only enables the transition of animation compositing technology from two-stage to single-stage but also reduces the requirements for training data, eliminating the need for annotation of the original data. The network model employs the distance between generated images and driving frames as supervision for training. The network can generate new animations based on a static image and a sequence of videos or continuous frames, unlike traditional style transfer techniques, focusing on the motion and pose from the driving video. As shown in Fig. 1, modeling the motion information begins by passing the source image and driving frames through a key point detection network, which employs the SoftMax function to output the same number of key points. The classified key points are used for motion prediction in the motion module. By mapping the key points of the source image to those of the driving frame, the motion trajectories of each classified key point are calculated. Optical flow, a pixel-level technique for predicting the movement trajectory of consecutive frames, is utilized in combination with first-order Taylor expansion for motion modeling. The estimated feature vector containing motion information is then combined with the appearance features of the source image to generate an explicit feature vector through a dense motion field network. For the image generation component, a generator from a generative adversarial network is employed for image synthesis. The first-order motion model can generate new images with different pose, incorporating the motion and pose from the driving frames, based on the style of the source image.

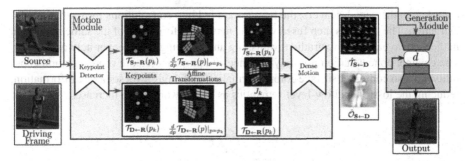

Fig. 1. First-Order Motion Model

The objective function used during the training of a first-order motion model:

$$Loss = L_{perceptual} + L_{gan} + L_{feature\_matching} + L_{equivariance} + L_{equi\,var\,iance\_value}$$

The objective function is as follows: Where $L_{perceptual}$ represents the perceptual loss of an image. The perceptual loss helps the network learn the contour structure and texture information of the images, serving as the primary loss for training the first-order motion model network. L_{gan} is composed of $L_{generator\_gan}$ and L_{disc_gan} as the losses for the generator and discriminator in a generative adversarial network (GAN). $L_{feature\_matching}$, as a feature matching loss, utilizes the output of the discriminator to minimize the feature distance between the generated image and the real image. $L_{equivariance}$ and $L_{equi\,var\,iance\_value}$ are losses for the motion pose and real image pose of generating images, obtained by estimating the Jacobian matrix loss of image key points.

3 First-Order Motion Model Animation Synthesis

3.1 Improvement of Hourglass Neural Network in Motion Estimation

The motion estimation in animation generation is divided into two parts, both utilizing a modified hourglass neural network module as the backbone [7]. The process initially involves image feature extraction and classification to estimate the key points of image motion. Sparse matrix of image motion is obtained, which is then used to construct dense optical flow matrix and occlusion mask. The dense optical flow matrix and occlusion mask are fed into the generator, combining the source image information and motion features to generate the image after motion transfer.

   In animation synthesis, the Hourglass neural network module is used as the backbone network for motion estimation, as shown in Fig. 2. F stands for feature and cat stands for concatenate. The feature extraction network employs a network structure pattern similar to a feature pyramid, with feature maps of different resolutions. The left side of the network serves as the encoder, gradually reducing the resolution from top to bottom and increasing the number of feature channels from top to bottom. The right side of the network serves as the decoder, with the resolution and number of feature channels changing in the opposite trend. However, each layer with the same resolution is concatenated with the corresponding layer on the left side. After the concatenation is complete in the decoder layers, the features are fed into convolutions for further feature extraction. The output is then fused with the network information of the same resolution in the next layer, reducing gradient vanishing and allowing for a deeper network design. The channel concatenation not only enhances the model's feature representation capability but also combines surface color information with high-level semantic information, reducing the loss of shallow-level semantics as the network depth increases.

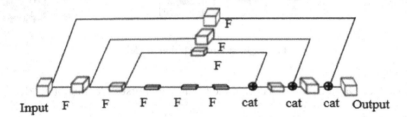

Fig. 2. Hourglass Network Module

Attention modules are often combined with networks [8]. The traditional attention mechanisms in computer vision can be divided into soft [9] and hard attention [10]. Soft attention can update the weight parameters of attention through the forward propagation and gradient backpropagation of the network. Hard attention, on the other hand, emphasizes the importance of specific information and its weight parameters are non-differentiable. This paper utilizes a type of hard attention mechanism, which adjusts the features based on the importance of each channel. This type of attention is known as Channel Attention (CA) [11], and its principle lies in the fact that different channels in a feature map contribute differently to different tasks. Channel attention can be divided into two steps: calculating the importance of each channel and weighting the channels of the input data. In the grid backbone encoding and decoding layers, CA modules containing channel attention are introduced to strengthen the connections between features.

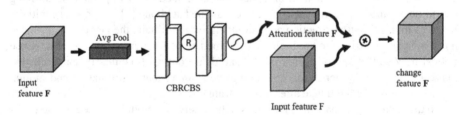

Fig. 3. Channel Attention Module

As shown in Fig. 3, the CA module is first implemented through an adaptive average pooling layer, which adjusts the size of the pooling window based on the size of the input feature map, better preserving the spatial information of the image. When a feature map X is obtained, with dimensions HWC, where H represents height, W represents width, and C represents the number of channels, the output enhancement coefficient is a $1 \times 1 \times$

C vector that represents the importance of each channel. The CBRCRS module uses two convolutional layers to calculate channel features. First, the feature channels are scaled by a factor of a, which requires calculating 1/a times, and then the inverse operation of channel number is performed to align the feature maps, i.e., performing dimensionality increase on the obtained feature vectors. This approach reduces the computational cost by 1/a compared to directly applying two dimension-preserving convolutions on the feature map. Batch normalization is applied during the convolution operation. Additionally, the Relu and Sigmoid functions are used as the activation and output functions, respectively, to obtain weighted feature coefficients. The obtained weighted feature coefficients are multiplied with the original channels to obtain the enhanced part of the feature map. Finally, the enhanced portion of the feature map is added to the original feature map to obtain the enhanced feature map.

3.2 Improved Generative Adversarial Network in FOMM

Estimating the motion between images to obtain dense optical flow images and combining the source images with the motion to generate image animations often requires the use of generative adversarial networks (GANs) [12] to achieve realistic results. GANs serve as framework models capable of generating data samples that follow the probability distribution of the original data.

Tanh-Improved Generator

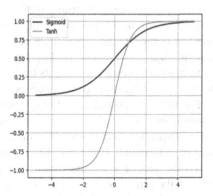

Fig. 4. Sigmoid And Tanh

Choosing an appropriate activation function introduces non-linear transformations to the neural network, thereby facilitating the generator to approximate the real data distribution more closely and enhance its adversarial capability against the discriminator. Different activation functions bring different non-linear transformations to the network. In computer vision tasks, it is necessary to select a suitable activation function based on specific tasks. Images generated using more appropriate activation functions exhibit greater realism and better generalization. Initially, the Sigmoid function was used as the output function of the network. The characteristics of the network's activation function can be observed from Fig. 4, where the Sigmoid function maps the input of the network layer to a continuous function between 0 and 1, aiding in network convergence. When the Sigmoid function is applied to large or small input parameters, the function's gradient remains relatively smooth. By utilizing steeper gradients, the network can achieve faster convergence, especially when using gradient-based optimization algorithms in the training of deep networks to find more definite descent directions. To address these issues, the Tanh function can be employed in image generation. The Tanh activation function varies between −1 and 1 and has a steep gradient, which helps in the gradient descent during network training.

Multiple Normalization and Adaptive Dual-Channel Fusion (See Fig. 5).

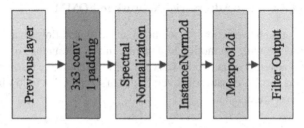

Fig. 5. Multi-normalization Down Sampling

The traditional down sampling module [13] primarily focuses on operations at the feature level, only performing weight normalization on the feature maps in batches or channels [14]. Adding spectral normalization to the down sampling operation, spectral normalization, a weight regularization technique in deep learning. The goal of spectral normalization [15] is to control the range of weights by limiting the spectral norm (maximum singular value) of the weight matrix of a network layer, thereby stabilizing the training process. The main idea behind spectral normalization is to normalize the eigenvectors of the weight matrix during each training iteration, thereby limiting its maximum singular value. This effectively controls the range of weights, preventing them from becoming too large or too small. If spectral normalization alone is used in the discriminator in the network, the generator and discriminator will become more stable, but the overall improvement of the generator by the discriminator will be slower, and the potential of the generator will not be fully stimulated. Instance normalization [16], which includes a scaling factor, can affect spectral normalization but also enhance the training of the discriminator. The combined use of spectral normalization and instance normalization helps control the range of weights, preventing excessive amplification or reduction of weights, and making the network more stable. Instance normalization can reduce internal covariate shift and accelerate the convergence process of the network. Therefore, combining spectral normalization and instance normalization into multi-normalization not only provides stability for the convergence of the adversarial network but also reduces the influence of outliers on the network's trends, helping the generator achieve better convergence and improve the generalization ability of generated images.

It is more important to use a reasonable discriminator output module to obtain the discriminator's discerning output for real and fake sample images. An adaptive dual-channel Fusion discriminator network output module is proposed to assist the discriminator in obtaining a variety of combinations to ensure output stability and accuracy. As shown in the diagram below, different from previous CONCAT and ADD connections for feature maps, two branches are created to expand the network's feature maps. The fused channels of these two branches are jointly transformed, using an adaptive mechanism as the fusion between image features. This enables learning of more reasonable and comprehensive features. When the discriminator assesses the authenticity of an image, it can learn the combination of features through different branches' responses to the feature maps. Finally, by blending the learned weights with the original features, a more accurate output is obtained, enabling targeted pixel-level feature enhancement. This, in turn, helps the discriminator better understand the distribution of image features and further assists the generator in generating more realistic images that conform to the original data distribution (See Fig. 6).

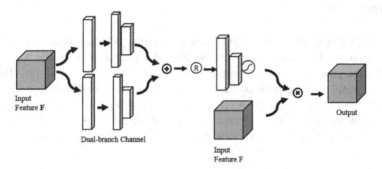

Fig. 6. Adaptive Dual-channel Fusion

Apply a Novel Generative Adversarial Network Function

In general, the loss function of a GAN consists of both the generator loss function and the discriminator loss function, which collectively drive the generator to produce more realistic probabilistic images and the discriminator to better distinguish between real and fake information, strengthening the ongoing adversarial process between the two parties.

$$L_{gen\_gan} = \frac{1}{KNM} \sum_{k=1}^{K} \sum_{i=1}^{N_k} \sum_{j=1}^{M_k} (1 - D\_G(i,j))^2 \qquad (1)$$

$$L_{disc\_gan} = \frac{1}{KNM} \sum_{k=1}^{K} \sum_{i=1}^{N_k} \sum_{j=1}^{M_k} ((1 - D\_R(i,j))^2 + D\_G(i,j)^2) \qquad (2)$$

$$L_{gen\_gan} = -\frac{1}{KNM} \sum_{k=1}^{K} \sum_{i=1}^{N_k} \sum_{j=1}^{M_k} (Max(0, \alpha + D\_G(i,j)) \qquad (3)$$

$$L_{disc\_gan} = -\frac{1}{KNM} \sum_{k=1}^{K} \sum_{i=1}^{N_k} \sum_{j=1}^{M_k} (Max(0, \beta - D\_R(i,j))$$
$$+ Max(0, \delta + D\_G(i,j)) \tag{4}$$

In the above formula, L_{gen_gan} represents the generator loss. L_{disc_gan} represents the discriminator loss. K represents the number of images scaled through a Gaussian pyramid, where the dimensions of each feature map are not fixed due to scaling at different ratios. N_k and M_k represent the width and height of each feature map, and α, β, and γ represent modulation factors. The original loss is measured using the squared distance to calculate the distance loss between images. Squared loss has high computational complexity, focuses on fine details of features, and is more susceptible to the impact of noise on the network. The discriminator becomes much stronger in the later stages of training compared to the earlier stages.

4 Experiments

This paper primarily adopts four rigid metrics as accuracy evaluation for the algorithm. Among them, the L1 metric represents the absolute distance between the images generated by the generator and the original real images, disregarding the direction and considering only the magnitude of the distance. AKD represents the average distance of key points between the real and generated images. AED represents the average Euclidean distance between the real and generated images. To ensure the directness of experimental results, EID applies weighted processing to the first three indicators (Figs. 7, 8 and 9, Table 1).

Table 1. Experimental Results Comparison

Methods	L1(‰)	AKD(‰)	AED(‰)	EID(‰)
FOMM	18.26	6.13	4.58	23.62
FOMM + Tanh	18.02	4.97	4.46	22.74
Ours-CL	17.57	4.67	4.33	22.07
Ours	17.47	5.26	4.15	22.18

The above is a comparative experiment conducted on the fashion dataset in the field of computer science. All experiments were conducted without data augmentation, and all data hyperparameters were kept the same, except for the fourth experiment which used a higher number of epochs. The experiments were performed using the same experimental setup, with the A40 graphics card used for training and the 3060 graphics card used for testing. Experiment 1, referred to as FOMM, represents the original author's method and its training results on the dataset. Experiment 2, labeled as FOMM + Tanh, involves modifying the generator's activation function from Sigmoid

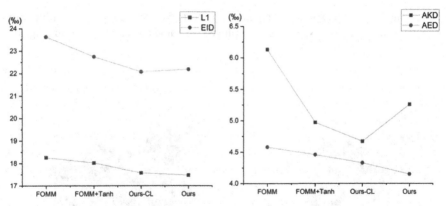

Fig. 7. Experimental Results Comparison

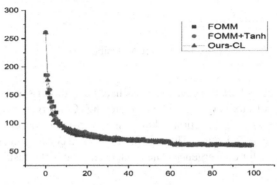

Fig. 8. Perceptual Loss

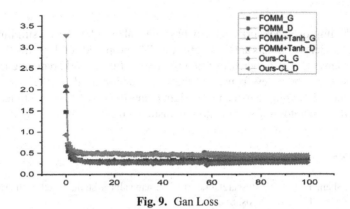

Fig. 9. Gan Loss

to Tanh. Experiment 3, denoted as Ours-CL, combines additional data by incorporating CA and adaptive dual-channel fusion output, using a multi-normalization down sampling module. The optimized experiment results outperform the previous ones, as evident from the outcomes. The above experiments employed the same constraint function (Fig. 10).

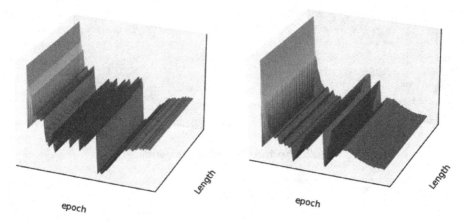

Fig. 10. Feature Matching Loss

The original network convergence process had a common issue, severe oscillation in the later stages of auxiliary loss feature matching. Convergence was modified by introducing a new constraint function, addressing the unstable convergence issue of the auxiliary loss before modification. The network model can converge to a better state, but it requires more time for convergence. The model achieved better results in terms of L1 and AED losses.

5   Conclusion

Although the improved network accuracy has been enhanced, there are still limitations, as the saved model parameters are relatively huge. The proposed new loss function cannot achieve a balance and also increases training time. In future work, reducing the model parameter size can be a key focus, and the loss function needs further improvement to balance the relationship between the original and improved loss functions, thereby promoting the generator to generate more realistic images.

References

1. You, K., Shen, Y., Tao, W.: Research on virtual human value systems based on the value chain theory. Wuhan Univ. J. (Philos. Soc. Sci.) (2023)
2. Isola, P., Zhu, J.Y., Zhou, T., et al.: Image-to-image translation with conditional adversarial networks. In: Proceedings of the IEEE Conference on Computer Vision and Pattern Recognition, pp. 1125–1134 (2017)
3. Chan, C., Ginosar, S., Zhou, T., Efros, A.A.: Everybody dance now. In: IEEE International Conference on Computer Vision (2019)

4. Wiles, O., Koepke, A., et al.: X2Face: a network for controlling face generation using images, audio, and pose codes. In: Proceedings of the European Conference on Computer Vision (2018)

5. Siarohin, A., Lathuilière, S., Tulyakov, S., et al.: Animating arbitrary objects via deep motion transfer. In: Proceedings of the IEEE/CVF Conference on Computer Vision and Pattern Recognition, pp. 2377–2386 (2019)

6. Siarohin, A., Lathuilière, S., Tulyakov, S., et al.: First order motion model for image animation. In: Conference on Neural Information Processing Systems (2019)

7. Newell, A., Yang, K., Deng, J.: Stacked hourglass networks for human pose estimation. In: Leibe, B., Matas, J., Sebe, N., Welling, M. (eds.) Computer Vision – ECCV 2016. ECCV 2016. LNCS, vol. 9912, pp. 483–499. Springer, Cham (2016). https://doi.org/10.1007/978-3-319-46484-8_29

8. Trinh, M.N., Pham, V.T., Tran, T.T.: An attention-PiDi-UNet and focal active contour loss for biomedical image segmentation. In: 2022 RIVF International Conference on Computing and Communication Technologies (RIVF), pp. 635–640 (2022)

9. Datta, S.K., Shaikh, M.A., et al.: Soft-Attention Improves Skin Cancer Classification Performance. arXiv preprint arXiv:2105.03358 (2021)

10. Hu, J., Shen, L., Sun, G.: Squeeze-and-excitation networks. In: Proceedings of the IEEE Conference on Computer Vision and Pattern Recognition, pp. 7132–7141 (2018)

11. Bastidas, A.A., Tang, H.: Channel attention networks. In: Proceedings of the IEEE/CVF Conference on Computer Vision and Pattern Recognition (CVPR) Workshops (2019)

12. Goodfellow, I., Pouget-Abadie, J., Mirza, M., Xu, B., Warde-Farley, D., Ozair, S., et al.: Generative Adversarial Nets. Neural Information Processing Systems. MIT Press, Cambridge (2014)

13. Springenberg, J.T., Dosovitskiy, A., Brox, T., Riedmiller, M.A.: Striving for Simplicity: The All Convolutional Net. CoRR, abs/1412.6806 (2014)

14. Ioffe, S., Szegedy, C.: Batch normalization: accelerating deep network training by reducing internal covariate shift. In: International Conference on Machine Learning, pp. 448–456 (2015)

15. Miyato, T., Kataoka, T., Koyama, M., et al.: Spectral normalization for generative adversarial networks. arXiv preprint arXiv:1802.05957 (2018)

16. Ulyanov, D., Vedaldi, A., Lempitsky, V.: Instance normalization: the missing ingredient for fast stylization. arXiv preprint arXiv:1607.08022 (2016)

Author Index

Printed in the United States
by Baker & Taylor Publisher Services